John Motley Morehead
and
The Development
of
North Carolina
1796–1866

The Reprint Company
Spartanburg, South Carolina

This Volume Was Reproduced
From A 1922 Edition
In The
North Carolina Collection
University of North Carolina
Chapel Hill

The Reprint Company
Post Office Box 5401
Spartanburg, South Carolina 29301

Reprinted: 1971
ISBN 0-87152-067-2
Library of Congress Catalog Card Number: 78-149347

Manufactured in the United States of America on long-life paper

1796–1866
From a portrait by William Garl Broune, 1859, in possession of John Motley
Morehead III, Rye, N. Y., showing the charter of the
North Carolina R. R. in his right hand

John Motley Morehead
and
The Development
of
North Carolina
1796-1866

By

BURTON ALVA KONKLE

AUTHOR OF
"The Life and Writings of James Wilson,"
etc.

WITH
AN INTRODUCTION
BY

HON. HENRY G. CONNOR, LL.D.
Judge of the United States District Court, Eastern District of
North Carolina

WILLIAM J. CAMPBELL
PHILADELPHIA
1922

PRINTED IN U.S.A.
PATTERSON & WHITE CO.
PHILADELPHIA

TO

WALTER ROY KONKLE

A

COURIER TO THE FRONT LINES

IN

THE THIRTY-SECOND DIVISION

AT

CHATEAU-THIERRY

Contents

Illustrations

Preface

In 1906, when the present writer was director of the patriotic effort to honor the chief maker of our national constitution, James Wilson, by removing his remains from Edenton, North Carolina, to Philadelphia, the leaders of that state were so generous and gracious in their cooperation, that I expressed the hope that both Pennsylvania and myself might render some reciprocal service in recognition of it.

Fourteen years passed before the opportunity came, when I accidentally came to know something of the career of this famous Carolina statesman, Governor John Motley Morehead, and his relations to the development of that great state. By a strange coincidence, his name was the earliest public name to fasten itself in the mind of the writer, as a mere boy in Indiana overhearing a conversation of his parents, in which occurred the expression "How could so good a man as Governor Morehead do it?"—meaning, thereby, join the secession movement. Doubtless the reason why this caught the Hoosier lad's attention in those middle 60s, was because he had never before heard that a secessionist could be "good," so he wondered about this unique case and remembered it. When the boy grew to be a man, however, and was nursed in an illness in the South, where he was writing some sketches, by the daughter of a Confederate Congressman and sister of a General in her armies, the veil fell from those same parents' eyes and they saw that goodness was by no means confined to one section; while the son came to have some of the dearest friends of his life in the Southland, and became one of the generation that knows no South, no East, no West, no North, but only one magnificent country.

To write a life of Morehead, therefore, became to one who, for twenty-five years had written on Pennsylvania's relation to national history, a unique adventure, made possible through the exigencies of the great war. That event came at a period when my six-volume, *Life and Writings*

of *James Wilson,* and my *David Lloyd and the First Half-
Century of Pennsylvania* were ready for press and hence
delayed. My *George Bryan and the Constitution of Pennsylvania* was then produced, and was issued in the spring
of 1922, while the present volume appears in the following
autumn. It is the purpose of the writer to issue the *Lloyd*
in the spring of 1923 and a new work *Thomas Willing and
the First Half-Century of American Finance* the fall of that
year, to be followed by the six-volume *Life and Writings
of James Wilson,* and following that *William Wilkins and
the Rise and Fall of Democracy in Pennsylvania.* The
process sounds much like a bombardment, which, as the
congestion of issue is due to the great war, may be considered perfectly natural.

In preparing the *Morehead* and its study of the great state
of North Carolina, many delightful friendships and courtesies should be mentioned if they were not so numerous.
A few must certainly be recognized, and first among them
are those of my friend Major John Motley Morehead III,
the distinguished scientist and engineer of the Union Carbide
and Carbon Corporation of New York, grandson of the subject of this volume, who, although not a resident of the state
for nearly thirty years, has become one of her honored sons,
a discoverer of that notable product acetylene gas, as his
equally distinguished father, James Turner Morehead, was
of carbide. Major Morehead issued his own beautiful volume, *The Morehead Family of Virginia and North Carolina*
in 1921, and his encouragement made the present volume
possible. In Raleigh the helpfulness of Chief Justice Walter
Clark, Professor R. D. W. Connor, Dr. D. H. Hill, Mr. R. B.
House, Col. Fred Olds, Col. J. Bryan Grimes, and others of
the Historical Commission; Marshall Delancey Haywood
of the Law Library; Justice Hoke of the Supreme Court;
Governor Morrison, Judge H. G. Connor of the United
States Court; Col. Samuel A. Ashe, clerk of that Court;
Miss Mary Hilliard Hinton; Mr. W. D. Self, clerk of the
State Corporation Commission; Mrs. H. S. Gay; and last,
but by no means least, State Librarian, Miss Carrie Brough-
ton, and her efficient and courteous staff to whom the writer

is greatly indebted for aid in his long work in that institution. In Greensboro also the aid of Mrs. Joseph M. Morehead, her son James T. Morehead, Esq., Mr. Victor C. McAdoo, John Michaux, Esq., Judge Wm. B. Bynum and Librarian Nellie C. Rowe and her staff of the Public Library and former Librarian, Miss Caldwell, must be acknowledged; as well as that of Mr. and Mrs. B. Frank Mebane, and Senator and Mrs. Walker of Spray; and Mrs. W. T. Harris of Danville, Va., as also Mr. and Mrs. Lindsay Patterson of Winston-Salem; John M. Morehead, Esq., of Charlotte; J. Lathrop Morehead, Esq., and Professor Boyd of Trinity College, Durham; Dr. J. G. de Roulhac Hamilton of the University of North Carolina; William Henry Hoyt, Esq., of New York; Mrs. J. Allison Hodges; Miss Emma Morehead Whitfield and Mr. Morgan P. Robinson of Richmond, Va., and Mrs. Gen. R. D. Johnston of Winchester, Va., cannot be passed by. Among these, the writer is especially grateful to Professor Connor and Mr. House for patient criticism of the text. He has also to express warm appreciation of the willingness of his valued friend, Judge Henry G. Connor, to write the introduction—a man of whom Bishop Cheshire has recently so beautifully said—"He stands so high that no man can be put above him and few on his level."

Finally, a word about the maps: These are chiefly new, prepared by the author from the best available sources, and, where originals do not exist, by a constructive process based on the principle that if a county is wholly derived from another county the latter must have contained the former—the only mode by which an approximate map of some counties can be obtained. The maps are designed for illustration of the text, however, not as minute and ultimate authorities, even though they have aimed at accuracy. That some frontier counties were created to extend to the Pacific ocean illustrates the vague notions of geography and the varying extent of British claims westwardly at different periods, not necessarily the legal bounds.

BURTON ALVA KONKLE.

Swarthmore, 30th January, 1922.

Introduction

As the result of repeated efforts by the people of Western North Carolina to secure amendments to the Constitution of 1776, a Convention composed of two delegates from each County, met at Raleigh, June 4, 1835. The members of this Convention were instructed by the Act, pursuant to which the people ratified the call, to reduce the number of Senators to not less than thirty-four nor more than fifty, to be elected by Districts composed of Counties in proportion to the amount of public taxes paid into the Treasury of the State by the citizens thereof, and to reduce the number of the House of Commons to not less than ninety, nor more than one hundred and twenty, to be elected by Counties or Districts according to their federal population, each County to have at least one member of the House of Commons. The adoption of other amendments was committed to the discretion of the Convention. The demand for a change in the basis of representation had, for more than thirty years, been a subject of deep concern, and at times intense feeling, to the people of the Central and Western Counties. The County system prevented making this and other changes necessary to bring the organic law into harmony with the growth of the State, and enable the West to secure a system of Internal Improvement with State aid. This aroused the fear of Eastern Delegates that plans would be adopted, fixing upon that Section, where the burden would be heaviest, taxation for the building of railroads and highways.

A prominent Western delegate said: "If the West had the power, a system of Internal Improvements would be commenced which would change the face of things and put at once a check to the tide of emigration which is depopulating the State."

A leading exponent and advocate of the Eastern view declared that "Highways, or other modes of transportation, would not benefit the West because nine-tenths of their land is exhausted and not worth cultivation, contrasted with hundreds and thousands of acres brought into market in the Southwestern States."

Swain, Morehead and other Western delegates, with Gaston from the East, led the contest for the change. Gaston discussed, with the ability and broad patriotism which always marked and controlled his course in dealing with every question, the origin and history of the controversy. The struggle of the strong men of the East and the West, who were called upon to settle this question, the merits of which are so clear to us now, resulted in the adoption of the Report, fixing the number of Senators at Fifty, elected from Districts formed upon the basis of property and taxation and the members of the House of Commons at One Hundred and Twenty, based upon Federal numbers—each County having at least one member, the remaining members being apportioned among the larger Counties. This plan was adopted by a vote of 75 to 52, the negative vote coming from the East. A sufficient number of Eastern delegates, under the leadership of Gaston, joining with the West, carried the question. It is impossible to understand the "development of North Carolina" from 1835 to 1860, unless we read the Debates in the Convention of 1835.

Morehead, as the advocate and wise leader of those policies, was elected Governor in 1840 and again in 1842. He was among the earliest, most enthusiastic and influential founders of the movement which culminated in the construction of the North Carolina Railroad and a system of roads extending from Beaufort to Charlotte and from Salisbury to the Tennessee line.

The story of the labors of Governor Morehead, to whom the title has been given of the "Architect and Builder of Public Works of North Carolina," is intensely interesting and stimulating to patriotic pride. This story is most interestingly told by Mr. Konkle in the following pages.

Recalling the pessimistic utterances of the reactionary sentiment of members of the Convention of 1835, we see the realization of the vision of Governor Morehead, Gaston and those who co-operated with them, as eloquently and truthfully described by one who has made a study of our history: "The traveler today, along the line of the North Carolina Railroad, sees the fulfilment of Morehead's dream. He finds himself in one of the most productive Sections of the New World. He traverses it from one end to the other at a speed of forty miles an hour, surrounded by every comfort and convenience of modern travel. He passes through a region bound together by a thousand miles of steel rails, by telegraph and telephone lines and by nearly two thousand miles of improved country roads. He finds a population engaged not only in agriculture, but in manufacturing, in commerce, in transportation and in a hundred other enterprises. He hears the hum of hundreds of modern mills and factories operating millions of spindles and looms by steam, water, electricity, employing more than fifty millions of capital and sending their products to the uttermost parts of the earth. His train passes through farm lands which, since Morehead's time, has increased in value more than ten fold, producing ten times as much cotton and a hundred times as much tobacco. From his car window he sees a thousand modern schoolhouses, alive with the energy and activity of one hundred thousand school children. He passes through cities of twenty to thirty thousand and towns of five to ten thousand inhabitants. Better than all, he finds himself among a people no longer characterized by lethargy, isolation and ignorance, but bristling with energy, alert with every opportunity, fired with the spirit of the modern world and with their faces steadfastly set to the future. The foundation on which all this prosperity and progress rests is the work done by John M. Morehead or inspired by him."

But my office is to introduce the author and invite the reader, who would know the mental, moral, political and social qualities and characteristics of the "rare individual, both architect and contractor, both poet and man of action, to whom is given the power to dream and the power to execute," of whom Mr. Konkle has made a thorough sympathetic study and of whom he has preserved a faithful and most interesting history to a closer acquaintance with his hero. Mr. Konkle has, by a careful, intelligent study of our records, made a permanent and most valuable contribution to the history of the State of North Carolina and her people.

H. G. Connor.

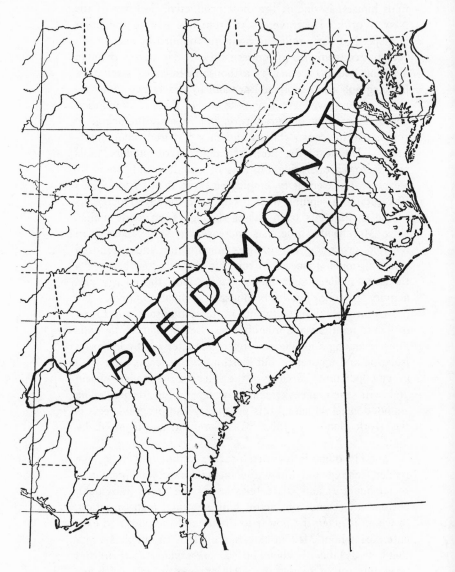

MAP OF THE PIEDMONT
Prepared by the author

MAP OF THE ROANOKE VALLEY
Prepared by the author

I

A Son of the Piedmont

1796

If on July 4, 1796, the Goddess of Liberty had already surmounted the dome of a Capitol and a Washington, yet to be, on the banks of the Potomac; and she could have raised to her eyes a seven-leagued field-glass and looked with superhuman view to the southwestward and beheld a strip of land about one hundred miles wide, lined with Appalachian foot-hills on the right and the water-falls of every river that crossed it on the left, generally about a hundred miles back from the ocean, and extending through four states and into Alabama at Montgomery—the capitoline deity would have covered in her purview a region that has a peculiar character and has acquired exclusive possession of the name "Piedmont."[1] And in her foreground, her glass would have easily picked out, among more than a score of rivers that cross it, with their rich valleys, one among the most rich and most extensive, in its windings, lacing together the two states of Virginia and North Carolina, prefiguring a time to come when bands of iron should replace it. This rich region is the valley of the Roanoke, which lies like a great wallet full of treasures toward the foot-hills, with its neck ready to pour them through Carolina into the Albemarle, if she should have a port to receive it or the water-falls did not choke the passage. And could so extensive a view permit the Goddess to see things more minute, she would have witnessed, in the very heart of the upper part of the valley in the lands between the lower two of three great tributaries, the Dan and Banister

---

[1] Technically, the name Piedmont is applied only to the western half; but the line of separation is so indefinite that the name is often applied to the whole.

1

rivers, on a farm in Pittsylvania county, Virginia, near the
Carolina border, the birth of a farmer boy, John Motley
Morehead, destined to be one of the great figures of Pied-
mont and national history.

His grandfather, Joseph Morehead, had been attracted
by the fame of the Roanoke Valley, from the ancient home
of the family in the head of the Piedmont, just below the
site of the future national capital, a region that was also the
head of that great peninsula between the Potomac and the
Rappahannock more commonly known by the not euphoni-
ous name of "Northern Neck"—a region made famous as
the birth-place of a Washington, Madison, Monroe and a
Marshall. Indeed the great Chief Justice was born only
five years before John, the youngest son of Joseph Morehead, and father of our subject, and equally near in the
same territory in Fauquier county, the latter's birth occurring on May 9, 1760. Joseph had named this son after his
aged father, John Morehead I, who had pioneered, like
the Washingtons, with the creation of successive counties
as settlement progressed up the "Neck," from his birth about
1689 in the old original Northumberland county, to King
George county created in 1720, to Prince William erected
ten years later, and finally to Fauquier, created just the
year before his grandson name-sake was born.

The tale of how John Morehead I came to be born at
the foot of the "Northern Neck" is one of the most romantic
in American annals.[1] The father of John Morehead I, was
Charles Morehead (or Muirhead), who is said to be a
younger son of David Morehead, or, as he himself spelled
it, David Muirhead, the distinguished London and Edinburgh merchant and colonizer, who appears, in 1630, to have
sent this son, Charles, over to Charles I's newly organized
colony of Virginia, as a factor at Kecoughtan (now Hampton), where Secretary of State William Claiborne was a most
enterprising figure, and for three years had been officially
designated to explore new lands for colonizing purposes.

---

[1] For fuller detail see the beautiful volume, *The Morehead Family of North
Carolina and Virginia*, by Major John Motley Morehead (III) of New York
City, issued in 1921.

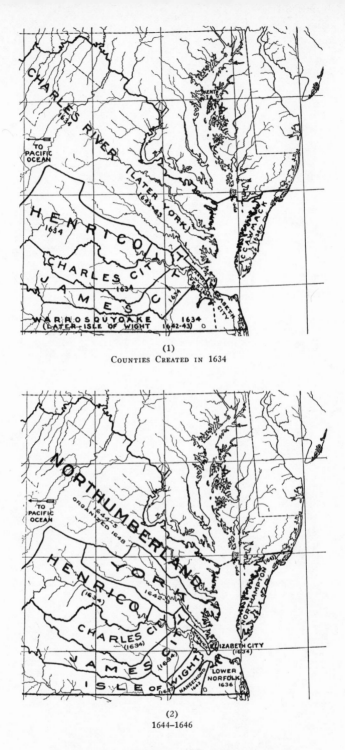

(1)
COUNTIES CREATED IN 1634

(2)
1644–1646

VIRGINIA COUNTIES CREATED FROM 1634 TO 1671
Prepared by the author
Kent Island is shown on Map No. 1 in Upper Chesapeake Bay

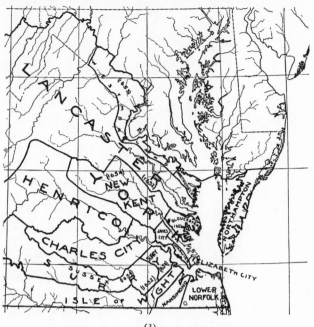

(3)
1652–1654

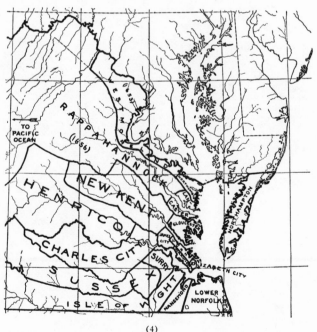

(4)
1656–1658

On one of his exploratory voyages northward, he was attracted to the largest island in the Chesapeake as a colonizing proposition and named it Kent Island, then far within the bounds of that colony and opposite the present site of Annapolis.

Forthwith he went to London and on May 16, 1631, secured a commission from Charles I, enlisted the capital of a few merchants as partners, one of whom, Thompson, had been a factor in Kecoughtan, and one Cloberry owning most of the stock; and finally Captain Claiborne, later in May, set out to buy Kent Island from the Indians and begin settlement. This was the first of many successive expeditions to the Kent Island colony; but within a year, Lord Baltimore, whose St. Lawrence colony had failed, persuaded His Catholic Majesty, Charles I, to give him the upper part of Virginia above the Potomac, which, to the consternation of the Kent Island owners, would place them under Baltimore, or confiscate all their laborious and expensive colonization. The vacillation of Charles I, which, was to yet cost him his head, precipitated a contest which covered several years and made civil war on the Chesapeake between the Kent Island company and Baltimore's new colony of Maryland. Merchant Cloberry was the only one of Captain Claiborne's company who was not discouraged at the prospect, and in 1634, when Baltimore's first colony arrived, he bought out the timid ones, and found more doughty partners in David Morehead and one or two others. They sent one of the partners, George Evelin, over to handle the matter diplomatically if possible; but Captain Claiborne was for war, not diplomacy, and the war continued in one form or another for a dozen years, long after the death of David Morehead, which occurred in September, 1642. Five years after his death, however, in 1647, the colony submitted to Lord Baltimore, although echoes of the conflict, legally, continued down to at least 1677.

Meanwhile the Crown seemed inclined to grant compensatory lands in Virginia; and Claiborne and others received estates in that part nearest the Maryland colony, namely, in the new county of Northumberland, covering all of the "Northern Neck" westward to the Pacific Ocean, and about half of the next peninsula below the Rappahannock, which was created about three years after David Morehead's death. Just how soon after this Charles Morehead moved up from Kecoughtan to his new lands in Northumberland county cannot be known, because of destruction of necessary county records in 1711, about six years after his will was probated by his eldest sons, who became executors, among other children, for his youngest son, John Morehead I, a child of his latest years, in the region of the Great Wicomico river near Heathsville.

The Morehead family, therefore, had been in Virginia for one hundred and sixty-six years, when the birth of John Motley Morehead occurred on the nineteenth anniversary of the Declaration, in the second administration of the first great Piedmont President of the "Northern Neck," George Washington.

But if the tale of their settlement in Virginia was romantic, it was not more so than the career of the family in Great Britain, whom Sir Walter Scott celebrated in his *Minstrelsy of the Scottish Border,* the valiant defender of the King, John Muirhead of Lauchope and Bullis, in the ballad entitled:

"THE LAIRD OF MUIRHEAD

"Afore the King in order stude
　　The stout laird of Muirhead,
Wi' that same twa-hand muckle sword
　　That Bartram fell'd stark dead.

"He sware he wadna lose his right
　　To fight in ilka field;
Nor budge him from his liege's sight,
　　Till his last gasp should yield.

"Twa hunder mair, of his ain name,
　　Frae Torwood and the Clyde,
Sware they would never gang to hame,
　　But a' die by his syde.

"And wondrous weel they kept their troth;
　　This sturdy royal band
Rush'd down the brae, wi' sic a pith,
　　That nane could them withstand.

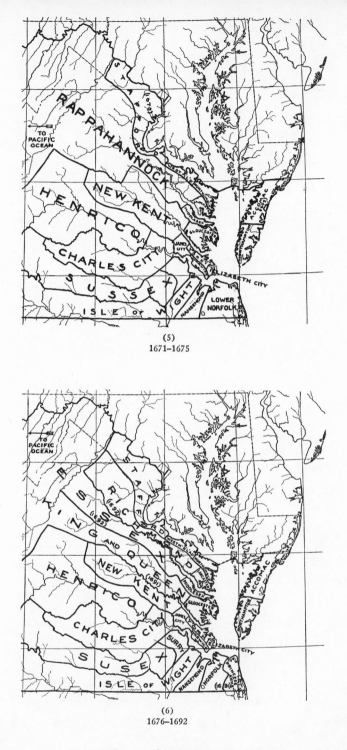

(5)
1671–1675

(6)
1676–1692

VIRGINIA COUNTIES CREATED FROM 1672 TO 1733
Prepared by the author
Where western limits were indefinite they were assumed, and sometimes stated to be to the Pacific Oc
according to Colonial claims

(7)
1693–1702

(8)
1703–1733

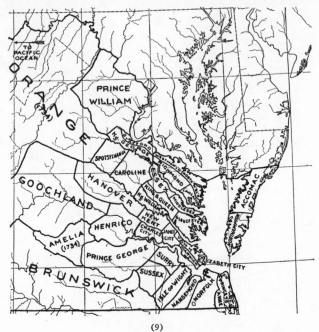

(9)
1734–1741

(10)
1741–1748

VIRGINIA COUNTIES CREATED FROM 1734 TO 1748
Prepared by the author
Halifax, 1752, west of which Pittsylvania was created, and Fauquier, 1759,
are also indicated

"Mony a bloody blow they dealt,
    The like was never seen;
And hadna that braw leader fall'n,
    They ne'er had slain the King."

The King, in this case, was James IV, and the battle, that
great one on the Flodden spur of Cheviot Hills, of September 9, 1513, so graphically described in the sixth canto
of *Marmion;* while John Muirhead, the Laird of Lauchope
and Bullis, was the officer in charge of the Crown lands of
Galloway and his clan body-guard of the King, and thus
lost his life against the forces of Henry VIII. This Laird's
father, who died seven years before, had been Knighted by
King James IV, Sir William Muirhead of Lauchope, and
his grandfather knighted by Richard III shortly before
1485, the first Sir William Muirhead of Lauchope; while,
during Columbus' voyages, one of the Muirheads, Dr.
Richard, was Secretary of State and, twenty years before,
another was Bishop of Glasgow. The clan began in Clydes-
dale before 1122, over four hundred years before the
"Laird of Muirhead" slept on Flodden Field with his King,
and Lauchope House had a new master, and what was left
of the clan, a new head.

Lauchope House, located some eleven miles eastwardly
of Glasgow in Lanarkshire, Bothwell Parish, about a mile
northeastwardly of Hollytown, was rebuilt in the early half
of the nineteenth century, "an old mansion," "elegant" and
"tastefully embellished," "a tower-house with walls of remarkable thickness," "the seat of a very ancient family, the
parent stem of the Muirheads," and "gave refuge on the
eve of his flight from Scotland, to Hamilton of Bothwell-
haugh, Murray's assassin at Linlithgow (1570)" in loyalty
to Queen Mary Stuart, and to the Hamiltons, with whom
the Muirheads inter-married.[1] The old Muirhead mansion
is still one of the beautiful country seats of Scotland, as it
was a tower of strength in the days of the Scottish Chief
who fell on Flodden Field.

For when John Muirhead I, of Lauchope died his son

---

[1] Lewis *Topographical Dictionary of Scotland,* 1846; Groome's *Ordinance
Gazetteer of Scotland,* 1903; and Muirhead's *Life of James Watts.* James
Watts, the famous engineer's mother was Agnes Muirhead, before her marriage.

John Muirhead II became head of the clan and master of Lauchope House; but it was the great-great-grandson of the hero of Flodden Field, James Muirhead II who had occasion again to bring disaster on his house and clan by his doughty strokes as a leader of unsuccessful Covenanter rebels who were proclaimed exiles in 1579, and thereby brought practical ruin on the family estates. Indeed he was so dangerous to the Crown that his son, James Muirhead III, of Lauchope, and other relatives had to go on his bond to keep the peace for the remaining thirty years of his life; and this son was the last of his direct line to own Lauchope House. It was a younger son, David Muirhead, born at Lauchope House, whose grandson, David Muirhead (III) became the distinguished London and Edinburgh merchant and colonizer of Virginia lands in the 1630s through his younger son, Charles of Northumberland county and the "Northern Neck," and the latter, thereby, brought into common use the Anglicized form of the name Morehead, which came to prevail throughout the "Northern Neck" and the Piedmont.

As in Scotland, the Moreheads inter-married with well-known Virginia and Maryland families, Charles' grandsons, Charles and Joseph of Fauquier county, both married daughters of a revolutionary heroine, Keren-happuch (Norman) Turner, who, like Molly Pitcher and Hannah Dustin, is immortalized in a statue; in her case, it is on the battle-field of Guilford Court House, near Greensboro, N. C., to celebrate the long horse-back ride from Maryland to act as nurse to her own and others wounded in that famous action.[1] One of her grandsons, under General Greene, was John Morehead, born in Fauquier county, Virginia, on May 9, 1760, as had been said, and he was married in 1790 to Miss Obedience Motley, a daughter of Captain Joseph Motley, a Church of England Welsh planter and trader of Amelia county, Virginia. Miss Motley, born in 1768, also had heroic and tragic experiences in that conflict: her father was a captain under Colonel George Washington in the French

---

[1] It is related of her that she improvised what amounted to the modern ice-pack to keep fever down, in the form of a mode of dripping cold spring water over the wounded.

LAUCHOPE HOUSE IN 1921

In Lanarkshire, slightly northeast of Hollytown, Scotland, ancient
seat of the Muirheads

and Indian Wars, and was present at Braddock's defeat, while six of her brothers were soldiers of the Revolution. As a child, she witnessed in the temporary absence of her father, the treachery of a Tory neighbor, who was leading a guerrilla warfare, and, deliberately cut an artery in the arm of her sick mother, lying in bed with an infant, so that she bled to death before aid could reach her; while some years later she heaped coals of fire on the head of her mother's murderer, by nursing him when he was accidentally brought to her home in a serious illness. She often told of her old nurse, to whose care this tragedy consigned the care of the young children: Rachel "had been an African Princess, and, being sent one day to drive the birds from the rice fields, was suddenly kidnapped, a bag thrown over her head, and herself carried away captive and sold as a slave in America. She was faithful and kind and became a real mother to the ten children when left to her care. There was a boy also, from Africa, among the slaves, and they talked with each other in their language. He often said he would go back to his people, for whom he sighed. One morning he was found hanging to a tree in the yard and Rachel explained that he had gone to his own country. The children wept for him, and only Rachel, whom they loved devotedly, could console them. She had flowers tattooed on her breast for beauty."[1] Miss Obedience, like her sisters, learned to spin and weave their clothes and the household cotton and linen.

It was she who was one of John Morehead's pupils when, on one occasion, he was teaching the young people dancing and he was so worried by her that he laid his bow on her shoulder and remonstrated with her—and made her his wife. They were a great contrast: he was versatile and many-sided; could officiate as a squire and marry people, pray with the sick and dying, preach a sermon of good Presbyterian doctrine, was a poet, a soldier, a planter, fond of the chase and social life. He hated slavery and tried to take measures against it; and has been described as a

---

[1] *The Morehead Family of North Carolina and Virginia,* by Major John Motley Morehead of New York, pp. 104–5, in the State Library, Raleigh, N. C.

man far ahead of his times, in morals and intelligence.
Many stories are told of him, even yet. His young wife
was more disciplined and practical; and when he thanked
Providence for whatever was sent, joys or afflictions, and
she remarked she believed he "would thank the Lord if
he broke a leg." "Yes, Biddy," said he with a smile, "I
would, because it wasn't my neck!" His parting benediction
when a child left home was: "Remember, child, death before dishonor." When about eighteen he joined the Revolutionary Army under General Greene, and was in the battle
of Cowpens, but was on a war prisoner's detail during the
battle of Guilford Court House. His old wooden cask-
canteen may yet be seen in the Museum on the battle-ground,
now a National Park. It was not until 1790, when he was
thirty years old, that he was married to Miss Motley, who
was herself but twenty-two, and they made their new home
where "Windsor," the home of Samuel Wilson now is near
the Henry County line, not far from the Dan River in
Pittsylvania county, also near the North Carolina line, west
of Danville.[1] They lived there but eight years, however,
while daughters came and their first son, John Motley Morehead, was born, as has been said, on July 4, 1796.

Their eyes had been turned longingly to a fertile section
slightly south of them, just over the North Carolina line.
Over a half-century before, in 1733, "Colonel William Byrd
of Westover in Virginia, Esquire," a famous early surveyor
and gentleman of the old school, wrote of it as "The Land
of Eden," in which he had "a fine tract." He tells of crossing the Dan river "about a mile and a half to the westward
of the place where the Irvin [river] runs into it," and passing over a barren highland, "on a sudden the scene changed
and we were surpriz'd with an opening of large extent,
where the Sauro Indians once lived, who had been a considerable nation. But the frequent inroads of the Senecas
annoy'd them incessantly, and obliged them to remove from
this fine situation about 30 years ago. . . . It must
have been a great misfortune to them to be obliged to aban-

---

[1] This location is furnished the writer by Mrs. Joseph M. Morehead of
Greensboro, N. C.

don so beautiful a dwelling, where the air is wholesome, and the soil equal in fertility to any in the whole world. The river is about 80 yards wide, always confined within its lofty banks, and rolling down its waters, as sweet as milk, and as clear as crystal. There runs a charming level of more than a mile square, that will bring forth like the lands of Egypt, without being overflow'd once a year. There is scarce a shrub in view to intercept your prospect, but grass as high as a man on horse-back. Toward the woods there is a gentle ascent, till your sight is intercepted by an eminence, that overlooks the whole landscape. This sweet place is bounded to the east by a fine stream call'd Sauro Creek, which running out of [into (?)] the Dan, and tending westerly, makes the whole a peninsula. I cou'd not quit this pleasant situation without regret, but often faced about to take a parting look at it as far as I could see, and so indeed did all the rest of the company."[1]

And one of their younger sons, who became a lawyer, scholar, and poet, years later, celebrated the region they chose near here in a poem of great beauty, entitled the *Hills of Dan,* in one verse of which he says:

"The world is not one garden spot,
      One pleasure ground for man;
   Few are the spots that intervene,
      Such as the Hills of Dan."[2]

And this spot which they chose, some five miles from the old home, and not far from the present site of Spray, Rockingham county, North Carolina, southwestward of Danville some twenty-five miles, they settled upon in 1798 when their son, John Motley, was a baby of two years.[3]   Here

---

[1] *The Writings of Colonel William Byrd, of Westover, in Virginia, Esqr.,* edited by John Spencer Bassett, 1901, pp. 306-7.   This beautiful spot, now called "The Meadows," is part of a large estate of many thousand acres, owned by Mr. B. Frank Mebane, of Spray, whose wife is a great-grand-daughter of John and Obedience Motley Morehead.

[2] *The Hills of Dan,* by Abraham Forrest Morehead, 1834, who, as he wished in the poem, does rest in the little family burial ground a few yards from the site of the old farm-house in which he was born, opposite what is now the Powell Store and "Corners," in Rockingham County, a few miles from Spray. The old farm-house was burned after his father's death and John Motley Morehead built a new one for his mother, which still stands.

[3] John Morehead, I am informed by Hugh R. Scott, Esq., of Reidsville, bought 200 acres on Horse Pen Creek, on May 29, 1798; 100 more the same year on Wolf Island Creek Fork; 100 more on February 14, 1799; and then numerous other tracts—all not far from Dan River on these various creeks.

they reared a family of five daughters and four sons, of which latter, John Motley was the eldest. Like Presbyterians generally, John Morehead and his family made much of religion and education. He, himself, built Mt. Carmel Presbyterian Church near his home and often, as has been intimated, he also did the preaching. They early determined likewise that their four boys should have a college education and then should teach their sisters in return; and not only so but that the older boys should aid the younger. It is doubtful if ever a family were a better example of what can be done in the home as a nursery of higher education; and who can tell how much this plan of John Morehead's country home has influenced the educational history of the State? One need not go much further than this to account for the educational philosophy and motive that the eldest son came to have after he had had a share in teaching both brothers and sisters in it; and the process was certain to make him not merely senior, but the recognized head of the family as the children grew to manhood and womanhood.[1]

While the primary instruction was proceeding in the home, John Motley had, in 1810, become fourteen years old, and, as Latin was the Apollyon which aspirants for higher education must first overcome and no academy existed in Rockingham county, at the time, Squire Morehead persuaded his neighbor's son, Thomas Settle, a young man of nineteen, who had studied Latin and Greek a few months in Caswell, the county to the eastward, and was just licensed to practice law in Rockingham, to teach his fourteen year old son, John Motley Morehead, the elements of Latin, at least, during 1810 and a part of the following year, at the county-seat of that county, Wentworth. "And then," said Hon. Thomas Settle, Jr., "between the teacher and his solitary student, commenced a friendship and intimacy which death alone terminated."[2] There is no doubt but that this

---

[1] These children were the five sisters and the four brothers, John Motley, born in 1796; James Turner, born in 1799; Samuel, who died in 1828, and Abraham Forrest, whose death occurred in 1834. All but Samuel became lawyers, James Turner being a distinguished one of the State and a Congressman and State Senator.

[2] Address before the bar meeting of Guilford County, N. C., in September, 1866. Justice Settle afterwards became a member of the Supreme bench of the State for a quarter of a century. His wife was a sister of Hon. Calvin Graves, of whom the reader will see more anon.

intimate relation between the young attorney and his Latin pupil from the Morehead plantation was to have much to do in determining the choice of profession of nearly all of the sons of John and Obedience Morehead. Certain it is, in that period of tutorship, young John Motley showed himself an apt pupil in the languages and that he got all that young Attorney Settle had to give and more. This result convinced Squire Morehead of the wisdom of taking immediate measures to put the young fifteen-year-old student in a proper school of higher learning.

II

Under Three Great Teachers

1811

In the year 1811, in Rockingham county, North Carolina, no one interested in higher education for his son would, for one instant, have to speculate where to find the proper school. Indeed the probabilities are that that very desire for higher learning in this region was largely due to the greatness of the primitive institution of Rev. Dr. Caldwell, not far away to the southward, for here was one of the greatest natural teachers that America has ever produced; and his school had been a famous one for nearly a half-century and that, too, under his own guidance—a North Carolina Eton or Phillips-Exeter and more, for it was practically an academy, college and theological seminary with this remarkable teacher as faculty.

Rev. Dr. David Caldwell was eighty-six years old in 1811 and still at work. Born in Lancaster, Pennsylvania, in 1725, he graduated from Princeton College the same year that John Witherspoon became President of it, 1761. Licensed as a preacher in 1763, he was sent out as a missionary, the year of the Stamp Act Congress, into the increasing settlements pressing southward down the Piedmont to North Carolina, and settled as pastor of two Presbyterian Churches, Buffalo and Alamance, in the big county of what became Guilford, three years before it was created in 177⟨1⟩, and his home was about three miles northwest of the present site of Greensboro, which in due time became the county seat. The young minister, now forty-two years old, had married Rachel, the daughter of Rev. Alexander Craighead of Mecklenburg county, and their home became, as has been said, an academy, college and theological seminary; while in 1768 he was installed pastor of the two churches, one of the new school and one of the old school, a relation that continued for over a half-century. His home, with himself and wife, became a veritable "seminary" to the whole South; for with a constant stream of boys from that section of the United States, always about fifty in number, he is said to have brought more young men into the learned professions than any one man of his time—lawyers, judges, statesmen, five governors, congressmen, physicians, ministers—nearly all of the Presbyterian ministry of the Carolinas and to the south and west, for many years, being trained in his school. Indeed seven of his pupils were licensed by Orange Presbytery in one day and only three or four members who admitted them but were also students of the venerable teacher. Nor was he merely a teacher and preacher, but a great man and leader, and he voiced the rising protest against British injustice and stood for the new principles of political science being wrought out in colonial aims at self-government so vitally different from those of the mother country. His home was in the center of that district which sought to secure redress of grievances from the notorious Governor Tryon, under the name "Regulators," and the Battle of Alamance occurred some twenty miles from his school. His influence consolidated the Revolutionary Whigs and he helped frame the Constitution of 1776 at Halifax, North Carolina. He was an intimate friend of the great Philadelphia physician-patriot, Dr. Benjamin Rush, under whom he had studied medicine as an aid to missionary work; and at the Battle of Guilford Court House, also not far from his home and at the edge of the county-seat yet to be created and named in honor of General Greene, he cared for the wounded of both sides. Lord Cornwallis considered him so great a source of inspiration to those who made this battle so costly that it has been described as having caused the surrender at Yorktown, that the British general camped upon his ground, destroyed his property, even his library, and proclaimed a price of £200 for his arrest. He rebuilt his home and school when the war closed and his last service for the state was in the convention of 1788, in which he opposed the new National Constitution. He was then sixty-three years old, and saw the National Constitution adopted by his state in November of the following year; and during the next month a charter was granted for the "University of North Carolina," which had been provided for in the constitution he had helped make in 1776. That he should be offered the Presidency of this new University was a matter of course, but he wisely declined it and clung to the great work of his life—which was not half done—for he was destined to almost top a century and was in educational harness until within five of that hundred years.[1]

That John Morehead and his wife were determined their first son, John Motley, should have the prized advantages of training under such a teacher, and that the sixteen-year-old youth was keenly ambitious to do so, in this year 1811, is borne out by the facts.[2] Years later the boy, then become famous, described his and his father's first interview with Dr. Caldwell: "In November, 1811," he writes on August 4, 1852, "my father took me, then in my sixteenth year, with a good common English education, from his residence in the county of Rockingham, to Dr. Caldwell's—a distance of some thirty miles, for the purpose of putting me under his care and instruction. I had heard so much of him as an instructor and disciplinarian, that I had conceived of him as a man of great personal dignity, with a face, the scowl of which would annihilate the unlucky urchin who had not gotten his lesson well. So I approached his residence with

---

[1] Dr. Caldwell died August 25, 1824, in his hundredth year, and his remains lie in the cemetery of Buffalo Presbyterian Church, of which, with Alamance, he was pastor sixty years. An adequate formal life of this great man is needed and at some point in the state, since there seems to be no portrait of him, a monument equal to that of any man in the state ought to be erected.

Maj. Joseph M. Morehead in a sketch of Caldwell for *North Carolina Day*, issued by the State Superintendent of Public Instruction in 1907, says Governor Morehead said of Dr. Caldwell that he was "a Jack-at-all-trades and good *at all.*" He also indicates that Dr. Caldwell's course in medicine was a "correspondence course," and, as we know, under Dr. Benjamin Rush.

[2] A tradition in the family has it that Mrs. Obedience Morehead was the one determined to educate her oldest son, and through him, the rest, and that she sold enough produce from the farm to do it. One of the songs she sang at her loom had these lines:

> "I raise my own ham
> My beef and my lamb.
> I weave my own cloth
> And I wear it."

It should be added, however, that some attribute most to John's qualities and some most to those of Obedience; and as usual both are right. It was the imagination of the one and the hard sense of the other that made John Motley Morehead what he was to become.

fear and trembling. We found, a few hundred yards from his house, and near a little mill on a small branch—built rather to serve as a hobby for amusement than for any more practical purpose, an exceedingly old gentleman, bowed down by some eighty-six or seven winters, enveloped in a large cape made of bear skin, with a net worsted cap on his head (for the evening was cool), and supporting himself with a cane not much shorter than his own body—this was Dr. Caldwell. My fears of him and his authority were at once dissipated. The moment he was informed of our business, he remarked that he had long ago abandoned his school, and had taught but little since, and then only to oblige a neighbor or two; that he had no pupil at that time, and did not wish to engage in teaching again. My father reminded him of his promise made, many years before, and while he was not teaching, that he would educate his oldest son for him. The Doctor replied jocularly that he did not consider that that promise bound him to live always, that he might comply with it; and that my father ought to have presented his son long since. My father made some answer at which the Doctor laughed heartily, and since in a broad Scotch accent, which he often assumed when he desired to be humorous, or to worry a laggard pupil with a bad lesson—'Weel mon, we must thry and see what we can do with the lad;' and turning to myself, said—'But mon, have ye an appetite for reading?' To which I replied, 'I am not very hungry for it.' The answer seemed to please him, and we then proceeded to his house.

"I took boarding in the neighborhood, and remained under his tuition until the fall of 1815 (losing a good deal of time, however, from the school), when I went to the University of North Carolina, and was admitted a member of the Junior class. As I had nearly completed the prescribed course in the languages under Dr. Caldwell, I studied no Latin or Greek at the University, with the exception of Cicero, and that I studied privately.

"I was not long in Dr. Caldwell's hands before I became satisfied of his remarkable excellence as a teacher. He had but little to amuse him, except hearing my lessons. I ap-

plied myself to my studies with great zeal, with which he
was much pleased; and often has he made me recite, from
four to six hours a day, parsing every difficult word, and
scanning nearly every line, when the recitation happened
to be in any of the Latin poets. Indeed you could not get
along with him, with any comfort, without knowing accur-
ately and thoroughly everything you passed over.

"The Rules of Prosody and Syntax in the Latin, and of
Syntax in the Greek, with all the exceptions and notes,
seemed to be as familiar to him as the alphabet. His memory had evidently failed to some extent; and I have sometimes found him, on my arrival in the morning, when I was
studying the higher Latin and Greek classics, looking over
my lessons for the day. He would apologize for doing so, by
saying that his memory had failed, and he was afraid I
might *cork* him; meaning that I might ask him questions
that he would not be able to answer. Hard words or difficult sentences in the various authors that he taught, seemed,
for the most part, entirely familiar to him; and often, when
he would ask me for a rule which I could not give, he would
attempt to give it; and the phraseology having escaped his
memory, he would bother at it, like a man with a tangled
skein, searching for the end by which it can be unravelled,
until some word or expression of his own would bring back
to his memory some part of the rule, and then he would
repeat the whole of it with great accuracy. Sometimes, when
he could not repeat the rule in English, he would say—
'Weel mon, let us thry the Latin;' and the Latin generally
proved to be quite at his command.

"Dr. Caldwell's course of studies in the languages—
Latin, Greek and Hebrew, as well as in the sciences, was
extensive for his day; and the facility and success with
which he imparted his knowledge to others, in such extreme
old age, was truly wonderful. Towards the latter part of
the time I was under his instruction, he had several more
pupils, and among them was a student of medicine; and I
noticed that he seemed just as familiar with that subject as
any other.

"During a part of the time I was with him, he found

great difficulty in reading, with the help of two pair of spec-
tacles; but his sight returned subsequently, so that he could
read the finest Greek print, without any glasses at all. I did
not, however, observe much change in his intellect.

"In stature I suppose he must have measured about five
feet eight or ten inches; and in his younger days, he probably weighed from one hundred and seventy-five to two
hundred pounds. He had a well formed head and strong
features. He was an exceedingly studious man, as his great
acquisitions in various departments of learning proved. The
prominent characteristics of his mind were the power to
acquire knowledge and retain it, and the power to apply it
to useful and practical purposes. By some he was thought
to be lacking in originality; but I think this questionable.
He certainly possessed a strong mind; but the late day at
which his education was commenced, the great extent and
variety of his knowledge, and the active pursuits of his life,
gave him but little time for that kind of reflection, without
which originality of thought is not apt to be developed.

"Dr. Caldwell was a man of admirable temper, fond of
indulging in playful remarks, which he often pointed with
a moral; kind to a fault to every human being, and I might
say to every living creature, entitled to his kindness. He
seemed to live to do good.

"It would be difficult to duly appreciate his usefulness
through his long life. His learning, his piety, and his patriotism, were infused into the generations of his day. An
ardent Whig of the Revolution, he taught his people the
duty they owed to their country as well as their God. Well
do I remember, when, in 1814, the Militia of Guilford were
called together in this town [Greensboro] to raise volunteers,
or draft men to go to Norfolk, to have seen the old gentleman literally crawl upon the bench of the Court House to
address the multitude, and in fervid and patriotic strains
exhort them to be faithful to their country. The sermon
had a powerful effect upon the soldiers. As an illustration,
I may mention that a Quaker lad, who had been strictly
educated in the faith of his denomination, after hearing the
sermon, entered the ranks of the volunteers, served his time,

returned to the bosom of his own church, which gladly received him, and lived and died an honored and esteemed citizen.

"From Dr. Caldwell's great age at the time I knew him, and the consequent failure of his voice (never I think a very good one), I could not form a very satisfactory opinion of his merits in the pulpit. All the sermons I ever heard him deliver were extemporaneous. But, if I were to hazzard an opinion in respect to him as a preacher, in the vigor of his manhood, I should say he was a calm, strong, didactic reasoner, whose sermons were delivered with an earnestness that left no doubt with his hearers that he was uttering his own deep convictions, and with an unction that bore testimony to the Christian purity of his own heart."[1]

The young student of seventeen, with his year of Latin and his experience in teaching his brothers and sisters, made rapid progress under Dr. Caldwell and was particularly good in the languages. He was there from 1811 to the autumn of 1815—about four years. It will be well to analyze just what this means, for it does signify a great deal. First it must not be forgotten that this famous school, not unlike the log-cabin days of Princeton, which was its model, had long been, as has been said, "academy, college and theological seminary" to many great men of the day; and that the young University was still a struggling institution, not quite having "found itself." Young John Motley Morehead and his father looked upon it in its old capacity; so that when he had Dr. Caldwell's course for 1811–12 and 1812–13, when a one-time lawyer of this general region, then of Tennessee, named Andrew Jackson, was soon to take part in the War of that year, he was advanced enough to have entered the Freshman year at the University. The decision, however, was to take not only his Freshman, but his Sophomore also, and even half of his Junior year, under the venerable and wonderful Doctor of Divinity, Medicine and Youth, with so wonderful a record as a maker of great

---

[1] *Annals of the American Pulpit,* by William B. Sprague, D.D., 1859, Vol. III, pp. 265–7. The letter closes: "Happy in the opportunity of thus bearing an humble testimony to the memory of my venerated friend, I remain, your obedient servant, J. M. Morehead."

men out of boys. One can imagine both father and son
weighing the pros and cons as to the respective advantages
of taking the rest of the Junior year and the Senior at the
old school or the new one. Nor must it be forgotten that
young John Motley was not many miles from his home in
Rockingham county or that he supervised the studies of his
younger brother, James Turner, and his sisters, in subjects
which he had completed.

As an illustration of what would have been required of
him if he had passed examinations in these classes in the
University, several years before, he would have taken up
preparatory work: Reading, Spelling, Webster's Grammar,
Arithmetic to the Rule of Three, Latin Grammar, Cordery
(a Latin primer), Æsop's Fables, and Eutropius, Erasmus,
Selectæ de Profanis and Vocables, Cæsar, Latin Introduction, Sallust, Ovid and Vigil's Eclogues, French Grammar,
French Fables, Telemachus, Gil Blas, Voltaire and Racine;
in Freshman work: Vigil, Latin Introduction, and Greek
Testament or Dialogues of Lucian, and the Odes of Horace;
in Sophomore work: Cicero, Geography, Arithmetic, Webster's Grammar, Syntax and Lowth's Grammar, the Satires,
Epistles and Horace's Art of Poetry; and half of the following Junior work: Ewing's Synopsis, Algebra and Ferguson's
Astronomy, or in place of the last mentioned: Junior Algebra, Euclid, Trigonometry, Heights and Distances, Navigation and Logarithms.[1]

There were probably other reasons why John Motley
Morehead and his father kept him here so long. The University was having a reputation for absence of discipline and
the students a kind of life that was not to be found in this
old school near the scenes of General Greene's and Cornwallis' conflict. Dr. Caldwell, says Dean Charles Le Raper
of the University Graduate School,[2] "was a thorough scholar
and had great tact in managing boys. He knew the correct
theories of life and education and had a wonderful faculty
in imparting instruction. His mode of discipline was very

---

[1] These, according to Battle's *History of the University of North Carolina*,
were the subjects of those respective examinations about a decade before. Vol.
I, pp. 168–9.
[2] *The Church and Private Schools of North Carolina*, p. 42.

peculiar to himself and very effective. He did not use the rod, nor is there any record of his ever having expelled a single student. His scholarship and character commanded their utmost respect. His disposition was of such a unique kind that he would give rebukes and corrections never to be forgotten; and such rebukes never won the ill-will of the pupil towards him. His countenance and manners, calmness and humor won their hearts. He knew how to inspire deep thoughts and great deeds in the boy. This was a school without a single parallel in North Carolina," and he adds that he knew of but one other such in the entire thirteen states. "Think," he continues, "of such a character in a log school house, a double-storied one with a chimney in the middle, which was built in his own yard, pouring out his deep life to about fifty boys or young men in those early times of darkness, and this, too, year after year for a long while"—practically a half-century, even allowing for its closing during part of the Revolution. He was beloved and venerated by every student and more than one has made a pilgrimage to his grave.

Such was the place that nurtured young Morehead for four profoundly influential years, when he decided, late in 1815, to go to the University of North Carolina and enter soon after Christmas in the middle of the Junior year, or as a "Junior Sophister" half-advanced. This institution, as the State University, had been provided for in the State Constitution of 1776, and chartered, as has been said, in 1789, with the adoption of the National Constitution, and its Presidency was offered to this venerable educator. They had endeavored to locate it, like they had Raleigh, the capital, as nearly as possible to the center of the commonwealth. They chose, therefore, a site about twenty-five miles northwest of the capital, "as the crow flies," on an elevation of Laurentian granite known as Point Prospect, or, more colloquially, "Piney Prospect," about 500 feet above sea-level and at the crossing of the old highway from Pittsboro to Petersburg, Virginia, and the one from Greensboro, through Raleigh eastward, to Newbern with its river flowing into Pamlico Sound. It was in an oak forest, with a wealth of springs and even the beautiful rhododendron of the mountains. At first designing the institution as one long building facing east—one exactly like the well-known institution on Dix Hill, at Raleigh—with a broad avenue from its main entrance to Point Prospect, they first built the north wing, which, when the Princetonians in the faculty became dominant, gave way to the English Quadrangle plan, so that the north wing became "East Hall," or "Old East," and by 1814 "Old South" facing north on the "Quad," was ready for students as the main building. Into one of its rooms, with four in a room, Dr. David Caldwell's half-advanced "Junior Sophister," John Motley Morehead, a fine big fellow of eighteen and a half years, with the Scotch sandy complexion and hair of his ancestry, was to come about a year or so later.[1]

When Dr. David Caldwell had declined the Presidency of the University, the trustees, doubtless hoping that he might yet be influenced, did not fill the office but gave executive functions to the Faculty, designating one of them as "Presiding Professor." In the very year that young Morehead was born, the then Presiding Professor Harris, wishing to be relieved, recommended the calling of a Princeton college-mate of his, graduated the year before he did, named Joseph Caldwell, but of no relation to the great Guilford county teacher. The young Princetonian was a native of New Jersey, a posthumous child of his Scotch-Irish physician father, and reared by his widowed Hugenot mother, who saw that he graduated in 1791 with the Latin Salutatory. Becoming a teacher, young Caldwell was soon recalled to Princeton as a tutor, meanwhile studying theology, and securing a license to preach in 1796. He accepted a unanimous call to become Professor of Mathematics at the new institution at the cross-roads of Chapel Hill, and buying a horse and sulky with box under the seat for supplies, he set out on a trip which was to last a month, coming down the Petersburg road onto the campus in the woods on October 31st, of that year. The primitive conditions discouraged him but put him on his mettle, and during the

---

[1] Battle's *Hist. of U. of N. C.*, Vol. I, p. 125.

following month he took up the work of his chair, and also succeeded his predecessor as Presiding Professor. Professor Caldwell had experiences in trying to avoid the office of executive, but his striking ability to meet crises in the growing University was so effective that, by 1804, the trustees were fully convinced that they had, in Professor Caldwell, not only a great teacher and an able executive, but, what was equally to the point, an educational statesman. It was due to the wisdom of the distinguished scholar, jurist and statesman, William Gaston, and another able trustee, Duncan Cameron, that this happy result was brought about. The new office was then first distinguished by the black gown. President Caldwell rose to the occasion and set before himself a new North Carolina Princeton, modifying the tendencies toward the sciences that had come through influences of General Davie and from the University of Pennsylvania. His progress in gathering a strong and permanent faculty about him was as difficult as the statesmanship that produced the physical side of the University; and the efforts to establish discipline and custom were no easier. It is not the purpose to enter greatly into the story of University development, further than to appreciate the influence of this great educator upon his new pupil.

One can hardly realize at this distance of time how much of an influence the French thought of Paine, Voltaire and others was, that took advantage of the great democratic movement led by Jefferson. They affected educational, religious and political theory in everything that came up in University life. One man at this time claimed that there was but one or two democrats among thirty trustees. All of this, however, only served to develop the statesmanship of President Caldwell, and he held his own with the ablest opponent. "It is the very nature of a place of public education," he wrote, "to polish and give play to the springs of human action, to spread abroad a desire of information, a spirit of active enterprise, and the instruments of interest, which must, without it, be buried in some distant part of the world." And his theory was exemplified in himself and his policies to a remarkable degree. He had much of the

modern university spirit, like that of Wisconsin, which
turned trained thought to development of the state in both
theory and policy, and application of the sciences—even
though the school was pathetically small at this time. One
of his graduates of 1799, Archibald Debow Murphy, at this
time a lawyer in Hillsboro, a few miles away, was even then
preparing to lead the state in almost every phase of public
development according to the fructifying principles of President Caldwell. The young man was at this very time preparing to advocate measures of public advancement in a
multitude of ways; but, of him, more anon. He had received many of these impulses from his friend the University
President and often longed for the academic shades with
him.

And President Caldwell, in 1810, saw that recognition
was given the venerable Guilford county teacher, then
seventy-five years old, by the degree of Doctor of Divinity;
and it is interesting, though pathetic, to see that the Faculty
consisted of but the President, one Professor and two
Tutors. These were critical days in every way, so much so,
that in 1812, the President insisted on being relieved of the
executive office. At this time, the *Raleigh Register* described
the institution: "In six months the Principal (South)
Building will be ready for the reception of inhabitants.
There will then be accommodations for eighty students.
There will be separate halls for the Dialectic and Philanthropic Societies, one for the library, and a Public Hall for
Prayers. Each of the Society libraries contains 800 to 1000
volumes. A society has been recently formed for the study
of sacred music. An organ ordered to be built in New York
is already finished. Public worship is held every Sunday in
Person Hall, which students are bound to attend. The
Faculty consists of a President, three Professors and one
Tutor. . . . The sessions run as follows: The first
from 1st of January to 24th of May. The second from
the 20th of June to the 15th of November." The expenses
of "diet," tuition, room-rent, servant hire, library, washing,
candles and wood, and bed total only $58.50.[1]

---

[1] Battle's *History of the University of North Carolina*, Vol. I, p. 230.

So he became Professor Caldwell again under President
Robert H. Chapman, a "Peace Federalist," who was inaugurated in January, 1813, at a time when the college
students were in no small measure neither "Federalist" nor
tolerant of "peace" with the hated British empire. And
they were for the North Carolina Tennessean who was
then carrying on a campaign with Georgia Indians, who had
been encouraged by the British, and preparing for the expected British attack on the Gulf Coast. The unhappy experiences of General Andrew Jackson in the west during
the year did not tend to lessen this feeling, and, just a year
later, January, 1814, the "Anti-Federalist" student element
made mid-night raids on President Chapman's stable, creating for him a horse with hair-less tail, hiding his cart,
over-throwing an out-house, secreting his gates, and finally
tarring and feathering the gate-post, leaving a written warning on the feathery entrance that Toryism in a certain high
officer might be dealt with in like manner![1] Ex-President
Caldwell was in no mood to stand idly by and endure this
procedure and he at once, forgetting his legal history, called
into use "general warrants" of the state that struck panic
to the hearts of students and parents alike. All elements
of the student body were examined, most of whom became
famous, among them being John Y. Mason, Francis A.
Thornton, Thomas J. Haywood, Francis L. Hawks, David
F. Caldwell, Charles L. Hinton, Charles Manly, and Willie
(pronounced Wylie) P. Magnum. The drastic action of
Professor Caldwell saved the day and the year. The institution was growing, too, for while the average attendance
of the collegiate department had been but 52 under President Caldwell, it was 88 under President Chapman; and the
graduates averaged respectively 6 and 16. Under the latter
also, the Bible became a required text-book in the courses;
and it was under his leadership that the Chapel Hill Presbyterian Church was organized. Like Ex-President Caldwell, who lost both wife and daughter during his term,
President Chapman lost his daughter; but he was honored,

---

[1] Battle's *Hist. of U. of N. C.*, Vol. I, pp. 234–5. The British burned the
Capitol at Washington in August following.

OLD SOUTH HALL
The Morehead room opposite one with last two second floor windows on the right

DIALECTIC LITERARY SOCIETY HALL, 1922

during 1815, with the degree of Doctor of Divinity by
Williams College, Massachusetts.

Therefore, the University was, in a sense, in a prosperous condition in January, 1816, with the stimulus of the
war of 1812–14 to all sorts of activity in education, religion,
internal improvement—especially transportation—and a
post-Revolutionary generation coming to its own, when
young John Motley Morehead, a Presbyterian and a Federalist in sympathy, entered the Junior Class "half-advanced,"
and took up his residence in one of the rooms in "Old
South" Hall.[1] One of the tutors under Dr. Chapman has
left testimony that he had "introduced a most salutary moral
change" into University life,[2] and doubtless young Morehead became an attendant of the church the President organized. The new Junior joined the Dialectic Society rather
than the Philanthropic, doubtless because that literary organization was then dominated more by Federalist members.
There was a mutual attraction between him and his Mathe-
matical teacher, Professor Caldwell, from the first, and
when the June Commencement arrived he was to see the
degree of Doctor of Divinity conferred on that member of
the Faculty. The graduate of that year to become most
famous was John Y. Mason, who became Attorney-General
of the United States and Secretary of the Navy under
President Polk (who was a student of the University at this
time) and was President Pierce's Minister to France who
became one of the authors, with Buchanan, of the famous
"Ostend Manifesto."

It should be remarked that practically continuous sessions of the University, excepting for a brief vacation of
about a month each at Christmas and in June, was due to
the fact that because of primitive transportation facilities

---

[1] The identification of this date has been made difficult by confusing and
conflicting statements of authorities, but it is believed this is accurate. The term
"first session" as applied to those beginning in January is also confusing in determining the middle of the Junior year, when commencement is held in June;
but the facts work out consistently. He was a Presbyterian adherent only.
    The "Old South" is now practically as it was in those days, even while
most of the University buildings are thoroughly up to date and being made
more so under the current administration. The picture of John Motley Morehead's room was taken in 1922.
[2] Rev. Dr. James E. Morrison, grandfather of President Charles W. Dab-
ney of Cincinnati University.

and long distance from home, the student came and staid continuously for the whole four years. This was, of course, probably not the case with young Morehead, for his home was only about fifty miles away, "as the crow flies." Apparently his brother, James Turner Morehead, was a Sophomore the latter part of the year, for he entered in the Class of 1819; and both were to witness a still more serious political out-break among the students on September 18th, so serious that it was to lead to President Chapman's voluntary resignation. A Newbern student, and of a family that worshiped at the shrine of the Sage of Monticello, had handed in an oration with a sentence or so of his "Republican"— as his party was called then—doctrine. This President Chapman forbade him to use in his delivery of the oration; but, on his appearance upon the platform the young Jeffersonian defied his Federalist President by using the forbidden sentences. Thereupon Dr. Chapman ordered him to sit down, but, encouraged by cries of "Go on!" and his prompter joining in the insurrection, he finished his speech amidst applause; and a large body of students met next day in the chapel and approved his conduct! Instantly the Faculty summoned 46 of them, suspended the orator and his leader, and two others. The rest were permitted to resume standing on a signed retraction of their offense; and among the signers were students who became known to fame as Chancellor William Mercer Green, of the University of the South, and Governor Wm. D. Moseley, first chief executive of Florida. As in other events of life, John Motley Morehead seems to have been one among those students who did not lose his head. He was also a senior, as was the offending Jeffersonian orator, and, as has been intimated, was a Federalist, which would probably account for his ease in retaining his poise. Public opinion, however, was so divided on the course of the President in carrying out the Trustees' rule that there should be no political speeches, that when, during the following month, some student made a bomb out of a brass knob and exploded it before a tutor's door, fortunately without injuring anyone although it exploded in the hands of one who attempted to throw it out,

President Chapman waited until the November meeting of the Trustees and resigned, the Board making it effective immediately. The Jeffersonian orator was a member of the Philanthropic Society, of which society a Dialectic member wrote at this time: "The poor Philanthropic members are to be pitied, for they have but thirteen members;" but another more cautious Dialectic later wrote that the membership "though increasing in numbers, degenerates in point of talent"—which shows that fraternity jealousy, like the poor, is ever with us.[1]

The Trustees again turned to Professor Caldwell on December 14, 1816, and again elevated him to the Presidency. This was a critical time, as the last session of young Morehead's senior year opened on January 1, 1817; but it was a great time in the commonwealth, for she had in her Senate one whose statesmanlike reports on plans for both internal improvement and public education, laid before that body on the 9th and 19th respectively, of the previous month, were soon to attract the attention of the whole country, and even be known abroad, setting up new and high standards in both, and certain to affect the plans for the University. This statesman and philosopher, one of the most striking and cultivated in the Union, was none other than President Caldwell's old pupil and friend and ablest supporter among the Trustees, Senator Archibald Debow Murphy. His proposals were along the same lines as those which De Witt Clinton was pressing in New York, state and city, but were far more scholarly and comprehensive, so far as the state was concerned; and these reports were only the opening guns of his campaign. Not less important than these, but due to the initiative of citizens of Rutherford, a county in the southwestern part of the state, was his constructive report proposing plans for a revision of the state constitution of 1776, which increasing settlement in the central and western parts of the state made imperative; while still another proposal of his was the colonization of free negroes,

---

[1] The two societies have come respectively, the writer is informed by Professor Connor, to be territorial in membership, the "Di" representing the west and the "Phi" the east. This would appear to the writer to be a natural outgrowth of political division of early decades.

who were increasing in number through individual emancipation, in some vacant parts of the great west. These papers were publicly printed and aroused the entire state; but at this point in this narrative only reference to his cooperation with President Caldwell in planning a more able Faculty need be considered and his consequent influence on John Motley Morehead, in the closing half of his senior year.[1]

The faculty was seriously crippled by the resignation of President Chapman, leaving it, technically, a University without a Professor. President Caldwell was of course a Professor, also; but for that session, January to June, 1817, his faculty consisted of Principal Tutor William Hooper, A.M., destined to become a Professor and college President, and Tutor William D. Moseley, himself a senior and destined to be Governor of Florida, and one other during that session, Robert R. King, but he was unpopular and resigned; so that during young Morehead's second half of his senior year, he was under President Caldwell's sole instruction, as were the other ten members of his class. The President, in 1815, had a salary of $1200, when Professor Caldwell had but $1000, and the Principal Tutor $500, with $300 and board each for the other two Tutors. These were somewhat increased under President Caldwell, and a search was being made for new professional timber in which they had their eyes on two Yale men, Denison Olmsted for the new chair of Chemistry, and Elisha Mitchell, then a Yale Tutor, selections again due to the scholarly Trustee, Hon. William Gaston. The former, however, was to have a year of further study, and the latter would not be available before February, 1818, so that President Caldwell and his Tutors constituted the Faculty the entire year of 1817.

Young John Motley Morehead gave his graduation oration at Commencement in June, and received his degree of Bachelor of Arts; but President Caldwell did not intend he should leave the institution yet. Principal Tutor Hooper, at this commencement, was promoted to full Professor of Ancient Languages, which had evidently been his chief field

---

[1] See Hoyt's *The Papers of Archibald D. Murphy*, Vol. II, pp. 33, 49, 56, *et seq.*; also Memoir in Vol. I, by Hon. William A. Graham, LL.D.

as Tutor, and the office of Principal Tutor was adolished.[1]
Tutor Moseley, A.B. (1817), was retained for the next
session and two additional Tutors were appointed by the
President, namely, John Motley Morehead, A.B. (also 1817)
and Priestly H. Magnum, A.B., who, with his brother, Willie
(pronounced Wylie), P. Mangum, A.B., had graduated in
1815.[2] Moseley, as Senior Tutor, considered himself a part
of the Faculty proper. Tutors Morehead and Mangum may
have had work with every class, in which case, John Motley
Morehead would have taught James K. Polk, a future President of the United States; William Mercer Green, a future
Bishop of Mississippi, and Chancellor of the University of
the South; Robert Hall Morrison, a future President of
Davidson College; and eleven other members of that notable
class; but he did have members of the classes of '19, '20, '21
and '22 and preparatory students; and among his Juniors
was his own brother, James Turner Morehead, whom he
had taught with other brothers and sisters in his own home.
His duties as instructor, therefore, were no new thing in
his experience, and the record is that he was an able Tutor
for that session and until the new members of the faculty
were installed at the beginning of 1818.

There is little doubt but that he had long since determined
to make the Law his profession, as his early Latin teacher,
Thomas Settle, Jr., had done; and now that he was ready to
begin its study, it was perfectly natural for him to turn, for
instruction, to that brilliant Senator Murphy of Hillsboro,
the county-seat not far from the University, whom it will

---

[1] Dr. Battle, in his otherwise excellent History of the University, makes
some very confusing statements about these events, but the facts seem to be as
here stated.

[2] The Mangums were prepared for the University by a very talented, educated free negro, named John Chavis, who prepared a considerable number of
sons of wealthy planters. Another free negro of the period, Rev. Henry Evins,
stopped in Fayetteville to do missionary work among the colored people; but
he was such a cultivated and powerful preacher that the white people came to
hear him so persistently that he finally organized them into a Methodist Church,
the colored people taking the gallery, and he became their pastor. As he became
old a young white minister became co-pastor and finally succeeded him. It is
said that inter-racial antagonism did not begin until the abolition movement
began; but considerable evidence exists that the real cause of it was the movement for independence under Toussaint L'Ouverture, some two decades before
this and its influence as an object lesson upon a younger generation of free
negroes and their associates. An uprising in Charleston sometime after this was
directly traced to this influence; and it would be further influenced, no doubt,
by the Bolivar movement in South America at this period, contemporary with
movements to check further emancipation or qualify it by causing them to be
transported.

be well to note more clearly at this point. The Senator was probably about forty-one years old, born about 1777 in Caswell, the county just east of young Morehead's home, and son of Colonel Archibald Murphy, whose plantation in the Dan valley was about seven miles from Milton near the Virginia border. He also was a product of Dr. David Caldwell's school, in which he remained until 1796, when the new University of North Carolina was started, and graduated after three years in 1799 with such distinction that he was made Tutor for one year and then Professor of Ancient Languages, a chair which he held for two years, during which incumbency he so perfected himself as a scholar of the highest character that he became distinguished throughout the State. He had begun legal study also under the direction of William Duffey, Esq., of Hillsboro, and, resigning, in 1801, to devote himself wholly to it, he was admitted to the bar by mere interview on the basis of his general ability. Notwithstanding he was to cross legal rapiers with such men as Henderson, Cameron, Norwood, Nash, Seawell, Yancey, Ruffin, Badger, Hawks and Mangum, he won a place in the front rank at this notable bar very soon. By 1804 he was taking such careful notes that he became Supreme Court reporter and was at this very time unconsciously preparing for the three volumes of reports yet to be issued.[1] His particular delight was in equity practice, which he often said was the application of moral philosophy to the affairs of men. In this field he had no equal in the entire State. In 1812 he was chosen State Senator from Orange County and for the next half-dozen years he was easily the leader in North Carolina government; and his broad and profound conceptions of public affairs caused him to introduce a new era in the State. Without doubt no man has greater claim to the title "Father of Public Improvement in North Caro-

---

[1] Mr. Murphy was clerk of the old "Conference" Supreme Court, and on May 26, 1819, was ordered by the new Court to deliver the records. Minutes of the Supreme Court, Vol. 19, of this date. The first North Carolina Reports was Haywood's of 1799, chronologically in date of publication; the second, Taylor's, in 1802; the third, Cameron & Norwood, in 1805; the fourth, Haywood, in 1806; then came Editor Gales', *The Carolina Law Repository*, legal miscellany, two volumes, in 1814 and 1816; next came Taylor's Reports of 1818; and Murphy's were issued—Vol. 3, in 1821, Vol. 1, in 1822, and Vol. 2 in 1826—a somewhat confusing arrangement if one is not informed, as they are not so numbered.

lina." Governor Graham, a follower of his in later years, says: "No man has ever brought into our Legislative halls a more ardent spirit of patriotism, a more thorough survey and comprehension of her situation and wants, or proposed bolder or more intelligent measures for her relief."[1] His reports, which as chairman of a legislative committee or of the Board of Internal Improvement, appeared, one or more every year from 1815 for the next eight years, covered, in masterly manner, such various subjects as water and road transportation, creation of trade centers within the State, a system of public education covering everything from primary schools and those for defectives, up to and including the University, and later even the history of the State. These papers are worthy of the best statesmanship of any land, and they became a great source of public instruction and public standards. If they had any fault, it would be that they were too comprehensive for their times, or that his was the work of the sower only, and that the executive reaper was yet among his younger followers.

His influence upon his own profession was scarcely less. He was a most successful teacher of the law. Thomas Ruffin, afterward a famous Chief Justice of the State, was not only a pupil, but a life-long intimate friend, and the brilliant Bartlett Yancey was another.[2] So, soon after February, 1818, John Motley Morehead gave up his tutorship at the University and began his legal preparation under the great lawyer and the distinguished public leader.[3] Whether Morehead lived at Hillsboro or not, is unknown; but it is

---

[1] *Memoir* by Hon. William A. Graham, LL.D., in the *Murphy Papers,* Hoyt, pp. 25, 26.

[2] Among Murphy's later students were: Governor Jonathan Worth, Col. James T. Morehead, Col. John A. Gilmer, William J. Bingham (the head-master of the celebrated Bingham School), Judge Henry Y. Webb of Alabama, Charles Pendleton Gordon of Georgia, and Justice Jesse Turner of the Supreme Court of Arkansas.

[3] It is interesting to note at this point, that on May 8, this year, lots were sold in the new town of Leaksville, Rockingham County—a town in which young Morehead was to become greatly interested—to the sum of nearly $25,000. *Raleigh Register,* current date.

Let it be noted, too, that on August 24, of this year, the corner-stone of the new National Capitol, to replace the one burned by the British, was laid, and Trumbull had his painting, *The Declaration of Independence,* ready for acceptance. Only 5 out of 55 of the signers were still alive, and yet the artist had been able, through himself or other artists, to get all but 10 of the 47 portraits from life. "The new United States Bank was erecting a building on land, that," says the *London Times,* "cost $1000 a front foot! a cost more than that of Carlton House, the home of the then British Prince Regent, or more than the Parisian palace of the King of Persia!"

probable that his work was done in Senator Murphy's office and fine library, and that he did much of the clerical work, as was the custom of those days. Near the close of that year, on the recommendation of Governor John Branch, there was a reorganization of the Judiciary under the leadership of William Gaston, that was to affect both the legal teacher and his pupil. The Judiciary Act of 1777 had created a "Superior Court," with six districts or circuits: 1. Wilmington; 2, Newbern; 3, Edenton; 4, Halifax; 5, Hillsboro; 6, Salisbury—to which were later added: 7, Morganton, and 8, Fayetteville; and it served the purpose of a Supreme Court until 1799, when a "Court of Conference," made up of these Judges, was created for Supreme Court purposes, the Superior Court becoming purely district or circuit courts. The "Court of Conference," in 1805, was given the name "Supreme Court," so that these Judges were both "Superior" and "Supreme" Court jurists—a fact rather confusing to the uninitiated. This, in 1806, caused the Judges individually to hold "Superior Courts" in each county twice a year, and six circuits were created. It was only in 1810 that these Judges sitting as a Supreme Court were authorized to select one of their number as Chief Justice, the first one being Judge John Louis Taylor of Fayetteville, who had been on the bench since 1798, and a quorum was any two of the Judges.

But during Senator Murphy's last session, after young Morehead had been with him nearly a year, a real and separate Supreme Court was organized. "The bill to appoint three Judges to hold the Supreme Court," wrote the Senator to his friend, Judge Thomas Ruffin, also of Hillsboro, on December 3rd, "has passed its second reading in both Houses. In the Senate 42 to 16 and in the Commons 80 to 44. The salary $2500. This will surprise you as it has everyone. It will probably be read the third time and passed in each house tomorrow. Tonight the enquiry everywhere is, who are to be the Judges?—I wish you were here to help our friend Seawell. I fear his chance is not good; great efforts are making for Taylor, and don't be surprised if he be elected. L. Henderson will be one, I believe. I was

waited upon this evening to know whether my name should
be used. I intend to be governed by circumstances. If I
see my way clear, poorly qualified as I am, I shall enter the
lists. I have been confined to my room constantly and know
nothing but from those who have business with me. James
Mebane tells me that L. Henderson, Gaston and myself will
be elected, if in nomination. He is well acquainted with the
members, and is influential. In all this you will know how
easily we may be deceived. One day more may give a
different aspect to things, and probably will. The salary of
the Circuit Judges will be raised to $2000. I think they will
probably be located. We have a liberal and intelligent legislature. When will you be down? No nomination is yet
made to fill the vacancy on the Bench. Nash, Toomer,
Paxton and Miller will all be in nomination. I can't even
conjecture who will be elected."[1]

The bill passed and on December 9th Senator Murphy
was nominated for the Supreme bench in the Lower House
by Mr. Mebane. The western ticket was: Henderson, Seawell and Murphy; but the eastern people, taking Henderson,
caused his election and that of Judge John Hall on Saturday,
the 12th of December, waiting until Monday, the 14th, to
elect the old Chief Justice, John Louis Taylor.[2] On the
following day a joint committee was chosen to select Judges
of the Superior Court, and on the 17th the resignations of
the Judges just elected to the Supreme bench were received.
One of the Judges, Lowrie, had died some time before and
the Governor and Council had found great difficulty in securing a successor, who was fit for it, the salaries were so
small and the circuit hardships so great. On the 18th
Judges John Paxton, John D. Toomer and Frederick Nash
were chosen to fill the vacancies; but on the 23rd of December Judge Thomas Ruffin's resignation was received and it
became necessary to elect his successor. Ruffin was proba-

---

[1] *The Papers of Thomas Ruffin*, Hamilton, Vol. I, p. 211. Judge Henry
Seawell was a Raleigh jurist of about forty-six; Henderson, of Granville, a
man of about the same age, later became Chief Justice; Congressman William
Gaston, of Newbern, about forty, had a greater national reputation than any
of the rest.
[2] *The Papers of Archibald D. Murphy*, Hoyt, Vol. I, pp. 122–3.

bly the ablest Judge in the State and, no doubt, had some hopes of a place on the highest tribunal of the State himself. Under the circumstances his logical successor, both from the point of ability and location, was Senator Murphy, and his choice was effected on Christmas eve, whereupon he became Judge Murphy of the Superior Court of North Carolina.[1]

Soon after holidays, the Superior Court Judges, excepting Judge Seawell, met and arranged their circuits, and early in February announced the result, as follows: 1. Edenton Circuit, Judge Daniel; 2. Newbern, Judge Nash; 3. Raleigh, Judge Seawell; 4. Wilmington, Judge Murphy; 5. Hillsboro, Judge Toomer; and 6. Morganton, Judge Paxton. The peculiar law that compelled continual change of Judges from one circuit to another and the varying hardships and inconveniences a given Judge would find in some of them gave occasion for heart-burnings, so that the Governor had to come in, in one case, and decided, about the middle of February, to send Judge Daniel to Raleigh and Judge Seawell to Edenton, away from home. It had a political bearing and Judge Seawell resigned and soon became Attorney General. That young Morehead followed Judge Murphy on his circuit is not probable; and how long he continued his intimate relations with his legal instructor into 1819 is unknown, because there seems to be no record of his admission.[2] It was probably late in the year, after his preceptor, as former clerk of the Supreme Court, had been directed, on May 26th, to deliver the records; after June 12th, when Judge Murphy was appointed Reporter for the Supreme Court and to publish the first three volumes, now known as Murphy's Reports; and probably after June 21st, when, by authority of "letters missive" from the Governor, he was appointed to sit on the Supreme bench, as a Judge of that Court in the temporary incapacity of any of its members. Judge Murphy was, therefore, a Judge of the Supreme Court on June 22

---

[1] It is a curious fact that no commission or record of one to Judge Murphy, as a Superior Court Judge can be found.
[2] The records of Guilford County Superior Court were nearly all destroyed by fire in 1870.

and 23, 1819, on December 13th, 14th, 15th and 17th of
the same year, and also in 1820, the first and only Judge of
this period to be so honored, and could claim the titles of
both "Justice and Judge."[1]   It was under such auspices
that young John Motley Morehead, now twenty-three years
old, closed his long period of preparation for life and the
practice of the Law.

---

[1] Supreme Court Minutes of these dates.
   The room in "Old South" Hall occupied by Mr. Morehead and others after
him, so that it is still known as "The Morehead Room," is on the southwest
corner of the second floor.   So late as 1891 the initials of the original occupant,
"J. M. M.," carved by him on the window sill, were plainly read.

III

Love as Well as Law

and

"Quiescere Non Possum"

1819

That a young lawyer should settle in the county-seat of his home county is perfectly natural, and especially if he should have taken his preliminary Latin under a young lawyer there, who was doing the same thing as young Lawyer Morehead had. The county was an old one, carved out of still older Guilford, in 1785, and both county-seat and county named after that friend of America among Englishmen, Charles Watson Wentworth, Marquis of Rockingham, the family name going to the former and the title name to the latter. North Carolina did not forget the Prime Minister who had repealed the Stamp Act and stood for their liberties, and his death, while again Prime Minister, only three years before the organization of the county, was fresh in their minds. Of course, this had been done before young Lawyer Morehead was born in that Virginia county named after a man of like character, William Pitt, but both names showed the keen patriotism of these two counties of the "Land of Eden," lying side by side in the rich valley drained by the Roanoke.

In Wentworth was his old Latin tutor, now just elected to the Sixteenth Congress, as successor to Bartlett Yancey, and leaving a lot business to his young Latin protegé. Congressman Settle had been in that able Legislature, led by Gaston and Murphy, while Morehead was in the University. He was only five years older than his old Latin pupil, and was an intimate friend, consequently an interesting example of the lawyer in public life. Mrs. Settle was the sister of a Cas-

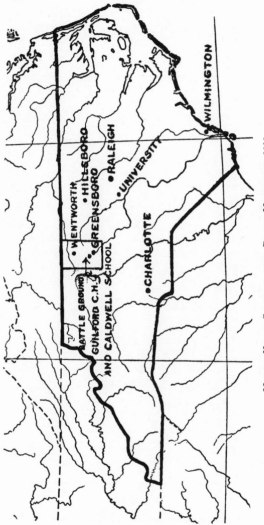

MAP OF NORTH CAROLINA WITH PLACES MENTIONED, 1819

well County boy of fifteen, in Bingham School, Calvin
Graves, who was soon to study law under her husband and
was destined to become an important factor in young Morehead's life. Mrs. Settle was to have a son-in-law, in the
same county, now a babe of but six years, bearing the name
David Settle Reid, and destined to become a Governor.
So Lawyer Morehead began his legal life in Wentworth,
and made his home with the younger Robert Galloway, "with
whom he lived during his residence here on terms of a perfect union of hearts,"—to use the words of Hon. John Kerr
years later.[1] He was but a few miles from his old home,
northward of the newly-projected town of Leaksville, and
his brother, James Turner, graduated this year from the
University and studied law under Chief Justice Taylor and
Judge Murphy.[2]

The two brothers saw much of one another as the years
proceeded and their horses travelled much down into Guilford County to the region of David Caldwell's school, near
the present Guilford Battle Ground National Park, where
these two old students of that school came to know, at
different periods, two young damsels at the small village,
there, of Martinsville, the seat of Justice of that county; and,
as it proved in the case of the two young attorneys, the
realm of another blindfolded deity, Cupid, who, like the
fates, were to determine this region as their home in the near
future.[3]

Guilford, unlike Rockingham, was a colonial county.
Its first inhabitants had settled there when it was still a
part of Edgecombe and Bladen Counties, in 1749; and
they were attracted by many things, fine forests, superb
water power, and an excellent diversified soil. Into the
central part that forms the present Guilford County, the
Scotch and Scotch-Irish came down the Piedmont from
Pennsylvania, Maryland and Virginia, and the Lindsay girls
were in this part, near Martinsville or Guilford Court House,

---

[1] Oration of Hon. John Kerr on John Motley Morehead, 1866.
[2] *Murphy Papers,* Hoyt, Vol. I, p. 25, and *Morehead Family of North
Carolina and Virginia,* John Motley Morehead III, p. 52.
[3] It should be noted that the younger brother's visits and interest were
some years later than those of John Motley.

as it was quite as frequently called. The settlers engaged in wheat raising and fruit culture, particularly, as did also the Germans from the Palatinate who settled the eastern part. The tobacco lands of West Guilford attracted the English Quakers as well as a band of Welsh; and others settled in the cotton country of South Guilford. Presbyterians from Nottingham, Pennsylvania, and South Carolina settled on the Buffalo and Reedy creeks, and were "Old School" in belief, while followers of Whitefield, the "New School," settled on the Alamance—causing the two churches over which David Caldwell presided so long. By 1766, Governor Tryon was able to say of this region: "I am of the opinion that this province is settling faster than any on the continent. . . . These inhabitants are a people differing in health and complexion from the natives in the maritime parts of the province, as much as a sturdy Briton differs from a puny Spaniard."[1] He even thought the region as "perhaps the best lands on this continent." These three elements make Guilford famous for its impression upon North Carolina. Governor Tryon was to find it out to his and their sorrow, in April, 1771, when, led by Guilford county men, calling themselves "Regulators," they refused to pay illegal taxes, and brought about the Battle of Alamance, which has been called the "first battle of the Revolution;" a failure, too, it was, just as "first battles" sometimes are.

Just ten years later the county was to be the scene of what has been called "the last battle of the Revolution," because it made that of Yorktown possible. For with the fall of Charleston in the spring of 1780, and the re-invigoration of the army by the new bank in Philadelphia, Washington was able to send General Greene to Charlotte later in the year, and in January, 1781, the latter's lieutenant, General Morgan, won the great victory at Cowpens, near the South Carolina line, and Cornwallis started for Greene's army. The winter and spring months were an exhausting game of

---

[1] Col. Records, Vol. 7, p. 248. The unpretentious little volume called *The History of Guilford County, North Carolina,* by Sallie W. Stockard, A.M., 1902, is probably the most useful single volume on this county, a volume made possible largely through the interest of Mr. Victor Clay McAdoo, of Greensboro, N. C.

chess on a gigantic board, but by March 14th, the American general was prepared to give battle near Guilford Court House, and on the 15th, that celebrated action resulted in a loss of one-fourth of the British forces, which so depleted them, that although the Americans had retired, Cornwallis' broken army had to hasten eastward for protection. Cornwallis called it a "victory," whereupon his London superior exclaimed: "Another such victory would destroy the British Army!" And Yorktown followed a few months later, and Guilford Battle Ground is now a beautiful national park.[1]

There had lived at this battle ground since 1772, Alexander Martin, a Princeton graduate, and the village at Guilford Court House took his name, Martinsville. He had been in public life since 1774 and was now Speaker of the State Senate, and upon the capture of Governor Burke, he became Governor, the first of six successive terms. But, in 1809, just before young Morehead had entered the Caldwell school, the county removed the seat of Justice to the exact center and named the new town in honor of the great American general, "Greensborough," which, in later days has been economized to Greensboro; and in 1819–20, young Morehead had cases here in the sessions of the Superior Court, while in 1821 the new town acquired a newspaper, *The Greensborough Patriot*. One interesting feature of Greensboro was the fact that it was between the slave-holding eastern part of the county and the Quaker western part, where the consciousness of the sin of slavery was increased by the

---

[1] This enterprise was a private one, long before the United States took it over, and John Motley Morehead's brother, James Turner's son, Major Joseph Motley Morehead, devoted so much of his life to it that a statue of him has been erected on the grounds. Scarcely less devoted was his wife, Mrs. May Christian (Jones) Morehead, a Virginian descendant of a founder of Baltimore, still resident of Greensboro, N. C. The following poem by him, on one of the monuments, represents the fine spirit of those who made this park possible:

"*Clio*

"*The Muse of History*

"As sinking silently to night
    Noon fades insensibly,
So Truth's fair phase assumes the haze
    And hush of history.

"But lesser lights relieve the dark,
    Dumb dreariness of night
As o'er the past historians cast
    At least a stellar light."

oncoming spirit of the Revolution and independence. In 1774, the Quakers, already the Quaker center of the State, began freeing their slaves, and the success of Toussaint L'Ouverture in freeing Hayti, led them to charter vessels to take the new freedmen there. Slaves were even bought in order to free them; and the number of free negroes that voted were not inconsiderable for a dozen years after this.

As has been said, however, the primary interest in the early visits of the Morehead brothers to the now ten-year-old county-seat, Greensboro, was in the environs in the home of the Lindsays, who lived at Martinsville and near Caldwell School. Of this family, one of the boys of the household, Robert Goodloe Lindsay, wrote, in later years: "Our great-great-grandfather came to this country from that portion of Ireland known as Scotch-Irish. The Lindsay blood is decidedly more Scotch than Irish. The Lindsays of Scotch-Ireland were descendants of David Lindsay, the head of the Scotch clan of feudal lords in Scotland before the fall of King James and Bruce, and portions of the family took refuge in Ireland. Afterwards some of them emigrated to America, and, with other Scotch-Irish colonists, settled in the lower part of Pennsylvania and Maryland; then a number sought new homes farther South. The greater portion of that number that came to North Carolina settled in Mecklenburg county, near and around Charlotte. Our grandfather pitched his camp in Guilford, in Deep River, about twelve miles west of Greensboro as it now stands. He never left the place he first settled upon, but raised his large family there, consisting of six boys and two girls: John settled in Davidson county, and has a large family of descendants; Samuel located in the south part of Guilford; William, near the old homestead; Andrew kept to the old homestead of our grandfather; David went to Jamestown; and my father, Robert Lindsay, took up his home at Martinsville, then the county-seat of Guilford county after the county was divided. He still continued to live at Martinsville, but did mercantile business at the new Court House, Greensboro. My mother [Letitia (Harper) Lindsay] continued to live at Martinsville until she married a Mr. [Henry] Humphries."[1]

Robert Lindsay, Jr., was a member of the first House of Commons under the commonwealth in North Carolina and had died just the year before young Morehead had settled in practice in Wentworth. Mrs. Lindsay was the daughter of Colonel Jeduthun Harper, of the Revolution, and was about ten years the junior of her husband. Her family, in 1819, consisted of Ann Eliza, the eldest, aged fifteen—the one in whom John Motley Morehead was interested; a son of thirteen, another of eleven, a daughter somewhat younger, a son of nine, a daughter of six, Mary Teas Lindsay, in whom some years later Attorney Morehead's brother, James Turner, was to became interested; and finally a baby son, three years old, who, years later, wrote the above account of the family. John Motley Morehead, of Wentworth, was only an occasional visitor, as he was rapidly becoming a very busy young lawyer in various parts of his circuit, that of Hillsboro, and was only looking forward to marriage, but not immediately.

He had begun buying his law-books, and, following the usual custom, he determined upon a suitable book-plate, with a motto, which he pasted on the inside of the front cover of each.[2] Such insignia, like a graduating theme, often are selected with wonderful intuition; and really do represent the life's chief characteristic in most cases, probably. A student of the Caldwells and Judge Murphy would be expected to have lofty ideals of life and the practice of the law, with a high regard for public duty. Judge Murphy at this very time, by his actual career, was as fine an embodiment of private and public life as was Cicero in the best days of the Roman Republic. Something over two years before, as

---

[1] *The Morehead Family of North Carolina and Virginia,* by John Motley Morehead III, of New York, p. 95.

[2] Lindsay Patterson, Esq., Winston-Salem, N. C., has his Reports coming down to about 1854. Some of the rest of his library is in the Public Library, Greensboro, N. C., among these books being a copy of Jefferson's *Manual of Parliamentary Practice for the Use of the Senate of the U. S.,* 1801, on the fly-leaf of which it is shown to have been presented by Jefferson to D. W. Stone and by him to Mr. Morehead on July 5, 1841. Another, Buller's *Trials at Nisi Prius,* was first owned by Wm. Fleming and then by Patrick Henry, while another containing Henry's book-plate is Coleman's translation of *The Comedies of Terence,* illustrated.

chairman of a House Committee on Inland Navigation, namely, in December, 1816, which resulted in surveys being ordered, in which he and President Caldwell took part, especially the proposal to connect the river transportation of the Cape Fear river, at head of navigation, with the Yadkin in the upper country, he produced his first able report. It resulted later, too, in his becoming President of the Yadkin Navigation Company. In this report he had said: "The true foundation of national prosperity and of national glory must be laid in a liberal system of Internal Improvements, and of Public Education," and intimated these were reserved for future thought. Following close upon it had been his report on Education later in the same month, in which he reviewed the excellent private schools and the University. "But," said he, "this general system must include a gradation of schools, regularly supporting each other, from the one in which the first rudiments of education are taught, to that in which the highest branches of the sciences are cultivated. It is to the first schools in the gradation" that he wishes to draw attention and make proposals covering every element in the population, even the deaf and dumb. This resulted in three commissioners as a board to digest a system of Public Instruction, of which also he was chairman, and his great report of November 29, 1817, while Morehead was yet a tutor, covered: 1. The creation of a fund; 2. An executive board; 3. Organization of schools; 4. Courses; 5. Modes of instruction; 6. Discipline; 7. Provision for poor children; and finally, 8. A Deaf and Dumb School. Still later in the same month, as has been noted elsewhere, as chairman of another committee, he showed how necessary it was that a new constitutional convention be called to equalize representation, which the great influx of population in the west had made viciously unequal. This proposal was defeated by the eastern members in the Senate, and this action touched probably the most sensitive nerve in the commonwealth, and it was felt from end to end of the body politic. About the same time he touched upon another sensitive public nerve, but with an alleviating hand this time, namely, with a proposal that might have made a negro State

ARCHIBALD DeBow MURPHEY.
From an engraving by John Sartain in
the *Murphey Papers*

on the Pacific Coast; and his resolution was adopted, but as
it was merely a national recommendation it came to nothing. It showed, however, the increasing sense of danger
in the growing number of free negro voters.

By the beginning of 1818, Chairman Murphy was able
to report, in an effort to create a fund, that what had been
done in inland navigation had increased the land values more
than ten million dollars. "North Carolina," says *The Niles
Register,* a national weekly of 19th July, 1817, "seems
roused to a sense of her many natural advantages. . . .
This State owes more to Archibald D. Murphy, Esq., than to
any, perhaps, of her many enlightened citizens. His name,
through his reports to the Legislature, etc., is familiar to our
readers; but he has many associates in his meritorious
labors." Already the several navigation companies had
made such improvements, that the *Register* announced that
tobacco from the Dan river, or upper Roanoke country, had
reached Norfolk in large amounts for the first time. About
the same time this statesman as chairman of a finance committee, attempted to solve the currency problems of the
State—a legacy of those who refused to re-charter that great
balance-wheel of finance, the Bank of the United States:
"About twenty years ago," he wrote on 17th Dec., 1817,
"we had no bank in this state: but we had a paper currency
issued by the State, supposed to amount to about three hundred thousand dollars. Every man whose recollection extends so far back, will admit, that at least one-half, of our
then circulating medium, was composed of paper currency;
and this fact seems to prove that our circulating medium at
that day did not exceed six hundred thousand dollars.
Until within the last six years, the banks of Newbern and
Cape Fear, were the only institutions of that description in
the state. The capital of both amounted to about four hundred thousand dollars, and the notes issued by them, not only
composed almost entirely *our* circulating medium, but they
overflowed into other states, and became considerably de-
preciated. The circulating medium, at that time required
for the state, could not have exceeded one million. When
the State Bank was established six years ago, with a capital

of one million six hundred thousand dollars, it was thought by many that that capital was larger than could be profitably employed in supplying the circulating medium employed by the state." He then shows that this State Bank's stock should be extended for relief in some way as the Newbern and Cape Fear Banks had, with extended charters, and that a Branch Bank of the United States Bank, re-chartered in 1816, was also nearly ready to open. Incidentally, he shows that at the time when banks west and south of New England suspended specie payments, notes of this State Bank of North Carolina, in a great degree, became a continental currency, and left the state dependent on the Banks of Newbern and Cape Fear [Wilmington]; but now that the National Bank was re-chartered and furnishing part of the currency, the outside currency is returning and caution must be used. His report on this subject of 21st November, 1818, was no less statesman-like; as was also that as chairman *pro tem.* of Commissioners, whose surveys were to connect up the river systems of the state, dated 28th November, 1818.

Judge Murphy's most elaborate treatment was issued as a publicist and for information of the Legislature in Nov., 1819, under the title *Memoir on the Internal Improvements, Contemplated by the Legislature of North Carolina, and on the Resources and Finances of that State.* It covered nearly a hundred pages, and was reviewed by Jared Sparks in *The North American Review* in January, 1821. It is impossible to speak too highly of this remarkable paper, which was being read and reviewed throughout 1820 and '21. It is probably the first statesman-like and adequate analysis of the fundamental problems of this great and unique commonwealth. It is probably not too much to say that here are the architectural plans and specifications of the state of North Carolina, so far as they could be foreseen and provided for in the second decade of the nineteenth century; and the architect, scientist and philosopher was Archibald Debow Murphy one of her own sons and a product of her own higher education under the two Caldwells.

To the general reader it furnishes probably the best conception of the North Carolina structural conditions and world-wide engineering on similar lines, of that day; but, as it is written for a foreign chief engineer, who had recently been secured, and also for the North Carolina influential public in order to secure adoption of the system proposed, it assumes in them a certain knowledge of the state and the times which will not be possessed by such a reader. In order, however, to arrive at that knowledge, it will be well to note some of the chief characteristics of what he does present:

He shows, for instance, that, for a State, as well as the individual, Pope's dictum—"Know then thyself"—was the beginning of wisdom. North Carolinians had known too much about her daughter, Tennessee, and the Ohio and Mississippi valleys, whither she had sent over a half-million of her population, because she knew not her own great resources. The War of 1812-15 had brought on a new generation and made Internal Improvement of resources the great slogan of the hour. The Legislatures of 1815, and those since, had awakened to it, but not enough. Two of the greatest needs were Transportation and home Trade Centers; and by the former he meant only water transportation, with short good roads to it, while, by Trade Centers, he meant a port of sufficient dominance to be a Financial center. As it was, there was a tendency to go to the Roanoke and two Virginia ports or the South Carolina rivers and Charleston, with one-third of her production. This made out-side financial, as well as trade centers and destroyed the unity of the state, and raised up no great consuming communities. Transportation, trade, manufactures, finance and banking were different phases of the one unity; and they were inseparable. He cited Pennsylvania as first realizing it and acting accordingly with marvelous results. New York's great canal was a beginning there, and Virginia had already established a fund. And what is more, Pennsylvania had so profited by her investment that in her returns from it she had been enabled almost to dispense with taxation. He analyzes the unique water-front of North Carolina and its problems of engineering, and the efforts to get a great engineer for whom the demand was greater than the supply, and the amateur efforts of home talent meanwhile. Surveys and maps were needed and settlement of boundaries. (Mr. Hamilton Fulton, the distinguished young British engineer, for whom this was, in part, written, had been secured in July, 1819.) The river systems are analyzed in relation to a proposed port, better, if possible, than Wilmington, which had great disadvantages; and a canal connection of those systems is a prime object. He points out the granite falls of these rivers at the eastern edge of the Piedmont, and their obstruction to traffic, in a great northeast and southwesterly sweep just eastward of Raleigh, as the chief inland problem. Allied to these were connecting roads and drainage of swamp lands.

These analyses were supported and enforced by excellent statistical tables: For example, net payments to the national government, as duties, etc., varied from $16,918.49 in 1808, the lowest, to $456,478.81 in 1813, the highest. Exports had ranged from $117,129, in 1808, the lowest, to $1,328,271, in 1816, the highest. For 1816, as an example, Wilmington led, with $1,061,112; Newbern followed next, with $84,281; Edenton next, with $71,484; Plymouth next, with $36,314; Washington next, with $33,933; Ocracoke Inlet, with $28,-165; and finally Camden, with but $12,982. North Carolina foreign trade tonnage, registered, varied from 10,167 in 1793 to 26,472 in 1810. Coasting tonnage, above 20 tons, varied from 2764 in 1793 to 13,184 in 1816. As an example of chief exports abroad from Wilmington in 1817: cotton was chief with 438,529 lbs.; Indian Corn next with 22,588 bushels; turpentine, tar, pitch and rosin next with about 18,000 bbls.; lard, over 20,000 lbs.; shingles, over 14,000 thousands; over 12,000 lbs. of hams and bacon; and lesser exports, the total value of which was $713,961.48. Fayetteville, at head of navigation on the Cape Fear, handled of domestic produce from the Pidemont, $621,900 worth of cotton and $400,000 worth of tobacco; $129,629 worth of flour; $77,460 worth of flaxseed; $50,000 worth of miscellany like bacon, lard, tallow, furs, etc.; a total of $1,331,398.

The population that produced this, was, in 1810:—555,-500, of which 168,824 were slaves; and they were dis-

tributed in leading counties as follows: total population:
1. Rowan, in the central west, had most, 21,543; 2. Orange,
near it, 20,135; 3. Wake, where Raleigh is, next, 17,086;
4. Lincoln, western also, 16,359; 5. Halifax, eastern Roanoke valley, 15,620; 6. Granville, another Roanoke county,
15,576; 7. Rutherford, west of Lincoln, 13,202; 8. Northampton, another Roanoke county, 13,082; 9. Chatham, near
Orange, 12,977; 10. Craven, the Newbern port county, 12,-
676—to name only ten of eighteen counties of above 11,000.
The counties which led in number of slaves were: 1. Granville, in Roanoke county, with 7746; 2. Northampton, also
on Roanoke, with 7258—exceeding the whites by about 1500;
3. Halifax, also on Roanoke, 6624; 4. New Hanover, the
Wilmington county, 6442—exceeding the whites by over
1400; 5. Warren, also on Roanoke, 6282—exceeding whites
by over 1500; 6. Bertie (accent on last syllable), also on
Roanoke, 6059—exceeding whites by nearly 1000; 7. Wake,
Raleigh county, 5878—scarcely half of the whites; 8. Franklin next to Warren and practically Roanoke county, 5330—
nearly 500 above the whites; 9. Edgecombe, adjoining Halifax, 5107, over 2000 less than the whites; 10. Craven, Newbern's county, 5050, over 200 less likewise—to name but ten
of sixteen counties having above 3000 slaves. The counties
greatest in white population were: 1. Rowan (also first in
population, but being thirteenth in slaves); 2. Orange
(eleventh in slaves); 3. Lincoln (below sixteenth in slave
rank); 4. Rutherford (far below sixteenth in slave rank);
5. Wake (seventh in slaves); 6. Mecklenburg (sixteenth
in slaves); 7. Guilford (with 9953 whites and only 1467
slaves); 8. Stokes; 9, Burke; 10. Chatham (fourteenth in
slave rank)—naming only ten of eighteen counties with
above 7800, all of which, possibly excepting Wake, the capital seat, being Piedmont or mountain counties, while seven
out of the first ten slave counties were on the Roanoke or
next to them, the exception being the Wilmington, Newbern
and Raleigh counties. The value of all the slaves in 1815
was $40,667,314, almost as much as the land which was for
tax purposes, $53,521,513. In that year there were twelve
counties whose land valuations were above one million dol-

lars: 1. Rowan ($1,870,142); 2. Halifax; 3. Orange; 4.
Edgecombe; 5. Northampton; 6. Wake; 7. Bertie; 8.
Mecklenburg; 9. Lincoln; 10. Granville; 11. Warren; and
12. Guilford, with 1,042,704. Of these twelve, half are
Roanoke country, four are central western and two western
near the mountains, or, practically half Roanoke and half
western, a fact of great significance. The whole number of
counties at this time was sixty-two.

The 1817 taxes, by counties, with fourteen paying each
above $2000: 1. Orange, with Hillsboro; 2. Wake, with
Raleigh; 3. Granville; 4. Rowan, with Salisbury; 5. Cumberland, with Fayetteville; 9. Edgecombe, with Tarboro;
7. Caswell; 8. Northampton; 9. New Hanover, with Wilmington; 10. Warren; 11. Bertie; 12. Halifax; 13. Mecklenburg, with Charlotte; and 14. Lincoln. Of these, eight
were in Roanoke country; three were Western and Cumberland and Wake were partly eastern and partly western,
with one being the port county of Wilmington.

The State owned $500,000 in bank stock and $112,500 in
stock of the following navigation companies: Roanoke, Yadkin, Cape Fear, Neuse, Tar River, Catawba, Lumber River
Canal, Roanoke and Pamtico [Pamlico] and Club Foot and
Harlow Creek. The Treasury disbursements in 1817 were
$207,081.51. By his analysis of revenue and expenditure,
he showed that there would be an annual surplus of $35,000,
which in 1822, would leave in the Treasury $265,234.58.

He then analyzes the statistics to show the state can have
ample funds to carry out this improvement system. The
Cherokee lands of probably "more than a million acres"
and the required loans of the two old banks are added
to these showing that the state, without taxation, had at
her command more than a million dollars. He then treated
in detail how these funds should be managed and proposed a Board of Public Works. To these he added a plan
of feeder roads in the mountains; and closed with an
analysis of the problems of the formation of alluvial lands
on the coast, with historical treatment from Herodotus down
to Proney, the French engineer, and Cuvier's *Theory of the
Earth*.

It will thus be seen that North Carolina had great problems and that, in approaching them, she had a great and skillful leader in taking the first steps in their solution, as a publicist and public inspirer and teacher, in this able lawyer, jurist and statesman, Archibald Debow Murphy, law preceptor and friend of young Attorney John Motley Morehead of Wentworth, in the county of Rockingham. Is it any wonder then, that, when the young man chose a book-plate and pasted its impressions on the inside of the front cover, it should contain a thought from Cicero's *De Republica,* and in the language of that Roman lawyer, and should read:

No. ——

John M. Morehead

— : o : —

Quiescere non Possum

which latter, being liberally interpreted, signifies that he is not able to live uninterested in public affairs? As he had been a disciple of Murphy in law, so he became one of his followers in statesmanship, destined to surpass his master in vision and powers belonging to another generation and a new time.

IV

Lost Atlantis' Legacy
OF
Problems to North Carolina

1821

Attorney John M. Morehead had been in practice in Wentworth about two years, when his inability to be uninterested in public affairs—the problems of state—and his excellent general ability became so evident, that Rockingham county, in the summer of 1821, when he was but twenty-five years old, sent him to the lower house of the Assembly, then called the House of Commons, as a successor of his old Latin teacher, Congressman Settle. And he went as a supporter of the program of Judge Murphy, and was familiar with his great report on the problems of the commonwealth. He brought to it a mind quite as comprehensive as that of his preceptor-statesman, and even more so; but with that comprehensiveness, he brought not less of theory, but more of organizing constructive power and a more severe regard for great realities. A suggestion of the visionary might characterize Murphy, and his career had failures in it; but Morehead's life was not characterized by failure and, by common consent of all, he was "a man of great vision." He was a remarkably well rounded man, physically, with his powerful frame and sandy, Scotch temperament, genial but serious, magnetic and gentle; intellectually, with the finest cultivation, a mind open to all sides of life, master of himself, capable of holding fine ideals in the proportions of truth, able also to see life whole, a strong writer and a powerful speaker; socially, able and inclined to meet pleb or patrician port to port and as though his vision of manhood was so keen that he minified the differences; and, morally, holding his ideals with a constant aggressive intuitive purpose and power to realize them. While some could hold

ideals in a speculative way, John Motley Morehead held them
in a process of realization. If his wagon was hitched to a
star, he kept the wheels to a well-paved highway. Vision
and action were undivorced, and he so lived in that kind of
a presence, that it produced the impression of a combined
modesty, boldness and wisdom, that makes him a difficult
character to picture. Not that this ripeness was complete
in this, his twenty-fifth summer, but the foundations were
all there; and he approached the problems of North Carolina with this kind of character.

And those problems were unique, among all the common-
wealths of the union, and even all countries of the world.
No land in the world had just such a combination of
problems, and no man was to enter upon their solution with
so great a comprehension, as he came to penetrate into them
more and more from year to year.

Let us see just what they really were—and, it may be
added, still are! And they are wonderfully interesting,
going back to what some have called "Lost Atlantis."

To find the problems of North Carolina, let us go to the
Island of Hayti, and go to the top of Mt. Tina. Here one
stands on the top of a mountain on a mountain, for the
Island of Hayti is itself the top of a submarine mountain,
as are all the West Indies up to the Bermudas—mountains
which themselves rise from a submarine continent; so that,
from the top of Mt. Tina, down its sides and down to its
base in the bottom of the ocean, is a height greater than Mt.
Everest by nearly two miles—about 10,000 feet greater, to
be more exact. The great depths about this submerged
continent, so near to the American shore, and by some supposed to be the lost Atlantis, gives a new meaning to that
more than seven-mile depth of waters that stream about its
sides into the Gulf of Mexico, continually acquiring more
head, and passing out along the front of Florida, Georgia
and South Carolina, about thirty miles out, and with a
velocity of about three miles an hour, and with so vast a bulk
that it is itself a feature of continental proportions.

As it reaches the front of North Carolina and begins
to pass out of the gigantic gateway between it and the Ber-

mudas, it both spreads out and meets the cold current down the coast; and the junction of these cold and heated bodies helps to make the storms of these waters most dangerous, while in earlier days, before the Stream was understood, its uncanny power to secretly move vessels out of their courses contrary to all reckoning, made this region a terror to mariners. But, if storms were produced by this junction, the pressure of the opposing streams upon each other and the coast of North Carolina, for centuries, caused all her rivers to slow up so much as they entered the ocean, that they dropped their silt and sand, which their succeeding waters at first built up into alluvial lowlands; and then, as these drew nearer deep water, the Gulf stream built up a barrier of the most perfect lacery of bars and dunes in front of the whole state to be found anywhere in the world. To introduce shifting bars and dunes into this stormy projection into the ocean, and the dark uncannily moving Stream, was to make this cape, which was given the name Hatteras, or "Hatteresk," from a tribe of Indians found there, famous throughout the maritime world as "the graveyard of the ocean."[1] The pressure of the volume of water

---

[1] The following excerpt from a poem by Joseph W. Holden, entitled "Hatteras," says:

"Yon lifeless skull shall speak to me,
This is Golgotha of the Sea!
And its keen hunger is the same
In winter's frost or summer's flame."

With this peculiar front on one end of the State, the other end has the distinction of having the highest mountain peak in the eastern half of the United States. The artist, Alfred S. Waugh, thus apostrophizes it in *The Greensboro Patriot*, 30th Oct., 1836:

"MT. MITCHELL

"Proud monarch of a cloud capp'd race,
Why hide from us your royal face
    And be but seldom seen?
Why do you thus in sullen mood
Around you dash the vap'ry flood
    As if you ne'er had been?

"Why o'er your sides the screen let fall?
Why shroud yourself in mystic pall
    And hide your height from view?
Is it that conscious of your size
You lift your head above the skies
    To bid the world adieu?

"Or that you fear the painter's art
Might from you take in whole or part
    Your glories newly known,
That thus from public gaze you flee
And show yourself to none but me
    From top of yellow Roan?"

from the rivers of North Carolina, penned up within this remarkable barricade, was not sufficient to preserve many open-
ings or inlets, or keep clear what were preserved; while it
built more lands and cut out new channels, as though according to the whim of the moment.   It was thus, that Sir Walter
Raleigh's Roanoke Island was formed just within the lacy
barrier, when there was an inlet near it; and it was these
obstacles that finally drove his enterprise to the Chesapeake.
For behind these barriers were two main bodies of water,
one, Pamlico Sound, over half as large as the Chesapeake,
and Albemarle larger than Delaware Bay, both nearly encom-
passing a great peninsula containing over 5000 square miles
of heavily over-grown swamp lands, while great flat alluvial
plains stretched back of these, the whole constituting about
two-fifths of the state, back to the falls of the various
rivers.

The front entrance of the state, therefore, had been almost closed by the sinking of lost Atlantis and her watery
offspring, the Gulf Stream.   The very best inlet in use in
1821 was that leading to Wilmington, and it had a channel
of but seventeen feet at high tide, and but eleven feet before
Wilmington was reached.[1]   The chief inlet to the Sounds
and their tributaries was Ocracoke, half way between Capes
Hatteras and Lookout, with the pressure of water so great
that there was no perceptible tide; while the bars allowed
vessels drawing only eight feet of water to enter.   The inlet near Cape Lookout, at Beaufort, had been held by many
to have the greatest possibilities, as it had fourteen feet of
water and a fine harbor within; but, to make it useful to the
Sounds, canal connections would be necessary, a not very
formidable undertaking.   However, to ask Wilmington, mistress of the Cape Fear river valley, to endorse the creation
of this effective rival, or to ask the rich Roanoke planters
to build up a port so far away, when Virginia's Norfolk or
Petersburg were so much nearer, was to ask the impossible,

---

[1] A Memorial from the Inhabitants of Wilmington to the Legislature on
December 3, 1822, says that before "the great storm" of 1763, the Cape Fear
bar allowed twenty feet of water at high tide, but this storm made a "New
Inlet," while in 1813 nearly a mile of the Cape was washed away, since which
the *bar* is all right, but the *flats* are worse, and they ask relief. Papers of the
Assembly, 1821-2, Historical Commission, Raleigh.

especially when the constitution of 1776 left these eastern leaders dominant in the state.

Herein was, therefore, the greatest peculiar problem of North Carolina—the obstacles to a great port. Its vital nature may be realized by thinking of a state's port as her heart and head. What were Massachusetts without her Boston; New York State without her city of the same name; Pennsylvania without her Quaker metropolis, Philadelphia; Maryland without her Baltimore; Virginia without her Norfolks and Richmonds; or South Carolina without her Charleston? The metropolitan port is the head, the heart, the organizing center of finance, and all great enterprise, the keystone of the state's arch.

As a consequence, when these obstacles drove Sir Walter Raleigh's enterprises to the Chesapeake, Norfolk became the port of chief entry into the northeastern corner of the colony on the northern waters of the Albemarle, and here grew up the first chief settlements.[1] As the grant of Carolina in 1665 stretched from that line below Norfolk down to include all of northern Florida, and westward to the ocean, there were some settlements grew up in the Cape Fear region over 150 miles beyond the swamps and penned in waters of the Sound, which was formed into Clarendon county, most of which was below Cape Fear. Consequently about 1689, the two settlements became known as North Carolina, meaning the Albemarle settlements and South Carolina, those below and about the Cape Fear river and cape. Some settlements began to occur between these on Pamlico Sound, one at Bath, becoming the center of a new county of the same name covering all the colony, except the two regions mentioned; so that up to 1722, when John Morehead I, was moving up the "Northern Neck" of Virginia, there had been three counties: 1. Albemarle, covering both banks of that Sound and the Roanoke and Tar valleys, of which Edenton became the chief town; 2. Clarendon, roughly covering the Cape Fear River valley, but abolished in 1667, of which Wilmington became the head; and 3. Bath, the space between, but after

---

[1] It should be added that many settlers in this region, when the boundary was unsettled, thought they were still in Virginia.

CAROLINA, 1665

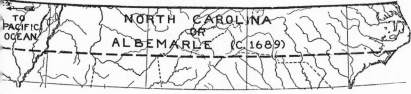

NORTH CAROLINA, C. 1689

MAPS SHOWING ORIGIN OF NORTH CAROLINA
Prepared by the author
Westward extension varied with variation of British claims

1667, covering all the rest of the colony with Washington town later to displace Bath, and the Neuse with the German and Swiss settlement of New Bern (later written Newbern) at the head of the estuary as chief inland port, both dependent on Ocracoke Inlet, with the Swiss town leading. These two big counties were divided into precincts, which in 1739 became counties themselves, thereby abolishing the two mother counties and creating fifteen: in old Albemarle, beginning at the east were: 1. Currituck; 2. Camden; 3. Pasquotank; 4. Perquimans; 5. Chowan—north of the Sound; 6. Tyrrell, south of it; 7. Bertie, westward; and 8. Edgecombe—extending southward nearly to Raleigh site and west to what is now Stokes county; while in old Bath, also beginning in the east, were, 9. Hyde; 10. Beaufort; 11. Craven; 12. Carteret; 13. Onslow; 14. New Hanover; and 15. Bladen—the frontier county extending to the Pacific Ocean. It will be observed, therefore, that the first eight, or Albemarle counties are those of the Roanoke and Tar rivers and Sound valleys and that they thus had a special community of interest at this early date which they were destined never to lose; but the latter seven, or Bath counties, were divided in interest because four of them—Hyde, Beaufort, Craven and Carteret—were more identified with Pamlico and the Neuse valley, while Onslow was between them and the two big counties of New Hanover and Bladen, which covered the Cape Fear River valley, stretching like a wide ribbon northwestward through the center of the colony almost to the mountains at the Virginia line. These two sections, therefore, had no community of interest—indeed, were essentially rivals.

All three, however, were also cut off, in some measure, from their back country, by the beginnings of elevation to what is called the Piedmont Plateau, a line roughly approximating a parallel to the coast, but with slight curve from near the first shoulder in the South Carolina boundary northeastward, east of Raleigh site, to somewhat below the Roanoke crossing of the Virginia line, where are a dozen miles of rapids. The Tar rapids are more scattered; those of the Neuse at Smithfield; and those of the greater Cape Fear at

Fayetteville, while her tributaries are lined with falls and rapids. All of which was not designed to encourage early immigration to these upper territories, by water.

All of this, however, leaves a great triangle, based on the South Carolina line, between the Cape Fear river ribbon-like valley and the mountains—almost one-fourth of the colony —unaccounted for, which is drained by two South Carolina rivers, the Yadkin and the Catawba, and were consequently unified in their community of interest with South Carolina, as much, if not even more than, the Roanoke and Tar valleys with Virginia—or would be when they came to be much settled. The mountains, too, "The Land of the Sky," were always turning their eyes toward the Mississippi valley with a unity of isolation of their own. And still, while these economic interests made this and the other divisions of the state at an early period, and ethnological and religious groups added to the complexity, a political grouping was to take place with increased settlement, that was to prove the more powerful, as shall be seen presently, for it was destined to unite the whole Piedmont plateau and the mountains as well, against the ancient eastern alluvial plains.

For Albemarle county was settled chiefly by English, many of whom were Quakers, while the Newbern settlement were chiefly German and Swiss, largely destroyed by the Tuscarora war of 1712-15; and the Cape Fear settlers, about the mouth of that river, were also English. The sturdy permanent element and larger than the latter two, however, and later, was first the Scotch Highlanders, who located at the falls of the Cape Fear, where Fayetteville became their center, and finally the greatest mass of Scotch-Irish and Germans, with many English Quakers, came down the Shenandoah, or the Piedmont, from Pennsylvania and Virginia, into the Piedmont and with such rapidity and in such numbers that it almost became like a new colony, encouraged thereto by the successive Scotch-Irish executives, Governors Johnston, Rowan and Dobbs.

The estimated population of these fifteen counties in 1739 was probably about 65,000, for the estimate for 1729 was 35,000 and 1752, was 100,000; but it rose to 200,000 at the

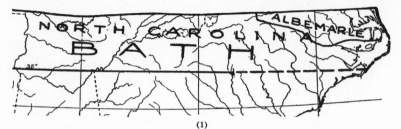

(1)

The Two Original Counties of 1696 created after and over Original Precincts

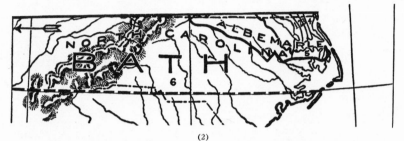

(2)

The Two Original Counties showing Precincts created from 1672 to 1705, Bath
a Precinct until 1696

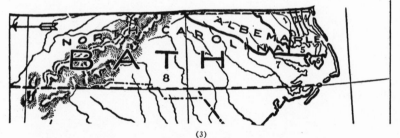

(3)

The Two Original Counties showing Precincts created from 1705 to 1712,
remainders of Bath and Albemarle serving as Precincts

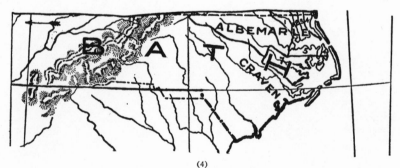

(4)

The Two Original Counties showing Precincts, 1712 to 1722

North Carolina Count
Prepared

Precincts (Counties from 1739): 1. Chowan; 2. Perquimans; 3. Pasquotank; 4. Currituck; 5. Al
1705), Craven (to 1712); 9. Bath (after 1712),

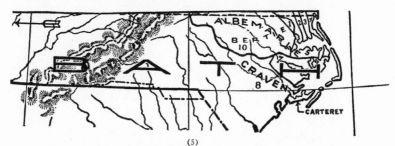

(5)

The Two Original Counties showing Precincts created from 1722 to 1729,
Albemarle ceasing to be Precinct

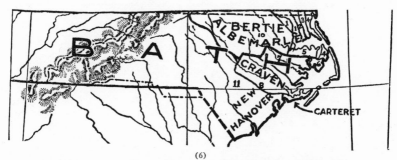

(6)

The Two Original Counties showing Precincts created from 1729 to 1734

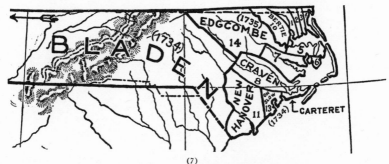

(7)

Map showing all Precincts transformed into Counties, 1739

(8)

Map showing all Counties created from 1739 to 1749

PMENT FROM 1672 TO 1749

thor

to 1729), Tyrrell (from 1729); 6. Hyde (after 1705), Bath (before 1696); 7. Beaufort; 8. Bath (to
(after 1722); 10. Bertie; 11. New Hanover; 12. Bladen

time of the Stamp Act, and 250,000 in 1771—five years before independence and union was declared. And this increase, while in a measure general in territory, was essentially an extension southward from the rich Roanoke
valley and its tributary the Dan, and that, too, from its
central and upper courses in the Piedmont. This vigorous
element has been said by some to have begun the Revolution in the Regulators' war about the time of the Stamp
Act in what was then Orange county—a western section of old Albemarle and a part of old Bath, extending out
to include what became young Morehead's old home counties—a struggle that lasted six years, and caused a great
exodus to North Carolina's trans-mountain territory to be
later known as Tennessee. It is reasonable to suppose that
the population, by 1774, was nearly 300,000, when a call
came for a Continental Congress and five men, chiefly of that
old Albemarle population, braved the British executives'
wrath and secured a convention even at Newbern, the seat
of his palace, and elected three Continental Congressmen,
one of whom was out of the same old county. Mecklenburg, Rowan and Orange, in the Yadkin-Catawba triangle,
and upper Cape Fear, westward, were the frontier counties
then, and their capitals, Charlotte, Salisbury and Hillsboro
took famous part when the guns of 1775 began to reverber-
ate. And, as has been said previously, it was here the closing conflicts of the Revolution occurred. Here it was, too, at
Hillsboro, after the flight of the British governor, in 1776,
that a provisional government was formed. In this old
Albemarle-Roanoke territory, too, at Halifax, on April 12,
1776, their Continental Congressmen were directed by solid
vote to secure independence and union. At the same place,
too, on December 18th, following, a constitution was adopted
by their convention.

What was done on that day, just a week before Christmas, created one of the greatest problems in the state's history; and it was to take nearly eighty years—the better part
of a century, to secure its solution. The population was so
distributed that the old principle of the Provincial Convention with each county equally represented, with representa-

tion from each town also, was continued in the new constitution of 1776.[1] No evidence has been found that this
method was considered vicious at that time; but by 1786,
when the population is estimated at 350,000, and, the increase was in the west, and the great principles of representation in a national government were fiercely discussed in
1787, and the immediately succeeding years, the west, or
Piedmont and Mountain region, began to challenge the inequality. This challenge, demanding new western counties,
of necessity, was met by the east, in an endeavor to retain
her power, by the creation of *un*-necessary counties, in her
territory merely as an off-set: if Caswell in the west is created in 1777, so must Camden be, in the east; and Wilkes
in the west must be off-set by Nash in the east; although
Burke was created in the west with no counterpart in the
east that year. In 1778, however, Gates was created in the
east, also Jones, whereupon Montgomery was erected in the
west. So in 1779, Lincoln, created in the west, was met by
Franklin in the east; and Rutherford and Randolph in the
west by Warren and Wayne, east, with Richmond on the
border. War and its aftermath kept them too busy the next
four years to create counties, but when Moore was created
in 1784, in the west, Sampson was erected in the east; while
the erection of Rockingham in the west in 1785 was balanced
by Robeson the following year. The National Constitution
kept them busy, but in 1788, when Iredell was erected in
the west with a vigorous challenge of this method, caused
by that constitution, no eastern one was created to balance it.
Three years later, 1791, the same thing occurred: the west
secured Buncombe and the east Lenoir, but when the west
secured Person, it was acknowledged a gain. Nothing was
done then for eight years, when, in 1799, the west secured
Ashe, but the east got Washington and Greene, which reduced the gain in the west. Over eight years passed again,
and in 1808, the east met the west's Haywood with Columbus. This was the status in 1821, when *Quiescere non
Possum* began to be effective as the motto of young John

---

[1] Free negroes were given the right of suffrage.

Motley Morehead, and he was elected to public life from one of those western counties, that of Rockingham, one of the westernmost of the old Albemarle-Roanoke group, when the west began to be restive with a constitution that could be manipulated in so absurd and unjust a way.

Furthermore, the lower Roanoke and the east were the region of great plantations and consequently of great slave population; and yet it was the Quakers in the northeast of old Albemarle that were the first to give vigor to the emancipation movement, which later was pushed with power by the Manumission Society of the Quakers in Guilford county in the west, which became Morehead's permanent home; but of this theme more anon. The federo-national ratio of races in voting, introduced with the constitution of the United States, in 1787, became a new source of complexity between the east and the west, where the slaves were so much fewer; and increased the resentments of both. The federo-national constitutional ratifying conventions of July, 1788, and November, 1789, at Hillsboro and Fayetteville respectively, in the first of which it was merely not ratified and in the second ratified, probably furnished no other problem, in these earlier years; and yet it was destined to furnish almost her greatest one. The new political science, which locates sovereignty in the individual, who creates state and nation with leased, revocable, limited sovereignty—the great discovery by America—was not yet generally grasped; and it was over a year after this ratification, that it was first formulated by James Wilson at the National Capital, in the College of Philadelphia (later the University of Pennsylvania), in his so-called "Law Lectures"—and then many, many years before it was widely understood and adopted, anywhere in the United States. Here again the old Roanoke-Albemarle country led and prevailed in ratification; but young Morehead's revered teacher, Dr. David Caldwell, did not believe it was "We the people," who made the constitution, in which, however, he only represented people in all the states who had not yet grasped the new political science; and stood as much in fear of "consolidation," or elimination of states, as the extreme Federalists did of anarchy. And yet, by that great fear the party of Caldwell and Jones, like that of Mason in Virginia and Bryan in Pennsylvania, and all those who wished states equally represented in the upper house and some pre-cautionary amendments, themselves contributed one of the greatest elements to the new political science, namely, protection of the minority by the upper house, and individuals in ways provided in the first amendments. In James Iredell, of Edenton, however, was represented North Carolina's final attitude, and in him produced the father of one school of constitutional thought, as James Wilson of Pennsylvania was of the other, until the American people came to see them as complimentary in a more perfect political science.[1]

This is not to say that North Carolina was not divided between these two schools, as were all the other states; or that even the old Roanoke-Albemarle country was not also divided, for it was; but the tendency to federo-nationalism was led by old Albemarle county at the earlier period and flourished more in the west, when that new population began to be more vigorous in leadership. Federo-nationalism in both periods meant primarily union; and union characterized the dominant element in all the period up to the entrance of John Motley Morehead into public life from Rockingham county.[2] It need hardly be said that reference is

---

[1] Hon. H. G. Connor and Mr. W. W. Pierson, Jr., in well-known articles, have made the point that the idea of independence of states, separately, is illustrated in the period from March until November, 1789, after the constitution became effective, but before the people of North Carolina ratified it; but North Carolina *did* ratify it, and at no time rejected it, and was merely in process of ratification and was a part of United States territory, nor exercised any national functions. The case of Rhode Island even cannot reinforce such an idea, because she also was a part of the territory of the United States, nor exercised any national functions. One is liable to forget that the Declaration was one of independence *and union;* that "the United States in Congress assembled" took over the imperial or national powers from Great Britain coincidently with the Declaration and no state thought of such a thing as exercising them alone. Disagreement with a *form* of constitution does not break up the meeting, for there is an automatic previous order that it becomes effective with a certain majority. That majority merely patiently waited for North Carolina and Rhode Island to think it over. Nothing is gained by trying to preserve the half-ideas that both Federalists and Republicans then had in their groping toward a real political science. Although James Wilson is more easily the father of the constitution than any other man, and has more nearly the right to the title of father of political science, yet he did not appreciate, until later, the great principle of minority protection through the upper house—a principle, which like the Federal Reserve System, keeps the nation from being led by an American Prussia-like majority in the northeast. The devotion to the union in North Carolina for the first three-quarters of a century is one of the most striking facts of her history.

[2] The term "federal" properly applies to union between states, as such, and so represents that part of the government called the Senate; but "national" applies to that part resting on "We, the people," etc., namely, the House; the executive is therefore a combination of the two, as is the judiciary. The more accurate term to describe our government is "federo-national."

not here made to partisan Federalism or partisan Republico-
Democracy; for in the partisan field, North Carolina joined
most other states in swelling the prestige of the sage of
Monticello and admiring the Hero of New Orleans as he
began to appear at the close of that conflict. In the midst
of these, however, the federo-national tendency still held.
No state was more proud of the union, and it was upon this
foundation that young Morehead based his leadership—the
same basis on which Johnston and Iredell built; but, as has
been said, this furnished no serious problem at this time.
North Carolina's problems were essentially from within, not
from without.

This political rivalry between the alluvial east and the
uplands of the Piedmont and mountains, was the basis of
most of her other problems: Education, Internal Improvement, Geological Survey, Transportation, Finance, Commerce, Land Reclamation, Agriculture, Manufactures. The
alluvial east with its great slave plantations, and their simplicity and self-sufficiency, could not arouse in themselves
an active interest in these great questions, which were a
matter of life and death to the Piedmont and mountains; and
this sluggishness, which could not be removed but by a political revolution, caused an exodus of vast numbers to the
western and southern states. And still the population in
1790 was 393,751, and at the end of that century, 478,103;
while in 1810 it was 555,500 and in 1820 was 638,829, just
the year before young Morehead entered the Assembly.
Nevertheless the effort of the west to induce the east to
provide for these elements of development in the commonwealth, except in a reluctant, meager manner, intensified the
west's political feeling and their determination to go first
to the root of the matter, namely, secure real representation
in the Assembly, such as was had in the National House of
Representatives or most other states. They well knew this
was transferring political power to the west, and with that
power, these things would be added unto them; but it belonged to them of right; and the same thing was in process
in the nation at large, where the west was preparing to

elect a President for the same reason and with the same phenomena of transfer of political power.[1]

This picture of the problems of North Carolina, supplemented by that of Judge Murphy, whom financial failure had overtaken the summer before, causing him to resign and return to practice at Greensboro, for a time, is that which was before the mind of John Motley Morehead, as he was chosen to go to Raliegh and take part in their solution in the House of Commons, as the lower house was then called.

---

[1] The session of the Assembly of 1819–20 was almost entirely given over to this fight; and this was taken up again in 1821.

V

Morehead Attacks
Educational and Constitutional Problems

1821

On August 9, 1821, the vote cast in Rockingham county elected Nathaniel Scales to the State Senate and John Motley Morehead and James Miller to the House of Commons. The results were of course not known from all the county on that day; but probably were within ten days, or by the 20th. By this time, also, it began to be evident that the twenty-five-year-old Lawyer and Representative of Rockingham county was concerned in another inauguration, namely, in the state of matrimony, for on August 25th, he went to the Court House in Wentworth, and with a relative of his fiancée, Jesse Harper, put up a marriage bond for $500 to Governor Jesse Franklin, and as he filled it out, did so with the usual prospective benedict's trepidation and con- fusion writing "Eliza" first, and then writing "Ann" over it, adding "Eliza Lindsay," in proper order.[1] Two weeks later, on September 9th, they were married at the Lindsay home near Greensboro, and the Representative of Rockingham county, with his Guilford county bride, had the unusual experience of becoming at the same time a resident of another county than that which he represented, for Mr. and Mrs. Morehead at once made a home in Greensboro, which was to prove permanent.

By the time the usual honeymoon was over, say some two months, or to be exact, on November 19th, Mr. Morehead was in Raleigh and present in his seat in the House of Commons at the capitol. This building was just two

---

[1] Marriage Bonds of Rockingham County, Historical Commission of N. C., at Raleigh.

years older than young Morehead, himself, having been
completed under Governor Richard Dobbs Spaight, in 1794.
It was built of local brick and the State Architect, Wm.
Nichols, who was making some changes and additions to it,
had been so perturbed by rumors to the contrary, during
the summer, that, in the *Raleigh Register* of July 27th, he
had assured the public that all would be ready for the
regular session. Presumably the young representative's
bride joined him in the "City of Oaks," as the capital was
well called in that day—a place of 2674 inhabitants, considerably over half colored, namely, 1497, of which about
one-seventh, 177, were free negroes. This left a white
population of only 1177. It was, however, the third city or
town, in size, Newbern being the largest, at 3663, of which
2188 were colored (268 free) ; and Fayetteville a close second, at 3532, of which 1614 were colored (277 free)—
strikingly different from either Newbern or Raleigh, being
the seat of the Scotch Highlanders who took less to slavery.
The capital was but slightly larger than Wilmington, at 2633,
with far over half colored, 1535 (only 102 free). These
were the larger places, Edenton, Salisbury and Washington
being scarcely more than villages, with 1561, 1234 and 1034
inhabitants respectively ; but of these Salisbury had the most
white people, while Edenton and Washington were considerably over half colored, so that Edenton's white population was only 634. These were the principal towns, so that
Raleigh had a very respectable place as a capital city, when
Representative Morehead of Rockingham, and incidentally
of Guilford, first entered there upon his public career.

The House of Commons represented counties only, not
population—its basis being practically the same as the United
States Senate, except that each of the six chief towns had a
representative, and also Hillsboro and Halifax, except
Raleigh and Washington.[1] Salisbury and Hillsboro sent
probably the ablest and most influential men, the former
sending Charles Fisher, who was easily the House leader,
while the latter furnished the Speaker, in James Mebane.

---

[1] This representation was specified in the constitution of 1776, when Raleigh
and Washington were not in existence.

CAPITOL AT RALEIGH, 1794–1831
Burned in 1831
From a painting by J. A. Marling, 1824, in the Hall of History, Raleigh

D. L. Berringer of Raleigh was also rather prominent, but Fisher was easily the leader of the House. He was only seven years older than Morehead, a native of Rowan county and educated chiefly by Rev. Dr. McPheeters of Raleigh. Educated for the law also, he was diverted from it, to the State Senate in 1818 and Congress in 1819–20, but was now returned to the House of Commons as leader of the west in their proposed attack on the old constitution, and was destined to so continue until the fight was won. Young Morehead enlisted under his banner.

In the organization of the House, young Morehead was assigned to his first committee on the 23rd of November; and it was no unimportant one either, namely, that on the settlement of the boundary between North Carolina and the states of Georgia and Tennessee, a necessity in the disposal of the Cherokee lands in that corner of the commonwealth. Four days later he was added to the committee on Correcting Bills on which day he first had occasion to express himself on a yea-and-nay question, voting with a great majority postponing indefinitely a bill relative to slaves executed for capital offenses. On the 28th, he made his first motion, namely, that the Judiciary Committee consider increasing of penalty on Sheriffs and other officers for failing to make due returns of writs, etc., and on the 30th presented his first bill, to alter an act of 1741 for restraining taking of excessive usury, and it passed first reading. The same day was to witness his first experience on the losing side, when he voted to postpone indefinitely a repealer of an act of 1820 providing for payment of costs when a slave was convicted of a capital crime; but on December 1st he was effectively against a bill fixing vacant lands at 5 cents an acre; while on the 4th he was one of a committee of two to join two of the Senate in conducting the election of a successor to Governor Franklin.[1] It was the 6th, before the gubernatorial deadlock was broken by the election of General Gabriel Holmes of Sampson county.

---

[1] It may be noted that as the Governor was elected by the Legislature under the constitution of 1776 and was given almost no powers, the chief executive became a mere figure-head and voice of the Assembly, unless, like Johnston, and Swain, later, he happened to be a strong personality.

The constitution of 1776 had provided for public education, but it was so nearly a dead letter, that efforts to make it effective had been in vain; but, Francis L. Hawks of, Newbern, afterward a minister, after the gubernatorial election was settled on the same day proposed a resolution for an inquiry into whether the Legislature had obeyed the constitution in establishing a public school system, and directing the formulation of plans, if it had not. Young Morehead's reputation as a student and teacher, as well as lawyer, marked him for fourth place, next to Charles Fisher, on a committee of sixteen. He was, therefore, recognized as a lieutenant leader in the proposed founding of a public school system for North Carolina. It was perfectly natural, also, that this newly born benedict should, on the same day, present a bill providing for recording of marriage licenses, as he did, and it passed first reading.

Mr. Morehead was very active. Governor Holmes was sworn in by Chief Justice Taylor on the 7th in the House, after which the Rockingham representative was made one of a committee of five to consider the needs of orphans. The red-letter day, however, was three days later, December 10th, for on that day Mr. Fisher, paving the way for the new educational program, put through a motion to consider the advisability of creating a fund to be known as "The Literary and School Fund;"[1] while he also put through a resolution for a vote of the people on a Constitutional Convention on the federal ratio, white and three-fifths colored.[2] Before this got into Committee of the whole on the 18th, several things occurred: Morehead lost his usury bill 100—to 25; Fisher got the State Library put in the west wing conference room; Fisher proposed a road through the Cherokee lands to meet one being built in Tennessee; arrangements were made to receive the new statue of Washington; Fisher

---

[1] The action on this fund seems to have been precipitated in part by the question then before Congress of disposing of public lands for educational purposes in each of the states. Maryland and New Hampshire had approached North Carolina on the subject and a committee had reported on it. *Raleigh Register*, Jan. 4, 1822.

[2] This subject had already been introduced in the Senate, but that body curtly refused to receive it, although they gave it somewhat more courtesy afterwards.

and Morehead failed in an effort to make a change in Davidson county; and lost and won in some yea-and-nay votes.

On the 18th, however, came action on the constitutional
question. The chief executive, at this time, might have
used the exact words of another in opening this session,
when, on referring to important subjects before it he used
these words: "Of these, the proposition to amend the constitution of this State, first introduced into the General Assembly, in 1787, and which has continued to command the
public attention for nearly half a century, is regarded as most
prominent. . . . The proposition to change the system in
1787, and the following year, was introduced and sustained
by some of the most distinguished statesmen of that era,
who were also conspicuous members of the Congress which
framed the constitution itself."

It may be explained, before quoting this executive
further, that North Carolina extended to the Mississippi
river in 1787 and 1788, and what is now Tennessee was
nearly covered by six counties, namely, the four shown in
the accompanying map of 1783: Sullivan, in the northeast
corner of what is now Tennessee; Washington, stretching
from that to the southern boundary; Greene, paralleling that
across the state; and Davidson, covering somewhat more
than the northern half of the rest of the state to the Tennessee river—the rest being unorganized; and finally the
county of Hawkins, carved from little Sullivan, and Sumner,
from Davidson, on January 6, 1787.[1]

"It was adopted in both instances by one branch of the
legislature," continues that executive, "and would most
probably have succeeded in the other, but for nearly unanimous opposition of the members from the counties which
now constitute the state of Tennessee. It was then, as at
present, the source of contention between the populous and
sparsely settled counties, and hence the change was universally desired by the maritime portion of the State. The
cession of our western territory to the general government,
obviated to some extent, the inequality previously com-

---

[1] *Colonial Records*, Clark, Vol. XXIV, pp. 826 and 830. The accompanying map is from one in Vol. XVIII, at p. 496, by E. W. Myers.

plained of, and restored temporary harmony to our public councils."[1]   Governor Franklin, however, did not even mention the subject and declined reelection.

The "temporary harmony" referred to, caused by the cession to the nation in 1790 of what is now Tennessee followed by its erection as that state in 1796, was only temporary; for the state's population rose from 393,751 in 1790 to 638,829 in 1820—an increase of 245,078 in thirty years, or about 25,000 every decade, but an increase that was so largely west of Raleigh, that the "populous" and "sparsely settled" portions gradually became reversed in location, the west becoming relatively more "populous" and the east relatively more "sparsely settled!"   Therefore soon after the census of 1810 appeared, the west began to want revision and the east to take the conservative position of the extreme west, or Mississippi valley counties of 1787!   And the past decade, with the census of 1820, had only intensified it and now the fight was on in earnest with Fisher of Salisbury in the lead and Morehead as chief lieutenant; and the fray began in committee of the whole on December 18, 1821. Mr. Fisher made a very able speech, in which he attacked the "sacredness" of the work of the Revolutionary fathers in making the constitution of 1776.   "Sir," said he, "the Provincial laws and customs were the materials out of which the Constitution [of North Carolina] was built, and the Constitution is little more than a compilation from these materials."   He was ably answered by Mr. Hawks of Newbern—the largest town in the state—and Mr. Alston of Halifax.[2]   Whereupon Mr. Morehead entered upon his defense and attack on the opposition.   This seems to be his maiden formal effort and is the earliest of his addresses which have come down to us.

In this debate on December 18, 1821, Mr. Morehead said this subject was one of great interest to the State, and on the decision of which no man could feel indifferent.   It is a

---

[1] Executive message of Gov. David L. Swain, 17th November, 1834.
[2] Hawks was two years younger than Morehead and both died the same year.   He had studied law under William Gaston, of Newbern, and was in the Assembly as a lawyer, although in 1827 he was ordained in the Protestant Episcopal Church and became one of the most distinguished divines in New York City.

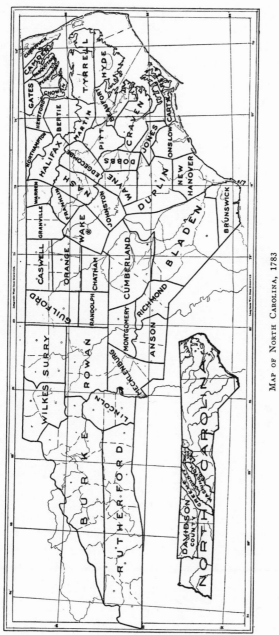

MAP OF NORTH CAROLINA, 1783

Prepared by the author

Showing four counties, now Tennessee, that voted against change of State Constitution in 1787–88

question which is calculated to call forth that kind of public feeling which is necessary for the welfare of the republic.

He "was sorry to see anything like party feeling introduced into this argument. He must tell the gentleman from Newbern (Mr. Hawks) that he had misunderstood the remark of the gentleman from Salisbury (Mr. Fisher), when he said we will have a Convention; it was not the language of *menace,* which he used, but of *prediction.*

"If he could prevail on his friends from the East to attend dispassionately to a plain statement of facts, he should have no doubt of convincing them that our present representation is unequal and unjust, though they might still doubt the policy of the proposed amendment.

"But the gentleman from Newbern has endeavored to excite an alarm in the committee, which was calculated to prevent a fair discussion of the merits of the question.

"The gentleman from Halifax (Mr. Alston) had compared some of our large and small counties to the States of New York and Rhode Island, under the General Government. [Mr. A. explained.] How are these States represented in Congress? Like the counties in this State in the General Assembly? No, sir; the United States are each of them distinct and independent sovereignties, whereas our counties are marked out by lines changeable at the will of the Legislature. Congress cannot divide a State, or interfere with it at all. Mr. Morehead hoped, therefore, this comparison will pass for naught.

"Do we," he asked, "see property represented in the General Government? No; the Senate is composed of men representing the sovereignty of the several States. Go, then, to the House of Representatives. Is there anything like property there respected? No; nothing but freemen, with the exception of three-fifths of other persons, which was a matter of compromise with the Southern States at the time the Constitution was formed.

"And is there any reason," he asked, "why property should be represented in this government? If so, how would gentlemen have property represented? How is the Senate at present composed? Is it not the representative of the landed interests of the country? Is not this a sufficient representation of property? Would you have your slaves represented as in the general government? Would you have property represented in both houses? If so, you would put it in the power of wealth to dispose of the destinies of your country.

"But the gentleman from Newbern says that Mr. Jefferson and Mr. Madison, whom he calls the high-priests of Republicanism, live in Virginia, where no person unpossessed of freehold property is permitted to vote for a representative; yet he says they do not complain, nor are their unrepresented people less ready to fight the battles of their country. Sir, in the late contest with Great Britain we have seen the sturdy yeomanry of Virginia *ordered* to Norfolk for her protection; we have seen them fall victims to the climate and to exposure; and they now lie mouldering in the dust, sacrificed by the laws of a country in which they had no voice; sacrificed by the laws of a State in which they were legislatively annihilated." He "admired the character of Virginia; he reverenced her sages; but he hoped he should not be considered as a political infidel, when he told the committee, he shuddered to think, that the poor freemen of his State should ever be excluded from the Legislative councils of the country.

"To whom," he asked, "did this country belong, when it burst the British fetters and became independent? It certainly belonged to the whole community, and not to the wealthy alone. Why, then, should the people be deprived of any privilege for which they jointly fought and to which they are justly entitled?"

He "believed, if he could assure himself that the situation of this State would always remain as it now is, he would not be in favor of calling a Convention; for no gentleman of that committee held the constitution more sacred than he did. He approached it with that awe, with which Moses approached his God while the thunders of Sinai were playing around him; he touched it with that diffidence with which the Israelites touched the Ark of the Covenant. But the foundation of our political Fabric is rotting; we must repair it in time, or in time it will tumble.

"What," he asked, "was the situation of things at the time when our present constitution was formed? The Eastern part of the State was almost the only part that was inhabited. The West had but few settlers. But our lands are now rising in value, and our population is every day increasing, while the Eastern part of the State remains much the same. Take us," said he, "poor as we are, and where is the boasted superiority of the East?" He apologized for this remark, but said, the moment this subject was introduced, the gentleman from the East made it a party question.

He said, "he had made a few calculations on this subject, which he would offer to the committee. In this estimate he had given Granville to the West [north of Wake county, the seat of the capital]. He had considered Wake as neutral, as she ought to be. She is as much the darling of the West as of the East. He had made his calculation first as the gentleman from Newbern wished it to be, according to Federal numbers.

"The total amount of population (including slaves and free persons of color) is 658,829. The whole Federal population of the State is 556,839. The Federal population of the 27 Western counties is 305,015, which, reckoning 2993 persons to send a member, entitles them to 102 members, instead of 81, which they now send. The Federal population of the 34 Eastern counties is 234,100, which entitles her to 78 members only, instead of 102, which she now sends. The Federal population of Wake county entitles her to six members. Representation, then, upon the Federal principle, entitles the West to 21 members more, and the East to 24 less than they now send to the Legislature, and Wake to 3 more.

"Go to the next principle of representation: that of free white population and taxation. The taxes of the whole State (exclusive of clerks and auctioneers) is $65,735.60. Taxes of the Western counties are $31,184.09; of the Eastern, $32,203.41; of Wake county, $2348.07. Estimating $353 for each member the Western counties will send 88; the Eastern, 91; and Wake, 6.

"Go to the next branch of the principle, that of free white

population, to which the opposers of these resolutions have the greatest objection, and the Western part of the State will be entitled to 31 more members than she has at present, and the Eastern part to 34 less.

"For the total white population of the State is 419,200, The Western counties have 253,235, which, allowing 2253 persons to send a member, will give her 112 members. The Eastern counties have 154,014, which will give to them 68 members. The white population of Wake, being 11,951, gives to her 5 members.

"So that upon the principle of free white population and taxation combined, the Western counties are entitled to 100 members, 19 more than at present. The Eastern counties, to 79 members, which are twenty-three less than at present. Wake county, to 5 members, instead of 3.

"Then compound the representation of the Federal population, free white population and taxation, and the Western counties are entitled to 101 members, 20 more than at present, and the Eastern counties will be entitled to 79 members, 23 less than at present. So that, upon the very principles upon which the opponents of the resolutions contend, the West evidently labor under important grievances. But wealth is sufficiently represented in the Senate to afford it self protection. The representation of our State should be upon the principle of free white population, requiring certain qualifications in the representatives, and in the electors of one branch of the Legislature, barely sufficient to protect wealth.

"Wealth fattens on the necessities of poverty; it can bribe; it can corrupt; and whenever it shall have a predominant weight in our government, we may bid farewell to the boasted freedom of our Republic, and ignominiously submit to the yoke of Aristocratic Slavery.

"The 34 Eastern counties having a free white population or 154,014, send to the Legislature 102 members; the 27 Western counties send 81 members, which, in the same ratio of the East, represent 122,229, leaving a balance of 131,024 free white persons together with all the negroes of the West, arrayed against the negroes of the East, and unrepresented.

Add to this, Sir, the vast extent of the West, the health of the climate, the territory acquired from the Indians, the vast increase of the value of the lands and wealth of the West from internal improvement; add these to the grievances under which we labor, and ere long they will become intolerable, not only to patriotism, but to patience itself.

"When I predict, under these circumstances, a Convention will be had, can the prophecy be doubted?

"We have now met the call of the gentleman from Newbern. Here is our grievance, which we wish to be attended to.

"No man would be more unwilling," said he, "than myself to touch the constitution, if I did not think the occasion called for it, and that the time is peculiarly favorable. The proposition before the committee ought not to be considered in the light of a contest for power. We do not ask from our Eastern brother anything to which we are not entitled. Nor would we ask for a correction of this grievance, if it were not constantly accumulating. For, to do our Eastern brethren justice, we acknowledge they have wielded their power with a great degree of justice and moderation, and it is hoped they will continue to do so.

"It will be to the East, if we are ever invaded. It may be expected your protection will not be found in your negroes; it will be found in yourselves, or in the strength of the West.

"For equal rights and privileges our fathers jointly fought, and bled and died, and their bones now lie hallowing the soil for the freedom of which they fell a sacrifice.

"But give us these, and when the demon of desolation shall hover around your borders, and the tragedy of Hampton is to be performed on your shores, call on your brethren of the West, and the mountains will roll their might to the main, carrying protection to your wives, your children, your homes and your country."

The speeches of Messrs. Fisher and Morehead were the objects of Eastern attack, and Thomas W. Blackledge of

---

[1] *Raleigh Register and North Carolina Gazette*, 1st Feb., 1822, from "Debate on the Convention Question," House of Commons, 18th Dec., 1821.

Beaufort was particularly vigorous, complaining that the westerners brought up this subject every year. Willis Alston of Halifax tried hard to head off the eastern and western division that seemed to be becoming more intense each year, claiming that it was un-natural; that the natural divisions were four, not two: 1. The old Roanoke-Albemarle counties, clear to the Tennessee line; 2. The Neuse and Tar valleys up to Wake and New Hanover; 3. the Cape Fear ribbon valley up to Stokes and Rockingham; 4. The rest from Columbus county westward. It was a vigorous fight and it classified Fisher and Morehead for life, but when the vote came on the 19th of December it was shelved by a vote of 81 to 47, every one of the counties east of Robeson, Cumberland, Wake (Raleigh) and Granville being against a convention as "inexpedient." Fourteen of these eastern counties paid less than their share of cost of government, while but five in the west were in like condition. The Senate treated the subject no better, indeed not so well; for when Senator Williamson of Lincoln county introduced a similar resolution, they practically refused to entertain it, although they reconsidered the next day. The result was that the great main object of the session was lost, on this 19th day of December, 1821.

While Mr. Morehead went to and fro in the business of law-making, he often saw Chief Justice John Marshall, who was then holding the national Circuit Court of this circuit, as had Justice James Wilson in the time of Washington. On the day before Christmas, too, he took part in the reception and dedication of the beautiful statue of the great first President, by Canova, in the rotunda of the capitol. This artistic creation from Italy had been made from the artist's original plaster model, probably the last work he ever did, for he died the following October. It represented the great American seated, dressed in the Roman toga, and engaged in writing his farewell address. It stood high above the spectator's head, on a large pedestal, on whose sides were bas-reliefs depicting leading victorious scenes in his life. It was destined to stand there for only a decade and to be beheld in admiration by multitudes, among them being

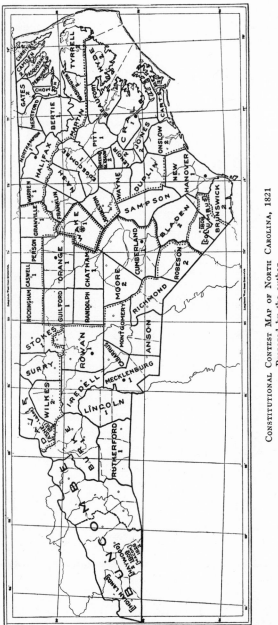

CONSTITUTIONAL CONTEST MAP OF NORTH CAROLINA, 1821
Prepared by the author

Counties in 1832 {
Paying over share of cost marked 1
Paying less than share marked 2
Paying about share no mark
}

≣ Line dividing East and West
: Lines dividing groups: 1. Roanoke; 2. Pamlico; 3. Cape Fear; 4. Western

Lafayette; for it was calcined in the destruction of that capitol a decade later.[1]   Not six months after this day, John Adams and Thomas Jefferson, as if in premonition of the deaths on the same day, the nation's natal day, too, exchanged philosophical letters on the subject of old age.   Representative Morehead and a new generation were coming to their own.

The session only lasted until the 29th, and but few other things were done of particular moment to Mr. Morehead, who fought the big eastern majority.   The new Board of Internal Improvement was chosen on Christmas Day, and Prof. Denison Olmsted was voted $100 to defray his expenses in a voluntary geological survey during the summer— a field in which this state was destined to take the lead. And on the next day a Board of Physicians was proposed, Morehead being one of the committee, but the Senate opposed both of these latter two projects.   He was also in the majority which tried to create an internal improvement fund;[2] as he was also on a bill to incorporate the Clubfoot and Harlowe's Creek Canal Company, a revision of the act of 1813, which was to connect the Beaufort Harbor with the Pamlico Sound.   On the last day he was one of the House nominees for trustee of the University, but the big eastern majority refused to elect him; and with the close of the year 1821 Representative Morehead of Rockingham county, became for all practical purposes, plain Lawyer Morehead of Guilford county, his future home.

---

[1] The original plaster model of Canova still exists in Italy, and the Italian King, in 1909, gave the state a replica in plaster, and it now stands in the Hall of History at Raleigh.   See Bulletin No. 8, N. C. Hist. Comm., by R. D. W. Connor.

[2] They succeeded in getting the dividends on state stock in the Newbern and Cape Fear (Wilmington) State Banks to the amount of about $25,000, voted.

VI

OTHER PROBLEMS FOLLOW
PERSONAL, SLAVERY, INTERNAL IMPROVEMENT, JUDICIARY
CRIMINALS AND DEFECTIVES, TRANSPORTATION
QUAKERS AND HISTORY

1822

The experience of Lawyer Morehead in challenging
the eastern counties was calculated to give a wise young
man of twenty-five years pause. It might naturally seem
to him that if wealth was so powerful, it might be well for
him to provide himself with it; even if Guilford county had
not already had able men whom she would see no reason
to displace with a young new citizen from her daughter
county to the north.[1] So, for the next four years, he devoted himself to his profession, and to other personal
problems quite as extensive, if not more so; for John Motley
Morehead's mind teemed with development in every line
that came under his observation, and everything that he
touched flourished. His interests at this particular period
were so many-sided, as they always were, and exact record
of them is so meager, that only general terms can be used
for the most part, at least for this period, even if more detail
in treatment of so public a career were desirable.

His profession as a lawyer, of course, came first and his
practice extended to County Courts; the Superior Courts
created in 1777, and covering the state with eight districts

---

[1] The western members, in 1822, called an extra legal constitutional conference to meet in Raleigh on November 10, 1823, and this body formulated
such a constitution as they thought the west would favor, but as Mr. Morehead
had no part in it, it need not be considered. Its quarrel over white and federal
ratio basis, and the success of the latter, did not appeal to men like Morehead
or his Quaker constituency; for it would have identified the middle with the
east and left political power as it was essentially. They recommended call of
a convention the next year but the Assembly, controlled by the east, ignored it.

at this time, his own being the Hillsboro District; the Supreme Court of North Carolina, which had begun its existence January 1, 1819; and the United States District and
Circuit Courts.   There is no record of his admission to the
bar of the National Supreme Court, and it is not known that
he had practice outside of the state.   He had a widely-
extended practice within the state, however, and, according
to one authority, was particularly distinguished in criminal
law.

The earliest incident discovered is one in which both he
and William A. Graham were associate counsel with his old
preceptor, Judge Archibald D. Murphy, and the writer,
Lyndon Swaim, one-time editor of the *Greensboro Patriot,*
says it was "near sixty years since" [writing under date
January 19, 1883, in the *Patriot*], which would make it near
1823, the period now under consideration.   It was in a case
locally known in Randolph county, in whose court the incident occurred, as "The Fishtrap Suit."   "John M. Morehead, then young at the bar, and I think also W. A. Graham,
still younger, were associate counsel," says Mr. Swaim.
"The suit made a great noise in the neighborhood, and I
heard the parties, the witnesses, the lawyers, etc., thoroughly
discussed.   Though a mere boy, the circumstances and the
personnel made a more vivid impression on my mind than
many a more important matter since.   Judge Murphy was,
in my eye, the central figure.   He was very small of stature,
thin and pale, with a kindly, kindling eye, and a gentleness,
nay sweetness of expression almost feminine.   He was
dressed with remarkable neatness, his coat hanging somewhat loosely upon his attenuated frame.   The lifting of his
hat as he stepped into the bar, his bow to the judge, his greet-
ing to every member of the bar and to the officers of the
court—nobody was omitted—was such an exhibition of self-
possession and grace as I had never witnessed before, and
such as, I yet verily believe, is seldom seen outside of a
Parisian *salon;* and the crowning charm was, he made
everybody feel that he was sincere.   His hand-shake, even
with a boy, left a pleasant memory.   There was no hurry
about it; he took time to attend to the matter in hand (pardon

the pun) ; the softly repeated pressure and the lingering glance of his dark eyes were magnetic in effect. I have never seen but one likeness of him, an engraving in the *University Magazine,* some years ago, probably from an old family portrait when he was very young. It was Raphael-like in rounded grace of outline and softness of expression. The matured face that I saw had the harder lines fixed by time and thought and care—nothing left but the gentle expression. The Fishtrap trial occupied most of the week. The points are beyond recollection. But I remember an observation made about Morehead. The second day's examination of witnesses was in progress, when Murphy remarked to Morehead, 'My young friend, you appear to be taking no notes of the evidence.' 'No, Sir,' he replied, 'I depend upon my memory.' The senior expressed his apprehension of the result. But when Morehead came to 'sum up' before the jury, his memory served him with remarkable correctness and particularity. His success in this case laid the first solid foundation stone in the building up of his reputation at the bar."[1]

"Mr. Morehead," says a member of the Greensboro bar of 1907, "was greatly devoted to the profession of law, and while he was eminent in the practice of the civil courts he was especially great and successful in the criminal courts, and his practice covered a number of counties. He was an acknowledged leader in the courts in which he practiced. He was retained in nearly all the murder cases in the part of the state where he resided and never had a defendant for whom he appeared convicted of murder or hanged."[2]

"When I entered the profession," says another distinguished lawyer of a later date, "I met him here [Greensboro] at the May term of the County Court, and found him occupying the position of leader on his circuit. I was pleased with his appearance, was attracted by his amenity and fascinated by his talents. His personal presence was imposing, his face beamed with kindness, and when he addressed the court

[1] *The Papers of Archibald D. Murphy,* Hoyt, Vol. II, pp. 432–3.
[2] Publications of The Guilford County Literary and Historical Association, Vol. I, p. 57, *The Bench and Bar of Guilford County* by Levi M. Scott.

and jury, I heard him with delight, and was filled with admiration."[1]

On January 17, 1822, he was among those whom conflict of new dates of the Superior Court, made by the Legislature, caused inconvenience and loss. Lawyer John M. Dick, of Greensboro, writing to Thomas Ruffin at Hillsboro, on the above date says: "You inform me that our legislature has legislated you out of two courts and express a hope that you are the only sufferer among your brethren. I am a fellow sufferer with you, and we are by no means alone, Mr. Little, Mr. Morehead and several others are much injured by the changes. I am legislated out of Orange County Court and the Superior Court of this county will sometimes conflict with the County Court of Randolph County."[2]

An eminent lawyer who was admitted to the bar about a decade later says: "When I was about to start out to practice law, I asked the advice of Judge Mangum. He named the courts which he advised me to attend. 'But, Judge Mangum,' said I, 'the oldest lawyers in the State practice in those courts, and have all the business. And I have neither reputation, nor friends, nor money.' 'No matter,' said he, 'go where there is business; do not fear competition. The examples of these great men are just what you need. If you want to find tall trees, you must go among tall trees.' I took his advice and proved its wisdom. I was soon in full practice; and never met those great men that I did not feel a longing to be like them—Badger, Nash, Devereux, Haywood, Graham, Morehead, Norwood, Saunders, Mangum, Waddell, Gilliam, Bryan, Miller, Iredell—an abler bar than that of the United States Supreme Court, as I have heard Mr. Badger say."[3] These were the courts in the northern part of the state—the old Roanoke-Albemarle and adjacent territory south and west. If to this list one adds William Gaston of Newbern, there were no greater lawyers in the state, in the period before the civil war, and most of these came to have

---

[1] Hon. John Kerr in memorial oration, 26th Feb., 1867, at Wentworth, N. C.
[2] The Ruffin Papers, Hamilton, Vol. I, p. 261.
[3] Hon. Edwin Godwin Reade, LL.D., of Raleigh, in an address before the North Carolina Bar Association on July 9, 1884, p. 12.

a national reputation. Morehead was recognized by these men as one of them, probably as early as 1825, and certainly was recognized as one of them by the profession and people at large.

It was in this latter year that he erected the residence on an elevation in the midst of an oak grove of the original forest on the edge of Greensboro, now at the corner of Washington and Edgworth streets, that became famous under the name "Blandwood," whose hospitality was so notable that "mine host" of the various Greensboro inns and taverns was often piqued at the loss of what might have been theirs. By the close of this year in the new home, Mr. and Mrs. Morehead had two children, one Letitia Harper Morehead, then two years old, while the second daughter, Mary Corinna, was born on November 27th of that year.

They had been but a few months in "Blandwood," when the people of Guilford county, in August, 1826, as though taking the establishment of that home as evidence of permanent citizenship, elected Mr. Morehead again to the House of Commons at Raleigh during the following summer. There were five candidates for the two places, Morehead receiving the highest, 1125 votes, and Francis L. Simpson 867, the three others falling below 777. The reason for this was the great questions that were to come up before the Assembly, for it was a great time. The rumblings of Jacksonism had begun to be heard, and North Carolina's attitude at this time was significant, for when the election was thrown in the national House of Representatives the previous year, she was one of the four states which voted for Crawford [Georgia, North Carolina, Virginia and Delaware], when seven voted for Jackson and thirteen for Adams.

It will be well to note the significance of this, for it is a complicated matter, and of great moment to Mr. Morehead and his constituency: In a certain sense it was a question of slavery and the Quakers' objection to it. This denomination had petitioned the Fifth Congress against slavery—the first North Carolina petitioned against it; and they utilized it again and again, until it was objected to when John Quincy

BLANDWOOD, GREENSBORO, N. C.
The home of Governor Morehead, erected in 1825

Adams defended them. They had exercised manumission so freely that the large element of free negroes was by some attributed almost wholly to them.[1] About 1800 a state law was passed that no negro should be freed except a bond be given that he should leave the state. By 1826 Quakers in North Carolina, led by the three Quaker counties of Guilford, Randolph and Chatham, which formed one district, decided on general manumission as far as it could be effected. On May 30, 1826, the *Raleigh Register* announced that beside 64 already sent to Ohio and 58 to Liberia, Dr. George Swaine, of Guilford county, had charge of over 500 more to be shipped out of the state: about 100 to Indiana and Ohio; 316 to Liberia; and 120 which were to embark at Beaufort for Hayti, in which colored republic there was great public interest as well as some apprehension. It was this subject also which led so many of the Quakers to emigrate to Indiana and in due time make it the greatest Quaker state in the union.

In December, 1823, the western party in the Assembly tried to instruct Congressmen to oppose the old Jeffersonian caucus method of nominating President, but the eastern members rallied and secured the recommendation of Crawford to the people. In 1824 the Harrisburg Convention nominated Jackson and Massachusetts had offered Adams, while Kentucky offered Clay. Thereupon the three Quaker counties of North Carolina, above mentioned, held a meeting at Greensboro and denounced the caucus, and endorsed their old defender, Adams, with Jackson as second choice. On May 3, 1824, Judge Murphy wrote: "I have been gratified at the prospects of General Jackson's friends in every county in my circuit, until I reached Guilford. That county is divided: Mr. Adams has, I think the majority. Mr. Crawford has the next greatest number of friends. Genl. Jackson has no active friend in the county, except Mr. Morehead. I do not therefore calculate much on Guilford."[2] In Novem-

---

[1] Brigadier General Jesse Spaight of Greene County, in a good speech said Friends were responsible for the element of free negroes that were a source of so much difficulty. *Raleigh Register*, Jan. 26, 1827.
[2] The Murphy Papers, Hoyt, Vol. I, p. 297.

ber, however, the western counties were for Jackson, "the
People's" candidate, forty-two of them, except the Quaker
counties and home of Mr. Morehead; these latter finally
joined the twenty-one eastern counties in voting for Crawford, in hopes of throwing the contest into the national
House of Representatives and there getting their favorite
candidate, Adams. The electoral vote of the State, when
given on December 1, 1824, was unanimous for Jackson;
but when it was up before the national House of Representatives, the North Carolina Congressmen voted an organization
vote: 10 for Crawford; 2 for Jackson; and 1, the member
from the Quaker district, had the pleasure of voting for their
favorite, John Quincy Adams, and seeing him elected, and
the old organization receive a stinging rebuke.[1]   Thus Mr.
Morehead's district, in which Jackson, his own candidate,
was second choice, voted for its first choice, Adams; but Mr.
Morehead, himself, was with the solid west against the east
and for the anti-organization unsuccessful candidate, General Andrew Jackson, who was also the Quakers' second
choice.   He was consequently in an excellent political position and a recognized power, to be reckoned with when he
entered the Assembly of 1826.

With this personal political prestige, however, he faced
a great lethargy among the eastern people regarding internal
improvement; they had transportation; it was the west that
wanted it, but they had not the political power.   Then, too,
the great leader of the internal improvement plans for river
and canal transportation, Judge Archibald Murphy, had lost
prestige through his financial failure, extending even to a
debtor's prison.   A few leaders were becoming thoughtful
about a new mode of transportation that was gradually becoming more and more a subject of experiment in various
parts of the world.   This was a mode of making a smooth
road on two wooden or iron rails laid parallel—an improvement on the old plank or corduroy roads on which the wood
was laid crosswise, instead of lengthwise.   It had been used
of course as early as the sixteenth century, and with the

---

[1] *State Rights and Political Parties in North Carolina,* Henry McGilbert
Wagstaff, Ph.D., p. 47.

advance in iron manufacture by 1820, malleable iron rails had been used very successfully in isolated instances in Great Britain. The first line in the United States was a short quarry one near what is now Swarthmore, Pennsylvania, at the Leiper quarries, in 1809—a quarry still in operation. This became the model for heavy carrying and the power was the horse or mule. In Great Britain some success was had with steam engines on the common road and by 1814 Stephenson had tried such an engine on the Killingworth tracks, although they did not supersede the horse; but, in 1825, the year before Mr. Morehead's election by Guilford county, a success was made on the Stockton and Darlington Railway in England, who had then about twenty-eight such small "rail-ways;" but the idea had not gained much ground in America except the tramroad like that at the Leiper quarries. The earliest note of a considerable extension of this idea appeared in Philadelphia during the winter previous to his election: "A great railroad is contemplated from Philadelphia," says the *Raleigh Register* of January 27, 1826, "to Pittsburgh, by way of Lancaster, York and Chambersburgh, a distance of 340 miles, with a branch from the neighborhood of Gettysburg to Baltimore, each state to be interested in proportion to its wealth and population, to be effected by steam power. It is calculated that a cargo of seventy-five tons might be carried on the proposed road, at the rate of six miles an hour, which would complete the journey in three days and three nights!"[1] This was Philadelphia and Baltimore's reply to the success of Governor Clinton's Erie Canal in gaining western traffic and making New York a rival. Some of the thoughtful in North Carolina, discouraged by the attitude of the east toward river improvement began to be interested in the new method of two parallel rails, with whatever power, and Morehead and his old University President, Dr. Joseph Caldwell, were among the number, though there was no public discussion at this time.

There was much discussion of another subject, however: On a certain occasion during the previous year a famous

---

[1] The exclamation point represents contemporary astonishment, although it may also be utilized for current amusement.

American said in an address: "It is said, that in England, not more than one child in fifteen possesses the means of being taught to read and write; in Wales, one in twenty; in France, until lately when some improvement has been made, not more than one in thirty-five. Now it is hardly too strong to say, that in New England, every child possesses such means."[1] This was published to pave the way for the reception of the report of the Public Education Committee of November, 1825, composed, among others, of Chief Justice Taylor and President Joseph Caldwell, who reported a system of public education for which the Literary and School Fund was founded. Likewise a committee on investigation of method of caring for insane and defectives was to report.

Closely connected with and underlying all of them was the state financial system. North Carolina, in 1804, had been among those states that feared the power of the Bank of the United States, a sentiment that led to the refusal of the Jeffersonians to re-charter it in 1811. In 1804 North Carolina had established two state banks, one at her largest town, Newbern, and the other at Wilmington, then known as the Cape Fear. In 1810 "The State Bank" at Raleigh had been chartered with the expectation that these two banks would become branches, but in 1812 they asked to be left independent and enlarged, and in 1813 were. The State Bank had only been chartered for five years; so in December, 1825, a new one had been created with mother bank at Raleigh and branches at Edenton, Tarboro, Wilmington, Fayetteville, Newbern and Salisbury.[2] And in these and the two old banks of Newbern and Cape Fear, the state had 5500 shares, then worth about half a million and yielding about $60,000 a year. This partial state ownership was like that of the Banks of the United States and England; indeed the custom was general, only about three states having it

---

[1] Daniel Webster, in an address at Plymouth, in 1825.
[2] Charles Fisher said on 2nd January, 1829, that the State Bank was organized because the currency was then composed of old Proclamation bills and Newbern and Cape Fear bank notes, and as the former were legal tender, the latter banks would use them to pay their own notes and so avoid paying specie. The State Bank was established therefore to make specie possible, as neighboring states had complained of the action of the two eastern banks.

otherwise. The State Bank *vs.* a Bank of the United States was coming to divide North Carolina as it was other states; and this was a part of the whole question of state *vs.* nation, or state fear of national power, complicated by needs of a national currency system. The tariff of 1824 entered into the complication.

These were the great subjects that confronted Representative Morehead of the Quaker district, who trained with Presbyterians, whose pastor had been his old teacher, Dr. David Caldwell, and usually attended the First Presbyterian Church of Greensboro, when it was organized on October 3, 1824, two years before. The Assembly of 1826 was differently organized from that of 1821, and the eastern majority put John Stanly of Newbern into the Speaker's chair. Mr. Morehead's old chief, Charles Fisher, of Salisbury, was there as before; but the mountains furnished the great leader of the session in David L. Swain of Buncombe, his native county. He had received, like Morehead, such a private education that he was able to enter the University in the Junior class in 1821. Studying law under Chief Justice Taylor, he was licensed in 1822, and in 1825 was elected to the House of Commons and contributed much to the great work of the Assembly. He was easily chief of the Assembly of 1826 also, when Mr. Morehead took his seat on November 26th, the second day of the session. Governor H. G. Burton drew their attention to a feature of internal improvement calculated to increase the available funds of the state, namely, the drainage and reclamation of swamp lands, which was destined to be a considerable source of future income to North Carolina. The Governor also laid before them, in more or less indignant terms some resolutions received from the State of Vermont. It seems that in 1824 the state of Ohio had proposed to Indiana and other states, and Indiana had approved a proposal for gradual emancipation of slaves, somewhat on the Pennsylvania plan of 1780; that Georgia had countered with a proposal of an amendment to the Constitution forbidding the importation of slaves into a state contrary to its own laws; and that Vermont had expressed its disapproval of it and willingness to cooperate with a proper course in gradual emancipation. This Governor Burton submitted to the Assembly with his somewhat indignant comments, to the effect that North Carolina was well aware of the gravity of the slave problem, quite as much as states that had no such problem. It should be added that the Ohio proposal differed chiefly from that of Pennsylvania, in providing colonization of all free negroes.

On December 27th, Mr Morehead was again put on the Committee of Education, and on the following day proposed a Joint Committee on Public Buildings. After holidays, on January 2, 1827, he proposed a joint committee to act on the Colonization Society memorial; and two days later, with leave, presented a bill, at the request of the Quakers, providing for emancipation of slaves under certain conditions. On this later day, however, he presented one of his own, namely, a bill to erect Courts of Equity to be held in each district by the Supreme Court Judges, taking it away from the Superior Courts.

On January 5, 1827, Representative Morehead had occasion to say something on his profession of the law, when he advocated a bill safeguarding clients of lawyers under twenty-one years of age. He felt "a pride in belonging to the profession of the law." He said some gentlemen did not believe that there existed a jealousy of the law but he "was of a different opinion."

On the 8th, he was among those who advocated the legal date of beginning the legislative session as the second Monday in December. On the 13th, Mr. Morehead, in advocating the bill to establish Courts of Equity, called it before committee of the whole and spoke at great length upon it, after which the tragic incident occurred of Speaker Stanly's sudden attack of a stroke of paralysis covering one side of his body; and the consequent appointment of General James Iredell as Speaker *pro tempore*.

Mr. Morehead was very active during this session and especially on this subject. He spoke at great length on the 16th, especially in behalf of necessity for such courts in the Hillsboro District. He said that "the white population of the Hillsboro District was more than one-fourth part of the whole state. The whole white population of the state being 419,200 and that of Hillsboro District 110,000; that Newbern and Edenton Districts together contained less than 84,000, so that the Hillsboro District contained 26,000 more than both of them, and yet each of the Districts were allowed the same time for holding their courts with the Hillsboro District." He also said that the Mountain Circuit contained a white population of 102,000; so that the two western Judicial Circuits contain upwards of 5000 free white persons more than are contained in the other four Judicial Circuits; and the consequence was, from the business necessarily arising from such an immense population that no time was found in those circuits for attending to Equity cases." He "thought it high time that provisions should be made for the relief of these sections of country at least." Mr. Stanly retorted that "If we have not white men [in the east] we have negroes. *We are cursed with them"*—and again he was attacked by the same kind of stroke as before. The committee reported it inexpedient to pass the bill—which, as shall soon appear, was merely one more phenomenon on the way to revision of the constitution, in the contest between east and west.

Fortunately a complete speech of Representative Morehead at this time has been preserved and well illustrates the vigor and ability of this young advocate of the growing counties of the west. "Mr. Chairman," said he the next day, "I had hoped, Sir, that some person would offer to the House some substantial reasons for striking out the second section of the bill [requiring the Equity Courts to be held by Supreme Court judges]; but in vain have I waited to hear them. Surely no gentleman of this House can doubt the great necessity of adopting some plan to improve the Equity system in the two western circuits; and is it possible that this House will give a silent vote against the plan proposed, without giving even a *reason* for that vote, or without suggesting some other plan that may meet the views of the House better than the one proposed? Surely not, Sir. That grievances do exist, is not denied; that they shall be redressed, certainly this House will not refuse. When, Sir, I arose before on this subject, I acknowledged the bill had imperfections, and asked the assistance of the House to bring it to perfection; but this assistance has been refused me, not by a positive denial, but by being withheld.

"It was said, the other day, by the gentleman from Newbern, our Honorable Speaker [Stanley], whose lamentable calamity no one deplores more than I do, Mr. Chairman, that the white population of the different circuits had been unjustly taken into calculation, without any reference to the great number of negroes in the eastern circuits, each one of which may form a separate subject of litigation, and without any reference to the great wealth and commerce of those circuits.

"It cannot be denied, that more litigation must necessarily arise among a population, each member of which transacts all the common concerns of life for himself, and appeals to the laws of his country for his protection and for his rights, than can arise among an equal population, many of whom are deprived of transacting their own business, and rendered incapable of making contracts, and whose complaints pass unheard, and wrongs unredressed.

"But, Sir, if the negro population is to be taken into consideration on this question, let us examine the subject, and see if this boasted superiority of the number of blacks of the East, over those of the West, does, in fact, exist.

"I will take the Newbern circuit, to which the gentleman belongs, and compare the slave population of that circuit with the same population of the Hillsboro circuit, to which I belong. From the census of 1820, the slave population of the Hillsboro circuit was upwards of 41,000, and that of the Newbern circuit only about 29,000; so that if the position be granted, 'that each of them forms a separate subject of litigation,' how satisfactorily does this comparison show that more litigation will necessarily arise in the one circuit than in the other. And that the Hillsboro circuit should have more litigation in it, than the Newbern circuit, is still better accounted for, by a comparison of the free white and slave population of each circuit, that of one being 151,000, while the other is only about 73,000, a difference of 78,000.

"I will now examine, Mr. Chairman, the relative wealth and commerce of the two circuits.

"I know of no way in which this comparison can be better made, than by the different sums which the treasury receives from each circuit; and the State should distribute her favors somewhat in proportion to the bounty she receives.

"It will be seen from the Comptroller's last report, that the amount of taxes and money received of Clerks in the Hillsboro circuit was about $16,000, while that of the Newbern circuit was about $9000; the receipts of the first circuit being nearly double that of the latter.

"So that if we take, Mr. Chairman, white population, black population and taxation, and compare them in every possible variety, as the criteria by which we may judge of the number of law suits that will probably arise, we must all come to this conclusion, that if the Newbern circuit requires a Judge a certain length of time to do the business of that circuit, the Hillsboro circuit must require the same Judge a much greater length of time to do the business of that circuit. We are told, Mr. Chairman, that the dockets even in these small circuits are larger: if this be a fact, Sir, is there a gentleman in this House, who can doubt for a moment the enormous accumulation of business on our Law and Equity dockets? And yet, Sir, is the relief proposed by this bill to be refused us, and no other offered?

"It was further said by the gentleman from Newbern, that litigation depended much on the habits and morality of the citizens; that if the people of the West could quit their frauds practiced in horse swaps, and would leave off counterfeiting bank notes and passing them, that then the dockets would not be so much crowded in the two western circuits. If, Sir, this be the true reason, why the dockets in the western circuits are large, then is there the greater necessity of having justice speedily administered, to redress those frauds and punish those offenders.

"While human nature remains as imperfect as it now is, we may expect fraud to be practiced and offenses to be committed; but I do not admit that more frauds and offenses exist in the western part of the State, in proportion to its population, than exist in other parts of the State.

"If we examine this subject, perhaps we shall find the reverse of this to be true.

"It will be recollected that in 1821, the gentleman from Newbern himself procured an act to be passed, authorizing a Court of Oyer and Terminer to be held in Newbern, to try the various offenders who could not be tried by the regular terms of the Superior Court. Whether these offenders were persons guilty of frauds, perjuries, counterfeiting or passing counterfeit notes, I know not; but if the little county of Craven, having a white and black population of only about 13,000 persons, cannot punish offenders in the regular terms of the Superior Court, but requires a special term for no other purpose but to punish its offenders; while the large counties of the West, some of them containing a population of upwards of 24,000 have never yet required a special term to punish their offenders, we must conclude that there is as much morality in the West as there is in some parts of the East. And this charge against the West would have come with as much propriety from any other quarter, as that from which it was made.

"So that, no matter what may be said to be the causes of much litigation in the western circuits, every person who considers the situation of the western circuits, must be satisfied that the business necessarily accumulates on their dockets from the diversified transactions of such an immense population.

"I again repeat, Mr. Chairman, that it will not be imposing on the Judges of the Supreme Court more duties than they can well perform. The bill has already been amended by striking out the 1st and 5th Circuits, because the business of their courts did not require any alteration. The 2nd circuit can not require this court any more than either of the others; and the Supreme Court sitting in this 3rd circuit is sufficiently convenient to try all Equity suits that may arise in it; so that one of these Judges can hold three courts in the two western circuits without employing much of his time, and this time would be employed in his term only once in eighteen months.

"If this plan is adopted, the business of the Supreme Court will be much curtailed. I have in my hand a statement of the Clerk of the Supreme Court, by which it appears that fifty-one cases have been sent to the present term of the Supreme Court, of which only twenty-five are appeals; the other twenty-six are Equity cases that have been removed to this Court, because they could not be heard in the court below.

"I hope, Mr. Chairman, the committee will refuse to strike out the second section of the bill, unless some gentleman will suggest an amendment that will better suit the views of the committee."[1] On the 19th, however, it was voted "inexpedient" 86 to 36, but Mr. Swain secured a resolution asking the Judiciary Committee to canvass the subject. The episode was merely another phase of the great underlying constitutional revision contest.

So also was the various phases of the negro problem more or less part of that contest. From this time on until the end of the session it came up in one way or another. For example, on January 23, 1827, a bill for freeing two negroes was before the House and Morehead voted for it, but it was lost 79 to 41, nearly two to one. On the 30th he fought a bill restricting entry of free negroes into the state and with somewhat the same results; but on February 2nd, he presented by request a memorial on the subject from the Quaker societies, The French Benevolent Associations of Jamestown, Springfield and Kennett, which was promptly laid on the table. On February 8th, his bill for emancipating slaves under certain conditions was finally indefinitely postponed 59 to 53; while on the same day he fought hard to indefinitely postpone a bill to prohibit trading in slaves, except under certain conditions named, failing 42 to 64. On the ninth, the efforts of Judge Murphy in his desire to have the history of North Carolina written, came to action when the Hillsboro Representative made a motion to take measures

---

[1] *Raleigh Register*, Feb. 2, 1827.

to secure copies of colonial records from London; and the
same day Mr. Morehead made a motion to grant Judge Murphy a certain amount to enable him to write a History of
North Carolina; but it was promptly laid on the table and the
next day he, and others, secured leave of absence for the rest
of the session.

The people of Guilford county, however, sent him back
again by their election of the summer of 1827, for that
summer was destined to be a turning point in the development of North Carolina and in the career of John Motley
Morehead. But before that occurred Mr. Morehead attended commencement at the University at Chapel Hill,
which proved to be a most remarkable occasion in one respect, namely, that eleven lawyers, in one block, applied for
the Master's degree and all received it, among them being
John Motley Morehead, M.A., and William A. Graham,
M.A., two young men who were destined to be closely
connected in the coming years.[1] About the same date a
prophetic proposal was made by a distinguished engineer
and architect to build a railway down the Piedmont 1050
miles from the national capital to New Orleans, which was
to be a wood rail covered with iron and capable of providing a six day trip, or even four days "under pressure."[2]
Then, shortly after Mr. Morehead's election in August, at
which he received 1603 votes and Mr. Simpson 1290, there
began to appear in various papers of the state a series of
public letters.

These were headed merely "'Communications," the first
was dated September 1, 1827, and a copy appeared in the
Raleigh Register of September 7th, and was signed "Carleton," the name of the home of the Prince Regent of Great
Britain, "Carleton House." These appeared at close inter-
vals to the number of twenty-two and the author spoke of
each one as a "Number." They were afterwards issued in
book form as "The Numbers of Carleton," and had great
power both in serial and in volume form. Following so
closely a great engineer's proposal of what has since become

---

[1] *Raleigh Register*, July 3, 1827.
[2] *Ibid.*, July 6, 1827.

Communication.

FOR THE RALEIGH REGISTER.

The people of North-Carolina have for for some years past evinced a disposition to facilitate the means of commercial intercourse, both foreign and domestic. It is an object in which they have felt themselves so deeply interested, that no small sums have been already expended for its accomplishment. The rivers Yadkin, Cape-Fear, Neuse, Tar and Roanoke, all witness, by the works commenced, and the monies disbursed, that such a wish has been alive in the public mind : and so well known are the many other attestations of it, that to be particular in their enumeration is unnecessary. It is practical proof that they have been deeply sensible of the disadvantages of their situation, and they have bee-

* * * * * * * * * * *

possible. If we would arrive at the greatest good of our country, personal or local interests must not be too strenuously consulted, ambition must not be narrow and selfish, but enlightened and well directed, and all our efforts and researches must be faithfully and intently turned upon the discovery and establishment of the truth. Could the people of N. Carolina, could her governor, magistrates, legislators and officers, all concur upon these principles, who can doubt that from that moment she would begin to grow conspicuously in individual happiness, and in strength and prosperity as a state.

CARLTON.

September 1st. 1827

FIRST NUMBER OF THE CARLTON LETTERS
Afterwards issued as *Numbers of Carlton*

the greatest Piedmont line from Washington south, it was a modest proposal compared with that, for it proposed a similar line merely from Beaufort Harbor across the central part of the whole state to the Tennessee line. It was avowedly presented because "a vast proportion of our enterprises for internal improvement [by water] have proved partially or totally abortive."[1] It was therefore a substitute for deep waterways and canals, precisely like the one proposed in Pennsylvania, where he had once lived, and railway projects, which he had seen in England in 1825, were no longer an untried thing. For the author of these public letters was none other than President Joseph Caldwell of the University of North Carolina, whose last illness was upon him about the time he closed the series.[2]

In these letters, he shows how railway experiments have proven them superior to canals; and by railways or railroads, as America preferred to call them, he meant only the road, not the power, for both horse and steam power were in use in England, but only horse power in the United States. They were less costly than canals, and far more reliable the year around; and, he writes, "It is continually evinced by present practice, that steam can be employed in transportation by a railroad"—implying if one should desire it, for horse power was the one in mind for actual use. Indeed he cites instances where a single horse "drew sixteen wagons, weighing upwards of fifty-five tons, for more than six miles along a level or very slightly declining part of the railway." He quotes Engineer Strickland of Philadelphia on the "locomotive," however, as an actual fact in England—a "gigantic automaton," he calls it. Then he takes up the cost of a railway commenced at Newbern, extended through Raleigh through the center of the state to Tennessee, to be built in seven years, which would require but $100,000 a year, divided equally between the state and private capital. He defends Beaufort harbor and the Harlow canal as terminals, using the tremendous growth of Rochester, N. Y., on the new Erie canal as an illustration. He then takes up

[1] *Numbers of Carleton*, 1828, p. 3.
[2] President Caldwell died at Chapel Hill, 24th January, 1835.

branch lines to all centers north or south of this railroad, and the cost of operation in horses, wagons and men, and foresees trade with all the world. He then tells what a railroad is, in detail, making much of the Mauch Chunk railroad in Pennsylvania and the report of the "Baltimore and Ohio Railroad Company" upon it. He also describes a Fund and predicts an Atlantic Coast Line from Amboy, N. J., to Savanah; and warns against Norfolk's efforts to get all North Carolina trade. His suggestion that one might "breakfast in Raleigh, dine in Newbern, and arrive in Beaufort in less than fifteen hours, including all requisite delays" had in it a note or triumph. He thereupon proposes that the next Assembly employ an engineer to canvass a route, and the people to call for a 37 cent additional poll tax; and thereupon quotes engineering authorities. In his issue of November 9th, just before the Legislature convened, he again defends Beaufort harbor, as if he had aroused a Wilmington hornet's nest, and shows the harbor to be only 26 miles from the middle point of the coast line. As this was his last number until spring, attention may now be turned to the Assembly and Representative John Motley Morehead's activities in it.

Raleigh capitol witnessed the gathering of the Solons on November 19, 1827, but two of their leaders were not present. Indeed this was not a House of a dominant single leader. Morehead was the equal of any of them and was no longer a lieutenant of Fisher of Salisbury, who was present again. James Iredell of Edenton was another until he was chosen Governor, while Newbern's successor to Stanley, William Gaston, was another who had been a member of both houses before. Swain had not been returned. Mr. Gaston was a native of Newbern, of Huguenot and English stock, his mother a Roman Catholic, widowed by the Revolution. He was educated at Georgetown, D. C., up to his Junior year at Princeton, and, graduating with high honors, studied law under Francis Xavier Martin. He succeeded to the business of (Chief Justice) John Louis Taylor, his brother-in-law, and soon entered public life in both Assembly and Congress, where young Daniel Webster declared him the leader in the War Congress of 1813. He therefore came into the House with the greatest prestige of any of them, for even Chief Justice John Marshall was to avow in his old age that if he was assured that Gaston would succeed him he would resign. He was a man of great purity of character, and was greatly beloved, but he was no more of a leader in this session than young Morehead, who was nearly twenty years his junior.

Mr. Morehead was not present until the 23rd, but he had already been put on the Standing Committee on Education, and on that day was also added to the Standing Committee on Judiciary, which was a most important one this session. On the 26th he was put on a Committee on Amending the Treasury Laws, one on connecting Albemarle Sound and the Ocean and one for a survey of a railroad to connect the Cape Fear at Fayetteville with the upper Yadkin river, on the 27th. On the latter day he himself presented a bill concerning bail and costs which was referred to his Judiciary Committee. On the 29th he was the one who proposed proceeding to the election of Governor, and he and others made several references to the Judiciary Committee. The previous efforts at gubernatorial selection having failed, Morehead and Blackledge joined the Senate Committee with no better success, but later in the day, December 5th, James Iredell was made Governor and on the following day Morehead was one of the committee of notification and arrangements. On this latter day, he was one of three candidates for Solicitor General. Judge Murphy had written Thomas Ruffin that Solicitor General Jones had resigned on December 8th, and that Morehead was talked of. R. M. Saunders had also written that the "contest would be between Nash, Morehead and myself;" but Morehead did not get it.

The month of December saw the Guilford representative very active and aggressive. On the 11th when a bill came up somewhat inimical to Quakers, Dunkards, Mennonites and Moravians, he fought for its indefinite postponement successfully, 62 to 51. On the following day, Brevard and Morehead were appointed on the joint committee to arrange election of a Public or State Treasurer, to succeed the late

Treasurer Haywood, and they were not successful. During
the month an unusual number of references of bills and
resolutions to the Judiciary Committee gave occasion for
Morehead to represent the committee in reporting almost
invariable rejection of them.[1] On the 14th, the Senate requested a joint committee on establishment of a penitentiary
and an asylum for insane and idiots, and the House made
Mr. Morehead chairman of their section of it. And when
someone presented a bill for repeal of the Common School
act of 1825, the majority sent it to Morehead's Standing
Committee on Education, where they knew it would be
properly interred. He himself presented a bill providing for
widows when they dissent from their husband's will, and also
a Guilford county bill, while he secured an amendment to
one protecting securities. On the 27th he helped vote down
an appropriation to improve the Cape Fear below Wilmington, but voted for it three days later. He also favored the
creation of Macon county in the west and on the 31st had
the pleasure of reporting out rejection of the repeal bill from
the Education Committee, which killed that movement. It
became plain to the public that Mr. Morehead was a defender
of the common schools, of Quakers and like bodies, of
widows, of defectives and insane, of slaves and free negroes,
the West, of the State's history, of judicial justice and exact
legal procedure.

    But on January 2nd, they were to learn that he was also
committed to the new project outlined in the Carleton Letters; for on that day, a resolution was offered requesting the
Governor to tell the Secretary of War of the desire of the
Legislature that a corps of United States engineers survey a
railroad from Newbern to Tennessee through Raleigh and
the central part of the state; and when it was read an immediate effort was made to postpone it indefinitely and it
failed 58 to 46; but when an immediate vote on passage was
taken that also failed but by only so narrow a margin as 52
to 50. This close vote was largely sectional as usual, but not
so much so as most sectional votes. Mr. Morehead was

---

[1] One of these was a proposition to prevent the education of slaves.

JOSEPH CALDWELL
From engraving by John Sartain of a Bust at the
University of North Carolina

among the 58 which procured its consideration, and was among the 50 who voted for its passage. This showed the influence of the "Carleton" Letters and also both a growing recognition of the probable efficacy of the new mode of transportation as well as discouragement over the failure of the old method, so far as North Carolina was concerned.

On adjournment on the 7th of January, 1828, Representative Morehead returned to "Blandwood;" but during the year the "Carleton" papers continued. In April he answered the fear that the very facility of railways would cause influx and competition, and soon followed this by examination of cost of a level mile, making it $2649. Funds are the subject of his next and his May numbers enforce the effect it will have on union; and shows from history how commerce grows. "We lay like a man of strength tied hand and foot," he writes. In July he takes up the action of Maryland, where, on July 4th, ground was first broken for a canal connecting the Chesapeake and Ohio—a distance of 400 miles—and also the first blow was struck for constructing a railway for the same purpose, more than 340 miles long. South Carolina already proposes three railroads from Charleston, namely, to Augusta, Columbia, and Camden; while the Massachusetts Assembly have just taken measures for a line from Boston to Albany. Here he first calls it "The Central Railroad," of North Carolina. Then he tells in detail the history of railroad development up to that time, and closes with the cry of Themistocles, the Athenian: "Aye, strike if you will, but HEAR!"

Thereupon on August 1, 1828, at Albright's, in Chatham county, over two hundred citizens of that county, Randolph, Guilford and Orange met and appointed a committee to formulate and issue an "Address" to the people of the State in favor of "A Central Railroad." Mr. James Mebane was made chairman. The address shows how increased population and consequently production have made stagnation because of no outlet or inlet to commerce; and urges popular meetings over the state to further the idea, and especially to ask the next Assembly to make an experimental railway from the market house in Fayetteville to the wharf a short

distance below at Campbellton, the port of Fayetteville, head
of navigation on the Cape Fear.   Also to ask the Assembly
to provide for survey of "The Central Railroad."   This "address" was prepared by President Caldwell as chairman of
a committee and it embodied in some measure the thoughts
of his main address before this meeting.   A committee of
three from each of the four counties, President Caldwell,
chairman, was appointed to carry on a correspondence and
provide promotion of the aims of the meeting.   The
"Carleton" papers were continued during the fall, appeal-
ing to the farmers and avowing "A Central Railroad" to be
"The Poor Man's Cause."   Mr. Morehead would naturally
have been in this meeting, but, if so, he is not mentioned
among those who were active in it.   Early in September the
Newbern Spectator announced a meeting to cooperate with
the Chatham meeting, on September 4th, at which meeting
William Gaston was made chairman of the promotion committee.   Even the *Wilmington Recorder* came out in favor
of it and praised the essays of "Carleton."   And on November 17th, even the chief executive, Governor James Iredell,
in his message, favored it; and in doing so, made probably
the most concise statement of the heart of North Carolina's
problems that has been made:

"There are three great outlets to the ocean," he writes
to the Assembly, "which nature seems to have indicated for
this State: one for the waters of the Albemarle, another
for the waters of the Pamptico [later Pamlico], and the third
for the Cape Fear.   The Albemarle Sound, in length about
seventy miles, with a uniform depth of not less than twenty
feet, receiving into its bosom, besides other rivers of no inconsiderable importance, the Roanoke, the noblest river that
traverses our State, finds its communication with the ocean
impeded by a sand bar not eight hundred yards in width.
All the produce which floats on its waters, after coming
within sight of the Atlantic, must seek that ocean by a narrow strait into Pamptico Sound, through that sound a distance of eighty or ninety miles, over dangerous shoals, and
through the Ocracock [later Ocracoke] Inlet.   Nine-tenths
of the navigation of that part of the State (as indeed of

every other part) are directed to New York as the best
market; and, by inspection of the map, it will be seen that,
in passing through Ocracock Inlet and proceeding to New
York, a vessel descending the Albemarle, must sail more
than one hundred miles to reach a point on the coast, not five
miles distant from that at which it was compelled to pass
into Pamptico Sound. The importance of opening a direct
communication from the Albemarle to the ocean, cannot be
urged in a more forcible manner than by stating the extent
of territory which would find a market for its productions,
and a diminished price of transportation through the channel. The Roanoke River is now rendered navigable for
bateaux from its mouth to the Blue Ridge, in Virginia, and
to Leaksville, in this State. In both States its branches are
susceptible of improvement to much higher points. There
is perhaps no river east of the Mississippi, which, in proportion to its extent, washes a more fertile soil. The rich productions of its adjacent territory have become, both in this
State and in Virginia, almost proverbial. In this State
alone, at least eleven counties would find it the most natural
and convenient highway to market. Add to these eight
counties, through which flow the Chowan, the Casbie, the
Perquimans, the Pasquotank, the North, the Scuppernong,
and the Aligator Rivers, each of a depth not less than 12 or
15 feet, which convey the produce of a highly fertile country, and which contribute to form or to swell the current of
the Albemarle; and you will see that the agricultural interests of nearly one-third of the State is deeply concerned in
the accomplishment of this work. . . ."

He then speaks of the shoal which was the greatest im-
pediment to navigation through the Ocracoke, namely, the
"Swash" and government experiments at running it. If
this failed, a ship channel to unite the lower part of Neuse
River with Beaufort Harbor, "perhaps the most commodious
harbor in the State," was the next most plausible project.
The Neuse's improvement almost up to Raleigh, which rendered a bateau navigation safe eight or nine months of the
year, was noted. Cape Fear outlet was noted next, and the
fact that all the western counties, that used North Carolina

ports at all, would use this through Fayetteville, as the highest point for steamboat navigation nine months of the year, with bateau navigation still higher, and with Wilmington as its port. He notes that the shoals below Wilmington are much improved and will soon form no obstacle. He advocated port perfection first, then river improvement; then roads or canals from western counties to Fayetteville and counties connected with the Roanoke and other rivers. He spoke conservatively of "Railroads" and experiments with them, especially the latest one to connect the Ohio with Baltimore. He favored a similar experiment with a "Railway" from Fayetteville to Campbellton, a landing on Cape Fear River, and he praised the "Carleton" papers.[1]

But if Mr. Morehead was not active in these preliminaries, it was because he was engaged in a far larger game, through which he would be able, in due time, to lift the project with greater power, for the gentleman from Guilford was then an Elector for General Andrew Jackson.

---

[1] *Raleigh Register,* 21st November, 1828.

VII

Measures for Development
and
Its Organ, a New Constitution

1828

On December 3, 1828, the members of the Electoral College of North Carolina met in the Senate Chamber of the old brick capitol at Raleigh. There were fifteen of them, about one-third of whom were venerable men with three-score-and-ten to their credit. General Mountfort Stokes was made chairman, and Hon. Willie P. Mangum was probably the most distinguished among them; then there were Edward P. Dudley of Wilmington, Richard Dobbs Spaight, Jr., both eastern men, and John Motley Morehead from the west. Four years before young Morehead had been the only active friend of General Jackson in Guilford county, and the east had been against this "People's Candidate;" but now the state was united on this political Lochinvar out of the West, and the Guilford county elector saw his favorite candidate of four years before not only the unanimous choice of this electoral college, but of that of the nation as well. The great fact, however, was that the east had turned and followed the west for the first time, in both state and nation. These men were the leaders of it in North Carolina. Morehead and Spaight conducted the balloting with a solid vote for Jackson and Calhoun. Indeed the state at large had gone overwhelmingly for the North Carolina lawyer who had become a Tennessean; only seven counties in the whole commonwealth went against him and one of these was Morehead's own county, Guilford, which went almost two to one for Adams, the greatest majority that candidate received.

The contest had been a fierce one all over the land. It was a period of breaking up, with a new generation coming

101

to the front. "This country," says the *Raleigh Register* of July 22, 1828, "bids fair to contain as many parties in politics as there are sects in religion. Formerly there were two national creeds, now we have nearly a dozen; and as they have multiplied so fast of late, it is impossible to predict how many there may be a few years hence." The feeling was intense also: At a Jackson barbecue in Pennsylvania, in the autumn, a toast was offered: "John Quincy Adams— may he take sick on Monday! Send for the Doctor on Tuesday ! ! Get worse on Wednesday ! ! ! No better on Thursday ! ! ! ! Die on Friday ! ! ! ! ! Be buried on Saturday ! ! ! ! ! ! And go to Hell on Sunday ! ! ! ! ! !!" The South Carolinians had the same feeling, but, on one occasion, expressed it more classically: "Adams, Clay & Co.—Would to God they were like Jonah in the whale's belly; the whale to the devil; the devil in hell; and the doors locked, key lost and not a son of Vulcan within a million miles to make another!" There was no such ebullition in North Carolina, for the revolution there had been so overwhelming that the result was a great rebuke to the State's Congressmen who had nullified the vote of their Electoral College of four years before.[1] It was also a victory for the western part of the State and in that much for John Motley Morehead of Greensboro; and it was prophetic of greater changes to come.

Busy as Mr. Morehead was in his profession, his mind teemed with all sorts of development; and the interest in railroads, which President Caldwell in his "Carleton" letters had awakened, was accompanied by a new belief in manufactures. The manufacture of cotton into yarn, at the falls of the Tar river, was the oldest factory, and it had recently shipped twenty bales of yarn, according to the *Tarboro Free Press*. Another factory was at Fayetteville, head of navi-

---

[1] Hon. Edwin Godwin Reade, in an address before the North Carolina Bar Association, in 1884, says that in April, 1828, two lawyers were to fight a duel because one of them had reflected on the character of Mrs. President Adams. The bearer of the challenge was told his principal was a scoundrel and he himself could have a fight if he wanted it. The bearer accepted it, but was just then already bound over to keep the peace in another matter, and this raised the question whether his bond would be forfeited if they went over the state boundary to fight. The two submitted it to Mr. Morehead and his old Latin preceptor, Thomas Settle, and in a written opinion they said it would forfeit the bond. The belligerents thereupon subsided.

gation on the Cape Fear, and another in the far west in
Lincoln county, west of Charlotte. On October 14th, the
Greensboro Patriot gave notice of a meeting to organize
manufacturing and to apply for incorporation of a new mill;
while on November 8th, a like meeting was held at Salisbury, Rowan county, and a similar one for both cotton and
woolen factories in the adjoining county of Iredell, at its
Court House, on the 17th. They cited the successful operation of the Tar river factory, and those at Fayetteville and
in Lincoln county. This had been, in great measure, stimulated by Charles Fisher's wool report of January 1st, previously, in which he had shown that the balance of trade for
several years had been so greatly against North Carolina,
that she was probably $10,000,000 behind. Why should she
buy flour in the north? Why buy pork in New York? Or
hogs in Kentucky and Tennessee? Cotton and tobacco were
the only things exported from the west part of the state and
rice and naval stores all from the seaboard. The introduction of the manufacturing systems and railroads, of course,
was the remedy. The state ships 80,000 bales of cotton at
$2,400,000, which, if manufactured, would bring $9,600,000!
—a gain of $7,200,000! It would give occupation, arrest
emigration, and build towns like Lowell, Mass., which, six
years ago, was nothing and now has 6000 population.

John Motley Morehead was also behind this public agitation during 1828, and was acting personally, too. Leaksville, near his old home in Rockingham county, was the head
of bateau navigation on the Dan-Roanoke and he, his father
and brothers owned land in the region.[1] He and his brother,
Samuel, established a big combination business there which
developed into various kinds of mills, cotton and otherwise,
general merchandise and supplies of all kinds. He later
had occasion to tell the people the relation of this enterprise to his temporary retirement from public life in 1828:
"The very extraordinary support which you gave me in

---

[1] This land was first acquired by his father, John Morehead, after Leaksville was laid out, on the belief that this town would become the head of Dan
and Roanoke navigation to a far more considerable degree than it ever has.
Spray was then a part of Leaksville. It was this investment, it is said, that
finally made John Morehead fail.

1827, after having been representative in 1826, was, to me, the most gratifying evidence of your approbation of the manner in which I had discharged the duties with which your kindness had entrusted me. My removal to Greensborough to settle myself among you, and the loss of my brother, to whose care I had entrusted, almost exclusively, the management of a considerable mercantlie establishment, the concerns of which devolved entirely upon me after his death, rendered it extremely inconvenient for me to solicit re-election in 1828; and which I could not have accepted without a personal sacrifice not required by my friends, and which my opponents had no right to demand.'"[1] This was his brother, Samuel, who died on September 17, 1828. There was one office, however, that, a few months after his brother's death, Mr. Morehead did accept. His friends had put him up for this office once before, without success, as has been seen; but early in January, after the aged Nathaniel Macon and Archibald R. Ruffin had resigned as Trustees of the University of North Carolina, the Assembly in an election on January 5, 1829, selected Mr. Morehead first among five new trusteees. Almost ten years later, they chose his brother, James Turner Morehead as Trustee, also; and the two served together for nearly thirty years, while John Motley, in serving the rest of his life, was destined to aid in guiding the development of his *alma mater* for but a dozen years less than a half-century, one of the longest services in the history of the institution. In that long period he served with such distinguished men as Archibald DeBow Murphy, William Gaston, Dr. Joseph Caldwell, Dr. James Mebane, Dr. McPheeters, Governor James Iredell, Chief Justice Thomas Ruffin, Secretary of the Navy George E. Badger, Hon. Willie P. Mangum, Hon. R. M. Saunders, Dr. Francis L. Hawks, Hon. Thomas Settle, President David L. Swain, Hon. Wm. A. Graham, Bartholomew F. Moore, Hon. John M. Dick, Gov. D. S. Reid, and many others, few or none of whom served so long. Nor was he a figure-head as a trustee, but for nearly forty

---

[1] A public "address" in the *Greensboro Patriot* of July 11, 1832.

The Original Cotton Mill
at Spray, N. C.

years—over thirty-eight, to be exact—he had a positive influence in the development of this great institution.

All of the general activity in manufactures and banking in 1829 and on was accompanied by activity in transportation and this centered to a remarkable degree about the Roanoke valley, of which President Caldwell had occasion to say, in the Senate of North Carolina late in 1829, while speaking of the Baltimore and Ohio raiload project, and the Georgetown and Ohio canal: "If we were to lay our hand upon the region of our own state, the brightest for affluence and efficient ability, it would fall upon the Roanoke with the portion of country that enjoys its privileges and prospects." And when during March, 1829, Delaware voted a railroad from New Castle on the Delaware Bay to head of navigation on Elk river at the head of the Chesapeake, when in April Baltimore and Ohio engineers returned from Europe announcing that steam "locomotives" were built that could pull up a grade four times any elevation on their survey, and that the Liverpool and Manchester railroad was to be built through to London as soon as Parliament passed an act; that the Baltimore line had experimented with a freight car loaded to 8260 pounds that *one man* moved easily; and that Massachusetts had in June authorized railroad construction across the state west and to Providence, R. I., and that 120 tons of railroad iron had just arrived in Charleston, S. C., for their new lines; that with the completion of the Dismal swamp canal, there were now eight vessels on the line between Weldon, at the Roanoke rapids, and Norfolk—then it was that a Virginia port rival to Norfolk, namely, Petersburg, on the Appomattox, not far from where it empties into the James—also a rival to Richmond—began taking measures to tap this rich Roanoke valley, not with canals, but with a railroad, and a survey was announced late in October, the objective also being Weldon.[1] This project was

---

[1] *Raleigh Register,* 3rd November, 1829. A month or so later the Liverpool and Manchester Railway had offered £500 for the best locomotive and the "Rocket" won. By the following June passengers arrived from Baltimore to Washington. A single horse drew a carriage weighing more than a ton, on which were 28 persons and they came at the rate of 15 miles an hour. "This was done, too, with much apparent ease, for the traces did not seem half the time to be strained at all." *Raleigh Register,* 3rd June, 1830.

destined to be the most influential event in the transportation history of North Carolina as well as Virginia; and soon led the upper Roanoke to demand a canal around the rapids above Weldon. It was inaugurated the following February. About the same time, October 28, 1829, a big meeting was also held in Beaufort to further the project of a ship canal to connect its harbor with the Pamlico and so with the Albemarle and Roanoke.[1]

Virginia was stirring North Carolina vigorously in another way, also, for the conservative eastern counties, which had heretofore quoted the Old Dominion's conservatism in not touching their constitution of 1776, could do so no longer. Agitation had begun in the spring and in April the aged Chief Justice Marshall had agreed to serve in the convention, while by June lists of delegates were published and in October the people of the Old North State began to read the proceedings of the convention and realize that the old constitution of 1776 in their sister state must go. Probably no one event was more calculated to revive the old east and west division in North Carolina over revision of her own fundamental law. President Jackson's election might consolidate the state for the moment, but the deep purpose of the Piedmont and Mountains to have proper representation was not to be denied much longer. Indeed, by June, 1830, proposals for a Convention were widely discussed, and the *Fayetteville Observer* drew attention to the fact that this ought not to be an east and west division—let it be as it was in 1787, when a Warren county man proposed it (Philemon Hawkins), or in 1788 when a Craven county representative, Richard Dobbs Spaight, urged it.[2]

This agitation was reinforced by the results of the new census of 1830, which showed injustice of representation was greatly intensified. The seven largest counties in population were all western, if Wake be included, and she often

---

[1] It is startling to most readers to learn that North Carolina had 3100 Indians within her borders at this time, out of the 312,300 in the United States. New York had still more and Mississippi had most. About 20,200 were between the Mississippi, Illinois and the Lakes; 94,300 between the Mississippi and the Rockies, above Missouri, and west of Arkansas and Louisiana; 20,000 in the Rockies and 80,000 west of them.

[2] *Raleigh Register*, June 24, 1830.

was: 1. Orange, the largest, with 23,875; 2. Lincoln; 3. Rowan; 4. Wake; 5. Mecklenburg; 6. Granville; and 7. Guilford—Mr. Morehead's county, with 18,735. Indeed, excepting Halifax, the next seven largest counties were western, too: 1. Burke; 2. Rutherford; 3. Buncombe; 4. Stokes; 5. Iredell; 6. Chatham; 7. Caswell, before an eastern county is reached. Furthermore, omitting Edgecombe, Craven and Northampton, the next six largest are also western: 1. Cumberland; 2. Surry; 3. Anson; 4. Davidson; 5. Rockingham; 6. Randolph. Two more, out of 36, above 10,000, in the whole 64, were western. The increase in population for the decade had been nearly 100,000 and mostly in the west. Newbern, 3796, was still the largest town, and Greensboro came up to 562. There was an increase of nearly 5000 in free negroes—nearly 20,000—the greatest number being in Halifax, the other counties having more than 500 each being Pasquotank, Craven, Hartford, Northampton, Guilford, Martin, Surry, Wake, Granville, Cumberland, Orange and Robeson. Halifax and Granville had the most slaves.[1]

The public mind was awakening to many new ideas: The confining of capital punishment to first degree murder was one; abolition of imprisonment for debt was another; there was wide-spread organization for more scientific agriculture; new transportation methods have already been noted; also manufacturing; in addition to these came mining; silk culture was also advocated; the advance of public education was not the least of these agitations, and colonization of negroes was an earnest theme. The tariff of 1828 had already brought much talk of nullification, by South Carolina particularly, but North Carolina had no sympathy with it. This so incensed the Charleston leaders that one of them succeeded in attaching the epithet "Rip Van Winkle" to the "Old North State" soon after; but that state had gone unanimously for President Jackson and he was not asleep on nullification. Indeed the North Carolina House of Com-

---

[1] By January, 1831, the Quakers had freed and removed 652 slaves with children at a cost of about $13,000.

mons, in January, 1831, passed a resolution against "this unhallowed thing!"

In this latter Assembly, fearing a fire in the old brick capitol, provision was made to replace the shingle roof with tin; and when the change was being carried out in June, 1831, the very thing feared, which tinners were at work with solder to prevent, was, on Tuesday, the 21st, apparently caused by one of the workmen, and the old brick capitol went up in flames, destroying the famous Canova statue of Washington in the rotunda. This comparatively insignificant event was the turning point in the development of North Carolina, strange as that may seem; and it was because it again raised the question of location of the state's capital and opened a Pandora's box of rivalries that were to involve the most vital questions to the commonwealth. For Fayetteville, daughter of Wilmington, on the Cape Fear, was ambitious to be mistress of the state, and Wilmington and the Cape Fear valley were in sympathy with it and the West saw in it a mode of furthering her two most important measures: a new constitution and central railroad. The former once settled, the latter would follow. The feature which made this possible was the fact that the capital had been settled at Raleigh by the state Ordinance of 1788, a convention measure and hence of the character of part of the constitution, which only a new convention could change. The matter was precipitated in the Assembly of 1831–32, held at Government House, or the executive mansion, at the foot of Fayetteville street just outside of Raleigh.

The beautiful chess-like game was as follows: First, on November 25th, Senator Seawell, of Raleigh, offered a bill to rebuild the capitol on Unon Square. Then, on December 8th, Senator Martin of Rockingham, 32 to 31, got it postponed a year. Next, on December 10, 1831, Senator Dishough of Onslow county, on the coast below Beaufort, called for a joint committee to consider a railroad or railroad and canal from Old Topsail Inlet, the entrance to Beaufort Harbor, through the central part of the State to the mountains, whereupon it was amended to include a Fayetteville-Yadkin valley road and one from Chatham, southwest to Raleigh, up to the Roanoke to join the Pettersburg road when it should be completed. These were assigned to the joint committee. On December 16th, James Harper of Greene, an eastern county, presented a bill in the Commons to rebuild the capitol in Union Square, Raleigh, and it was referred to the committee of the whole House on the 21st. On this latter day before the Commons proceeded to the capitol matter, William Gaston, the distinguished Newbern member, reported from the joint committee bills to incorporate the "North Carolina Central Railroad Company," Beaufort harbor to Newbern, Raleigh and the west, and the Cape Fear-Yadkin Railroad. Immediately thereafter the committee of the whole House began consideration of the rebuilding of the capitol. It began to be evident that the West, headed by Mr. Morehead's old district, which was both a Cape Fear valley and a Western district, had decided to hold over the East a threat to join the lower Cape Fear Valley and remove the capitol to Fayetteville, unless the East joined the West in securing a new constitution and a central railroad from Beaufort harbor. Even on the 8th of December, Senator Seawell saw the combination: "Who," said he, "are the people who find fault with the constitution? The people of the West, who want more power; the people of the Cape Fear, who want the seat of government. The small counties on the Cape Fear, with a black population, in some instances greater than the white, are by this compromise to surrender the right of representation to the West, provided the West will cede them the seat of government. . . . I perceive, Sir, by the newspapers, that our enterprising brethren of the West contemplate the project of a railroad from the back country to Old Topsail Inlet. God speed their undertaking and give it success." Senator Toomer of Fayetteville, answered him: "The scepter is passing away from Judah," said he, "empire is marching westwardly; in that section population is increasing. We have seen the grandeur of the eastern, and enjoyed the splendor of the meridian sun; we must now admire his beauty in the west. Fifty-five years have devolved since the constitution was formed. During that period many changes, moral, political, and physical, have occurred in the condition of our country, and the character of our people. Yes, a new country has appeared, and a new population has arisen in the west." So when it came up in the Commons on the 21st, 22nd, and 23rd of December, William Gaston made one of the most impassioned pleas of his life for it. He said there were but 13 smaller Cape Fear valley counties of the 64 that had any real interest in it, but there were 30 that abhorred it and would not stand for it in the end. He said it was being done by a dominant Jackson party, upheld by Crawford adherents—another political combination. He said these 13 counties were selling their equality of representation, their birthright, for a mess of pottage! And when he finished, the battle was lost to those who wanted the new capitol—in Raleigh—68 to 65. The 68 were: from Anson, 2; Ashe, 2; *Bladin,* 2; *Brunswick,* 2; Buncombe, 2; Burke, 2; Cabarrus, 2; Caswell, 2; Chatham, 2; *Columbus,* 2; *Cumberland,* 2; Davidson, 2; *Duplin,* 1; Guilford, 2; Haywood, 2; Iredell, 2; Lincoln, 2; Macon, 2; Mecklenburg, 2; Montgomery, 2; Moore, 2; *New Hanover,* 2; *Onslow,* 1; Orange, 2; Randolph, 2; Richmond, 2; Robeson, 2; Rockingham, 2; Rowan, 2; Rutherford, 2; *Sampson,* 2; Stokes, 2; Surry, 2; Wilkes, 2; *Wilmington,* 1; *Fayetteville,* 1. The italicized names are those which joined Wilmington and Fayetteville for the West. This was the first successful battle of the West, unless the Jackson West's capture of the Crawford forces could be called the first. It should be observed, however, that this 68-to-65 vote was merely negative, so far as capital removal was concerned; and that Mr. Gaston and other eastern men had served a warning on Wilmington and the lower Cape Fear in the form of a Beaufort harbor-Central Railroad Bill.

It was now to be a struggle between the Cape Fear and lower Roanoke for the favor of the West, which boded well for both a new constitution and a Central Railroad. For the West had said merely "The capitol question is still open, so far as the Commons is concerned; we will wait and see what you will do." Thereupon, they put forth further opportunity of test, when Senator Dick of Guilford county, on the 28th, presented a preamble and resolutions calling for

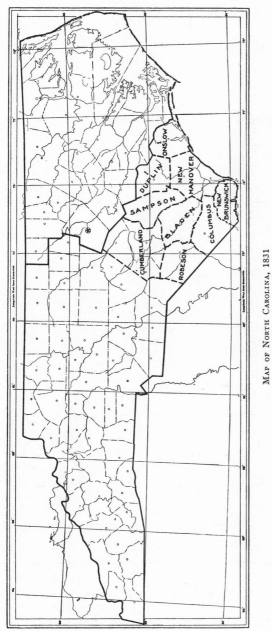

MAP OF NORTH CAROLINA, 1831
Prepared by the author
Showing eastern counties that joined the west, 68 to 65 votes, Duplin and Onslow divided

the election of a Constitutional Convention, a chief feature of which was practical representation according to population by giving the largest counties four votes each and the rest graduated down to one each for the smallest. Two days later the Central Railroad bill was pushed forward and on January 6, 1832, the main bill was passed, but not the completed bill. Thereupon the Senator from Granville, on the 9th, tried to reintroduce the capitol bill and, after a fight that lasted to the 11th, it was ruled out by but one vote, remaining postponed until next Assembly. This was the West's notification that the capitol question must await the outcome of the convention question; and it was well they did so, for on January 4, 1832, Senator Louis D. Wilson of Edgecombe made a determined effort to have it postponed indefinitely and succeeded by a vote of 42 to 21. So both capitol and convention were postponed for another year, and the honors were even, between the east and the west, with the West in possession of her railroad bills.[1]

A curious feature of the situation, however, was the fact that Raleigh's friends, so confident of keeping the capital, had anticipated the Fayetteville-Campbellton "Experimental Railroad" of a mile or so, and in February, 1830, had secured incorporation of their own "Experimental Railroad," designing to run it from capitol or "Union Square" to the quarry, a mile or so southeastward, to also haul stone for the new capitol, when it should be ordered. It went eastward from the capitol, on Newbern, to Bloodworth, then south to East Hargett, then east to Tarboro and south again to the quarry. All railroads were "experimental" ones; but by "experimental" they meant not only mechanical experiment, but psychological and political experiment. They proposed to have not merely a railroad track and freight wagons, but "handsome cars on it for such ladies and gentlemen as may desire to take the exercise of a Railroad airing," a feature that was accomplished not

---

[1] The year 1831 was characterized by slave insurrection to an unusual degree. In August there was one in Virginia and in September one in the counties of Duplin, Sampson, and others near Wilmington were nipped in the bud. These followed one in Charleston that was apparently started by Haytian negroes.

many months later.[1] This feature was designed to convince
Solons and other North Carolina visitors to the capital, by
actual experience with a railroad, what a good thing the
North Carolina Central Railroad would be; for the progress
of the Petersburg and Roanoke Railroad toward the Roanoke valley, and the effect it was having on the shipments
from the Roanoke, even before it reached there, was causing
intense thought on the subject in the southern part of the
state and in Wilmington especially. Before the close of 1832
Halifax was saying she was getting goods and shipping them
much quicker, even though it was only 30 miles from
Petersburg, and a good way from the Roanoke, yet.

In view of these things, it is not strange that John Motley Morehead's motto, *Quiescere non Possum,* should become acutely active in his consciousness, for by the time
"The Experimental Railroad" was organized in July, 1832,
the friends of President Jackson had nominated him for
Presidential Elector again. Of this *The Greensborough
Patriot* of July 11, 1832, says of the Jackson connection in
that place, after coming out for that ticket, "then for
dulcifying the *pill* which the Divil would hate to swallow,
without something to give it a *relish,* 'a member' very gravely
asserts that John M. Morehead, Esq., stands pledged to support the above ticket. If this pledge was given *at all,* it
must have been given in *confidence,* to 'the member' alone,
for we never heard such a thing in these Capes! It is true,
the gentleman in question has been nominated by the friends
of the present administration, as an elector on the *Jackson*
ticket; but Van Buren was never named, and only *remembered* to be *depised,* in the several meetings which made
and sustained the nomination. Mr. Morehead is properly
pledged to support the Jackson ticket, *if chosen as an elector;* but who ever authorized 'the member' to cram Van
Buren down his throat?"

---

[1] *Raleigh Register,* 28th December, 1832. The first meeting of stockholders
was on June 29, 1832, and the organization took place at the Raleigh Court
House on July 6th, with Joseph Gales as President. By September 10th, their
iron rails were at Petersburg and by January, 1833, the road was finished, and
possessed two cars and three horses. Minutes of the Managers' Board, Historical Commission, Raleigh.

On the same day as the above, Mr. Morehead issued a "Circular to the Freemen of Guilford County," in which he says: "Fellow Citizens: The very extraordinary support which you gave me in 1827, after having been your representative in 1826, was, to me, the most gratifying evidence of your approbation of the manner in which I had discharged the duties with which your kindness had entrusted me.

"My removal to Greensborough to settle myself permanently among you, and the loss of my brother, to whose care I had entrusted, almost exclusively, the management of a considerable mercantile establishment, the concerns of which devolved entirely upon me after his death, rendered it extremely inconvenient for me to solicit a re-election in 1828; and which I could not have accepted without a personal sacrifice not required by my friends, and which my opponents had no right to demand.

"Our late worthy Senator having declined a re-election, I became a candidate to represent you in the next Senate. I was induced to do so for diverse reasons:—Our next legislature will be a very important one;—Matters in which the state and yourselves have the deepest interest, will, no doubt, be agitated. The subject of holding a convention, to revise and amend our constitution, and remove the seat of government, if it shall be the people's will; the establishment of a bank, by which the interest of the state and her citizens shall be advanced and secured, and a sound and sufficient currency, now so much needed, be afforded for all commercial purposes;—Investments in railroads, on a plan, wild and extravagant, or prudent, economical and judicious; and an appropriation for rebuilding your capitol; and diverse other matters of equal or minor importance.

"You who pay the least attention to the interests of our State, know that the next session will present an important crisis in our affairs. And you must be satisfied that at no time, has it been more desirable that the West should send to our next legislature the whole force of her moral and intellectual strength. And it is to be lamented that some of the most efficient, able and distinguished members of the last session, from the West, are not before the people for a re-election.

"Some of you, my fellow citizens, as well as some other citizens of the state, were kind enough to signify to me the favorable opinion that I could be of service to my country and state in the next legislature, and that I would in some degree, add to the weight and character of the Western representation. This favorable expression was accompanied with a request that I would tender my services to the people. Believing it the duty of every citizen to render service whenever required, I came to the conclusion to tender you my services, however much it might be against my inclinations and interests, if no other citizen should do so.

"At May term of your court, having understood that it was probable Jonathan Parker and Francis L. Simpson, Esqrs., would be candidates in the Senate, I applied in person to Mr. Simpson, between whom and myself the most friendly relations have existed from our first acquaintance, to know whether he had any such designs, at the same time assuring him of my determination not to become a candidate, if any other person of respectability did so. Mr. Simpson replied, that he was determined Mr. Parker should have opposition if he became a candidate; and that he would oppose him unless I would do so. I again stated to Mr. Simpson that I was determined not to become a candidate, if himself, Mr. Parker, or any other respectable citizen chose to do so—as I was determined to have no contest with any person. To this Mr. Simpson replied, that the friendly relations which had existed between us forbade our opposition; and he was kind enough to say, that my becoming a candidate met his entire approbation. He also assured me in the most positive and unequivocal terms, that he would not become a candidate for the Senate if I would tender my services. I thanked him for his renewed but not unexpected evidence of his friendship, and assured him that I should become a candidate, if Mr. Parker, or some other citizen did not.

"Not until Friday of the same court, did I know certainly

that Mr. Parker would not offer; and no other citizen coming forward on that day, I tendered you my services.

"And I assure you, fellow citizens, that I should have been again proud to represent the intelligent freemen of Guilford, if it had met their approbation—if I would have done so with honor to myself and usefulness to them. And as an earnest of the future, I would have referred you to past services I have rendered you. During the two sessions I had the honor to represent you, I have not heard the first complaint; and I was not, during that time, a mere *cypher,* counting only when on the *right* of a *figure!*

"Scarcely had my name been announced, when the ever busy tongue of slander commenced its *worthy* work. The public ear was filled with suspicions, jealousies and slanders, the most ridiculous and unfounded. And there were some, whose good opinion I desire and respect, affected to give some credence.

"In all communities there will be a noisy herd, who utter a senseless clamour and gladly listen to, and circulate everything that is destructive of a neighbor's character. If I had found the opposition to me confined to this class, I should certainly have disregarded it; but when I find those, whose good opinion I esteem, attributing to me unworthy and unfounded motives for tendering to them my services, and, instead of giving me their support, pursuing me with jealous suspicions—I have for them, too much regard, to any longer trouble and disquiet them.

"I desire to render services to my state, and the honor of representing the freemen of Guilford, is, and will be at all times, to me, a *sufficient motive* to tender them my services, whenever I may deem them acceptable. And I shall deplore the condition of our common country, when the feelings of patriotism shall become so far extinguished, as not to be a sufficient inducement to serve the public—and when, to receive the suffrages of freemen, shall cease to be an honor.

"I find myself unexpectedly opposed by Mr. Francis L. Simpson. This is an opposition which no man could have anticipated after what had passed between us unless he were *much better acquainted* with *Mr. Simpson,* than I confess I was!

"Whether the idle clamours against me have offered him temptations he could not resist; whether a fickle disposition could not bear the yoke an honorable pledge had imposed; or whether an anxiety to play the bravo, flourish the candidate a few days and then retire, as on a former occasion—has been the cause of his course, I know not.

"But whatever the cause may be, I sincerely regret it;—not that I could have anything to fear from such a contest. The language which you have heretofore spoken through your ballot-box, to both of us, when canvassing for the same seat, was too intelligible for the most consummate vanity to misunderstand. And even if anything was to have been apprehended, in a *fair* and *honorable* contest—*now,* that apprehension would be *certainly* removed!

"The same busy tongue which has traduced me, and abused you, will attribute my withdrawal to an apprehension of the result of the contest. Can you expect anything else from that mind, in which a noble emotion never arose—in which a generous sentiment, a disinterested motive, honest candour, or veracity has no abiding place?

"I stated to you, my fellow citizens, in my first declaration, that I wished not to have a contest for the place—I am still determined to have none; and beg you to consider me no longer a candidate before you.

"To have been your representative by a respectable majority; and yet to have been opposed and suspected by an honorable minority, would have rendered my seat unpleasant, particularly at a time when every Western representative should be untrammelled; and should unite all our intellectual energies and strength for the advancement of our common good.

"A seat in the legislature is pleasant to him who is content to obtain it by any and every means, however degrading or unjustifiable—who is content to screw himself into some obscure corner of the legislative hall, equally incapable of *originating* or *sustaining* any great and useful public measure, and from his snug retreat, to cry 'Aye' or 'No' to every question put, *regardless* of the propriety of the vote he is giving—but *regarding strictly* how he thinks it will *go down at home;*— who draws his pay—chuckles over it— returns home—and tells what wonders 'we have done!'—but never tells that stubborn truth:—'*I got my pay, but I did not earn it!*'

"Far different are the feelings of that honorable member who takes his seat, deeply impressed with the magnitude of the responsibility he has assumed—who reflects, under the obligations of an oath, that he is legislating upon the lives, the liberties and fortunes of his fellow men; and that after ages may be affected by an error in his course—who votes for the public good, regardless of popular clamour, returns among his constituents, convinces them of their error, and again receives their support.

"While a portion of the community remain ignorant and unsuspecting, for the artful and designing demagogue to play upon and deceive; and the more intelligent give ear and countenance to idle clamour and unfounded reports, you will find your legislative halls filled with the former class of representatives, while the latter never attempt to stem that torrent of scurrility which lies between them and an honorable seat.

"If you have anything on earth to give your children, vest it in the head—in every sense of the word, *it is a life estate.*

"If you have talents, wisdom and integrity among you, and that you have there can be no doubt, I conjure you, fellow-citizens, if you ever intend to employ them, to do so *now.* A more propitious time will never arrive.

"Most joyfully will I join with you, to place that one of you, most distinguished for these attributes, in that seat I so lately sought to occupy—indulging the fond hopes, that the able and distinguished individual, who may occupy it, will do honor to himself and his constituents, and will sustain and advance the interests of our beloved country.

"Accept, fellow citizens, a renewal of my thanks for the

confidence you have heretofore placed in your fellow citizen
and humble servant.

"John M. Morehead.[1]
"Greensborough, July 11, 1832."

In this address are evidences of the large mould in which
John Motley Morehead was cast. His was the spirit of the
statesman. The West at this critical juncture could not
afford to allow dividing contests, and he personally would
not be the subject of one in the presence of such a great
opportunity to get a new constitution and the lesser organs
of the transformation of North Carolina. On the other
hand, he showed the bold fearlessness of the master surgeon,
probing to the seat of disease and following it with knife
and scalpel. Likewise, as a modern surgeon, he used the
anesthetic of a fine and lofty feeling, gentle humor and good
will. But all his efforts came to naught so far as the Assembly of 1832-33 was concerned, for although so progressive
a westerner as Judge David L. Swain of Buncombe was
chosen Governor, when on December 3, 1832, Senator Martin of Mr. Morehead's old home county of Rockingham
presented a preamble reciting people's desire for a new constitution, election of Governor by themselves, and a possible
change of the capital from Raleigh, to which was added a
resolution providing for vote on a convention in August,
1833, it did not succeed, while on the 17th, action was begun
on a House bill to provide a new capitol in Raleigh. On the
18th, and on the 20th, fights for and against the latter bill
were made by Senators Leake and Martin, the Raleigh
capitol party winning in each by a vote of 33 and 36, against
27—the solid new constitution block.[2] So when Mr. Morehead, as an elector on the overwhelming Jackson-Van Buren
ticket—again against his own county which went for Clay
and Sergeant—he knew the constitutional contest was again
delayed.

When, however, during the Christmas holidays, it was
realized what had happened, the friends of the Convention

---

[1] The result was that Candidate Parker was chosen Senator.
[2] The defections from the vote of 1831 came from such counties as Bladen,
Duplin, Onslow and a few others.

in the Assembly, met on January 4, 1833, and elected General Polk of Rowan chairman, and it became evident they were there for but one thing, namely, to find a mode for the people of North Carolina to express themselves on the desire for a convention. Among them were some eastern men who realized the gravity of the situation and felt that now the capitol question was settled, the West's demand for the North Carolina Railroad, already surveyed from Newbern to Raleigh by Engineer Francis W. Rawle of Pennsylvania, and a new constitution were due that section. These were men like William Gaston of Newbern, David Outlaw of Beaufort, William H. Haywood of Raleigh, and others. This unofficial constitutional convention recommended that election officers take the unofficial vote of the people and forward returns to the Governor, and that officer in turn to the Assembly; that a committee of four issue an "Address" and explain the amendments sought and that county committees of three aid these purposes. The four for the "Address" were Richmond M. Pearson, Romulus M. Saunders, William H. Haywood, Jr., and Thomas Dews. The local committee for Guilford county was Mr. Morehead, George C. Mendenhall, John M. Dick, and F. L. Simpson; and the rest were men of like character; so that it was plain that this unofficial constitutional convention was not going to be an inefficient one.

While awaiting their action preparatory to the August elections attention may be turned to other momentous events. One might dwell long on the nullification movement led by South Carolina but as fiercely and impatiently resisted by her sister Carolina were is not so well known a part of national history. The action of President Jackson, in this matter endeared him to the old North State, even when she opposed him on other scores; but the subject of railroads was as much uppermost in men's minds as that of the revision of the fundamental law. While in the previous November, Halifax had said she was getting goods more quickly than ever because of the Petersburg thirty miles of railroad that didn't even reach them, and a toll-bridge bill for the Roanoke at Weldon was passed on January 3rd

[1833] and the Virginia bill for a Portsmouth and Roanoke Railroad was also passed to enable it to reach Weldon—Portsmouth notice of rivalling Petersburg for the Roanoke valley trade—it was announced on February 15th, that the Petersburg road was complete, with a locomotive, for 41 miles, and that tri-weekly four-horse coaches from Raleigh took passengers to it at Belfield. The Raleigh "Experimental Railroad" from the new capitol site to the quarry had been completed on January 4th, at which time Engineer Rawle's formidable estimate of $5000 a mile for the North Carolina Central Railroad from Beaufort harbor to Raleigh and $9000 for the Yadkin line came out as a great discourager of the project. This led to the *Raleigh Register* proposing an extension of the "Experimental" line to the Neuse River, and, by March, Granville county held a meeting at Oxford proposing a railroad through that place to connect with the Petersburg and the proposed Portsmouth-Norfolk road at Weldon. Fayetteville was working hard in January and February raising $200,000 for the Cape Fear and Yadkin Valley road; while in April the Granville people had another meeting, this time proposing that the line have Blakely on the Roanoke as an objective, instead of Weldon, and go westward through Warrenton and Oxford. They told of how two cars and about forty people were easily drawn by two horses; how the road across New Jersey, from the Delaware at Bordentown to Amboy toward New York, had a locomotive and eleven cars with 200 people carried at 15 miles an hour! By April the old capitol ruins at Raleigh were being removed and the "Experimental" line getting ready to haul stones from the quarry. A traveler visiting Newbern, in June, notes that the Petersburg line has thoroughly convinced that section of railroad efficiency; that in Orange county railroads was the "talk of every third man;" that the Neuse people's slowness is forcing the northern counties to connect up with the Petersburg road, and proposes a line from Raleigh to Smithfield on the Neuse, 18 miles, which, if made as cheaply as the "Experimental" line, at $2800 a mile would cost but $68,000. The *Raleigh Register* editor on same date, June 11th, proposes an extension of the "Experimental" line to South Washington in New Hanover county, about 75 miles, and make that the head of navigation instead of Wilmington.

By this time, the committee of the unofficial constitutional convention at Raleigh issued their "Address" on June 18th [1833]. This was a strong presentation: They said that 33 counties with only 156,000 population elect a majority of the Assembly when 31 have over 316,000 population; that the 33 have only an $8000 land tax while the 31 have $17,000; that the 33 elect a majority, with all taxes only $24,000 as against 31 with twice that amount; that half of the 33 do not pay enough to even pay their own members' salaries—two-thirds taxed by one-third to pay minority for controlling the majority! that 40 counties do not pay taxes to equal their share in public expenses, yet elect two-thirds of the Assembly! that the 40 do not contain an average population; that 46,600 people have no larger share in government than 9000! In 1776 the 36 counties had 115 members, but in 1833 the 64 counties have 199—double the size an Assembly ought to be; so that there has been an annual deficit of $12,000 to $17,000 for years! They propose: 1. Reduction in size of Assembly; 2. Biennial meetings only; 3. Popular election of Governor; 4. No borough representation; 5. And a new mode of amendment. They point out that New York, Virginia, New Hampshire, and Georgia have already revised their old constitutions.

The main burden of their paper, however, was an argument for a *limited* convention. Indeed, they distinctly avow that "no *unlimited convention* is asked." They remind the people that the conventions to merely accept or reject the national constitution were limited; that the New York convention of 1801 was limited; likewise the Virginia convention and those of New Hampshire and Georgia. The North Carolina constitution, they say, is silent on a mode of revision; but, they add "in this country," sovereignty, "is lodged with a *majority of the people*," and these can determine that mode, keeping in view *justice* to the minority, the *right* of the majority, and the interest of both. It was a most able and disinterested paper and was destined to point out the way to final settlement of the generation-long controversy.[1]

Coordinate with this and the railroad agitation, was the establishment of a new Bank of North Carolina provided for in January [1833] to take the place of the old State Bank whose charter would expire in 1835. It was to be capitalized at $2,000,000, one-half of the stock to be taken by the State; and with a head bank in Raleigh were to be branches in leading centers over the state—a recurring necessity because of the President's new attack on and final destruction of the Bank of the United States. On January 8th of this year, Governor Swain appointed commissioners to take subscriptions to the new Bank of North Carolina in the leading towns, and he made Mr. Morehead chairman of the Greensboro body, composed of Messrs. Lindsay, Humphries, Maxwell and Parker. "Senex," whose series of papers was pleading for the new constitution, incidentally but ably touched upon the bank question, saying that since the State Bank was created in 1812, $2,000,000 had "taken wings and flown away."[2]

Various matters came to a strategic head on Independence Day at Raleigh, when the laying of the corner-stone of the new capitol was also made the occasion of what might be called a "Transportation Convention,' but was entitled "Internal Improvement Convention." As the new capitol, in a very true sense, represents the new North Carolina of a new constitution and modern development, it may be well to take more careful note of it, as the corner-stone was laid on this 4th of July, 1833: That it should epitomize the effort to unite North Carolinians in both a constitutional and transportational way is unique. The Scotch architect, David Paton of Edinburgh, took charge not long after the corner-stone was laid and had much to do in determining its character. It is about twenty feet longer, north and south, than east and west, so that it can be said to front both east and west, but the east front is most used as front, at the head of Newbern Avenue, named for the city whose able

[1] *Raleigh Register*, 18th June, 1833.
[2] *Ibid.*, 11th June, 1833, "Senex" No. IV.

citizen, William Gaston, had so much to do with harmonizing the conflicting elements which raged around this capitol for and against a new constitution and some unifying mode of transportation and trade centers. The greatest height, the dome, is 97½ feet. Built completely of stone from the Raleigh quarry, it is of Grecian Doric style, copied from the Temple of Minerva, or Parthenon, of Athens of 500 B.C., its octagon tower forming the rotunda and being capped by a crown similar to that of the Lanthorn of Demosthenes. The proportions may be realized when it is known that the columns of the east and west porticos are over five feet in diameter. The vestibules and corridors are decorated with Ionic columns, and the rest with groined arches on Doric columns and pilasters. The Governor's rooms are in the southwest corner, and the Senatorial and Representative Halls are in keeping with the rest of this noble Greek structure, which cost the state over a half million dollars—a capitol of which even the 20th century North Carolina may well be proud. But only its corner-stone was finished on this day by the company which met at "Government House," as the executive mansion at the foot of Fayetteville street was then called, and served as temporary capitol. Governor Swain presided at the function in the morning, as he did at the more important one at Government House in the afternoon.

This Convention was a peculiar one, composed of some of the strongest men of the state, and especially of the east, for it was essentially an eastern convention: out of 20 counties represented, only Chatham, Orange and Wilkes could properly be called western, as Cumberland, Wake, and Granville were sometimes one or the other. Governor Swain was properly from the west, though credited to Wake county. Gaston, of Newbern, was always a great harmonizing force, and he represented a constituency committed to the North Carolina Central Railroad and a new constitution, if it could be wisely done. Raleigh sent George E. Badger, James Iredell, Dr. William McPheeters, the Haywoods, Judge Seawell, Charles Manly, Editor Gales, and others of like standing. Orange, from the west, had such men as Nash, W. A.

Graham, W. J. Bingham, and similar characters. Mr. Morehead and his brother, James T., were there from Greensboro.[1] It was as though Newbern, Raleigh, Hillsboro and
Greensboro—the mid-Carolina centers—had got together
to find a golden mean between the desires of the Roanoke,
the Cape Fear, and the Yadkin and Catawba, which were all
fearful lest they be left out in the play for a favorable
seat, when the great new god—the Locomotive—entered
North Carolina with his procession of passenger and
freight cars. Under such circumstances, it required great
skill to find just what they could agree upon. Transportation was the real subject, but they used the term "Internal
Improvement;" and it was evident that while they saw the
rising tide of sentiment toward railroads—the cry of the
west, they clung to the water side of transportation
tenaciously; that was a fixed quantity, while the railroad
could go anywhere and cause a revolution in the importance
of position on water routes. Almost every community of
any wealth saw opportunity to itself to build a railroad
to its nearest market. Consequently the burden of this
convention was favorable to new transportation; that funds
should be created by the state for it; that the state should
take two-fifths of the stock of any enterprise in this line
when the other three-fifths were privately subscribed. To
this end an "Address" should be issued; proceedings should
be laid before the Legislature; committees of correspondence
be appointed in each county; and a full convention be held
on the fouth Monday of November, 1833. Editor Gales of
The Register thought it "perhaps not going too far to say
that it was the most talented, respectable and dignified body
ever convened in North Carolina for any purpose."[2]

President Swain made William Gaston chairman of the
general committee of 20, and on July 20th announced his
elaborate committees for each county, in one of which, that
for Guilford county, Senator Parker was chairman and Mr.
Morehead one of the members. Then ten days later the
Gaston general committee issued its address: it dwelt on the

---

[1] *Greensboro Patriot*, 31st July, 1833.
[2] Issue of July 9, 1833.

contrast with other states which had surpassed it in development; "The great wants of our state then are emphatically good marts of traffic and the means of cheap transportation," said the "Address." Then they showed that natural water routes could be developed, and when these could not, the canal and railroad must enter. Sacrifice by individuals and aid by the state was the slogan; and a great Convention in November. It was a strong appeal to forget the mistakes of the past and move forward, and worthy of the pen of William Gaston.

Thereupon a movement arose in Raleigh to immediately make an effort to get subscriptions for that section of the "Central" railroad between Raleigh and Waynesboro (later Goldsboro) on the Neuse, to be extended later to Beaufort or Wilmington or both. Governor Swain was active in it, while Gen. Edward B. Dudley and others of Wilmington, early in August, secured a public meeting and appeal to the counties between them and Waynesboro and Raleigh for subscriptions to a railroad to Waynesboro to connect with a Raleigh line. They announced that they already had $173,000 and aimed at $180,000. "Citizens of Fayetteville!" said the *Observer*, "Will not such facts as these rouse you to action?" Waynesboro and Pittsboro followed with subscriptions. On August 2nd, at Smithfield, Johnston county, $22,000 was subscribed in a mere election crowd. Newbern meetings called a district convention at Kinston in September, and by 27th August Waynesboro territory had raised $60,000 for a Wilmington road to Raleigh by way of that place and Smithfield. This was all voluntary, but stimulated by the Raleigh Convention of July 4th. A meeting on the 29th of August at Pittsboro, Chatham county, was somewhat divided, but was for improving the Cape Fear above Fayetteville; and on the 27th of August Beaufort city's meeting decided on a railroad from there to Trenton—thus passing by Newbern—and urging Onslow and Jones counties to aid them in it. The *Wilmington Press,* in September, showed that $400,000 had been subscribed for a Wilmington and Raleigh Railroad—a port-to-capital road—*via* Waynesboro, already by various interests along the route. The Kinston meeting, presided over by Governor Swain, late in that month raised $30,000 for a railroad from Beaufort to Waynesboro (later Goldsboro). The Wilmington activity, however, did not satisfy the western people, and the upper Roanoke country and tributaries began intense activity for a road from Weldon, to which the Petersburg railroad was nearly complete, westward by way of Oxford, in a meeting at Hillsboro on September 9th. The Beaufort and western idea, represented by Governor Swain, and the Oxford and western desires, represented by Judge Thomas Ruffin, came in conflict, when the latter was elected President over the former by a vote of 26 to 16. The result was the avowal for such a road and that a charter should be sought entitled the Roanoke and Yadkin Railroad Company. It is curious to note that nearly all of these plans wanted Mr. Morehead to head their committee in Guilford county, as did this Hillsboro Railroad convention; but there is more evidence that he was most interested in the North Carolina Central Railroad plan from Beaufort and in the unofficial vote for a Constitutional Convention. He was, therefore, not at the Hillsboro Railroad Convention, although they appointed him head of their Guilford county committee.

The wide-spread interest in railroads, all over the United States, was indicated by the appearance this month of *The American Railroad Journal* in New York; and it was proposed to run the New York and Erie Railroad directly through to Chicago and to complete it in seven years. The line from Washington to New York was all provided for, except the part between Baltimore and Port Deposit on the Susquehanna; and there was prospect that there would soon be a railroad from Maine to New Orleans, with branch lines from it—a great Piedmont line being in view at this early date. This great movement was taking on so many complications in North Carolina, however, that it was evident the coming Raleigh November Convention would be a great battle ground. Johnston county had a meeting favoring a road from Fayetteville and Smithfield to Halifax, which did not look favorable to Wilmington's plans. The

Salisbury meeting of October 17th, seemed inclined toward Fayetteville also, though it deferred to the Raleigh convention of November.

The months of October and November, 1833, were a pregnant period. The action of President Jackson in ordering the removal of national deposits from the Bank of the United States and the use of Roger B. Taney to enforce it startled the whole union and no part more so than North Carolina. It meant the flowering of a great anti-Jackson movement in this state, as vigorous as the anti-Nullification movement was for him. The Assembly was to meet and it was to be a notable one, before whom was to be laid the unofficial vote of North Carolina on a new Constitutional Convention. In addition to this was the great Transportation Convention to meet in Raleigh. But before turning attention to these let it be noted, that Mr. Morehead, besides being a great lawyer in active practice, and the recognized head of his counties' activities for the North Carolina Railroad prospects, the Bank of North Carolina subscriptions, and a Jackson leader, he was interested in the Humphrey Cotton Mills at Greensboro, which had just received a steam-engine from Pittsburgh; had two great plantations at Leaksville, one of which he farmed under his own direction; and on October 16th [1833] in the *Greensboro Patriot* advertised as one of the firm of Barnet & Morehead, his partner having built the first mill in 1813, a plant composed of a saw-mill, oil mill, carding mill, cotton gin, blacksmith shop, general merchandise, and supplies store, and their own line of boats on the Dan River. These became his own property later on the death of his partner. And his devotion to private affairs did not signify that his motto— *Quiescere non Possum* hung in any less prominent place on the walls of his mind. It did, however, indicate that he realized that there was to be little public progress in other lines until the fundamental basis of such progress was secured—namely, a new constitution. This was true, not only because it was right; but because, notwithstanding the few leaders of that section with broad ideas like William Gaston, the east acted on local interests and were unable

apparently to grasp the broad unifying conception of the
state as a whole. Mr. Morehead's conceptions were well
known and in no sense vague. As Washington had once
said in the apparently hopeless days of the early 1780s on
the same subject, that the people must suffer still more before they would *feel* enough to *act,* so John Motley Morehead might have said in the early 1830s regarding all
questions, and especially the one concerning a new state
constitution.

The meeting of the Assembly on November 18th [1833]
gave Governor Swain an opportunity to state the great
questions before the people, but while ably stating the secon-
dary ones he was notably silent on the one great primary
one of a new constitution. And this was not because he did
not consider it primary, himself, but because he saw from
the character of the present Assembly, especially the lower
house, that the people had little to hope from it. Furthermore, the death of Chief Justice Henderson gave that element opportunity to remove the great power of William
Gaston from the active arena of public leadership to the
sequestered shades of the Supreme Court. Governor
Swain was re-elected and he dwelt upon what he called the
"excitement" in every part of the state on "Internal Improvement," which practically always meant "transportation."
He showed that real improvement had been made since
Murphy's original movement in 1818–19; but asserted that
the railroad would be "the commencement of a new era in
the annals of physical inmprovement." One can feel the
intense jealousy of every corner of the state in his scrupu-
lously cautious general territorial terms in reference to it.
To increase the educational Fund he dwells upon the over
2,500,000 acres of fertile swamp land, three-fifths of which
was state property, and the whole was one-twentieth of the
extent of the state and probably one-eighth in fertility urging its reclaimability, and as an educational Fund measure.
The currency and bank questions were acute, and the Bank
of North Carolina charter was not inviting to capital, and
must be made to; for a bank must not be created to escape
taxation, but to regulate the currency. He dwells also

upon revision of the statutes from the earliest one of 1235 and the first "revised code" of 1715 and thought almost everything before 1777 might be discarded—but he said nothing about a new constitution.

November 25th, however, was the red-letter day of the session, for on that day the Governor presented to the Assembly Chairman Thomas G. Polk's report on the results of the unofficial vote of the people on a Constitutional Convention. This report showed "that, in thirty-three counties in North Carolina more than thirty thousand freemen have voluntarily demanded of their immediate representatives a change in our State Constitution." Furthermore, these returns "exhibit a vote, which is by several thousand over a majority of the largest poll ever held in North Carolina for the election of a President of the United States."[1] A large majority of the people of North Carolina had therefore demanded a Constitutional Convention.

On Saturday the Internal Improvement Convention at Raleigh laid before the Assembly their program: 1. A ship channel connecting Beaufort harbor with the Pamlico and Neuse river, to avoid Ocracoke Inlet; 2. A railroad from the sea to Tennessee; 3. A Roanoke-South Carolina railroad above the falls of rivers; and 4. A canal or railroad from Edenton to Dismal Swamp canal. This was a $5,000,000 proposition. Four Roanoke counties had voted against it, but 44 counties and towns had voted for it. It was vague and was of no value to the Roanoke country, and had in it nothing to hold them back from connecting up by railroad with Petersburg and Norfolk; and it left the Wilmington-Beaufort rivalry on the door-step in plain sight!

And what did the Assembly do with these two momentous programes? It spent the longest period in session in the history of North Carolina to that date, namely 57 days, adjourning from Government House, or the executive mansion, on January 13, 1834; and yet the organization of a bank system and charters for a few privately owned railroad propositions was all that was done with great questions.

---

[1] *Raleigh Register*, 3rd December, 1833. Letters dated 25th November.

The transportation program failed because of the fight over the constitutional question, chiefly. The Senate was inclined to accept a convention program of a limited kind and had even passed it on final reading, but the House by five votes only rejected it. "If the people of the Eastern counties," wrote Editor Gales of *The Raleigh Register,* "knew the excitement which exists in the West touching this matter—if they were aware, as their representatives in the Legislature must be, that unless the grievances complained of be speedily redressed, the yeomanry of the West will take the remedy into their own hands—if they were enlightened as to the defects which exist in our constitution, and were convinced of the utter hopelessness of achieving anything for the advancement of the State, while these evils are without a remedy—if, we say, proper exertions were made to inform them on these points, they would cordially sustain the course of those who have 'dared to be honest in the worst of times.' That the people of the West will ultimately obtain the relief for which they are seeking is as certain as that their demand is founded in equity. Then let us meet our brethren half way—let us arrange our differences in such a manner, as will secure to them *their* legitimate rights, without making *us* 'hewers of wood and drawers water.' "[1] On the 11th of January, immediately after the Convention bill was rejected by the House, friends of the measure held a meeting to provide an organization to go to the people and urge them to *instruct* their representatives to provide for calling of a convention at the next Assembly. Senator Robert Martin of Rockingham was, as usual, active in it; Fisher of Rowan proposed the resolutions, and the Executive Committee chosen were Wm. H. Haywood, Jr., of Raleigh, chairman; Judge R. M. Saunders and Editor W. R. Gales of the same city; Wm. A. Graham of Hillsboro; James Seawell of Fayetteville; and Wm. R. Hargrove of Granville county.

As this was destined to be the last reactionary legislature obstructive of a new constitution, it will be of interest to

---

[1] Issue of January 14, 1834.

note an analysis of it, by occupation: of the 199 members of the Assembly, 147 were married and 52 single men. The great bulk of them, 145, were farmers or planters, while the next greatest single block was 31 composed of lawyers. Seven merchants came next and six physicians, with six of no occupation at all, evidently retired. Two blacksmiths, one tailor, and one tavern keeper made up the rest.

These law-makers were convinced of one thing, however, and that was the desirability of railroads, as a private enterprise; they were not even yet convinced that public money should be put into them. Speaking of the Raleigh "Experimental Railroad," Editor Edmund Ruffin of *The Farmer's Register* of Richmond, said on November 26th: "This little Railroad has doubtless had much effect in promoting the present zeal for similar and more extensive works. We are much more ready to be impressed by what we see, even if we hear truths demonstrated, and made undeniable; and very many, who have come to the seat of government from every quarter of the State, have been first convinced of the advantages of railways by seeing the enormous masses of stone conveyed as fast and as easily as the empty cars could be drawn on good common roads." Consequently they passed bills to incorporate a "North Carolina Central Seaport Railroad Company," "The Wilmington and Raleigh," and the "Greensville and Roanoke"—a Virginia road to connect at Belfield with the Petersburg road from a point above the falls on the Roanoke, later to be called Gaston, "The Roanoke and Yadkin," "The Campbellton and Fayetteville"—a short experimental railroad at Fayetteville to her river wharf, "The Cape Fear, Yadkin and Pee Dee," and the "Roanoke and Raleigh." These were all to be, like the "Experimental Railroad," at Raleigh, private enterprises, unsupported by the State, and when, in January, 1834, the Raleigh road declared a ten per cent. dividend, it gave great encouragement to these various railroad projects. They were likewise encouraged by progress elsewhere; for example from Washington to New York there were 37 miles of the Baltimore and Ohio to Baltimore; 41¼ miles from the latter city to Port Deposit; then 31¼ miles of the Oxford

Railroad to the Pennsylvania Railroad; then the latter road
into Philadelphia at Broad Street for 46½ miles, or 156 miles
from the National Capital to Philadelphia. Then a mile up
Broad Street by the Northern Liberties and Penn Township
Railroad; then 27 miles from there to Trenton; then the
Delaware Bridge and New Brunswick turnpike, 26¼ miles;
then the New Jersey Railroad to Jersey City, 30 miles; and
finally 4 miles across the Hudson—a total of 244½ miles,
very much of which was completed. In England there were
a dozen new roads projected; next door, in South Carolina,
was a locomotive hauling each way every other day, and the
road was making money.

With all the local projects in North Carolina there was
one region that proposed the Beaufort-Tennessee or "North
Carolina Central Railroad," namely, in 1827 when President
Caldwell, as "Carleton," advocated it, and at Jamestown on
June 28, 1828, in a district meeting urged it, and that was
Guilford county.[1] From that time to July, 1834, they had
had four meetings of this county Internal Improvement
Convention, but the one of July, whose public address appeared in the *Greensboro Patriot* of July 14th [1834],
signed by Andrew Lindsay and Dr. David Worth, called
upon the people to begin building the railroad from Beaufort to Newbern and Raleigh by subscribing 3/5 of the
capital; but also announced that nothing could ever be done
until the constitution was revised, as the East was opposed
to transportation improvement.

This was followed on the 19th, by the appearance in the
Greensboro Patriot of a unique public letter, signed "Clinton," referring no doubt to Governor De Witt Clinton of
Erie Canal fame, and purporting to be from Beaufort. It
was the first of a series and is so similar to the style and
ideas of John Motley Morehead that it is given in full:

"Gentlemen: A request has been made to county committees of correspondence and others who feel an interest

---

[1] President Caldwell had spoken in the first of these meetings and he also
spoke in a Hillsboro meeting on May 27, 1834, in which he urged that the State
was without debt, had a capital of $800,000, and even $500,000 after the $300,-
000 bank stock was taken out; so that the State could easily take the two-fifths,
especially when private capital stood ready to take the three-fifths. *Raleigh
Register,* 10th June, 1834.

in the improvements of the state of North Carolina, to communicate their plans to the public previous to the next session of the legislature. I shall therefore submit my plan to the farmers of North Carolina. If I only inherited one-half of Girard's fortune I would amuse myself with making a grand central railroad from the port of Beaufort to the Tennessee line. In the first place I would employ an experienced engineer: M. Robinson, H. Allen, or A. A. Dexter might probably be engaged; and such assistant engineers as they might deem best qualified to carry on the work. I would then take them out on Beaufort bar—let them sound the bar outwards and inwards, and satisfy them that there was 22 feet [of] water at ordinary high tides. And then we would sound the channel up to Fort Macon, about two miles, with from four to five fathoms water, good harbor, and safe anchorage, as soon as you get within the bar. From Fort Macon we would sound up to the mainland, near Shepherd's point, about two miles, by which they would be satisfied that the lowest cast of the lead in this noble channel is 22 feet, and near Shepherd's point this channel terminates in a large harbor or basin, with from four to five fathoms water, and good anchorage. This harbor is protected by a powerful port. Here then at Shepherd's point, my engineers would commence their level, and proceed in the best, most practicable, shortest and most level route, to Morganton in Burke county, and thence by the most practicable route to the Tennessee line. I shall consult my own interest in selecting the best and shortest route. I cannot consent to run this road zig-zag through every little town between Beaufort harbor and Morganton. The main road must be as straight as possible, to facilitate the speed of the locomotive engines and freight and passenger cars. A straight road will last much longer than one in which there are frequent curves. Let all the county towns near the main railroad make branches into it as soon as possible.

"The more branches, the better for the farmers—and the merchants, also. Most of the farmers who make small quantities of produce will sell it to the merchants in the interior towns near the railroad. As soon as the engineers

could get ten miles of the road levelled, I would put it out to
contractors at a public sale, after due notice. These contracts should be made with the lowest bidder, fairly and
honestly. And proceed on in the same way as soon as another ten miles is levelled. I should proceed a little south
of the lakes, to near the line of Onslow county: There
would be a slight curve in the road—and thence straight to
Trenton or near it. By this route I should avoid crossing
Newport river, and also Trent river near Newbern, where it
is navigable. No engineer will attempt to cross a navigable
river, when he can possibly avoid it. The citizens of Newbern could make a short branch railroad to join near Trenton. At the close of the first year, say 1835, I would have
the road finished to Trenton, and two Locomotive steam
engines, with a sufficiency of passenger and freight cars
travelling on it. The distance from Shepherd's point to
Trenton is about 45 miles. From Trenton I would run the
road in a straight line to Haw river and cross that stream
by a stone viaduct, near Haywoodborough. From Trenton
to the Haw river is about 100 miles. I would 'go ahead' the
second year, and at the close of 1836, would have the line
from Shepherd's point to the Haw river in operation. The
ground is so favorable in this division of the road and timber
so convenient, that I do not feel a doubt of completing this
division by the close of 1836. In 1837 and 1838 I would
push on the railroad to Morganton in Burke county, about
one hundred and forty-five miles.

"In this division it is necessary to make good stone viaducts across the Haw, Deep, Yadkin and Catawba rivers.
All these viaducts could be built while the other parts of the
road were in progress. In the year 1839 I would carry the
railroad from Morganton to the Tennessee line, in Buncombe county, where the French Broad river passes through
the Bald Mountain. When I get to the Tennessee line, I
shall think it is 'glory enough' to have accomplished this
great state—I have a mind to say—national work.

"Clinton."[1]

---

[1] Whether the series were all written by the same hand can not be known;
indeed the second article, on Oct. 1st, avows it to have been written by a resi-

On October 1st, he writes: "I agree with Dr. Caldwell in the opinion that a road can be made for five thousand dollars per mile, including locomotive, passenger and freight cars. But it is prudent to allow something for contingencies —say 250,000 dollars—which makes in all the sum of two million of dollars.

"If I had the funds I would commence the work and only ask of the legislature the same rates of toll which are received on the Charleston and Petersburg railroads. Time would soon demonstrate that I had a fortune equal to any man in the United States. But, as I have not the honor to be the son of Girard, how shall the funds be raised? Let the next legislature authorize the Governor and treasurer of the State to borrow in London, or elsewhere, one million dollars, redeemable in 25 years. A late number of the *London Mercantile Journal* says: 'so abundant has money become that discounts in some cases have been obtained at the extreme low rates of 1½ per ct. per annum.' The current rate is, however, 2 and 2½ per cent. Certainly if money is so plenty in London, it could be borrowed for four cents, including brokerage and all expenses. The money could be deposited in the new state bank subject to the order of the treasurer of the State countersigned by the comptroller.

"The contracts on the railroad when executed and approved by the chief engineer, would be certified by him and the commissioner or commissioners, presented to the comptroller and treasurer, who would take receipts and issue drafts on the State bank for the amount. The engineers and commissioners to be debarred by severe penalties from any interest directly or indirectly in any contracts to be executed on the railroad. The legislature could, by joint ballot, appoint one or three commissioners to superintend the construction of said great central railroad; with such compensation as would command men of unquestioned talent for

---

dent of Beaufort. At any rate the first and second so well represent Mr. Morehead that it is possible it was his custom to spend a part of his summers there; they serve well for illustration of the best thought of this early period. Dr. J. Allison Hodges, born on the Lower Cape Fear river, tells the writer that it was the custom of such families to be at the shore together one month of summer and at the mountains another month, so that it is entirely possible that Mr. Morehead had "lived" there, in that sense, for many years.

such an important work. Then let the great work be immediately commenced, and prosecuted with all possible
energy to its final completion. While it was going on, the
citizens of Wilmington and Newbern, with the aid of two-
fifths subscribed by the state, could push forward their
branches to connect with the central road, probably at Trenton. Wilmington, which is the second best sea-port in
North Carolina, would thus by a branch of 60 miles be connected with the main road and Newbern by a branch of 20
miles in length. Then would the farmers of our state who
are the main pillars of society have a choice of the markets
of Beaufort, Wilmington and Newbern.

"Beaufort is as healthy as any sea-port in the United
States. In this respect it is far superior to Petersburg and
Norfolk to the north or any sea-port to the south of this."
And he devotes a remarkable paragraph to this feature, after
which he details the profit of the road, the advantages in
fresh foods from a distance, like sea-foods, similar branches
like those to Wilmington and Newbern, the completion of
road and branches as they proceeded westward, the development of one great port, steamship lines abroad and
consequent commercial development. The two letters are
strikingly predictive of what the Greensboro statesman was
to actually undertake and persuade the state to undertake
also.

These July operations were followed on August 13th
[1834] by a discussion at a public meeting in Greensboro
held under the auspices of the Raleigh Internal Improvement
Committee of the previous November, of which Mr. Morehead had been appointed a member, but it was ineffective.
After election, however, a Greensboro meeting was held on
the 15th of August in the Presbyterian Church to listen to
the successful candidates at the late election talk. And
although John Motley Morehead was neither a successful
nor a defeated one, he was called upon; and it became practically the signal for his re-entry into public life. "He said
he appeared before them in a character different from that
in which his predecessors had presented themselves. He
was neither a candidate *elected,* nor a candidate *beaten,*

but as the *town* was already sufficiently represented, he had stepped forward as a candidate for the *country*. He was very sorry that questions of importance were always presented to the consideration of the people, when they were disqualified, by excitement, for deciding correctly. It was not the proper way for candidates to vindicate their conflicting sentiments among the people just before the election; because each one would have his *personal* favorites, who would go for them, principle or no principle. Hence the result of an election was no test of any principle.

"He maintained that it was not for candidates to say what they were in favor of; but it was the proper business of the people to elect men who were intelligent, firm and untrammelled; to consult together and determine, among themselves, what they wanted done, and then command their servants to perform it! He never had any confidence in anything that a candidate might say, either about *principle or* policy—as his object was to say anything that might advance his hopes of success.

"He therefore, as one of the people, feeling no interest in the matter but what ought to be felt by every citizen in the State, called upon them to assemble at the Court House in this place, on the Tuesday of November Court, to take into consideration the subject of Internal Improvement; and either determine upon some plan proper to be pursued, or else put the matter forever at rest. He said every man who ever had a dollar, or whoever expected to have a dollar, or whoever expected his children to have a dollar, ought to attend this meeting, that all information on the subject might be thrown together in one common stock, for the benefit of all; and that an aggregate of public sentiment might be made out as a guide to our Representatives.

"Mr. Morehead was cheered by the people in a spirit which clearly indicated their hearty approbation of the course he had proposed, and we hope that every man, rich and poor, learned and unlearned, will make up his mind to attend on that day, in order that the question may be fairly settled, so far as this county is concerned. We know the question is one of vital importance. If it be for the interest of the State to improve it by Railroads, it ought to be known, and the work commenced; if otherwise, the project ought to be promptly met and put down."[1]

This meeting was held on November 15th, and it was so well attended and considered of such importance that the Court adjourned for it. The occasion was one of the most important in the history of the state, for it virtually became the announcement of a new leader with a definite program, from which he was never to deviate and in which he was destined to lead his state to its adoption. With a long and powerful address he introduced a set of resolutions designed to definitely instruct the representatives of Guilford county just what to do, as he had proposed doing in the previous meeting. They are so important that they are here given in full:

"*Resolved,* that the spirit of Internal Improvement, which pervades every State in the Union, should not be permitted longer to slumber in this State; and that it is the duty which our State owes to herself and to her citizens, forthwith to arouse that spirit, and to put it into energetic and successful action.

"*Resolved,* that the State contains within herself the elements of a great and powerful State, in the mildness of her climate, the fertility of her soil, the variety of her productions, the exhaustless stores of her innumerable mines and minerals, and in the intelligence, industry and patriotism of her citizens; and that nothing is wanting to bring these elements into immediate action, but a system of wise and liberal legislation, by which the energies of her most enterprising sons shall cease to aggrandize other States, by emigration.

"*Resolved, that this State has one of the best harbors in Beaufort harbor, south of the Chesapeake; and that a Railroad, from that place to the city of Raleigh, should be forthwith commenced by the State* HERSELF; *that she has the means to execute this work speedily; that, by the exe-*

---

[1] Quoted from the *Greensboro Patriot* by the *Raleigh Register* of 2nd Sept., 1834.

cution of the work, ALL *her citizens—even the most ignorant and narrow minded—must become convinced of the practicability and utility of such improvements.*[1]

"*Resolved,* that by the construction of this Road, access will be opened from the interior to our best harbor; facilities and powerful inducements will be offered to individuals, to invest their capital in the construction of lateral roads to Newbern, Wilmington, and other places, and the extension of that road westwardly, through the center of the State.

"*Resolved,* that a steamboat navigation, if practicable, should be opened through the Club-foot and Harlow's Creek Canal between the waters of Beaufort harbor and the waters of Pamlico and Albemarle Sounds.

"*Resolved,* that it is the duty of every State, in all works of general utility, to execute them at public expense, or at least, to contribute largely to their execution.

"*Resolved,* that it is expedient that a general law be passed whereby the State shall pledge herself to take two-fifths of the stock in any company that shall or may be hereafter incorporated for the purpose of internal improvement, whenever individuals shall subscribe and secure the payment of the other three-fifths.

"*Resolved,* that we view the conduct of the Legislature of our State, upon the subject of Internal Improvement—by merely passing acts of incorporation, in which the collected wisdom of the State refuses to invest one dollar of the public wealth—as a mere mockery of our wants; and as wholly impolitic, unjust and unworthy the State, and contrary to a wise system of legislation.

"*Resolved,* that inasmuch as all the funds and revenues of our State are subject to the disposition of our Legislature, we deprecate, exceedingly, that *Manger* policy by which they are hoarded up, and rendered useless, while the best interests of the State are *starving* for want of their judicious application.

"*Resolved,* That we cannot enough deprecate that system of demagogical legislation, which proclaims unlimited con-

---

[1] Italics by the present writer.

fidence in, and friendship for Internal Improvement, manifested by acts of incorporation, whereby *individuals may do* what the *State should do*—and whereby a miserly care of the people's money is attended with the usual concomitants of all miserly acts—degradation, poverty and suffering!

"*Resolved,* That in the opinion of this meeting, if each American citizen had been permitted to fight just as much as he chose for his freedom; and each State had not, in her sovereign political character, declared her citizens a free people, we should have continued to be, until now, the subjects of Great Britain:—and it is further the opinion of this meeting, that our citizens must remain the subjects and slaves of thraldom and poverty, unless our State, *herself,* shall again declare them free, by adopting a system of Internal Improvement that shall bring into action all her energies.

"*Resolved,* That a copy of the Proceedings of this meeting, and of these Resolutions, be transmitted to our Representatives in the present Legislature, with a request to lay them before each House thereof.

"*Resolved,* That our Representatives be instructed to vote, on all subjects of Internal Improvement, according to the true spirit of the foregoing Resolutions; and that we shall hold them responsible, without specific instructions, for the judicious exercise of their votes on all questions relative thereto.

"*Resolved,* That the foregoing proceedings be published in the *Greensboro Patriot,* and that all Editors in the State, friendly to Internal Improvement, be requested to publish them also."[1]

This was the signal of preparation for action on the backbone question of transportation that should follow the almost certain reference to the people by the next Assembly, of the question of a constitutional convention. For the *Carolina Watchman,* early in July, had said: "If the General Assembly does not submit the inequalities of our Constitution to the people in some formal mode—we of the

---

[1] Reprint in *Raleigh Register,* 9th Dec., 1834.

West are determined to go to work without the behest of
that body. We admit that the experiment is dangerous—if
the people were less virtuous, it would be imminently so—
but we think the spirit of our fathers which bore them
through the trials of the Revolution, is still sufficiently with
us to secure us against the perils of faction. Mark it, my
dear Sir, cost what it will, the experiment will be made
immediately after the rise of the next Assembly, if some
measure of Reform does not pass. We are determined to
try it before another hot Presidential contest shall come on
to absorb State politics. We say this in the very best
feeling, not as a threat, but as a warning. We would be glad
to avoid the alternative, and it is but right that we should
try to do so—for this purpose, we ask our brethren of the
Press in the East to repeat this caution—for this purpose
an attempt at liberal concession will be made by Western
members at the next Assembly—and then, if the alternative
is forced upon us, WE WILL GO AHEAD!"[1]

As to the position of the *North Carolina Watchman*
amongst the press of the commonwealth, let an interesting,
though partizan statement of a powerful journal of that day
in the western part of the state, *The Greensboro Patriot,* be
given, for Editor Swaim was almost as important a figure in
the state press as Editor Gales at Raleigh. "The *Milton
Spectator* is already out of the question;" the statement proceeds, "the *Fayetteville Journal* is fluttering like a wounded
pigeon—the *Rutherfordton Spectator* has worked itself into
an interminable fog—the *Wilmington People's Press* is sort
of *Boo!* and sort of not *Boo!* The *Newbern Sentinel*
CLUCKS now but to hang its wings in despair on the morning of our political resurrection! and the *North Carolina
Standard* [Raleigh] 'conceived in iniquity and brought
forth in sin' will die a natural death with the extinction of
Col. White's pursership in the navy. Thus, 'we have met
the enemy and they are ours.' On one side stands the
Raleigh Register, venerable for its age and consistency; the
Star, once in bad company, but now on the side of the

---

[1] Reprint in *Raleigh Register,* July 29, 1834.

people and the constitution; the *Oxford Examiner,* not to be sneered at by modern Toryism; the *Fayetteville Observer,* an untrammelled asserter of truth and correct principles; the *Western North Carolinian,* once tainted with the heresy of nullification, though now threatening death and desolation to the usurpers of imperial power; the *Carolina Watchman,* like a faithful sentinel, sounding the alarm at any approach of danger; and last, though not least, the *Newbern Spectator,* scoring the trammels of party discipline and soaring high above the temptations which have led the *Standard* into ways of error and falsehood, stands like an everlasting pillar of truth in the midst of a wicked and perverse generation. When to these can be added the *Southern Citizen* [Editor Swaim's proposed new periodical], with its twenty-four ponderous columns, and two thousand subscribers, the cause of the people must triumph. Jacksonism will go down into its socket and disappear; and Van Burenism will pass away as a dream in the night."[1]

The significance of the political upheaval plainly to be seen in this picturesque view of the Carolina press is well expressed by a Beaufort correspondent of the *Newbern Spectator,* so highly praised by Editor Swaim: "We are generally Whigs—or Rebels, if you insist on it, in this county [Carteret]. We cannot and will not support a collar man for Congress. We are in favor of Clay's Land Bill—we are in favor of a National Bank, to regulate the currency—we are in favor of the cause pursued by a majority of the Senate of the United States—we are opposed to the Kitchen Cabinet—we are opposed to the election of Martin Van Buren to the Presidency—we are opposed to the corruptions of the Post Office Department—we want to see this Augean stable cleansed—we are opposed to the usurpation of the Executive, and his violation of the Constitution and laws of Congress—we are opposed to the union of the purse and the sword in the same hand—we are opposed to the practice of President Jackson of appointing members of Congress

---

[1] *Greensboro Patriot,* 24th Dec., 1834.

to office. This practice, if not rigorously opposed, will soon destroy what small remains of liberty we possess."[1]

This great wave of national political tide was serving to help float both the movement for a constitutional convention and for railway transportation. And yet it would be no easy matter, for the alluvial soil of the east was heavy upon the bottom of the ship of state, and localism was a barnacle not easily removed. Nor did John Motley Morehead of Guilford underestimate these difficulties or expect a commonwealth to be remade in a day. However, he expected it to be rebuilt; and indeed considered the process was well under way.

---

[1] Reprinted in the *Raleigh Register,* Aug. 5, 1834.

Probably it ought to be added that Judge Gaston's elevation to the Chief Justiceship, as noted in this chapter, was not altogether political, but for the good of that high bench, as Judge Connor has shown in his address on Gaston.

VIII

REVISION OF THE CONSTITUTION
AND
TRANSFER OF POLITICAL POWER
TO
THE WEST

1835

Probably the earliest reference in the North Carolina press to a new political uprising in the nation was that on June 10, 1834, in the *Raleigh Register* giving an account of a celebration at Alexandria, Virginia, on the 27th of May of a victory over the administration party by a combined opposition which everywhere had taken the name of "Whig." The Alexandrians cheered the "Whigs of '34" as following in the footsteps of the "Whigs of '76!" And the name was commonly used all through the campagn of 1834 in North Carolina which was to have so much influence on local questions in the coming Assembly of 1834–35. The Whig cry was no louder, however, than the Wilmington cry, through their Committee of Correspondence on June 17, 1834, against the Raleigh Convention program of November, 1833, which favored, as has been seen, the North Carolina Central Railroad from Beaufort to Tennessee and a Roanoke-South Carolina line, *above the granite falls of rivers,* which offered as great an obstacle to rail grade as to navigation. This Wilmington Committee defended their port with some important statistics, and it had among its members men like General Edward B. Dudley. Their cry was against a Virginia-South Carolina railroad above the falls as permitting those two states to "bleed" North Carolina; "but," said they, "if there is any general plan to be adopted by the Legislature, and to be preferred above

144

others, we would advocate the construction of a Railroad from the port of Beaufort through Newbern to the city of Raleigh, thence to Fayetteville and Hillsboro, or in any other direction that may be more favorable, so as to reach the remote "west." They further add that *"after the completion of this work,"* they would support any cross-state proposition if it were generally desired.   This was a great victory for the North Carolina Central people and was made possible in some measure, no doubt, by the disaffection of Johnston county in favor of the above-falls-Fayetteville line instead of the Wilmington-Raleigh line.   By July 15th, the Raleigh committee directed Gavin Hogg to answer the Wilmington address and on August 12th, the Wilmington committee retorted with vigor.   This controversy became essentially a Raleigh-Wilmington one, because the Raleigh leaders of the November Convention were accepting the verdict against Wilmington as a possible great port, and had cast their lot in with Beaufort and were still trying to hold the Roanoke and Yadkin regions.   So that so far as Wilmington was concerned this question was quite as vital as the new Whig politics or the new constitutional convention.

The election of the new Assembly in August reflected the political revolution in some measure.   The Whigs were able to elect the Speaker of the House, a western man, but the Jacksonians elected the Speaker of the Senate.   On November 18th [1834], Governor Swain, in his message, which was longer than usual, devoted first and chief space to the constitutional convention, as he said circumstances were different from those of last year.   In a most able, convincing historical as well as logical and compromising treatment, he showed how this system of inequality in representation inherited from our British Colonial status had been either abolished or drastically modified by every state except Maryland and North Carolina and that it did not appeal to the national convention of 1787.   He dwelt on the desirability of limiting action, but that a wise compromise would win them "the lasting gratitude of posterity." Not to do so would leave the baneful spirit among them that had defeated all progress in wise and liberal legislation since the beginning. While giving this subject first place he reiterated his beliefs regarding transportation and the port of Beaufort. He also announced the opening of the Bank of North Carolina. Probably the best known men in the House were Graham of Hillsboro, General Dudley of Wilmington, Wm. H. Haywood, Jr., of Raleigh, M. E. Manly of Newbern and James Seawell of Fayetteville.

On the 19th of November [1834], the first motion to refer any subject of the gubernatorial message was that on convention to a select committee, which was announced on the 21st as Messrs. Craige of Rowan, Barringer of Cabarrus, Haywood of Wake, Outlaw of Bertie, and Clark of Beaufort City, but on the following day Graham was appointed in place of Haywood, resigned, making three western men to two eastern, showing that Mr. Haywood declined to play the rôle of Justice as a representative of the capital county. The result was as it should be: the west was to have her Convention, but it would be on as conservative lines as a compromise could make it. On November 24th Mr. Outlaw asked to be relieved and Mr. Potts of Edgecombe county was substituted, not affecting territorial representation. Chairman Craige's committee made a Convention report on December 4th, which passed first reading and was made the order of the day for a week later. On the 9th Mr. Manney of Carteret (Beaufort) thought this a good time to introduce a bill for a railroad from Beaufort to the Tennessee line to take the place of the North Carolina Central bill which had not been effective thus far. It was referred to the Internal Improvement Committee, and was a bill "to *construct* the Central Railroad," and was evidently along the lines laid down by President Caldwell at Hillsboro. The political fight over instructions to U. S. Senator Willie P. Mangum prevented the ordered discussion of the Convention report, but on the 18th both the Convention and the Central Railroad bills were set for discussion the following week. It was the 23rd before a discussion in committee of the whole was secured without definite result, and likewise on Christmas

Eve; but on the 26th, it was decided by a vote of 74 to 52 that it should be re-committed to a select committee of one from each Congressional District—which would be on a Federal ratio basis. This had been proposed by Mr. Kittrell of Anson and he was made chairman, with Barringer of Cabarrus, Weaver of Buncombe, Waugh of Surry, Cotten of Chatham, Poindexter of Stokes, Haywood of Wake, Dudley of Wilmington, Pugh of Bertie, Bragg of Warren, Norcom of Edenton, Whitfield of Lenoir, and Smallwood of Beaufort county. This gave six western men and six eastern, with Mr. Haywood of Wake, the capital county, again to be asked to play the rôle of Justice, and on the 27th they reported a substitute bill, which was accepted by a vote of 68 to 61, favored by the west, with a certain number of harmonizing eastern men. Immediately following this vote the east tried to remove the provision of election of Governor by free white voters, but it was held in 94 to 35, whereupon they tried to remove borough representation, but lost it by the practically original vote of 68 to 60. Thereupon a Brunswick representative tried to open the capital question by giving it into the Convention's hands, but he was promptly overwhelmed by a vote of 108 to 19. It was finally passed second reading and ordered printed by a more conservative vote of 66 to 64. On the 30th, General Dudley offered an amendment to the charter of the Wilmington and Raleigh Railroad which was significant. On the 31st, by a vote of 66 to 62, the Convention bill passed third reading and was sent to the Senate. This was a dangerously small margin.

The Senate had had a bill under consideration but laid it on the table to receive the House bill on January 1st [1835] and on the 2nd began its consideration and promptly made a few slight changes and one important one, namely, by reducing the House membership limits to between 90 and 120 and leaving the borough representation to the Convention. It was then passed by the narrow margin of 31 to 30. On January 3rd, third reading was had and after many efforts to amend it in various ways it was passed by the same vote, 31 to 30, practically as it was, and returned to the Commons. The House took up the amended bill on the 5th and after a determined fight by some, which was resisted by a large majority, the Senate amendment was accepted by the equally big majority of 86 to 36, and the Senate so informed. The House later wanted to add a supplement providing that judicial salaries be not diminished during continuance in office, and sought a conference committee to which the Senate agreed, and by the 9th the bill was finally passed and provision made for printed copies of the bill for circulation; thereupon the Assembly closed its long session on January 10, 1835.

It will be well to take note of the leading features of this act, for it determines the essential features of the new constitution in advance; and what is determined satisfies neither the east nor the west. Thus it was a compromise that it soon became evident both east and west would accept as the solution of the half-century old controversy. After providing for the modes of securing the convention on a House of Commons basis, it provided that the people should vote for or against a Convention to be bound by the following propositions: 1. A Senate of but 34 to 50 members, elected by taxation districts; 2. A House of but 90 to 120 members, "exclusive of borough members," which the Convention may exclude as it will, the basis being the Federal population, except that each county must have at least one representative; 4. Use discretion as to free negroes voting, the holding of both State and national offices, equality of capitation tax, and nine other provisions, one of which was election of Governor by the people, and a mode of ratification. The supplement provided for Judiciary revision. The vote was to take place on April 1st and 2nd [1835] next; and if favorable the Governor should provide for election of delegates. Twenty days later, as if feeling that his work was done and that with the coming of the new constitution all things else would be added unto them, including "Carleton's" Sea to Tennessee railroad, President Joseph Caldwell passed away and men said: "A great man has fallen!" Contemporary with this event, also, the Alabama "Whigs" nominated Judge Hugh L. White of

Tennessee for President against the Tennessee President's candidate, and the "Whig" movement was abreast of both constitutional and transportation reform.

While these events were in progress, Mr. Morehead was leading public action against the Jacksonian Baltimore Convention, being the chief speaker in a Guilford county meeting on May 19th [1835], at Greensboro, which was thereby led to denounce it by a vote of 93 to 3. During the meeting he twitted Mr. Shepperd on "Confessing the sin" of supporting the "powers that be," meaning Jackson and Van Buren, "as he [Morehead] was himself a sinner of the same description about that time; but that since then he had become heartily penitent." He had already spoken in other counties with similar results. On May 13th, the editor of the *Greensborough Patriot* had said: "We are anxious that John M. Morehead should be in the Convention by all means. His interest is identified with the west; and his ability to defend any proposition he may bring forward to sustain that interest renders it peculiarly important that he should have a seat in that body. . . . In this case we need our strongest men—our *heaviest metal!*"

He was again in public life, and the people knew what he would do in convention.

The meeting at the Guilford County Court, on the constitutional convention, had appointed a committee of ten, of whom Mr. Morehead was one, to address the public. This address was issued on February 25, 1835, and among other things, it emphasized the fact that *five* western counties named, with greater white population than *nineteen* named eastern counties, had but fifteen representatives, while the latter had fifty-seven; that five western counties having more black than white population than sixteen eastern counties, had only *fifteen* representatives, while the latter had forty-eight; that Guilford had a greater white population than five eastern counties, yet she sends but *three,* while the latter have fifteen! Orange county, but slightly less in white and black population than five eastern counties has but *three,* while the five eastern counties have *fifteen! Twelve* eastern counties paid only two-thirds of what *five* western counties

paid the State treasurer. They showed that western counties were actually paying the salaries of eastern county
members! The new convention would make a constitution
based on taxation and federal population; and while the
proposed limitation of the powers of the convention were
not all that was to be desired, yet the proposals were fair to
all, and some things like election of executive by the people
was in line with more direct popular control. "The opportunity is now offered us [on April 1st and 2nd] to put
ourselves on an equality with them [the eastern counties];
and to give the west a decided preponderance, which it ought
to have in the legislature."

The April election occurred and with the result not so
unlike the unofficial ballot of near 30,000, namely 27,550 for
and 21,694 against, making a majority of 5856, with every
county voting, and having votes both for and against,
even to a solitary one in Rutherford or two in Rowan against
to so few as four for in both Tyrrell and Greene or five and
six in Hyde and Martin respectively. And the remarkable
feature of it was that this majority vote of 27,550 was given
by 26 counties, while it took 39 counties to furnish the
minority vote, or 13 more than the majority! The location
of them is shown on the accompanying map. The greatest
number against in any one county was that of Johnston,
Edgecombe coming next and Beaufort and Wayne counties
following; while the greatest for was Lincoln, Orange coming next and Rutherford and Surry following. Wake, the
capital county, went over 2 to 1 against. Probably Halifax
gave the greatest number for of any eastern county, unless
Granville be called eastern; and probably Caswell gave the
largest against, among western counties, unless Cumberland
be called western. Guilford was 1271 for to 143 against.
The Governor appointed May 21st for the election of
delegates who were to meet in the capital on June 4th.
Guilford County sent John Motley Morehead and Jonathan
Parker.

Government House, the temporary capitol at the foot
of Fayetteville street, Raleigh, was the objective of every
thoughtful man in North Carolina as the new delegates

gathered there on the afternoon of June 4, 1835. Editor
Gales, of the *Raleigh Register*, said that "the people, laying
aside political feeling, have in almost every county, selected
their most experienced, most talented and strongest men—
men who would confer dignity and honor on any station."
"It may be said," he asserted in the issue of June 9th,
"without the fear of contradiction, that the Convention, as
a body, will not suffer by comparison with any similar
assemblage in the Union, which has preceded it." Here
came the venerable Nathaniel Macon of Warren, now coming probably to his last great public service, as he had come
to his first, when the place was merely "Wake Court House,"
in 1781. Craven sent Judge William Gaston and Greene
sent Richard Dobbs Spaight. Governor John Branch came
from Halifax, General Alfred Dockery from Richmond,
Governor Swain from Buncombe, Calvin Graves from
Caswell, Charles Fisher of Rowan, General Alexander Gray
of Randolph, Judge Henry Seawell of Raleigh, D. M. Barringer of Cabarrus and others of like character.

Even before permanent organization was effected, Judge
Gaston, as often before, became the voice of a great
majority, 86 to 22, to enter upon the work in the spirit
of the Assembly's limitations of it, now, by endorsement,
the people's limitations, also. Thereupon the patriarchal
Macon was unanimously chosen President of the Convention. Mr. Morehead's first effort was on June 5th, desiring
to economize in printing, and Mr. Fisher supported him and
he won his point of election of a Convention printer and
Gales and Son, of the *Raleigh Register,* were chosen. He
then offered resolutions assigning different subjects of the
Act to select committees, but differing ideas upon the
matter led to adjournment and to use of the Presbyterian
Church for a future meeting place. The idea of Weldon
Edwards of a Procedure committee as first in order was
offered as similar to Virginia and New York plans, while
some preferred a Committee-of-the-whole plan used in the
national constitutional convention; but, by a vote of 64 the
Edwards plan failed and Morehead again called up his plan;
and Judge Gaston again became a decisive factor and actually

secured the adoption of the Edwards resolution, and Morehead as well as Gaston, Edwards, Fisher and others active
in the matter were appointed on the Congressional District
committee of thirteen.   This occurred during the first session in the Presbyterian Church, a brick structure on the
site of the present one at the southwest corner of Capitol
Square, of which Rev. Dr. McPheeters was pastor.

Before Judge Gaston made the report of the Procedure
committee, some discussion was had on whether visitors
should be allowed elsewhere than in the galleries, then the
report proceeded to provide for committees much as Mr.
Morehead had proposed: 1. On representation in Assembly; 2. On processes of amendment, ratification and
ordinances; 3. On borough representation; 4. On vote of
free negroes; 5. On holding both state and national offices;
6. On capitation tax of white and slave; 7. On militia and
local justices' selection and removal; 8. Assembly mode of
election of officers; 9. On the 32nd article; 10. Assembly
vacancies; 11. On frequency of Assembly meetings and election of Secretary of State; 12. On gubernatorial election;
13. On Attorney General's election; 14. On judicial impeachment; 15. On local Justices' disqualification; 16. On
judicial disabilities; 17. On judicial salaries; 18. On private
legislation; and 19. On confining Judges elected to judicial
offices only, while still on the bench.   At this point occurred
that invariably interesting pair of proposals: attacking all
subjects alike *vs.* first selecting the simple great subjects
in committee of the whole.   This latter was proposed by
Governor Branch, and others brought up almost all the
various methods so familiar to students of the convention
of 1787.   On taking up the first resolution, however, an
eastern member tried to change the Congressional District
basis to a judicial district one, and on Morehead's attacking
it, it was lost 75 to 51, but the committees were doubled
to 26, instead of 13, and Morehead was placed on the Assembly representation committee, and his motion to meet at
10 A. M. every day closed the session of Monday, June 8th,
at the corner of Salisbury and West Morgan Streets.

An effort on the 9th to get statistics on the election

brought out some interesting facts: Among others, Governor Swain said the April vote, "thin" as it was said to be, was the greatest in her history, with one exception— the Presidential vote of 1828, when it was 51,776, while that of April was 49,244. But on Wednesday, the 10th, the Committee of the Whole took up borough representation, for which Judge Gaston made the most notable plea, and as usual Governor Swain brought out some interesting history, namely, that it was the course of the borough members which brought this Convention into existence in the Assembly. He thought the country would not be just to the towns; and said he had hoped district representation would take the place of county representation, and so break up, by district lines, an imaginary line between the east and west. These two probably strongest, most liberal leaders of the Convention, one of the east and one of the west, both for borough representation, was a rather remarkable fact, except that one was from the largest town in the state, and in the east, and the other from the extreme west, at that time. And when Fisher of Salisbury confessed his practical decision to vote for abolition of borough representation had been suspended by what he had heard, one may know the discussion was a powerful one; and his own description of borough election fights was, unconsciously no doubt, one of the strongest points against them, for he said it was not true of county election. His conclusion seemed to favor some eastern boroughs, but he was against western borough representation, and he was from Salisbury. Meares of Sampson county made good points for representation of marine boroughs—in fact it was Newbern, Wilmington and Fayetteville, marine towns, which desired separate representation most. Of course they would be represented in the Senate, but that was not enough. "The interests" of that day were in the marine boroughs. Some gentlemen even advocated it on the old English basis. And then the Roanoke and Albemarle spoke up through Governor Branch and others, and they were against the borough. One of them indeed said: "Halifax, Sir, is gone—Edenton is going—and Newbern is

not far behind"—so their power to vote did not protect them
as boroughs! Mr. Toomer made a powerful plea for the
boroughs, noting that South Carolina, Virginia, New York
and Massachusetts, in their revised constitution, retained
borough representation. At the end of two days, a vote
on excepting the three marine boroughs was negatived, and
abolition was also negatived, and it was sent, 103 to 23,
to the committee of 26 as it was.

On June 12th, negro voting was taken up in Committee
of the Whole—meaning of course free negroes. Mr. Daniel
of Halifax precipitated the question by a resolution to have
them vote, if with a freehold of $250. The greatest attack
upon it was by Mr. Bryan, of Carteret, who insisted that
freeing slaves did not confer political rights. "North
Carolina," said he, "is the only Southern State in the Union
that has *permitted* them to enjoy this privilege." He insisted that "this is a nation of white people," and, whether
one agreed with him or not, his was a powerful plea. In it
he anticipated almost all the difficulties that have grown out
of this great question. He didn't want North Carolina to
become "an asylum for free negroes." It was finally decided
by a close vote of 61 to 58 to withdraw the vote from free
negroes; and on the following day it was taken up in open
Convention. Here again discussion was able and vigorous.
Mr. McQueen of Chatham, drew attention to the fact
Connecticut gave them no vote, likewise Ohio. Judge Gaston favored not removing the vote, and Mr. Morehead
favored voting for Commons alone, with a $100 freehold.
Thereupon a vote was taken, 66 to 61, in favor of abrogation
of the vote, Mr. Morehead being one of the 61; and with him
such men as Fisher, Gaston, Branch, Swain, Seawell, and
others of like character. It was plain that the British and
probable French freeing of slaves in the West Indies and
the occasional insurrections had some influence in the settlement of this question, as well as some northern movements
of this period—and yet it was done by a narrow margin of
but 5 votes, and the division was not territorial; it seemed
to be wholly an individual sentiment or conviction.

No time was spent on No. 5, as all were agreed two

offices should not be held by one person at one time in state
and nation; and No. 6 on equal capitation tax was held in
similar attitude, but it succeeded in bringing out that occasional expression of suspicion that suggested an atmosphere
of armed peace between east and west; and thus June 15th
was ushered in with the question of members in each house,
in Committee of the Whole.   This was the vital point of the
whole Convention. "It has been said," exclaimed Spaight of
Greene, "that unless the Convention would agree to fix the
number of 120 members for the House of Commons, 50
having been agreed to for the Senate, the West would not
accept of the Constitution. A fair course," said he, "would
be to give the West ascendency in the House of Commons,
and the East ascendency in the Senate."   He acknowledged
the right of the majority to rule, but said "there were checks
and balances for the security of the minority; and when this
should cease to be the case, our Government would be more
odious than the despotism of Europe. In the North," said
he, "they have small Senates and large Houses of Representatives.   In the South the number of the Senate is much
larger, and possess all the legislative power of the other
House."   He avowed that emigration was not from North
Carolina alone, but from all eastern states, and was due to
cheap land sales in the west.   He said there was not only
an eastern and a western interest, but a Roanoke, a Cape
Fear and a Neuse interest. Great differences were expressed as to property controlling in the Senate, and population of some sort—whether white or federal ratio—in the
House.   Governor Swain answered him that 120 for the
House and 50 for the Senate was the compromise in view
in the Act—which, by the way, became the Magna Charta of
the Convention—between East and West, and he thought
this Convention had a majority to carry out that compromise
in good faith.   This was what it was for.   It continued
through the next day, too, and came close to being a question
of Counties *vs.* Districts.   It was bitterly fought on both
sides.   Mr. Bryan, of Beaufort city, as usual clarified the
subject, by admitting that the East and property was to
dominate the Senate; the real difficulty was in the House,

for any number between 90 and 120, mentioned in the Act, would give the East power there; so it was somewhat immaterial what number between was taken. He praised Judge Gaston's tabulations, and showed that the plan would give, in the House, six to eight majority for the West, in the Senate four for the East and, in joint session, four for the West— but he wanted three eastern boroughs represented. President Macon occasionally expressed himself, but as if fearful of a new Pandora box. Mr. Fisher of Salisbury, saw fit to answer his statement that all changes in government were "from better to worse;" after which he reminded the Convention most ably, that the assertion, that the West was pressing for *power,* was false; they were pressing for a *principle* which would operate justly all over the state. He noted the fact that the West was homogeneous, while the east had three sections always jealous of one another. He thought it immaterial, what number between 90 and 120 was taken, so far as a majority to the west was concerned; it would go there anyhow, and that was what they were here for! He believed the east and west division would disappear with the new constitution.

The Convention was still engaged in the subject on the 18th, and for the first time Mr. Morehead indicated his deep interest in keeping at it until it was settled. He was wisely letting the East have its say, for was he not witnessing a fulfillment of his demands and predictions of 1821? Was not the battle already won, and could not the vanquished wisely be permitted to work out the details? The Magna Charta Act and its ratification by the people in calling this Convention were the real Constitution of 1835; it was already theirs. Let the East work out the details; and no man was more influential or able in it than Judge Gaston of Newbern. He now made his first great address of the Convention. He showed how the East-West division had arisen first over location of the capital, then the Seaboard *vs.* the West. This was perpetuated in a new slogan: "A new Western county, a new Eastern one." Now it must cease, in a justice to the West, for the People have bound all members with an oath to do so. "Some things we *must* do.

Some things we *may* do.   There are others we *cannot* do."
He was magnificently interpretative, giving that fundamental conception of our political science, which is so rarely
appreciated; and yet he showed the deeply rooted English
ideas of the east on property and limited suffrage.   Such
studies make one realize how the new American political
science, underlying the Declaration and the Constitution,
had, and still has to fight its way against the antiquated system of Great Britain.   Even so great a man and scholar as
Judge Gaston took it for granted that the Senate should represent property, and the ordinary man had no right to vote
for it.   The English term "Freeholder" was more sacred
than the Jeffersonian Declaration as to men born free and
equal.   He revealed the East's great fear lest the West on
coming to its own, should vote Eastern wealth for transportation.   His analysis of the federal ratio, instead of white
vote only, was most able.   "Slaves are human beings," he reminded the West.   As the Senate represented mixed property
and person, so the House must represent mixed persons and
property.   A slave is both property and a member of society, he said.   Every Southern state had one of the
federal ratio in the national House.   How could they want
it less for the State?   The opposition to 50 to 120 was
merely because it was slightly different from the old 1 to
2; but this was merely because *taxation* made 50 and *population* made 120, if each county was to have at least one
representative.   In fact, the excess that 120 is over 65,
is the population basis, and it is a compromise the West
has accepted; the 45 members, only, represent the population proportion, and it must not be reduced, so long
as the Senate is 50.   Those, who would make it 100, would,
if Person and Robeson counties were Western, make the
House stand 47 to 53; if neutral 47 to 51; if Eastern 49 to
50; but with 120 the first would be 55 east to 65 west—the
second 55 to 61, and the third 59 to 61.   To make it so close
as 100 would make it, was not fair to the West or to the
oath of this Convention.   This matter was settled and no
half-settlement would answer, nor would it be made.
"Make it right, so that it may last."   Wealth had many

forms, and the West would yet rival the East in its possession. He analyzed the excess-member question ably, but reminded them that the Act settled the matter that they must
go to counties according to *respective* numbers; so that he
suggested county election for counties not having excess,
and district for those having excess. Judge Gaston closed
with a beautiful comment on North Carolina, but he made
one statement that showed him not to be the man of vision
that Morehead was: "The laws of Nature forbade North
Carolina from attaining great commercial eminence, or
rivalling in wealth some of the other States of the Confederacy." The method he proposed was adopted and reported
to the Convention—the product of two weeks' work, for the
Convention confirmed it. Thus far it was plain that no man
was so nearly the father of the constitution of 1835, as
Judge Gaston, so far as its construction was concerned;
but so far as the voices that represented the demand of the
West was concerned, the fathers of it were Fisher and Morehead in 1821. Nothing had been added in the past fifteen
years to what they had uttered; and this Convention was
constructing what was then asked for, in the main.

The three weeks longer, that it was destined to sit, would
have no such important question to settle, as the one just decided; and yet what occurred was to be a great and plainly
recognized change in the spirit of the Convention. The
chief bone of contention had been removed, and the state
stood upon a new basis. The West had come to her own,
but left the East, or minority, an organ of self-protection
in the Senate, just as had been done in the national constitutional convention. North Carolina had again endorsed the
great American doctrine of minority self-protection. The
final vote on the 120, on the 19th, showed that the Convention stood 75 to 52 for it—a very vigorous majority; and
this was no doubt due chiefly to Gaston, the "Peace-Maker,"
the rôle he, himself, avowed he wished to play. To reinforce this settlement, a vote of 120 to 4 for holding to 50
for the Senate was had, and all doubt removed as to the
vitality of the settlement.

The biennial meeting of the Legislature was easily

settled on the 20th to the accompaniment of an interesting Jeremiad by President Macon, to whose venerable mind the course of the Convention, and especially of Judge Gaston were anathema. It was therefore most interesting to see the new order recognized promptly, on Monday the 22nd, by making Mr. Morehead chairman of Committee of the Whole. The biennial matter was again fought when it was attached to the original resolution on representation, but again confirmed by a vote of 85 to 35. Then came that sensitive subject, borough representation, on the 24th, and it was fought over for two days, but the "Peace-Maker," although followed, in wanting representation, by such men as Fisher and Morehead, lost his battle 73 to 50—practically the same majority that settled representation in general.[1]

Representation was now fully settled, it would seem; but it was plain that the Convention was in a mood to leave no dark corner of it uncleansed; and action to that effect was precipitated on Friday, the 26th, in taking up Article 32, namely, the subject of religious disabilities in office-holding as most thought, of Roman Catholics and other non-Protestants. Mr. Fisher, of Rowan, was called to the chairmanship of Committee of the Whole. This Article, for sixty years, had been essentially obsolete, for Catholics held both legislative and judicial offices; indeed the "Peace-Maker" of this very Convention was a Roman Catholic, and as some would say, "the noblest Roman of them all;" but, essentially obsolete as it was, profound sentiment surrounded it in many quarters. It was a theme for flights of oratory, and men like Weldon Edwards of Warren, Bryan of Beaufort city, President Macon, Shober (the Moravian) and Rayner took advantage of it, eloquently. This was the one theme on which President Macon could see the constitution changed and not be from "better to worse." To one man on this floor in the Presbyterian Church at the southwest corner of capitol square, it was a personal question,

---

[1] A very interesting suggestion is made by A. B. Andrews, Esq., of Raleigh, that it was the Roanoke valley—meaning the lower Roanoke—which punished the marine boroughs by taking away representation, for aiding the West to get a new constitution. The favor of such men as Fisher and Morehead to the boroughs gives ground for its plausibility.

probably more than to any other—a man now on the highest
bench in the state, the man, who, at this moment, was doing
more than any other one man to construct this new constitution, namely, its avowed "Peace-Maker," Judge William
Gaston of Newbern.   At the beginning of the fourth day in
Committee of the Whole he began an address that must
ever be considered a classic in constitutional annals.   He
showed that the article was inconsistent with the Bill of
Rights and did not forbid Catholics from holding office, according to the most careful thought of thoughtful men.   The
article was not understood, as it was, nor could it be;
let it be made plain, whatever it was to mean, and he would
abide by it.   His idea was that its meaning hung on positive
denial of truths of the Protestant religion.   It has been held
to disqualify Atheists, Deists, Jews, Catholics, Quakers,
Mennonites, and Dunkards, at least.   The Convention is directed to make it plain.   His historical treatment was superb.
He noted how Maryland, Rhode Island, and Pennsylvania
were "the only countries," before the Revolution, in which
religious equality was established, and the Declaration of
Independence and Union made it all but universal among
the States, North Carolina alone having the sole relic in
Article 32.   He insisted that as a Roman Catholic he owed
"no allegiance to any man or set of men on earth, save only
to the State of North Carolina, and, so far as she has parted
with her sovereignty, to the United States of America."
His plea to the West, which stood for equal representation
was most earnest, and he closed with a plea for full freedom.   Many more speakers followed him on July 1st, the
last one, except a word from Governor Swain, being Mr.
Morehead.

The Guilford delegate said he should have remained
silent, except that such censure had been passed on all who
would retain the article.   "Because we are in favor of retaining in the Constitution something like a Test for office,
we are charged with bigotry and illiberality.   In every
Constitution," said he, "certain qualifications are made necessary for office.   In the amendments proposed by this
Convention to the Constitution, certain qualifications are

provided for the members of both Houses, and why not place some guard against inroads on the religion of our country? We, the other day, refused to a class of freemen the right of voting, because the color of their skin happened to differ from ours. Why was that done? Not because it was just, but because it was expedient. But when we prefer keeping a guard upon our religious rights in the Constitution, we are called illiberal bigots, fanatics, etc." Mr. Morehead could not "say he was a Christian, because he made no profession to be such; but he was as free from bigotry and fanaticism as anyone. ——— If no care is to be taken to preserve the sanctity of Religion in our country, why keep up the custom of administering oaths? Why administer an oath to an Atheist? He would not be bound by it." It had been said that there were no such beings in the country. He believed there were many such. He was therefore in favor of retaining the section in question. If any amendments were made to it, he should prefer that offered by the gentleman from Wilkes, and now under consideration. He agreed with the gentleman from Cumberland (Mr. Toomer) that it had been settled by the highest authority, that the 32nd Article did not exclude Roman Catholics from office, since the General Assembly had recently selected a distinguished gentleman of that profession to fill one of the highest offices on our Judicial Bench. He had been admitted to his seat without a single whisper of objection from any quarter, but on the contrary, with the general approbation of the whole country. Mr. Morehead added that he wished every man in North Carolina could have heard the able defence and explanation which the gentleman from Craven (Mr. Gaston) had given to the Convention, of the Roman Catholic Religion. He wished it, because he was satisfied that it had been greatly misrepresented and misunderstood. He knew it was generally believed in the part of the country in which he was best acquainted, that the Catholics here owned allegiance to the Pope. He was glad to hear this positively contradicted by the gentleman from Craven. He would add another remark in relation to what had fallen from the gentleman from Buncombe some days ago, in relation to the late Rev. Dr. David Caldwell, of his county. Mr. Morehead said there never was a truer Whig than Dr. Caldwell, nor one that had the good of his country more at heart. He mentioned several striking instances of his ardent zeal during the Revolutionary struggle, in evidence of this fact. And Mr. Morehead, when it came to a vote on substituting "Christian" for "Protestant," was in the minority of 51 to 74, along with Governor Branch, General Dockery, Spaight of Greene County, Judge Seawell, Judge Toomer of Fayetteville, and others of like standing. Judge Gaston had won again. Even so, however, Judge Gaston was voting to keep Jews and Atheists out of office, and it was extremely probable that this would occur to some as unjust, before the Convention rose.

July 2nd was a scarcely less auspicious day than the 26th of June had been, for the question was then raised as to whether the distrust of the people and distrust of the Executive shown in the old constitution was to stand. The annual choice of Governor by the Assembly indicated a purpose to center all control in the Assembly, so that the Governor was merely a species of executive officer dependent on the legislature. Here again the old British conceptions were in evidence, as well as repudiation of the checks-and-balance system between legislative and executive departments. While it did not affect power between east and west, it was part of the same political ideas, and was scarcely second in importance to the future of the commonwealth to that of proportional representation itself. The West proposed to elect the Governor in the same way they were to elect the lower House; for they purposed having an executive in sympathy with measures the House should secure. Not that the Governor had veto power, for he had not, but that he should, like the lower House, be the voice of population and, consequently, the West. And the curious thing about it was that it was an eastern—extreme eastern man, Mr. Jesse Wilson of Perquimans, on the Albemarle, who proposed the resolution. And the very first speaker said he had heard no complaint against the sixty-year-old mode of choosing the Governor; and he was possibly right; but the call for population repre-

sentation in the Assembly, which would have given the West
its choice anyhow, carried with it as a corollary, like election
of the executive; for both were merely means to an end,
namely, the will of the majority of the people in development
of North Carolina. *The defeat of development was the
motive of constitutional revision,* rather than any senti-
mental or academic political theories of popular equality; so
great was the hold of the old British conceptions of political
representation upon the people. They were far behind the
new American political science expressed in the national constitution, but not so far as Pennsylvania had been before
their constitution of 1790. This latter, the work chiefly of
James Wilson, chief father of the national constitution and
first to present the new political science, as a science, had
been formed on the new science; and all that great body
of settlers in western North Carolina who came from that
state after 1790 had those ideas. That they influenced the
thought of the west there can be no doubt. In this particular
question, however, North Carolina was no doubt somewhat
influenced by her daughter, Tennessee, who had in her recent
constitutional revision done the same thing. Indeed the
first speaker, Mr. Daniel of Halifax, said he had lately met a
Tennessean "who said that two Candidates were travelling
through the State on an electioneering campaign, at expense
and trouble to themselves, and to the great annoyance of the
People," and he hoped not to see such a phenomenon in
North Carolina. He of course could not know that there
were members present then who should soon be doing that
very thing for the first time in the history of the State. He
cited Pennsylvania, New York and Massachusetts as warnings.

Others followed: President Macon said that a Governor
that could do no more than a North Carolina executive was
of not enough importance to bother about it; but if he had
a veto power, as many have, he thought the People ought
to elect him. Some feared that the only question people
would ask would be: "Is he an eastern or a western man?"
Judge Gaston recognized the inseparableness of this and the
new House basis, and its inevitableness. He also noted the

utter absence of power in the "Old North State's" executive; he was merely and strictly executive, with neither
appointive or veto powers, and so to vote for such an office
was no great privilege, that 60,000 voters should bother
about: it would be different if he had power. He dreaded
the election machinery. He thought it broke the compromise between east and west, because it would compel free
white voting, not the federal ratio. Judge Gaston again lost,
74 to 44, almost the usual majority; and with him were men
like Bryan, Edwards, Macon, Seawell, Toomer and others of
like standing.

On July 3rd, the Senatorial districts and House election
arrangements prepared by a committee were accepted, and it
was decided to keep at work on the 4th, on which day, the
Volunteer Militia celebrated with noisy procession past the
Presbyterian Church so effectively, that, while it irritated
Mr. Morehead, who thought it deserved a reprimand, it
actually resulted in persuading the Convention to honor the
day by adjournment, the day being Saturday. On the 6th,
however, the future method of amendment was taken up.
It was natural that the West, which had struggled so hard to
get revision, should want a more easy mode of amendment,
and it was even proposed that only majorities in two successive Assemblys, the second elected on this basis, could
secure its presentation for ratification by the people. The
Convention's course in turning down Judge Gaston's position
three times was beginning to raise his apprehensions, and
since he was so great an instrument in securing the present
revision, he wanted a conservative amendment process for
the future. "In what sense," said he, "ought majorities to
govern? That the deliberate will of the People ought ultimately to prevail, no one will deny; but that the temporary
will of the majority, which may be produced by the efferves-
cence of the moment, ought to do *whatever it pleases*—set up
and pull down Constitution from day to day—no man can
be so extravagant as to desire." In this comment, he expressed the permanence of American institutions—which
makes ours the oldest government on earth. If the West
did such a thing, he considered himself deceived. "There

are many reasons," he said, "why the claims of the West did
not sooner succeed. He owed it to the East to say, that
never until lately were these claims fairly before the East.
—— Sometimes the West connected the removal of the
Seat of Government with their claim for equal representation—and sometimes they advanced their claims in connection with other propositions which actually reflected on the
understanding of those to whom they were addressed." He
said no other state had such loose provisions. In this he
won the day for two-thirds votes in the Assembly, 107 to 17.

Mr. Morehead astonished the Convention by a vigorous
unequivocal denunciation of requiring *viva voce* voting for
public offices in Assembly, which came up next; but he was
disagreed with, 82 to 38. He was pleased, however, when,
immediately thereafter, July 6th, Judge Gaston suggested
that since the majority against giving free negroes the vote
was so small, it might be reconsidered. Before the Revolution, he thought there was hardly a freed negro in the State,
and such as there were, were mulattoes, children of white
women, and thereby free. The act of 1777, providing for
control of emancipation plainly noted it as a recent phenomenon. A few days since he had seen the certificate of John
Chavis, a colored minister, that he had taken the oath of
allegiance at Mecklenburg, Va., on December 20, 1778.
Legislative acts entitled freed negroes to all rights of colored freemen, *i. e.,* mulattoes, sons of white women. He
therefore proposed an amendment, restricting, but not with-
drawing the vote. Mr. Holmes, of New Hanover, cited the
case of San Domingo, where in 1791, slaves who became
free through meritorious services, the removal, some years
later, of the voting rights then conferred upon them was the
chief cause of revolution. A Perquimans member said no
free negro, in his region, had ever been allowed to vote. Mr.
Fisher proposed a less severe amendment. Objection was
made that no free negro was allowed to enter any state,
except he give bond for good behavior, and Ohio forbid
his entrance at all. A vote would cause confusion. The
Gaston amendment was voted down, 64 to 55, and Mr.

Morehead was one of the 55, results not essentially different from the first vote, but more favorable to the minority.

Judge Gaston made an attempt to reopen the county-district method of voting for the lower House, but in vain; and then Mr. Morehead brought up the impeachment article which provided that the Chief Justice should preside, as in national proceedings of like character; but they wanted no one but Senators concerned in this judicial act. Mr. Morehead did secure one amendment, however, namely, one on holding state and national offices; but he failed in another, namely, the abolition of private laws, and it was Judge Gaston's influence which defeated him. Mr. Wilson, of Perquimans, made an impassioned plea to remove the word "Christian" before "Religion" in Article 32, but in vain. The general report on form of amendments for submission was adopted, 81 to 20, on the evening of July 10th. The usual acts of courtesy were performed on the following day, when President Macon avowed he had never witnessed such good order and decorum in any body with which he had been connected, and he expected this to be "the last scene of my public life." With a closing prayer by the pastor of the Presbyterian Church, in which this great act of justice to the West had been consummated, the Constitutional Convention of 1835, for North Carolina, ceased to be.

In a word what were the results: 1. Equalized representation; 2. biennial sessions; 3. Popular biennial election of executives; 4. Attorney General's term to be limited to four years; 5. No borough representation; 6. No vote of free negroes; 7. *Viva voce* Assembly vote for public officers; 8. Removal of Roman Catholic disability to hold office, definitely; 9. Two-thirds Assembly votes for amendment process; 10. Mode of impeachment of officers; 11. Removal of judges for disability; and 12. Restriction on private laws. The new order of representation provided one member for each of 9 counties, with less than the federal ratio; Brunswick, Columbus, Chowan, Greene, Jones, Tyrrell, Washington in the east and Macon and Haywood in the west. The remaining 111 members are on a ratio of 5399, that gave 32 counties each one member, 17 counties two each, and 7 counties three each—not allowing for fractions permitting another member. The latter counties—those given another member on fractional excess, were 24 in number: of these 15 went to the 32 with one member, while 7 went to the 17 with two members, and 2 went to the 7 with three members. These additional members, as between east and west, were not very equal. The two three-member counties, which thereby got four, were western, Lincoln and Orange. The seven two-member ones, getting three, were five western—Burke, Chatham, Iredell, Surry and Stokes—and two eastern—Granville and Halifax; while on the other hand almost all of the 15 given to the one-member class were eastern. Therefore only Lincoln and Orange had four members. Those having three were: Guilford, Mecklenburg, Rowan, Rutherford, Wake, Burke, Chatham, Iredell, Surry, Stokes, Granville and Halifax. Those having two were: Anson, Buncombe, Cumberland, Craven, Caswell, Davidson, Edgecombe, Randolph, Rockingham, Wilkes, Beaufort, Bertie, Duplin, Franklin, Johnston, New Hanover, Northampton, Person, Pitt, Sampson, Warren, Wayne, Montgomery, Robeson and Richmond. The rest had but one representative. As property was so largely the basis of the Senate, it was only a question of a short time when the West would be equally dominant in that body.

The Convention had barely adjourned when news came of the death of Chief Justice John Marshall, whereupon North Carolina came out boldly and vigorously for the Roman Catholic "Peace-Maker" of the Convention as his successor. It was a premature wish, however, for it was to take over a half-century before the people of the United States were able to take such an attitude. That the new constitution was more his work than that of any other one man is self-evident. That Mr. Morehead recognized him as leader is also self-evident, and, as a rule, supported him on the great committee of which both were members. That Morehead would have gone farther than Gaston is also not to be questioned, nor that he recognized that Gaston led Cape Fear and Neuse sections of the east against the Roanoke, or the commercial boroughs of the southeast against the planters of the Roanoke. A sub-conscious, if not conscious, basis for this, was undoubtedly the Newbern-Beaufort-Raleigh hope for a Beaufort-to-Tennessee railroad. The Caldwell idea of the west had become the Gaston idea of the east, the lever by which the State was to be lifted. That this was Mr. Morehead's objective, rather than any especially academic ideas in political science, there can be still less doubt; for this new constitution was preeminently a means to an end, just as Judge Gaston himself was. The statesmanship of the Murpheys, the Caldwells, the Fishers, the Moreheads and other western leaders, whose eyes were on the building and development of the commonwealth, were the real cause of this new fundamental law. They were the designers; Gaston the chief builder, after their plans—plans which had been forced upon him and his eastern friends almost at the point of revolution. And it had been the whole burden of Morehead's public life, his heritage from his great teachers and heroes, Murphey and Caldwell. The order for the Constitution of 1835 had been given in the West and the general design made there, but its mechanism was built chiefly by eastern hands.

Its ratification was not to be voted on until November, so that the general elections at once overshadowed all else. The "Whigs of '34" were now merely full-fledged Whigs, and were carrying the banner of Hugh L. White of Tennessee against "Van Burenism." It was a period of the rise of the national "West" as well as the State "West;" Arkansas and Michigan were asking to become states. The growth of the Whigs everywhere was amazing. North Carolina was divided nearly equally between the two—the idolizer of General Jackson not long since! General Harrison's friends were becoming active; and with this uprising came also, in the North, aggressive propaganda for the abolition of slavery. These themes were in the minds of all in November, when the new Assembly met and the vote on ratification was taken. This vote of the people was a magnificent proof of the need for revision, for the tre-

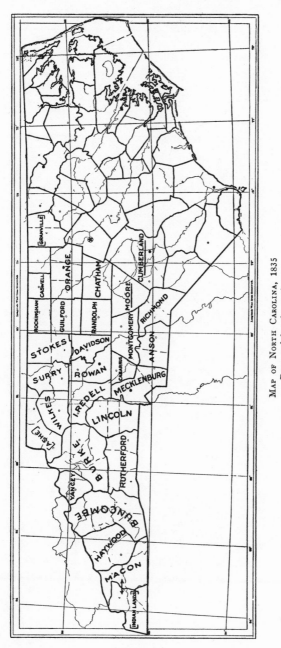

MAP OF NORTH CAROLINA, 1835
Prepared by the author

Showing vote for Constitutional Convention, 27,550 (26 cos.), and against, 21,694 (39 cos.); and ratification vote, 26,771 for, with 21,606 against, Ashe and Granville changing for, and Moore and Cumberland against

mendous number of 39 counties were against, nearly 40
against, to 26 for; and yet 26,771 were for and but 21,606
against, making 5165 majority for ratification! The only
difference between this vote and that for calling the convention was that the latter majority was somewhat larger, 5856.
In other words, the two votes for, were 27,550 and 26,771;
the two votes against were 21,694 and 21,606; and the
majorities 5856 and 5165. The chief difference was that
several hundred were so sure it would win that they did not
vote, while less than a hundred were won to the eastern
cause. Therefore, on December 3, 1835, Governor Swain
proclaimed the new constitution to be in effect from and
after January 1, 1836.

And what was the immediate result? The Assembly
had its shortest session within memory, adjourning on December 22nd. Their most notable work was to amend the
Wilmington and Raleigh Railroad act of 1832, changing the
line to run direct from Wilmington to the Roanoke, leaving
Raleigh out; for not only Petersburgh was running trains to
Weldon, below the Roanoke rapids, and, by way of the
Greensville and Roanoke, from Belfield, were running to a
point above the rapids now called Gaston; but a new "train
of cars" was announced for December 1st on the way from
Portsmouth to its successive termini on the way to Weldon.
Wilmington, therefore, proposed to make haste and take
its share from the rich Roanoke. The Gaston terminus,
therefore, on the Wilmington people's leaving out Raleigh,
caused her to secure incorporation of the Raleigh and Gaston
Railroad Company, and the Raleigh and Fayetteville Railroad Company. The Weldon Toll Bridge increased its
capital to $75,000, to get ready for the big business. These
were the answer to the new constitution, of the people of
Wilmington and the Roanoke, for they expected the west
to move for the North Carolina Central or Beaufort to Tennessee railroad.

IX

John Motley Morehead
AND
The Rise of the Whig Party
IN
North Carolina

1836

Immediately on the close of the Assembly on December 22, 1835, the Anti-Van Buren or Whig members met in the House of Commons hall, at Government House, foot of Fayetteville Street, and resolved upon organization of a party ticket to be known as Whig. General Polk, of Rowan, took the lead in this as in the unofficial constitutional convention of 1833, although Col. Andrew Joyner of Halifax, was made chairman. They nominated White of Tennessee for President and formed a Whig Central Committee headed by Charles L. Hinton, an address committee headed by General Polk, provided for county nominations of a Whig candidate for Governor, and for county committees of five each. When these were appointed the list showed almost none of the old leaders, except General Polk in Rowan, Mr. Morehead in Guilford, General Dockery in Richmond and a few others, but its organization was complete in every county.

But whether Whig organization, which was almost as vigorous in most other states as in Carolina, was more active, or railroad promotion more so, is difficult to say. On January 2, 1836, Raleigh held a meeting of all those interested in a railroad to the Roanoke terminus of the Greensville and Roanoke Railroad at Wilkins Ferry, now called Gaston. Judge Cameron, Charles Manly, George E. Badger and others led the enthusiasm and $150,000 was

Portsmouth & Roanoke
RAIL ROAD.

THE Public are informed that **Sixty Miles** of this Road are completed and ready for the Transportation of Passengers and Produce.

A Train of Cars

WILL LEAVE PORTSMOUTH DAILY, (commencing **this day,** *Tuesday, the first of December,* at 9 o'clock, A. M.) and arrive at MARGARETVILLE, (the present termination of the road,) to dinner, whence passengers will be conveyed in

FOUR HORSE
POST COACHES
TO HALIFAX, N. C.
Arriving in time for the
Southern Stages, via Raleigh &c.

FIRST PICTURE OF A TRAIN IN A
NORTH CAROLINA PAPER
Raleigh Register, 15th Dec., 1836

subscribed, whereupon the President of the Petersburg Railroad announced that he was authorized to put down $150,000 for citizens of his city. This made immediate organization possible; but the Wilmington people were equally in earnest and at the same time announced a subscription of $200,000 for their road. The Gaston road organized on February 4th. Five days before, on January 30th, Raleigh Whigs started the local nominations for President, Vice-President and Governor and determined on Hugh L. White, a native of North Carolina; John Tyler of Virginia, and for Governor, General Edward B. Dudley, of Wilmington. A general understanding existed among the Whigs of the State that there should be unity on these men, so that the campaign should be wholly against Van Burenism and Jacksonism, whose ticket was headed by Spaight, both eastern men, and designed to divide the east, prospects of which was almost certain.

On February 16th, General Dudley accepted and slightly less than a month later, 14th March, he was also chosen President of the Wilmington and Raleigh Railroad Company. The success of the Raleigh-Gaston organization seems to have made the board change its policy and go to Raleigh, for this meeting decided to at once begin work at both ends, Wilmington and Raleigh. The Raleigh-Roanoke road, designed to go to Weldon from Raleigh was active but not so far successful; so that the commitment of the Raleigh people to the Gaston, or abovefalls route, no doubt temporarily influenced Wilmington to go to Raleigh, with an idea of heading off any Raleigh-Fayetteville alliance. The decision did not last long, however, chiefly, it is said, because Johnston county would not subscribe. This course was stimulated, too, by the Raleigh-Gaston line calling in 8% on its stock on June 7th and actually getting to work on the Gaston end; and also because the Raleigh-Fayetteville road was becoming active, while the Richmond and Petersburg and Richmond and Fredericksburg roads were building so fast, that Wilmington feared lest the through line might be diverted west of her by Raleigh activities. The fact that stocks of all com-

pleted roads in the United States were above par served to
make them attractive investment as well as public improvement. The Hartford and New Haven was to begin operation on August 15th; and 48 miles of the Richmond and
Fredericksburg was in use in November, with only 16
miles more to complete. The Raleigh-Gaston road had
35 miles out of Gaston contracted for by October and
would have 50 before the end of the year. By November
the Wilmington-Weldon route was settled and 30 miles surveyed and 35 under contract. They took over the Halifax
and Weldon road as part of this line. Then came a new
idea from Virginia, not unlike the Greensville-Gaston
branch of the Petersburg to tap the upper Roanoke above
the falls. This was to tap the still farther upper Roanoke
and Dan valleys from Portsmouth to Danville, paralleling
the Roanoke, under the name Roanoke, Danville and Junction Railroad proposed in December—a project that was to
appeal greatly to Mr. Morehead's district, because it would
be their nearest line, although it would bind them com-
mercially to Virginia. By this, the latter state, which
was capturing the lower Roanoke already, would capture
the back country to the north, as South Carolina was already capturing it to the south by water and proposing to
do by rail. Indeed so early as 1833 a North Carolina
convention proposed a line to Louisville and Cincinnati
through the mountains and now Charleston was actively
at work on the Louisville, Cincinnati and Charleston Railroad and was at this very time, through her agent, attempting to enlist North Carolina in it, showing that the Yadkin
road, from Fayetteville to Beatties Ford, would make it as
much a Wilmington as a Charleston road, in the east, and
be a great thoroughfare for the west. The agent's letter to
the Governor noted the increase of commerce that was
bound to come with passenger travel. "Before the railroad," said he, "was made between New York and Philadelphia, about 80 or 100 passengers daily was the usual
number; now it has increased to between 1500 and
2000. . . . Between Charleston and Augusta, a single
stage three times a week, was more than sufficient for the

transportation of passengers. Since the establishment of the railroad, the average of passengers to Charleston has gone as far as 500 per week."[1] This was something that would sooner or later awaken Wilmington to the mere first-aid nature of her Weldon line, as a state measure.

During the summer, however, politics grew, what might be called, "White Hot;" for, as Tennessee had been the first to champion her and North Carolina's son, Jackson, and North Carolina and Pennsylvania had been first to second that cause; so now Tennessee was first to turn from him to her and North Carolina's other son, Hugh L. White, and again the same seconds followed her! The Whigs were growing as fast as the new Washington monument plans, under the leadership of ex-President James Madison, who died on June 28th in the midst of them; and the stars in the national flag, which would increase to just double the original number, with the transformation of Arkansas and Michigan from territories to States. And John Motley Morehead, twice a Jackson elector, now became in July a White, or Whig elector from the Sixth District, and with him were, for the most part, a new set of leaders, Judge Toomer of Fayetteville, Charles Manly of Wake, John Giles of Rowan, Dr. James S. Smith of Orange, and others equally new, so that Mr. Morehead was probably the best known among them. And the August election gave Guilford's vote to General Dudley for Governor, 1145 to only 475 for Governor Spaight, the administration party candidate. It was typical, for 32 counties, *both east and west almost equally,* gave Dudley 31,829 votes, or 5007 majority over Governor Spaight, with 26,822 votes.[2] The east and west seemed broken up forever! They were both divided: the coast counties from Carteret to Camden went Whig almost without exception, and even Halifax and Northampton. The central part, Warren to New Hanover, went for the administration, as did the Charlotte country, three

---

[1] *Raleigh Register,* 3rd Jan., 1837.
[2] Technically, when official count was made, 62 counties gave Dudley 33,993 and Spaight 29,950, Chowan, Gates and Burke not counted, for various reasons. So that Dudley's technical majority was 4043. If they had been counted, it would have been 4729. The 5007 figures were the actual, but not technical votes; so that the map has been made from it, as truer to the movement.

mountain counties, and three upper Roanoke ones on the Virginia line. Judge Gaston's county went with them. The Whig gubernatorial victory was so great that, when it came to the Presidential vote, many took it for granted and didn't vote at all![1] Over 10,000 Whigs did not, and nearly 2000 Democrats, so that White lost, 21,218 to 24,878, a difference of 3660. The House of Commons was similarly affected, the Whigs securing 59 members and the Democrats 61, so that here, too, the east and west lines were broken up. As Judge Gaston had predicted, the national lines in politics had overshadowed state lines. For, strange to say the Whigs secured a majority of four in the Senate, so that with the Senate and Governor and joint ballot, the Whigs were victorious; and there was even a good chance of a tie in the House. Surely 1836 was a year of revolution in the politics of North Carolina! Mr. Morehead's brother, James T., was made a Senator.

When it came to organization of the Legislature in November, 1836, it is interesting to see how east and west still persisted, but under political names of "Van Buren-ites" or Democrats and Whigs; for that central bulk of Democratic territory eastward from Raleigh was leader of the one, and that central bulk of territory west of Raleigh led the Whigs. And, although the state went so largely for the Whig Governor, General Dudley was an eastern man; and the smallness of the margins in both Senate and House enabled the east to utilize various influences to their advantage. For example, speakership candidates in the Senate were an eastern Democrat and a western Whig; and with only 48 present, the two candidates not voting, gave 24 for the Whig and 22 for the Democrat, electing the Whig, and with one vacancy to be filled, the Senate then stood, 25 Whigs and 24 Democrats! The House margin was not quite so small, but nearly so, properly 61 Democrats and 59 Whigs, and yet when the Whigs put up Wm. A. Graham of Hillsboro, the west, against Mr. Haywood of Raleigh, the east, they lost 53 to 60, showing that some

---

[1] Even so the opposition majority to Van Buren, in the nation was over 18,000, which was significant for the future.

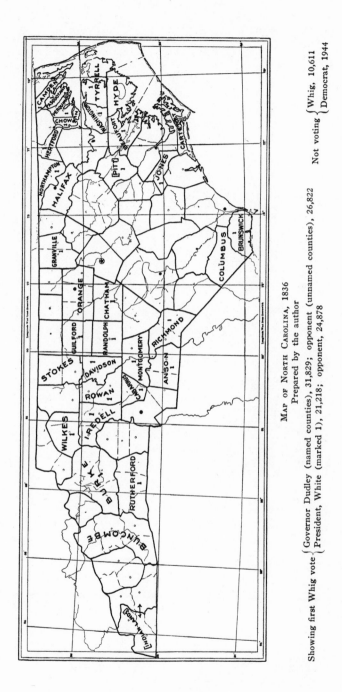

MAP OF NORTH CAROLINA, 1836
Prepared by the author

Showing first Whig vote {Governor Dudley (named counties), 31,829; opponent (unnamed counties), 26,822   Not voting {Whig, 10,611
{President, White (marked 1), 21,218; opponent, 24,878   {Democrat, 1944

in both cases, merely joined the majority. The Whig Senate leaders were Polk, Morehead (J. T.), Dockery, Bryan of Beaufort city and a few others, while the House Democratic leaders were equally new men. The result was that, on joint ballot the parties were so equally balanced that anything might happen—with a Whig majority of two in the Senate, as there finally came to be, and a Democratic majority of two in the House. And yet, while such a condition favored the east, it was a tremendous party revolution for North Carolina that promised much for the future; and was an equally wonderful eastern victory in the midst of a sectional state revolution in which the east was properly a loser! The activities of the old legislative election of Governor were now transferred to the election of United States Senators; and the small margin let loose an amount of contest of seats on various grounds and resignations and apparently even death, that characterized this Assembly above probably all its predecessors. The result was that a Democratic United States Senator, Judge Strange, was chosen, by a majority of four votes; and the new Senator would be asked to act on the proposition of the Minister from the Republic of Texas, just arrived in Washington, that that republic become a state in the American union, to become the only state that ever exercised national sovereignty as a commonwealth. And, as Mexico proposed forcibly to resist this course, the new Senator was destined to help sow the seeds of a foreign war.

The cap-stone of Whig, though not unmixed Western victory, was the inauguration of Governor Dudley at Government House, foot of Fayetteville street, on January 1, 1837, at noon, in the House of Commons Hall. The noble new capitol at the other end of the thoroughfare was in course of construction, but it was not destined to be ready* for the first Whig executive; and in this hall which was properly the Executive Mansion, he outlined his policies. They noted that the state, fifth in population among the twenty-six, needed all manner of internal improvement, from education to transportation. With only a third of the banking capital of neighboring states to the south, they need more, as the root of progress. The new distribution of federal surplus promised nearly two millions and would be an aid, but his main idea was increase in capital of the present banks; for he was not in favor of State aid in transportation; in which respect he was thoroughly eastern, and thereby laid foundations for a new determination in the west. Governor Dudley was a very high type of man—a moderate and a harmonizer, but he was by no means designed to carry out the purposes of the west. Under his influence, the Assembly was almost wholly occupied with financial measures, reorganization of State finances, in which Representative Wm. A. Graham led. The session was 64 days long—one of the longest and most important in results, for it adopted the two-fifths state-aid plan for the following railroad projects: Cape Fear and Western (Fayetteville-Yadkin), the Wilmington and Weldon, the North Carolina Central (Beaufort harbor, to go to Fayetteville); and adopted reorganization of the education board on the basis of reclaiming swamp lands and bank stock; redemption of State paper money of 1835, revision and publication of code modified, new assessment law, militia self-election, abolition of imprisonment of honest debtors, and some others. The favor to the Louisville-Charleston Railroad project was marked and banking facilities were granted to it. Meanwhile, the legislature had also incorporated a Raleigh southwestern road as extension of the Gaston road, which latter line was making great progress in construction, 50 miles having been located and nearly all under contract, with a force of seven hundred laborers. With its new extension it desired to tap a region midway between Charlotte and Fayetteville, going through Anson county, its name being the Raleigh and Columbia Railroad. These things put vigor into Wilmington, and by March, she had won the two-fifths state aid; had one locomotive and another on the way from England, expecting to have 30 miles completed at the south end before the end of the year, 85 miles to Waynesboro (Goldsboro) graded, and 20 miles completed at the Weldon end. By April trains on the Virginia line to Gaston were running—and bridges were building over the Roanoke both at Gaston and Weldon. By July (1837) the Gaston road had 70 miles surveyed to within 15 miles of Raleigh, 60 miles under contract, 50 miles to be ready for rails in November, and the first 10 miles out of Gaston to be laid at once, while the laborers had increased to about 1200. The Portsmouth road was ready to send its cars over the Weldon bridge as soon as it was completed and the same road was able to announce an accident in which two were killed, while Supreme Courts were locating responsibility and damages. In the midst of all this the *Newbern Spectator*, in Judge Gaston's town, was calling vigorously for the state to note great improvement in Beaufort harbor and to undertake a sea to Tennessee railroad. The quarry road at Raleigh and the Petersburg road had served a good purpose; the railroad in North Carolina was an accomplished fact, and the gold at the end of the rainbow was the riches of the Roanoke valley; but it will be observed all of this rail activity, except that proposed by South Carolina was almost wholly eastern and southern; not in the great central west that had brought about this revolution, at all. Indeed it seemed to cover almost every part of the state but their own, and to deliberately share their trade with other states, when it was not a desperate effort merely to save a share for themselves. This was because the time was not ripe for leadership of that great central west to lay down its program.

The coming leader was himself growing in power and wealth. John Motley Morehead was forty-one years old, and about him at "Blandwood," in Greensboro, was growing up a numerous farmily: his eldest child, Letitia, was a girl of fourteen, and, like his father, he desired for his family a higher education, and it was time his eldest child was entering upon it. His next child, however, was also a daughter, Mary Corrina, a girl of twelve years, likewise almost ready; while Ann Eliza II, his third child, named for her mother, and but a couple of years behind at the age of ten years, Mary Louise, seven years of age, and Emma Victoria, a babe about one year old, convinced him that whatever his plans for higher education of his girls might be, they must necessarily be large plans, and plans for female education, rather than male, since he had but one son, a child of four years, John Lindsay.[1] For the son, Caldwell Institute, established by Presbyterians, of whom President Caldwell of the University was a leader and named for him, had been opened in January, the previous year, and had just been chartered by the Assembly and was already most successful.   There had been a small private girls' school in Greensboro for a number of years, and, during the previous year, a talented lady, Miss Mary Ann Hoye, had had charge, and he had placed four of his daughters under her guidance.   But this was not the advanced education he had in mind.

There were large ideas abroad in Greensboro at this time: The editor of the *Patriot* was working out plans for a southern periodical as ambitious as Morris' and Willis' *New York Mirror*.   The Moravians had a girls' school of higher education at Salem, a few miles westward, and the Friends had a Boarding School at New Garden to the eastward; while the Methodists, with a little school for children at Greensboro, had, during the previous January, applied, with others, not only for a new North Carolina Conference, but for a female school of higher education for it at Greensboro as a Female College.   Mr. Morehead decided he himself would take Miss Hoye as a nucleus and create a school of higher education, not only for his own daughters, but for the girls of the South as well.[2] He had become interested in the fact that the novelist, Maria Edgeworth, had done so much for Ireland that she had become the inspiration of Sir Walter Scott in doing the same for Scotland in his Waverley novels, the books of both authors being great favorites in his home and town; and he chose as a name for the proposed institution, Edgeworth Female Seminary.[3]   As his plans were on a large scale it required

---

[1] The daughter named for his wife was born February 8, 1827, and died Oct. 7, 1876.

[2] The girls' school in which Miss Hoye taught, however, continued for some time after she left it.

[3] Miss Edgeworth was still living, although Scott had been dead for five years, and the novels of both were "best sellers" of the day.

EDGEWORTH FEMALE SEMINARY
Greensboro, North Carolina
From an old woodcut

the next three years to get ready for the opening. He purchased a large tract of land from his home, "Blandwood," north to West Market Street, to what became the site of the Methodist Female College. At his own expense also he erected the seminary itself, a large four-story brick structure, and laid out the grounds in picturesque design. It might well look as though the spirit of an Edgeworth, that inspired a Scott, might be preparing decades later to inspire an "O. Henry," who was also to sit at the feet of a woman teacher of Greensboro who was herself an Edgeworth graduate. This will indicate the kind of vision, ability and wealth that John Motley Morehead was to bring to public affairs when the time was ripe.

One reason for this delay was the sudden announcement in Washington on May 12th, that the banks of New York, Philadelphia and Baltimore had suspended specie payments, and the panic was so great in New York, that two regiments of soldiers were called out to preserve order. Said one witness of it in New York: "I have witnessed excitement and distress produced by Yellow Fever, Cholera, and the great Fire, and I assure you, if they were all concentrated and caused to take place in one day, the excitement and distress would not equal that now felt in New York *every day!*"[1] There was no doubt in the minds of men like Mr. Morehead and other Whigs, that this was the natural result of the Jackson destruction of the regulatory financial system of which the United States Bank was the head and had been, with its predecessors, the first Bank of the United States and its predecessor (the present oldest institution of the kind in the nation, The Bank of North America, both of Philadelphia) for over a half-century; nearly ever since the Yorktown surrender, except for an interregnum of four years, 1811–16, the President of the first two banks, Thomas Willing, being known, for this period of about thirty years, as "The Old Regulator" of American finance. This system, designed by James Wilson, and adopted by both treasury heads, Robert Morris and

---

[1] *Raleigh Register*, May 16, 1837

Alexander Hamilton, was built up by that remarkable man,
Thomas Willing, the only man ever compared to Washington, and that, too, by no less a man than the great
lawyer, Horace Binney. The destruction of that system,
without offering any regulatory system in its place, may be
compared to what would happen at the present day if President Harding were to destroy the Federal Reserve system.
The State banks tried to bear the burden, but were unable
to do so, and legislatures everywhere were hastily summoned. The Bank of North Carolina, which had super-
seded the old State Bank, held out until May 19th, when it,
too, suspended specie payments. Currency and even government drafts had no value. "So much," said the *Raleigh
Register* of May 23rd, "for this grand 'Experiment' with
the curency, which, it was ever and often promised, should
fill the purse of the poor man with Benton yellow boys, and
supersede altogether those dirty rags, called paper money."
The Whigs held that it all came about from President Jackson's demand that the Bank of the United States remove
a man from one of its branches who was opposed to his
election and the Bank refused; whereupon in 1834 he began
his attacks upon it, which, in three years, had destroyed
it and the financial system, with these lamentable results.
The Democratic leaders held otherwise and spoke of the
"money power," as later generations speak of "the interests" or "corporations." And yet the American system
was like that of every other great country in the world and
had made American money respected everywhere, as it is
under the Federal Reserve system today; but the difficulty
was that "The Old Regulator" was not replaced by a new
regulator of some kind.

Nothing could have happened more fortunate for the
immediate future of the Whigs, either locally or nationally.
On July 4, 1837, the Whigs of Ohio called for a national
convention in June, 1838, at Pittsburg, Pennsylvania, and
the Whigs of North Carolina put up William A. Graham
for Congress, for election on August 10th, while other districts put up Whigs also and Stanly of the Third was
elected on July 27th. Whigs everywhere made great gains

upon the administration members, which, among themselves, were divided into conservative and what was called
"Loco Foco" wings. It was September before a Bank Convention was proposed to consider resumption of specie
payments; and President Van Buren ready to propose a
Sub-Treasury system, while postage and duties were demanded in gold by the national government, which enabled
them to pay members of the national government in specie.
Upon which the Whigs exclaimed: "Gold for the Government! Rags for the People!" Thereupon the President's
state, New York, went bodily for the Whigs; and on the 8th
of November, at Alton, Illinois, occurred the first bloodshed
of the Abolition movement, in the death of Rev. Owen P.
Lovejoy in a riot. The bankers' convention in mid-winter
did not think it advisable to set a date for resumption,
which set it forward at least until their next meeting in
April, 1838. The administration charged this action to
another Philadelphia state bank, the Bank of Pennsylvania,
which had become the leading one—said to have more
specie in its vaults than all the New York banks put together; but the real reason seems to have been an inability
to support such a movement, in parts of New England.[1]
At any rate the critical situation remained and contributed
to the Whig cause, while the growing acuteness of the
Abolition movement in both Whig and Democratic ranks in
the north, involved the situation still more. The aggressiveness of the latter movement made a new self-consciousness
in both North and South, so that hereafter they should be
spelled with capital letters; and a like aggressiveness was
in the slave-holding states, determined to hold their present
standing by securing a new Southern State in the South for
every new one in the North.

And these midwinter national phenomena of 1837–8 were
accompanied by significant local ones in North Carolina.
On December 5th, the Wilmington & Raleigh (as its

---

[1] New York quotations on bank notes of exchange on other cities, in January, 1838, are interesting: The lowest rate was that for Philadelphia and
Charleston, 1½ to 2. The next closest to these was Boston, 1¾ to 2¼. Baltimore followed with 2 to 2½. Richmond and New Orleans had next place with
2½ to 3. Augusta and Savanna had 3 to 3½; Cincinnati had 5 to 6, and Mobile,
5¼ to 6. It is difficult to realize these relations today.

corporate title still stood) or Wilmington & Weldon Railroad, which had taken over the Halifax & Weldon line, announced that "The Engine with Train of Coaches and Cars" was now leaving Halifax every morning, going by way of Weldon to Portsmouth to meet the boat for the national capital. This was the first regular train to run any material distance in North Carolina. The Wilmington road had advertised her port business in May, previously, showing that 152 vessels to foreign ports and 150 coastwise ports had taken out nearly a million dollars' worth of exports in the previous six months—$999,937.16, to be exact. To see such progress in transportation as this from Wilmington, Weldon, Raleigh and Gaston, and prospects at Fayetteville, Yadkin and the Louisville, Cincinnati & Charleston, affecting nearly every part of the state but her own, it was not strange that, in January, 1838, the *Patriot* of Greensboro, should be the first Whig organ to announce that Governor Dudley would decline re-election, and to issue a call for Guilford county Whigs to hold a convention to nominate a Whig successor, whose plans of progress covered the great central west. The call alarmed the Whig *Register* of Raleigh, which could not believe that Governor Dudley would decline: "We would therefore say," wrote Editor Gales, "to the Guilford Whigs (whose name is legion) *bide a bit!*"[1] And by February 19th, the Whig editor at the capital was able to announce that Governor Dudley would run again. On January 30th, Governor Dudley had written Ex-Governor Swain, then President Swain of the University, asking his advice on standing for a second term, saying he did not want it, but "had never given authority for any such announcement." Some of his friends thought he could not retire "with safety to the party," although he himself believed "any other Whig candidate would unite the same vote."[2] On his announcement through the *Raleigh Register* that he would stand again, the *Standard* of the same city, the Democratic organ, plainly said they would hesitate to put anyone up against him. The reason

---

[1] *Raleigh Register,* January 22, 1838.
[2] Swain Papers, Hist. Comm. of N. C.

First Picture of a Raleigh & Gaston Railroad Coach
May 30, 1838

for this, though not stated, was plainly that the lower
Roanoke and Cape Fear valleys were holding together in an
eastern combination against the west; and Governor Dudley's letters to President Swain soon after, trying his best to
get the latter to become President of the Fayetteville and
Western Railroad project, shows the strong hand that Wilmington is playing, with Fayetteville as her partner and
sub-port feeder from the west. In keeping with this
purpose, was the effort to swing the Beaufort-Newbern-
Waynesville "North Carolina Central" south to Fayetteville,
instead of to Raleigh and the west. In short, Wilmington
was striving to unite the conservative east with railroads,
and the lower Roanoke was willing that she should. When
Governor Dudley consented to stand for a second term,
it was a matter of course that he would be elected: in the
west, because he was a Whig, and in the east, because he
was an eastern conservative in state matters, or sufficiently
so to develop the east through railroads, as he was President
of the largest road designed to bind the east together. It is
well to take careful note of these circumstances, for they
not only present the occasion for Guilford county's haste
to get rid of their present Whig executive, but also the large
size of the contract before them when they should succeed.[1]

This haste in Guilford was not looked upon indiffer-
ently by the east. Contemporary with it was a plea in the
Newbern Spectator that a British vessel had passed out of
Beaufort harbor in thirty-five minutes in *"twenty-three feet
of water on the bar!"* The writer deplored the neglect of a
great railway effort to utilize this great port. On May
12th, the Raleigh and Gaston road made an announcement
more notable than that of a train to Portsmouth, namely,
that trains were now running from Littleton in Warren
County, over the Gaston bridge and to Petersburg, connecting with trains by way of Richmond and Washington for
New York, the "Great Mail Route," in 39 hours—or 48 in-

---

[1] The Raleigh *Standard*, Democrat, says on December 4, 1839, that a
Whig caucus, during this Assembly of '38–'39, agreed on Mr. Morehead as the
next candidate for Governor, and that "everybody knows it." No public expression of it occurred, however, until the following August at Greensboro.

cluding all stops. Travellers from Greensboro and the west are assured that this line lands them in Washington 24 hours ahead of any other line. Then about June 1st, a writer in the *Fayetteville Observer,* who avows his belief that Wilmington should be made the importing center of the State and that a railroad should be built from Fayetteville to the west, calls for a "commercial and agricultural" convention at Greensboro on July 4th next. Thereupon, on June 12th, the *Raleigh Register* notes that *The Carolina Watchman* describes a considerable public sentiment in the west in favor of extending the Raleigh and Gaston from Raleigh westward. By June 18th, Wilmington had had a meeting to promote it and called upon Raleigh, Newbern, Halifax, Fayetteville, Salisbury and all the other leading towns to cooperate. *The Wilmington Advertiser* taunts the *Raleigh Register* with hesitation which Editor Gales is compelled to deny, but qualify, in favor of certain "local" predilections, well understood; but, on June 25th, he calls a meeting to forward it. Then *The Western Carolinian* presents some inviting manufacturing statistics of great moment to railroads to the west: Cotton factories now actually in operation number practically a dozen, nearly all in the west, namely (passing by the oldest one at Tar River falls in Edgecombe county), one near Lincolnton owned by John Hoke; one at Fayetteville owned by Mr. Mallet; and another there owned by Benbow & Company; one in Greensboro, steam power, owned by Mr. Humphreys; one at Milton owned by a company; one at Mocksville owned by Thomas McNeely; one or more in Orange county owned by companies; one at Salem, steam-power, owned by a company; one in Randolph owned by a company, and one at Lexington, Davidson county, owned by a company. Besides there are over a half-dozen more now building—all in the west; one at Rockfish, near Fayetteville, owned by a company; one in Richmond county owned by a company; one near Leaksville, on Dan river, a stone building, owned by John M. Morehead, Esq.; one in Surry county, on Hunting Creek, owned by Mr. Douthet; one in Montgomery county owned by a company; and one, ten miles northeast of

A GEORGIA TRAIN OF 1838
From a five-dollar State bank bill

Salisbury, owned by Fisher and Lemly. There were rumors
of three or four others projected. Three years before great
quantities of cotton yarn came from the north; now, not
only did "not a hank" come in, but North Carolina was
already beginning to ship out, even to New York; and undoubtedly coarse cotton fabrics would soon rival the north.

And then came the Greensboro Convention on July 4th,
with Governor Dudley presiding. Again they covered up
the word "transportation" with "Internal Improvement."
Wilmington, Fayetteville, Guilford, Chatham, Randolph,
Davie, *Salisbury,* Lexington, *Hillsboro,* and Rockingham—
those in *italics* being towns—were represented, Mr. Morehead being one of the Guilford delegation, the strongest
present. It is notable that Governor Dudley did not put
Mr. Morehead on one committee, and that he advocated
the Fayetteville terminus. It is notable that to the Governor's general committee was assigned the canvassing of the
best route for the "Central Railroad." The only specific
thing decided upon, however, was a Raleigh Convention
for the second Monday in December next.

Contemporary with this event was the announcement
that Philadelphia banks would resume specie payment on
August 1st; and that the Democrats finally decided to put
up a candidate for Governor, Ex-Governor John Branch;
but it was done with so little enthusiasm that the result was
a foregone conclusion. Governor Dudley was good enough
for the east, even if he was a Whig. For, under his inspiration, Wilmington was making tremendous efforts to
make herself the acknowledged commercial center of the
state. They showed that Wilmington's total outgoing tonnage surpassed even Norfolk by about 5000 tons; that
North Carolina's entered tonnage was nearly 5000 above
Virginia; and that Wilmington owned more tonnage than
Richmond, Petersburg or Edenton by about 2000 above the
highest, Richmond. And in August, the Railroad President Governor of Wilmington was re-elected by the tremendous majority of 17,041 votes! Wilmington stock
was rising and her two wings were Whigs and Railroads,
with a powerful rudder named East; but there was a very

evident apprehension that Guilford county was liable to
puncture the aeroplane's gas tank—to use a figure not, of
course, current then; and that one never could tell what
Raleigh might do.   In October the Raleigh and Gaston
people were trying to borrow money in New York to complete their road; and they also announced that their Raleigh
and Columbia road had enough subscriptions to get a charter.   *The Greensboro Patriot* at the same time announced
that place's purpose to establish a bank, and Fayetteville
was to put in the same town a branch bank.   In November
"Mentor" in the *Raleigh Standard,* Democrat, fought the
Columbia road idea, in favor of Wilmington, of course,
while *"Rip Van Winkle,"* in the *Register,* fought him, and
incidentally dropped these illuminating sentences: "To the
West," said "Van Winkle," "this matter presents itself with
peculiar force, and if they do not arouse themselves at this
attempt, by a sectional interest to force them into sectional
measures, *it may be too late.*   They have been trifled with
long enough, and it is time their hitherto neglected claims
should be listened to and complied with; and I hope every
county west of Raleigh will be fully represented in the proposed Internal Improvement Convention, about to be holden
in this place."

As that meeting was to occur during the Assembly, it
was a comforting fact that that body had a comfortable
Whig majority: "We hail the triumph of the Whigs," wrote
Editor Gales of the *Register* on December 3 [1838], "as the
triumph of Republican principles, as the prostration of men
who have made themselves odious by their persecution,
their exclusiveness, and their political imbecility."   He be-
spoke Whig generosity to the foe, however.   Seven days
later, the 10th, thirty-eight counties' delegates—some counties like Cumberland, Beaufort, Guilford, Randolph, Wake
and Wayne having as many as a dozen members—gathered
at the Methodist Church in Raleigh as successor to the
Greensboro Convention—but Mr. Morehead was not one
of them.   It was an able convention, compared favorably
with that of 1833, and Hon. Romulus M. Saunders was
chosen President.   Needless to say every section asked for

its favorite water or land transportation, all of which were
referred to a general committee of thirteen, which reduced
them to a minimum and adopted a program of liberal state
aid to the two railroads in process of construction—the Wilmington road and the Gaston—and the projected enterprises: the Fayetteville-Western, the Nags Head Inlet,
Beaufort Harbor to somewhere on the Wilmington-Weldon
(incidentally praising the harbor as unrivalled, as was
shown by its use in the late war of '12), which would be
called major projects, and such minor ones as a Raleigh-
Fayetteville, and a Waynesboro(Goldsboro)-Raleigh railroad and a Neuse river improvement above Newbern.
Various efforts to change this were made, among them to
the first class, a State-built turnpike to Greensboro, but this
last was reduced to a survey. The financial side was taken
up and a loan of $3,000,000 was recommended to carry out
the plan, and a committee ordered to present the matter
to the Whig Assembly. If Mr. Morehead balanced his
national Whig principles against this local Eastern program, as he of course did, the explanation of his absence
from this Convention is not far to seek. The east had
actually captured the Whig organization through the course
of Governor Dudley's Wilmington-Fayetteville and western
program, with an Albemarle-Nags Head Inlet and Beaufort
Harbor-Raleigh bait! It remained to see what the Whig
Assembly would do with it. That can be told in few words:
Nothing; except the loan to the Raleigh & Gaston Railroad
—a loan, because its state stock-holders were made liable.
The redeeming feature of the Whig Assembly, however,
was its presentation to the School districts of a constructive
common school program for their acceptance, which seems
to have been largely the work of President Swain of the
University.

An incident occurred before the Assembly adjourned
which showed the Democratic, or Van Buren party, anticipating the logical next step by Guilford county, began the
attack on Senator James T. Morehead. They found in the
Quaker Memorial against slavery, which was presented
by request by Senator James T. Morehead of Greensboro,

a morsel of great sweetness, and in this difficult fight against the Senator's brother's undoubted candidacy for Governor they made continual use of it.   In defending both Moreheads *The Greensborough Patriot* of February 18, 1839, described the authors of the Memorial: "in much the larger portions of the State the peculiarities of the Society of Friends are not understood, nor even known.   Their principal settlement is in this county, and we are well acquainted with their manners, habits and modes of thinking.[1] They are a peculiarly quiet, unobtrusive, orderly and intelligent people, and have their distinctive traits, which they have sustained for ages.   They refuse the fashionable modes of speech and dress; support their own poor; celebrate their own matrimonial rites according to the simple forms of their own society only; pay particular regard to the rights and influence of women; are forbidden in their discipline to hold public office; interfere with the rights of no person, and refuse to wage war, even in self defense.   They own no slaves.   They are opposed to slavery.   To use a phrase of their own—they bear a continual testimony against it. Yet they are not Abolitionists, in the sense in which the term is taken in the South.   They would be as far from encouraging disobedience or rebellion among slaves, or from consenting to their sudden and unprepared liberation, as the most devoted advocates of 'Southern rights.'   They have been in the habit of petitioning the legislature for the 'termination of slavery,' for a series of years past.   The representatives of the people of Guilford have uniformly presented their memorials, knowing at the time that their prayer would be utterly fruitless—unheeded—forgotten— yet they discharged their 'bounden duty' to a respectable part of the constituency.   Judge Dick (who, before he accepted the judicial bench, was the champion of the Van Buren party in this county), when a representative, presented these memorials—and would, we doubt not, do so again under the same circumstances."   This indicated the

---

[1] They centered about "New Garden," now Guilford College, the seat of the Quaker institution of that name about a half dozen miles west of Greensboro, as it is now spelled.

feeling on every hand that Guilford was to furnish the
next gubernatorial candidate; for with all the Whig Congressional conventions during the spring, no candidate for
Governor was named.

This was due in some measure to the Whig fight for
Congressional seats, which was most successful; but the
first to enter the gubernatorial field was, as before, old
Guilford county. She even anticipated the call for a state
convention for that purpose. At her county Whig convention on August 20, 1839, it was *"Resolved,* that we
esteem our fellow-citizen, John M. Morehead, Esq., as a
republican in manners, in conduct and principle; a gentleman and citizen of pure and elevated character—a statesman of eminently practical mind, and of enlarged and liberal
views of public policy—a patriot devoted to the welfare of
the State, and identified in all his interests with the honor
and prosperity of North Carolina; and that we recommend
him to that convention and to the people of the State as in
every way worthy to be her *Chief Magistrate,"* while they
yielded to the decision of the convention.[1]

Orange county followed. Moore county, on the 31st,
said: "He is a patriot and statesman of generous and enlarged views of public policy, and closely associated in all
his interests, with the honor and prosperity of North
Carolina," and so they recommended him to the coming
convention. Cumberland Whigs joined with them. Whigs
of Surry followed. The *Newbern Spectator* said the East
was falling in line: "Mr. Morehead has a large stake in the
welfare and prosperity of the State. *Its interests are his.*
He owns many slaves, is deeply embarked in manufacturing
and mining, and possesses talents and acquirements fully
adequate to the duties of the high station to which the
people seem inclined to call him. He is besides, *a Western
man,* and justice demands that we support a gentleman of
that section, in reciprocation of its recent aid in electing
a citizen of the east." Indeed the *Spectator* went so far as
to say the east would be disappointed if Morehead were

---

[1] *The Greensborough Patriot,* 27th Aug., 1839.

not nominated.[1] Stokes County Whigs joined them on October 8th and Caswell on the 1st, and indeed by this time
forty counties had acted. Rockingham, the county of his
boyhood, on the 29th went so far as to speak of him as
"a native of Rockingham, whose plain republican manners,
superior intellect, political honesty and practical talent as a
statesman, eminently qualify him for chief executive of our
State."[2] Then came the State Convention of November
12th, which, "having been inspired with a deep and lively
sense of the eminent practical vigor, sound Republican
principles, unblemished public and private virtues, ardent
patriotism and decided abilities" of Mr. Morehead recommended him to the people of the State. This followed the
recommendation of the committee whose "attention has been
forciby engaged by the practical energy, the sound Republican principles, the distinguished intellectual vigor, and
fervid patriotism which are embraced in the character of
our cherished fellow-citizen, John M. Morehead of the
county of Guilford. Born, reared and educated among the
honest yeomanry of North Carolina, all his heartfelt sympathies are with the people of this State. Severely disciplined by a constant performance of the practical business
of life, possessed of enlarged and liberal views of the policy
of the State, and having inflexibly adhered to the principles
of the republican creed of faith in every political emer-
gency which has thus far passed over the State, we
recognize in John M. Morehead a citizen in every view of
his character, whom we deem eminently acceptable to the
people of North Carolina as a candidate for the office of
Governor of the State."[3]

---

[1] *The Greensborough Patriot,* 8th Oct., 1839.
[2] *Ibid.,* 12th Nov., 1839.
[3] Both the Rockingham and State Whigs of course made the natural error
of not knowing that he was two years old when he came to that county, and was
born in Pittsylvania County, Va. Indeed the North Carolina "wish, father to
:he thought," to have his birthplace in the Old North State has its adherents
even to this day, and even among some of his relatives! Unfortunately, unlike
Homer, the facts place him in Virginia by birth.
  As the Raleigh *Standard,* Democrat, of December 9, 1835, says, no other
candidate was offered, although it intimates that some would liked to have been.
It is in form of innuendo, however. *The Star,* a Raleigh Whig paper, of 11th
December, '39, says Mr. Morehead was spoken of as far back as the Legislature of November, 1838, because of universal western enthusiasm for him and
this was what decided the Raleigh convention—namely that no one else would
satisfy the west.

Mr. Morehead was notified by letter dated November 13th, and on the 25th he penned his letter of acceptance as follows: "Gentlemen: Your communication of the 13th instant has been duly received, announcing to me, that the Convention of Delegates of the Whig party, assembled in the City of Raleigh on the 12th inst., has unanimously selected me as the Candidate of the Whig party for Governor of the State, at the ensuing election.

"This flattering testimonial of respect, emanating from so respectable a source as that Convention, does not fail to impress me with a lively sense of the honor done me by that body; and, if there were no other reasons to influence my course, the respect I have for the wise heads, the pure hearts, and the well-established Republican principles of those who composed that Convention, would make me hesitate long before I would gainsay their wishes.

"But I know I shall be pardoned by that Convention, when I say that considerations, higher than those already suggested, combine in making up the decision to which I have come.

"I view the Convention as emanating directly from the people, and as reflecting *their* wishes and *their* will. They have found themselves grossly deceived by those in whom they heretofore placed confidence. They were promised everything, *every thing,* that the simplicity, purity, honesty and economy of our Republican Institutions could require. Instead of finding those pledges fairly redeemed, they have witnessed with mortification and regret, the Federal Executive, repeatedly endeavoring to fix upon them the complicated machinery of his Sub-Treasury and that, too, after they have repudiated his notions and rejected his scheme. From manifestations in the late Presidential Tour, we may again expect the wishes of the people to be set at defiance, and another attempt made to force this scheme upon them.

"If this attempt is again made, the issue will be fairly made up between the President and the People—to say whether HE or THEY shall govern.

"On the one hand we shall behold the President and his official myrmidons, greedy for the onset, with their banner unfurled, bearing the insulting inscription—'*To the Victors belong the Spoils*'—on the other, we shall see the People—*Freemen*—the sons of the Whigs of the Revolution, who knew no 'Victors' and who offered no 'Spoils,' but the havoc committed upon invading legions.

"If the same spirit now burns in the bosom of the sons, that animated the sires, the issue cannot be doubtful. The star-spangled banner will be thrown to the breeze, and the glorious motto—'*E Pluribus Unum*'—shall float in triumph; and the minions of power and of corruption will vanish before the blazing indignation of an injured people, like the morning mists before a glorious sun.

"The People were promised by the last administration, in the footsteps of which the present was to tread, the cleansing of the 'Augean stable,' and the same purity that characterized the purer days of the Republic. In the days of Washington, Jefferson and Madison qualifications for office were honesty and capacity. 'Is he honest?' 'Is he capable?'—and office-holders were strictly enjoined from becoming political partisans, and from interfering in elections. In the present day, behold the melancholy contrast! The qualifications now are, if we judge by the result, unquestionable dishonesty, utter incapacity to discharge the duties of the office, but extraordinary capacity to serve 'the Party;' entire unwillingness to pay the people their money, but great readiness to pay the levies made upon salaries and embezzlements for the support of 'the Party.'

"Posterity will certainly do the present Administration the justice to say, that no prior one has manifested more signal ability in the selection of its officers for the purposes of *the office,* than the present has manifested in the selection of its officers for the purposes of *the party.* And if there be any doubt upon this question, reference to the extraordinary abstractions from the Treasury, and to the nuisances committed in most civil communities by official political brawlers, will certainly remove that doubt.

"The People were promised honesty and strict accountability from the Officers of Government; and by way of earnest in redemption of that pledge, one Tobias Wat-

kins, a defaulter of some $4000 under the Administration
of Mr. Adams, was ferreted out, hunted down and incar-
cerated; and the people well hoped that all other public
swindlers would be dealt with in like manner.

"They have been told again and again, 'by Authority,'
that 'all was well'—that the Government was greatly
blessed in the ability and faithfulness of its Public Officers;
but recent investigations have brought to light corruption,
dishonesty, and official dereliction, that are truly startling
and alarming. And the people, to their sorrow, have learned
that a falsehood 'by Authority' is more pernicious to
their interests, than a falsehood 'without Authority.' And
they verily believe, if they shall ever be so fortunate as to
have another Administration, that will bring defaulters to
justice, all the Penitentiaries attached to the Sub-Treasury
Bill will not hold the Tobiases that will then be discovered.

"Economy is a word that seems to have been stricken
from the nomenclature of the present Administration. It
has become a bye-word and a jest. The Expenditures of
the Government, increased from thirteen to thirty odd
millions, show what the party in power mean by the word.
An empty Treasury and a bankrupt Government tell the
people how grossly they have been deceived.

"The people are at length awakened from their lethargy
and security, and aroused to their danger. They no longer
regard glossy messages and partizan demagogues. They
have have determined to think and act for themselves.
They are moving in their primary Assemblies. They
are determined, by united action, to put an end to
that misrule, which has bankrupted the Government, corrupted its Officers and brought universal distress upon
every class of the community, except embezzling Office-
holders.

"Your Convention was the offspring of that determination; and no person can unite with the people more
heartily than I do 'in the great struggle' for correct principles, which the Whigs are now endeavoring to maintain.

"At no period of my life, could this call have been made
with more inconvenience to myself, than the present; but

as it is the wish of the people that I shall be their Candidate, I 'accept the nomination.' And, for this expression of their kind consideration, I pledge them whatever of ability and of zeal I possess, in the noble cause in which we have embarked.

"Before closing this communication, I desire to submit a few remarks in relation to two subjects in which North Carolina has much at stake. I allude to the Public Lands, and to the subject of Abolition.

"North Carolina ceded to the United States a large Territory. She is equally interested, with the other States, in all the Public Lands. Her interest in these Lands is worth millions upon millions; and if she could receive her share of the proceeds of those Lands, every poor child of the State could be educated, and every work of Internal Improvement successfully prosecuted. The President has left us nothing to hope from that quarter, and it remains for the people to say whether *his will* shall govern them, or *their will* shall make him cease to govern—whether HE shall be sovereign, or THEY shall be sovereign. As a North Carolinian, I will never consent to surrender this ample patrimony of our old North State.

"On this subject of our domestic institution of Slavery, I should suppose there could be but one opinion in the South, among men who have capacity to think.

"The emancipation of our slaves among us would lead to consequences too direful for contemplation. And no man will meet with more uncompromising hostility, than I will, the very first fanatical or unconstitutional aggression made upon this institution, guaranteed to us by our Federal Compact.

"The people's attention should be drawn to the fact, that some rickety understandings, and hypocritical politicians, are continually conjuring up the awful charge of a union between the Abolitionists and the Whigs—not because they have such apprehension, but to prevent the discovery of an actual union and cooperation of the Abolitionists with the present Administration, ever since they received that withering rebuke at the hands of Mr. Clay.

"For weal, or for woe, my destiny is fixed in North Carolina—my prospects for future prosperity are attached to her soil—and whatever I now have, or ever expect to have, will be protected by her institutions.

"For your kind expressions of regard towards me, accept, gentlemen, individually, my sincere thanks, and for the distinguished honor done me by your Convention, accept collectively, and in their behalf, the profound acknowledgment of your most obt. serv't

"John M. Morehead."

There was an absolutely clear expression on every national subject for which the Whigs and Mr. Morehead stood. His attitude on slavery, at least on its abolition, could not be more explicit. His record as to free negroes voting had been unequivocally and vigorously in favor of it, as it had been for the education of the negro. He had slaves; but he had, like his brother, and Democratic representatives like Judge John M. Dick of Greensboro, presented the usual Quaker memorials against slavery, when requested by that part of his constituency. Like multitudes of Democrats, as well as Whigs, Mr. Morehead did not believe in slavery; but it was a system entwined in our institutions, even in the national constitution; therefore, he was likewise neither for wholesale abolition. In short, he was for the constitutions of state and nation and American institutions as they were and had been from the beginning, and considering slavery a curse to the American people, but an existing fact. Such a position was not to be understood, however, either by defenders or by attackers of slavery; the proslavery Southerner or the Abolitionist Northerner; and he was not the only leader who was destined to be misunderstood; who was to hold to the constitution until it should be properly amended. Such men, however, were liable to be between the hammer of the Abolitionist and the anvil of the large Slave-holders; those far away from slaves, but mad for their freedom, and those in the midst of a slave population, often larger than their own, and fearful of a holocaust—an uncontrolled Frankenstein. Mr. Morehead held the same position as the man who, as President, refused to

touch slavery so long as the constitution was preserved;
and who, as all students of history now know, was himself
between the same hammer and anvil: between those who
were able to call the constitution a league with the Devil and
a covenant with Hell, and those who so far agreed with them
as to be ready to join in breaking it. On these points his
position was unmistakable. That he was for a national regulatory bank was no less certain; his language was too vivid
on that point to be misunderstood, as it was on the personal
government of Jacksons and Van Burens.

On the state issues, however, there was a possibility of
his being misunderstood. He was a western man, to be
sure; but he was not a man merely for the west. Localism,
or sectionalism, had prevailed in North Carolina since the
death of Murphy and President Caldwell; even a Gaston
was unable wholly to cast off its shackles, and a Swain stood
helpless against it. Mr. Morehead's first entry into the
arena of the commonwealth was as a disciple of Murphy,
and his second as an advocate of the measures proposed by
"Carleton," the pseudonym of President Caldwell. He
carried their banners boldly—so boldly indeed that he had
been a marked man ever since. Theirs was not a benumb-
ing localism or sectionalism, but a statemanship for the
whole commonwealth; and not merely for the whole, as
superior to a part; but for the organic nature and stature
of a state with a unifying development. The vision of a
Murphy and a Caldwell seemed to have been forgotten in
the sectional struggle for dominance, or the desperate effort to staunch the flow of Carolina's commercial blood into
the arteries of neighboring states. There was an instinct
among some of the people that this builder of factories,
opener of mines, developer of farms, advocate of justice,
friend of both races, and creator of a school of higher education for women was the man to turn to at this juncture.

Three weeks after the new Whig candidate for Governor penned his letter of acceptance, and white common
schools were preparing to open all over North Carolina, Mr.
Morehead, on December 16th, issued an announcement,
which appeared first in the *Patriot,* that "Edgeworth

School," as he then called it, would open for the first time on January 1, 1840, with Dr. S. P. Weir as Principal and Miss M. A. Hoye, late of Princeton, vice-Principal, former Principal of the "Greensborough Female Academy." It was designed to be a school of higher education for young women throughout the South, and was soon destined to have pupils from West Virginia to Texas. In an announcement of 29th October, 1839, he says the Edgeworth grounds contain about twenty acres adjacent to his own residence, and that he designs it to be "a school of the first class—and it shall be such—or it will be abandoned."

When "Edgeworth School" had been in operation about a month, the editor of the *Patriot* had the following to say of it—the only description of the interior known. "The building occupies a retired, though not remote situation, on a gentle rise of ground, at the western part of the village. It is of brick, fifty-six feet long by thirty-eight in width; two stories, with a basement and attic; covered with tin. The cornices, doorways, and attic windows (which latter stand out to the view with good effect) being finished in a chaste and uniform style of architecture—a stately and feminine appearance is imparted, which strikes the passer-by as peculiarly appropriate. The interior is arranged and fitted up in a style of neatness and elegance, and with a view to the health, convenience and comfort of the pupils. Each of the principal stories is divided by a spacious passage, containing a flight of stairs. On the left, as one enters from the street, are the recitation rooms; and on the right, rooms of the same size, yet having large folding doors between them, which, when thrown open, give to both apartments the advantage of a spacious hall. The attic story is occupied as a dormitory, and its spacious dimensions, and airy situation adapt it well to its purpose. Connected with the main building, is a smaller one, containing an apartment for the sick, a dining room, and other apartments necessary for a domestic establishment. When the extensive grounds surrounding the School shall be enclosed, and improved as contemplated, by the laying out of walks, and pruning the native growth—it will make a temporary *home* for the pupil,

the recollection of which will be called up with pleasure in
all her after life." He then adds: "Success to it!—success
to the Caldwell Institute!—Success to the contemplated Female Collegiate Institute! and last, *but not least,* success to
Common Schools in our County and our State!" This might
be considered an omen of a new period to be ushered in by
the new State leader, candidate for its highest office, a
Whig—and much more.

X

A

WHIG LEADER AND GOVERNOR

AND

THE FIRST RAILWAYS

1840

The newly nominated Governor, John Motley Morehead, the candidate of the Whig west, was not a member of the Harrisburg Convention, or more serious effort would have been made to nominate Senator Henry Clay of Kentucky instead of General Harrison and John Tyler of Virginia, at the December meeting, 1839. And he had not long to wait to know whom the Democrats would name to join him in the first state canvass in the history of the commonwealth, like had already been begun in Tennessee; for in January his rival to be, Hon. Romulus Mitchell Saunders of Caswell county, also accepted a nomination. Judge Saunders should have been a Whig, as he studied law under Judge Hugh L. White of the Tennessee Supreme Court. He was five years older than Mr. Morehead and was about that length of time ahead of him in public life in both houses of the Assembly and in Congress. He was Attorney General in 1828, but on his appointment in 1833 by President Jackson to the French Claims Commission, resigned; while on his completion of that service in 1835 he became a Judge of the Superior Court. He therefore came into the campaign with great prestige, and the forthcoming canvass was bound to be a most remarkable contest.

While preparations were making for entering upon it, however, some great events were introductory and destined to be a considerable aid to it as well. These were the completion of North Carolina's first two railroads in March, when the first train passed over the whole Wilmington and Weldon Railroad on the 7th of that month.[1] Closely following this event, on the 21st of that same month, the first train from the north over the Raleigh and Gaston Railroad steamed into the capital, to rival in interest the little "Experimental Railroad" to the quarries which had served so well to convince the state of the feasibility of these larger ones. The *Raleigh Register* of 24th March, thus celebrates it:

"Phizzz—zzz—zzz"

"This is as near as we can come in type towards expressing the strange sound which greeted the ears of the assembled population of our city on Saturday evening last. About 6 oclock of that day, the first steam locomotive that ever snorted amongst the hills of Crabtree reached the limits of our city and was enthusiastically welcomed with every demonstration of joy. The bells rang, the artillery roared and the people cheered. *Huzza!* Huzza!! HUZZA!!! The Raleigh and Gaston Railroad is completed and no mistake. The passenger cars are expected here tonight, and we jolly Cits can now amuse ourselves with Railroad incidents until the Assembly meets. 'Last bell, Sir, last bell! Hurry, Sir; hurry, Ma'am!'— 'Where's my trunk? I carn't go till I see my trunk—a round top, kivered with flowered paper.' 'All safe, Ma'am!—all in the baggage car.' Phizz-zzz-zzz — ding, dong, bell — ding, dong, bell. 'Make haste, make haste!' 'Oh my! Mr. Zeigenfuss, I've dropped my bag!' 'Get in, Ma'am!' 'Gracious, you've almost jerked my calash off my head.' 'Please Mr. Zig'— Phizz — clack-clack-clack — lack-lack-lack—ack-ack-ack—ck-ck-ck—K-K-K—*Away they go!*

"Magnificent enterprise! We have now actual demonstration of *that*, which no man would have believed thirty years ago to be within the compass of human power. Truly has it been said, that the last few years have unfolded more

---

[1] The last nail was driven at 12.00 noon and the first train from Wilmington reached Weldon a 9 P. M. The road was 160¾ miles long, the longest road then in all the world. For a town of but 3500 people, Wilmington's achievement was most remarkable.

that is novel, vast and wonderful, than the whole eighteen
centuries of the Christian era.

"The Raleigh and Gaston Railroad is 86 miles in length,
and has been constructed altogether by individual stockholders, the State having uniformly declined embarking in
the enterprise.   More than usual difficulties have presented
themselves in the progress of the work, over and above the
natural obstacles, but they have all vanished before a determined purpose and never-tiring energy.   The whole line
is now finished, is said to be admirably built, and reflects
high credit on the President, Engineer, Assistants, and indeed, all connected with its construction.   We hail the
rumbling of the first locomotive as the glad omen of future
prosperity to our city and country, and feel that we shall
not be disappointed."[1]

It was natural that Wilmington and Raleigh should
formally celebrate these events, and the President, Dudley,
should invite his successor to join them at the former city
on April 15th.   Mr. Morehead would have entered upon
his campaign sooner had it not been for a critical illness of
his wife, but when the crisis was passed, she insisted that he
proceed on his duty.   He had accepted the Wilmington invitation and was speaking on April 7th, at Germanton, in
Stokes county, where he himself was temporarily ill.   By
the 15th, when he was at Wilmington he had issued the
following eastern itinerary: 1. Waynesboro, the 18th; 2.
Kinston, 20th; 3. Trenton, 21st; 4. Newbern, 23rd; 5.
Washington, 27th; 6. Halifax, 30th; 7. Jackson, May 1st;
8. Edenton, May 4th; 9. Hartford, 6th; 10. Elizabeth City,
7th; 11. Camden C. H., 8th; 12. Currituck C. H., 9th; 13.
Windsor, 12th; 14. Williamston, 13th; 15. Nashville, 16th;
16. Louisburg, 18th; 17. Oxford, 20th; and Raleigh, May
22nd.   The address at Wilmington in connection with the

---

[1] *Raleigh Register,* March 24, 1840.   The Wilmington & Weldon road was
161 miles long and at their celebration which began on the 9th and lasted several days a gun was fired for each mile.   Water from the Roanoke, Tar and
Neuse Rivers were brought and formally mixed and Wilmington was elabor-
ately illuminated at night.   This was then the longest completed road in the
world.   The Raleigh and Gaston road had four engines, its largest one, "Tor-
nado," was made in Richmond, weighed 6½ tons and hauled 30 loaded cars.
The Raleigh people celebrated, in a splendid three-day session, both the
completion of their railroad and the new capitol, beginning on June 10, 1840.

celebration was not replied to by Judge Saunders, who had
sent his regrets; but it became a most auspicious opening
of the Whig campaign.

One of the best contemporary pictures of the Whig
gubernatorial candidate, was that of a correspondent who
witnessed the forensic battle between Judge Saunders, his
Democratic rival, and himself at Snow Hill in Greene
county on May 14, 1840. "This has been a great day for
Snow Hill," he writes. "Never since the days of the
Giants, have our white sand-banks been the arena of so
great intellectual war, as we have witnessed today." Then
describing how the two rivals came in after a 56-mile ride,
while the Presidential-Elector, James W. Bryan, was speaking, he shows Mr. Morehead opening the debate, which
"continued until candle-light." "As a Whig," the correspondent explains, "I may be pardoned for believing that
Mr. Morehead bore away the palm. His broad good-
humored countenance, lighted up with perfect good humor,
is occasionally irresistible. He has winning ways to make
men love him. The strength and energy and unwavering
directness with which he marches up to, and attacks the
positions of his adversary, levelling stroke after stroke in
precisely the right place, tell with tremendous effect. The
caution and care with which he fortifies his own positions,
make it no easy matter for him to be out-generalled. The
indignant denunciations which he pours out upon the powers
that be, for their mal-practices, falling upon minds, believing
or strongly *suspecting* them to be true, uttered with an air
of honest scorn, which his hearers are convinced cannot be
assumed, create an impression hard to be removed. But
he who supposes that General Saunders is but a play-thing
for Mr. Morehead, or for anybody else; he who thinks he
cannot and does not ably defend himself, have mistaken the
man. Some parts of his speech were truly eloquent, and
worthy of a better cause; and none will more cheerfully
say so than the Whigs. In his youthful days, Gen. S. was
a patriotic Whig, and so deeply imbued with good feelings,
that even his connection with this blighting administration
has not been able entirely to destroy them. They occasion-

ally burst out even now, and, like the verdant spots in the desert, are welcomed with heart-felt pleasure in proportion as they are unexpected and rare. The debate was conducted with fairness—and, with a single exception, with courtesy and kindness, that exception, I know, a cause of regret to both of those gentlemen, as it is to their friends. 'It was a hasty spark, and soon was cool again.'

"On one subject, however, Gen. Saunders did not give satisfaction, even to his friends. Mr. Morehead stated that he had heretofore called on his competitor to say what were his views in relation to the Public Lands, and that he had declined to give them. He today called emphatically for his opinion on the subject, but, like the spirits from the vasty deep, they would not come. He did not and would not, though repeatedly asked to do so, say *one word* about the matter, only 'that he *had not time* to talk about it.'

"If we can judge from the deportment of the two competitors, the Whig cause must succeed. Mr. Morehead is certainly buoyant with hope. General Saunders *may* hope, too, but if he does not carry about him a somewhat dejected air, there is no truth in Physiognomy.'"[1]

Of Mr. Morehead, *The Carolina Watchman* had recently said: "There are few men who can combine so many popular qualities as John M. Morehead. Highly gifted by nature, he has acquired much scientific and practical information. With an eloquence, strong, clear and convincing, he combines the rare qualities of genuine wit. He is honorable to the 'minutest tittle—brave, manly, generous and affable. His morality has never been questioned. His social qualities would be a hindrance to almost anyone else in their march through life, but no blandishment of pleasure —no allurement of ease can stay his progress when business or duty calls. He is such a man as we delight to honor, and such a one as the people are always willing to advance. But such as he is, it must be said to his honor, he has made himself. He was once a poor boy on the banks of the Dan River, working to get a little money to enable him to go to

---

[1] *The Raleigh Register*, May 19, 1840.

a Latin school. Now he would confer distinction on the office for which he is presented to the public. We, therefore, say that in this, as well as in many other things, the Convention has done well.'" Among other things said of him were the following: "Without fear and without reproach;" "carries his recommendation in his countenance;" "perfect gentleman, able civilian and sound politician;" "shook hands with the unwashed;" "the plow-boy of Guilford," and the like.

Without attempting to follow the details of the canvass, a few instances may be used as illustrations:

The gubernatorial canvass in Granville county seat, Oxford, May 20, 1840, is thus described: "The discussion of the candidates lasted till night. We were all delighted beyond our calculations. Judge Saunders opened the debate, spoke three hours and a half, and delivered a speech that did him much credit; for a Van Buren man, it was candid and open. We were somewhat uneasy, and began to think his ingenuity could not be successfully answered. But, soon after Mr. Morehead rose to reply, we found our fears were groundless. His speech was admitted, on all hands, to equal, if it did not surpass any speech ever delivered here. At times, his audience were enchained by his eloquence, and then again amused, beyond expression by the introduction of humorous caricatures of the Powers that be. In his replies to some of the remarks of Judge Saunders, he was very caustic and severe, which produced some interruption by the Judge. But nothing was gained by it, as Morehead's facts were so strong, and illustrated by so much good temper and good humor, that they could not be successfully resisted."[2]

A little later, on Friday, May 22, 1840, they met at the capital city and spoke in the old Baptist Church. Here "Mr. Morehead opened the discussion," says the editor of the *Register*, "and exposed in a masterly manner the corruptions and extravagances of the Administration—the dangerous features of the plan reported by the Secretary of

---

[1] March, 1840.
[2] *Raleigh Register,* 26th May, 1840.

War, for establishing a *Standing Army*—which plan, obnoxious as it was, received the approbation of the President. He pronounced it a fit instrument to make slaves of us all—particularly when united with the Sub-Treasury—a measure which struck at the very root of our credit system—reducing all prices to a specie standard, and enabling the President, by an increase of his already immense patronage, to exercise an improper and corrupting influence over the elections. He exposed with great ability the malfeasance of the Secretary of the Treasury in permitting defaulters to continue in office, after the heaviest defalcations, in some instances, without even requiring bond for the security of the public revenue. He replied in the most indignant terms, to the charge of being an Abolitionist, which was brought against him by a certain leader of the Van Buren party, in a meeting held in this place a short time after his nomination, and reminding 'the Party' that the same process by which this *Orator* sought to prove him an Abolitionist, would fix it on nearly all their own leaders in the Convention. Messrs. Branch (who was run for Governor by the Van Buren Party), Marsteller (Collector of the Port of Wilmington), Daniel (Judge of the Supreme Court), Parker (late Van Buren elector), Quinn, Graves, Morris (run by 'the Party' against Mr. Deberry), Montgomery (Representative of 'the Party' from this District), Kimbrough Jones (who was presiding at the very meeting the *Orator* was addressing), and many others, 'good and true' men to the Administration, gave the same votes that he (Mr. M.) did. Many parts of Mr. Morehead's address were truly eloquent, and frequently his caustic sarcasm and pleasant humor elicited the applause even of those who were opposed to his political principles. We do not recollect ever to have listened to a more powerful and interesting political speech. The open, candid countenance of the speaker, the earnestness of his manner, united with the strength and clearness of his arguments, were calculated to produce conviction on the minds of all who were not blinded by prejudice."

Judge Saunders' speech is then described, after which,

"Mr. Morehead rejoined briefly, when a humorous sparring between the candidates, producing much amusement, concluded the conflict of the day."[1]

In June he began his western itinerary in the county next north of Guilford.

A good description of Mr. Morehead's style in speaking, during the gubernatorial campaign, has come down to us from an "Observer," who happened to hear the two at Wentworth, Rockingham county, the boyhood home of the Whig candidate: "Mr. Morehead is more rapid in his speaking, yet his enunciation is equally distinct and impressive as his opponent's. His language is strong and forcible, and never wanting at his call;—unlike the spirits of Hotspur—the words will 'come at his bidding.' By his great command of language, with the fact of his speaking more rapidly than Mr. Saunders, he is enabled to say much more in a given time. His gestures are better, more varied, and more energetic than his competitor's; and on the whole he is a more interesting speaker: but decidedly his superior in the opposite qualities of pathos and humor. Indeed these last seem to be totally *without* the range of Judge Saunders, whether from choice or necessity, I know not: while Mr. Morehead is peculiarly happy in both. Each of them spoke about three hours. . . . Mr. Morehead made an able reply; in which it appeared, as the Danville Reporter remarked—he had *Morehead,* a *better head*, and a *better* cause, than Judge Saunders. . . . and the *denouement,* when he spoke personally of himself, was truly pathetic. He is, I understand, a native of this county, and resided at this place when, poor and friendless, he commenced the practice of law; and in alluding to this circumstance and other personal circumstances, he could not well have been surpassed. It is said that one 'cannot speak eloquently of *self,*' but in the face of this maxim, I say he was truly eloquent; never were my feelings so completely carried with another's. He conformed, too, to the Horatian precept in the 'Art of Poetry,' *'Si vis me flere, delendum est, primum*

---

[1] *Raleigh Register,* 26th May, 1840.

ipsi tibi,' 'if you would have me weep it behooves you first
to weep.' Mr. Morehead did actually shed tears, and the
sympathetic tears stood in the eyes of many of the audience.

The effect was electric; and I will venture to say there
was scarcely one who did not feel the force of this eloquent
appeal.'"

By the midde of June, the Guilford Tippecanoe Club had
built a portable "log cabin" with "Hard Cider" attachment
and were familiarizing themselves with such songs as the
following, as were all other Whig districts in the state:

"HARRISON AND TYLER FOR THE UNION

AND

"MOREHEAD FOR THE 'OLD NORTH'

('Rosin The Bow')

"Old Rip will fight under this banner,
    With the pluck of a soldier that's true;
He'll not be the hindmost in battle
    With him of old Tippecanoe.

"Old Rip will soon wake from his napping,
    And make every spoiler look blue,
With a hearty hurrah for Jack Tyler
    And a round for old Tippecanoe!

"Old Rip will call at his log cabins,
    And rouse out the voters a few,
Whose thunder will tell next November
    For the hero of Tippecanoe.

"And when he's fixed up in the White House,
    The farmer and patriot true,—
We'll drink in the mug of hard cider,
    The health of old Tippecanoe.

"Then, adieu to your Swartnants and Prices,
    And little leg-trousers, too!
He'll sack every rogue of a spoiler—
    He sacked 'em at Tippecanoe.

"In the halls of our wise legislators,
    To his country he ever proved true;
At Meigs, at the Thames and the Raisin,
    And also at Tippecanoe.

---

[1] *Greensboro Patriot,* 16th June, 1840.

"Then, success to the Son of old Guilford!
    The old Rip, ever faithful and true;
'Old Virginny,' success to thy Tyler!
    And triumph to Tippecanoe!"[1]

Guilford sent a fine delegation on July 4th, to the great
Whig celebration at Salisbury, composed of the Guilford
Tippecanoe Club and the Guilford Guards, who, at 6 A.M.
of the 2nd, with their Log Cabin on wheels and about 2000
people went to Edgeworth School, where the ladies of the
School, headed by Miss Hoye, presented the Club with a
beautiful banner, on one side of which was a Log Cabin
with "Republican Simplicity vs. Loco Foco Arrogance" and
on the reverse side a barrel, presumably of hard cider,
surrounded by a green wreath and thirteen stars, with
"Once more to the rescue, dear friends, once more;" while
the staff was surmounted by a model of a plow. The procession then stopped in front of Dr. Mebane's, where the
Guards were likewise honored with a banner, presented by
Miss Mary Corinna Morehead, as the work of herself, her
sister and Miss M. E. Mebane. It had on a white field an
American Eagle, with a scroll in its beak—"On to Victory,"
and on the reverse the legend "Merit Wins the Prize" enclosed in an elaborate wreath. The presentation address of
both Miss Hoye and Miss Morehead were responded to by
Mr. Ralph Gorrell and Mr. John A. Gilmer, respectively.[2]
The procession contained the Log Cabin, drawn by six white
horses, and the chimney was made to emit smoke, while a
barrel marked "Hard Cider" was strapped on behind and
the cabin draped with deer skins, raccoon skins, buck horns,
and many relics of Guilford battle ground, from which the
poles of which the cabin was made were cut. They also
had a canoe drawn by four white horses. Other Whigs
followed with large blue silken sheet variously inscribed
on one side: "The Sons of Old Guilford," "Against the

---

[1] Clippings in possession of the Misses Caldwell, Greensboro, N. C. "Old
Rip" of course is "Rip Van Winkle," Senator Preston's (S. C.) jeering name
for North Carolina when she refused to endorse nullification.
[2] Greensboro Patriot, 14th July, 1840. These flags are now in possession
of the Greensboro Public Library. Miss Mary Corrina Morehead was but fifteen years old and her sister, presumably Miss Letitia Harper, was two years
older.

Standing Army," "Against the Sub-Treasury," "Against Van Buren;" and on the other "The Sons of Old Guilford," "For Harrison and Tyler," "For John M. Morehead," "For Retrenchment and Reform." This was the spirited part they took in the great Salisbury celebration of about 12,000 people on July 4th. They were helping transform the Van Buren *Baltimore Republican* sneer, that if the Harrisburg nominee, Gen. Harrison, "had a barrel of hard cider and a pension of $2000, he would sit the rest of his life contentedly in a log cabin," into a slogan of victory! And this was a sample of what was occurring in most counties of the nation!

On Mr. Morehead's return from his mountain canvass on July 6th he answered some detractors as to his vote on the laws prohibiting immigration of free negroes into the State, in 1826; he said he voted against the bill first because of the 5th section, but on third reading he succeeded in getting that removed and another Wilmington man secured the removal of three other sections, whereupon he voted for the bill as it was passed into law. Incidentally, he said the Salisbury meeting was the largest meeting ever held in the State and never had such enthusiasm pervaded the Whigs.[1]

Then on August 13th, came the state elections, and, said *The Patriot:* "THE OLD NORTH STATE GREETS THE UNION WITH THE THRILLING FORCES OF TRIUMPH!!" "To the eminently practical mind and eloquence of John M. Morehead, our distinguished Countryman, more than to any other man in the State, is to be attributed this triumph of TRUTH — of PRINCIPLE — of THE PEOPLE!" Guilford went 1742 majority and the state went 8080 majority for him, or 44,508 votes with both houses of the Legislature.[2] Thereupon his old county of Rockingham on September 19th announced a festival in honor of their old-time son

---

[1] *The Patriot*, Aug. 11, 1840.
[2] On the day of his election a second son, James Turner Morehead, named after his brother, and bearing the same name as his distant cousin, Ex-Governor James Turner Morehead of Kentucky, was born.

Governor-elect Morehead stimulated almost every enterprise he came in contact with. Amongst multitudes of enterprises he had a share in was the Greensboro Tannery, owned by Morehead & Willis, who on Sept. 8, 1840, advertised for an expert in that line.

and invited all the surrounding counties' Whigs to join them at Wentworth on the 29th of October. The Caswell County Whigs announced a similar program for October 1st, and the *Patriot* and other papers which had headed their columns with: "For Governor, John M. Morehead. For President, William Henry Harrison. For Vice-President, John Tyler," now headed them only with the Presidential names in preparation for the November election; and on October 5th, the Whigs held a great convention in Raleigh in which delegations from the counties vied each other in its most picturesque banners and emblems. "Whig in 1776 and Whig in 1840" was one of the most common. On the second day of the Convention it was that there was sung a song, written to a favorite concert air of several young ladies who requested it of Judge Gaston, the now famous song of the commonwealth, "The Old North State Forever," which was thereupon first published in *The Raleigh Register:*

"THE OLD NORTH STATE FOREVER

"Carolina! Carolina! Heaven's blessings attend her!
While we live, we will cherish and love and defend her;
Tho' the scorner may sneer at, and witlings defame her,[1]
Our hearts swell with gladness, whenever we name her.
      Hurrah! Hurrah! The Old North State forever!
      Hurrah! Hurrah! The good Old North State!

"Tho' she envies not others their merited glory,
Say, whose name stands the foremost in Liberty's story?
Tho' too true to herself, e'er to crouch to oppression,
Who can yield to just rule more loyal submission?
      Hurrah! &c.

"Plain and artless her sons, but whose doors open faster,
At the knock of the stranger, or the tale of disaster?
How like to the rudeness of their dear native mountains,
With rich ore in their bosoms, and life in their fountains?
      Hurrah! etc.

---

[1] This doubtless referred to the gibe of Preston of South Carolina, who was incensed because North Carolina wouldn't follow his own state in nullifying measures a half dozen years before and called her "Rip Van Winkle."

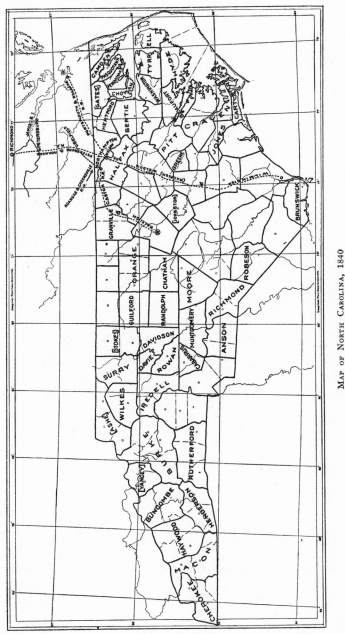

MAP OF NORTH CAROLINA, 1840
Prepared by the author

Showing railroads and Whig vote {
Governor Morehead (named counties), 44,508; opponent (counties not named), 36,428
President Harrison (named counties), 46,628; opponent (counties not named), 34,168
}

"And her daughters, the Queen of the forest resembling,
So graceful, so constant, yet to gentlest breath trembling,
And true lightwood at heart, let the match be applied them,
How they kindle and flame? Oh none know but who've tried them!
    Hurrah! etc.

"Then let all who with us, love the land that we live in,
(As happy a region as on this side of Heaven)
Where Plenty and Freedom, Love and Peace smile before us,
Raise aloud, raise together, the heart-thrilling chorus—
    Hurrah! Hurrah! The Old North State forever!
    Hurrah! Hurrah! The good Old North State!

The big Wentworth festival followed and it was here
that Governor-elect Morehead explained why, although he
had canvassed the state "from the mountains to the sea,"
he did not set out on the campaign as early as he expected
to do, the reason being that she who was dearer than life to
him "was sick unto death;" that as soon as the physician
said she might live, and before she could turn herself in bed,
she said to him: "Go and do your duty to your country!"
Thereupon the people enthusiastically gave three times three
cheers for Mrs. Morehead. Again, like Homer, Rockingham tried to claim him as her native son—which he was, essentially, since he was but a two-years-old babe when his
family moved across the river a few miles into another
state.

The fame of the new Governor-elect spread over the
country and an elegant new steam-boat launched at Cincinnati, was christened "Gov. Morehead" in his honor.[1] At
a dinner to Secretary of the Navy Badger, in Raleigh, Congressman W. P. Mangum's Washington letter was read and
it contained a toast to "John M. Morehead—the able and
patriotic Executive; his friends *will* not forget him—his
enemies *cannot*." To this Governor Morehead responded in
a happy vein, a part of which was prophetic, namely, when
he said he "trusted that he should in his effort to direct
Internal Improvements of the Old North, and to cultivate

---

[1] *Greensboro Patriot,* 8th December, 1840. This may be true; but when
one knows that Kentucky had Governor James T. Morehead from 1834 to 1836,
only four years before, one wonders whether it might not be named for him,
especially as he was slated for the U. S. Senate as colleague of Henry Clay, at
that time.

its intellectual condition, so entitle himself to their respect, that neither *they,* their children, nor their children's children *could forget him.*"[1] And he might have added— "posterity."

Following these festivals came the national election in which "Old Guilford," "The Old Dominion," as it was often called by the Whigs, even increased the Harrison vote to 1886, or 144 more than for Morehead. The Whigs swept the land. At the Assembly in Raleigh, which then met, Mangum and Graham were made national Senators. The electoral college of the State gave all fifteen votes to Harrison, the majority in the commonwealth being 12,594. The new Whig Assembly was the first to meet in the new capitol and the new census appeared, showing North Carolina with far the smallest increase in population since 1790, namely, but 18,469—about one-fifth of that of the preceding census, one-fourth of that of 1820 and nearly the same ratio for those of 1800 and 1810. The increase in slaves was but 455; while there were 22,724 free persons of color. The white population was 487,298 and the slave population 246,917—a total of 756,939.[2] The financial disorganization of the past decade and the attractions of the west accounted for this meager increase; and consequently the great Whig revolution and the great impetus to the railroad movement. This was the condition that accompanied the Guilford county Governor-elect and his family at the close of 1840, when they arrived in Raleigh to locate in the renovated and restored "Government House," at the foot of Fayetteville Street, used for the past decade by the Assembly, since the destruction of the capitol in 1831, and now to again become the Executive Mansion. For the new Whig Assembly. whose session was now nearly over, had moved up to capitol

---

[1] *Greensboro Patriot,* 23rd Nov., 1841. The Governor's salary at this time was $2000 only. The Justices of the Supreme Court received $500 more. The free white population of North Carolina at this time was 484,870 and the free colored population, 22,732, a rather strikingly large number, while the slaves numbered 245,817—practically half of the white number. The total of all was 753,419.

[2] North Carolina's increase was 2%, the same as Virginia, South Carolina and Delaware. Maryland was still lower and Connecticut lower than Maryland. These were lowest of all the states. The great increases were in the west and the greatest in the northwest, Michigan being as high as 590%, altho' Arkansas and Mississippi were very high.

THE GOVERNOR'S MANSION, 1840
at the foot of Fayetteville St., Raleigh
Drawing by Miss Emma Morehead Whitfield, Richmond, Va., from a
photograph in the Hall of History, Raleigh

square in preparation for their new Governor. Nor did the *Greensboro Patriot* think much of the work of that Assembly; but spoke of it as an "honorable, dignified, fidgety, diddling, do-nothing assemblage," whose greatest achievement was adjournment. It did, however, come to the relief of Governor Dudley's railroad with a $300,000 loan and support of the credit of the Raleigh & Gaston; created three new counties in the west; improved the school laws; provided for a State Library, and last, but not least, improved the incorporation act of 1836 of the North Carolina Railroad Company, providing for individual subscription of $1,000,000 to build a railroad from Beaufort Harbor to the Wilmington road presumably at Waynesboro (Goldsboro). The asylum acts—orphan and insane—did not pass. But, all this was under the close of Governor Dudley's term.

The new capitol, the stately Greek temple that still stands stained with over four-score years of time, was so nearly complete that not only the new Whig Assembly was the first legislature to meet in it; but on January 1, 1841, at high noon, the ancient oaks of the original forest which surrounded it witnessed the gathering in the hall of the House of Commons, Governor Dudley leading, in which the first inauguration of the chief executive was to take place. Chief Justice Ruffin, whose bronze statue now graces the Supreme Court building, administered the oath to the second Whig chief of the state, whereupon Governor Morehead delivered a brief inaugural.

"Gentlemen of the Senate and House of Commons," he began, "In obedience to the requisition of the Constitution, I have appeared before you and have taken the oath prescribed, before I enter upon the duties of the Executive Office, to which I have been called by my fellow citizens of North Carolina.

"I assure you it is with unfeigned diffidence that I enter upon the discharge of these high duties; and if I may not hope to bring as much ability into the Executive Chair as now leaves it, I will yet endeavor, in the discharge of my official duties, to rival the zeal of him whose seat I am now about to occupy: And I shall be more than fortunate, if at the expiration of my term of service, it may be said of me, as it may be well said of him, 'Well done thou good and faithful.'

"I desire to discharge my duties as it becomes the Governor of the State, *and of the whole State;* I desire to be the Executive of the People, *and of the whole People;* and it shall be my constant endeavor so to discharge those duties, that the laws suggested by your wisdom—and by the wisdom of those who have gone on before you—shall be so administered that all the beneficial results anticipated may be fully realized.

"I shall be happy to cooperate with you in bringing into active operation all the elements of greatness and of usefulness with which our state is so abundantly blest.

"Other States have outstripped us in the career of improvement, and in the development of their national resources—but North Carolina will stand a favorable comparison with most of her sister States, in her national advantages—her great extent of fertile soil—her great variety of production—her exhaustless deposits of mineral wealth, her extraordinary water-power, inviting to Manufacturers—all, all combine to give her advantages that few other states possess.

"Whatever measures you may adopt to encourage Agriculture, to induce the Husbandman, while he toils and sweats, to hope that his labors will be duly rewarded; whatever measures you may adopt to facilitate Commerce, and to aid Industry in all the departments of life to reap its full reward, will meet with my cordial approbation.

"And I am happy to find that the action of one of your bodies has anticipated a suggestion that I had intended to make: I allude to the subject of opening Roanoke Inlet. This is a work, if practicable, of the first importance to North Carolina; it is a work in which the State is deeply interested—recent surveys, conducted by scientific skill, have shown that the work is practicable, and if so, it should be *certainly executed.*

"The Commerce and Navigation of the Nation would

THE CAPITOL
Raleigh, North Carolina
as it is today, unchanged since 1840

be greatly benefited by it—and if there be any work which
the Federal Government ought to execute, and which steers
clear of all Constitutional objection, this is the work.
Thousands of dollars are yearly spent to improve the navigation of rivers within the limits of some of the States,
whilst this would be an improvement by which the Atlantic
itself would be introduced within our borders.

"If the General Government cannot execute a work of
this description, or if it can and will not, then do we derive
but little advantage from our Federal association; we
should not ask the execution of this work by the General
Government as a boon, but demand it as a *right,* and I hope
the time is not far distant, when the application of North
Carolina to the General Government for her rights, will not
be disregarded; therefore, whatever duties you may choose
to assign me, to bring this subject to the attention of the
General Government, will be most cheerfully performed.
As there may be another session of Congress before our
legislative body may meet again, and as is probable no
action will be taken on the subject at this session of Congress, I would respectfully suggest that any communication,
which you may direct to be made, should be made to the
next session of Congress as well as to this.

"It is equally our duty, fellow citizens, to attend to our
moral and intellectual cultivation, for upon this depends
our continuance as a free and happy people. Our State
possesses in her University, an institution that will compare favorably with any other in the Union, at which a
portion of our youth can be well educated—we have a number of Academies and other high Schools at which another
portion can receive excellent educations; but it is to our
Common Schools, in which *every child* can receive the rudiments of an education—that our education should be mainly
directed. Our system is yet in its infancy—it will require
time and experience to give to it its greatest perfection; our
Literary Fund should be carefully husbanded and increased,
and I doubt not, in due time, the Legislative wisdom of the
State will perfect the system as far as human sagacity can
do it. And no part of my official duty will be performed

with more pleasure than that part, which may aid in bringing about that happy result.

"Nothing so surely indicates tne happiness and prosperity of a people, as numerous School-houses well filled,
during the week; and Churches well crowded on the Sabbath, and the latter is sure to follow the former. If we
desire to perpetuate our glorious political institutions, we
must give to all our *people* moral and intellectual cultivation
—that man who improves his intellect for six days of the
week, and, on the seventh, endeavors to give it the proper
direction, from the precepts of our Holy Religion, who
learns to do unto others, as he would they should do unto
him—*that man will never become a Tyrant—and he can
never be made a slave.*

"Believing, as I do, that comity and good feeling should
exist between the General Government and all the members
of the Confederacy—I shall endeavor, while I have the
power to preside over North Carolina, on every occasion
that may offer, to meet them with that courtesy to which
they are justly entitled—and which a due self-respect and
the dignity of our State require should be shown.

"I will cheerfully yield to the General Government all
the powers to which it is entitled, from a fair and proper
construction and interpretation of the Constitution—while,
on the other hand, I shall carefully maintain, protect and
defend the rights which pertain to our own State.

"I shall be extremely careful to see that North Carolina, when she speaks in her sovereign character, has a
right to speak—and when she does so speak, *through her
great seal—the emblem of her sovereignty—while I have
the honor to control it—it must be—it shall be respected.*[1]

"The days of our political existence, under our present
happy form of government, are numbered, when States shall
permit *their sovereignty to be contemned and their great
seals to be scoffed at and disregarded.*

"In a word, fellow-citizens, whatever measures you may

---

[1] These expressions were due to many acts of Presidents Jackson and
Van Buren, which were the cause of the Whig uprising.

GOVERNOR JOHN MOTLEY MOREHEAD
in 1841
From a print in possession of Lindsay Patterson
Winston-Salem, N. C.

adopt to advance the prosperity of our State, and the happiness of our citizens, will meet with my hearty cooperation.

"I cannot conclude my remarks without congratulating
you and myself, upon the time and place of our meeting.
This splendid edifice has nearly approached its completion.
You are the first legislative body that ever had the honor
to assemble in its splendid Halls. I am the first Executive
that ever had the honor to be installed within its durable
walls. It will endure as a monument, for ages to come, of
the munificence, liberality and taste of the age in which we
live. There is a moral effect produced by the erection of
such an edifice as this—it will serve, in the chain of time, to
link the past with the future. And if ever that proud spirit
that has ever characterized us—which has ever been ready
to assert its rights and avenge its wrongs—which exhibited
itself at the Regulation Battle of 1770—which burnt with
more brilliance at the Mecklenburg Declaration of Independence in 1775—and which totally declared for Independence
in 1776—even if that proud spirit shall become craven in
time to come, and shall not dare animate the bosom of a
freeman—let it look upon this monument—*and remember
the glorious institutions under which its foundations were
laid, and the noble people by whom it was reared*—and
then let it become a slave *if it can.*

"May it endure for ages to come—may it endure until
time itself shall grow old—may a thousand years find these
Halls still occupied by Freemen, legislating for a free and
happy people."[1]

The new Governor in a new capitol, representing a new
political life in the state, was now about to fulfil so far as
was in his power, the ideals he had voiced in this body in
the old capitol twenty years before, with such vigor and
determination that he was now the first choice of that west
as soon as it found a voice.   He had been twenty-five years
old then; now he was forty-five, and was a national figure.
His predecessor, while a Whig, was essentially a compromise
eastern man; but John Motley Morehead was no compro-

---

[1] *Raleigh Register*, 5th Jan., 1841, and elsewhere.

mise candidate. He had won North Carolina, as a Whig and man of the west, in the greatest political contest ever waged in the commonwealth. Not that he was the first chief executive from the west; for six western men had been Governor of North Carolina before him, out of the twenty-six under the commonwealth. "Old Guilford" had furnished one of them, Alexander Martin, whose home was its first county seat, and he had served twice and was a Federalist; but Governor Morehead was the first western man since Governor Martin, who had not been chosen as a Democrat, or, as they were often styled in earlier days, "Democratic Republican." His election, therefore, was more of a revolution in North Carolina than any event since the era of independence began; and this was what attracted national attention to him, and likewise gave him a new prestige over other executives of the state, because it made him the recognized political leader as well as Governor. A North Carolina chief executive was severely an executive, with almost no other powers; the receptacle of power was in the Assembly. As also a political leader, however, Governor Morehead acquired more power potentially than previous executives; and to this was added the force of his unique personality and his infectious enthusiasm. Since this Assembly would not meet again, and the next in two years might not be Whig, his duties for that period would be purely executive, and he was handicapped at the beginning.

One of the most interesting of these latter, was a requisition on him from Governor A. G. McNutt of Mississippi, first presented to him while he was attending the inauguration of President William Henry Harrison at Washington on March 4th. He then drew attention of the Mississippi agent to grave defects in the requisition for a man charged with stealing and carrying off a slave, such as no copy of an indictment nor the use of the state seal as required by national law. The requisition was dated February 10th, and on March 17th it was again sent by the agent with the defects still existing, whereupon Governor Morehead made a detailed reply on these points and sent them to Jackson. From that time on no less than twenty papers and letters

passed between the two executives. On October 7, 1841,
Governor Morehead said, in a letter: "Therefore the Executive of Mississippi has no right to make the demand, nor
have I the right to make the arrest."   For as the case proceeded it became evident that not only were the papers
defective, but that it was a case of persecution for another
cause. The matter covered almost a year, and while it was
in course Governor Tucker became the Mississippi executive, and in a letter of January 31, 1842, announced the
voluntary surrender of the man Sanders which closed the
incident. The case was discussed in the Senate of Mis-
sisippi during that long period, when Senator Ives of that
state, in defending the course of the North Carolina executive, said that he had the honor of a personal acquaintance
with him and that if the Whigs recovered their ascendency
of early 1841, Governor Morehead "might yet preside over
a republic as well as a state!"   This seems to have been
the first suggestion of his name for the Presidency of the
United States, but it was by no means to be the only one.
This, however, was some time after his inauguration in
January, 1841.

     With this latter event came news in February, that specie
payments would be resumed in North Carolina and her
sister states northward, Maryland taking the lead, as if to be
ready for the inauguration of President Harrison in March.
This was hardly disseminated, when reverse news came
that the United States Bank of Pennsylvania had suspended
specie payments which would cause suspension in all states
southward—a course that was charged to New York banks.
North Carolina was cheered, however, by news of Mr.
Badger's selection as Secretary of the Navy in the Harrison cabinet, a Newbern and Raleigh jurist recognized as
one of the greatest lawyers in the United States, and in the
same class as his fellow townsman, Judge Gaston. This
was a Morehead year, for besides a Governor Morehead
and Senator Moreland in North Carolina, Kentucky sent,
as successor to Senator Crittenden, who became Attorney
General at Washington, a western representative of the
family, Ex-Governor James T. Morehead, so that there were

two Senators James Turner Morehead, at this time. But it was also a year of blasted hopes for every Whig everywhere, for on April 4, 1841, President Harrison's death was announced, and President Tyler's first announcement of his policies left one subject as a source of apprehension to every Whig, namely, his attitude toward restoration of the United States Bank to regulate the currency. To test that apprehension, Henry Clay, as chairman, reported a bank bill and by August 6th it had passed and been sent to President Tyler. Ten days later the Whigs of America received a shock more vital, if possible, than the death of their late President, for it was the announcement of the political death of President Tyler in his veto of the Clay bank bill! The act was softened slightly, however, by his signature of the repeal of the Sub-Treasury bill but he again irritated them by vetoing a somewhat similar bill for a "Fiscal Corporation" on September 9th, when they knew they had no longer a Whig President, and began to suspect him of creating a "third party." Then came the resignations of his Whig cabinet, except Secretary of State Webster, and formal Whig denunciation of Tyler as their President. The next logical step was for a sentiment to spring up for Henry Clay as the next Whig leader, because of his bank bill to cure the financial ills from which the country had suffered so long.

While these events were in progress in April, Governor Morehead was at Greensboro arranging the removal of his family to Raleigh and installing them in the Executive Mansion at the foot of Fayetteville Street, where he had made such improvement as he was accustomed to have at "Blandwood." And among his improvements was an ice-house, which, because of the want of more serious issues, his political opponents were to make locally famous! The Governor's family now consisted of eighteen-year-old Miss Letitia Harper Morehead, "sweet-sixteen" Miss Mary Corinna Morehead, and fourteen-year-old Miss Ann Eliza (II), with a boy of eight, John Lindsay Morehead, named for the Governor's father and Mrs. Morehead's family, a girl of five, Emma Victoria Morehead, and the election-day

babe-in-arms, James Turner Morehead, named after the
Governor's younger brother, Senator James T. Morehead of
Greensboro. The older daughters, of course, spent the
school year at Edgeworth Seminary. The Executive Mansion was placed in as attractive condition as the Governor
had been accustomed to keep "Blandwood," which was one
of the notable residences of the state; and his life now was
spent at both ends of Fayetteville Street. In the Executive
office at the southwest corner of the first floor of the new
capitol, Governor Morehead had inherited from his predecessor a free colored messenger and attendant, Lunsford
Lane, who had purchased his freedom of Mrs. Sherwood
Haywood of Raleigh, and who, after six months with Governor Morehead, found it necessary to leave the state because of general feeling against free negroes, and he
became a well-known lecturer in the Abolition agitation in
the north.[1] The Governor and his family spent three weeks
in August at his old home.

His first aggressive work was in connection with the
reclamation of Swamp lands in the Sound peninsula.
Governor Morehead's appointment of Ex-Governor Dudley to this service, although he soon resigned, led to their
personal examination of those lands, and on Wednesday,
June 16, 1841, the borough of Washington, Beaufort county,
gave them a complimentary dinner at which Major Thomas
H. Blount presided. Among the toasts was one—"Our distinguished guest, Governor Morehead: He has introduced
into the administration of the state, the 'go ahead' principles
which have illustrated his private life." In his response he
showed that glowing faith in the possibilities of North Carolina for which he was so well known, dwelt upon the importance of the reclaimed swamp lands, credit for which he
gave to his predecessor as a bold and original conception,
designed to raise the common school system through its
wealth.[2] By September the Governor was able to advertise
50,000 acres of swamp lands on the watershed of Hyde
county between the two sounds, into which two canals six

---

[1] *Lunsford Lane*, by Rev. Wm. G. Hawkins.
[2] *Washington Whig*.

miles long drained them. They were to be sold at auction
on the Pungo canal on November 30th—at which, it may
be added, none were sold because no bid was equal to the
required minimum. His interest in this, however, was
bound up in his interest in the common schools, because it
was the basis of funds for that purpose. He therefore put
able men on this board and that on common school funds as
well, and gave both his personal attention.

He was at Chapel Hill at the University Commencement
as President of the Board of which he had been a member
for over a dozen years and during the summer issued, as
President of the Literary (or Common School) Fund, the
county incomes from it—a total of $54,608.99, from which
such counties as Orange, Rutherford, Guilford and a few
others received largest amounts. It was this fund the Governor was trying to increase in sale of reclaimed swamp
lands. It was expected that the next one would be twice
that amount. Indeed Governor Morehead's stimulating
suggestive spirit unconsciously permeated every department
of the state's thought and activity. He spent two weeks in
October in Greensboro and on his return early in November
attended a meeting of the Wilmington and Weldon Railroad, representing the state, and a public dinner to Ex-Secretary of the Navy, Mr. Badger, at Raleigh, in which he
responded to a toast to himself. About this time the effect
on agriculture and commerce for about fifty miles each
side of the new railroads was beginning to be so noticeable
that some leaders like Mr. Gales of the *Raleigh Register* began advocating a turnpike from Raleigh to the Tennessee
line. The enthusiasm over the growth of public schools
was so great that it was believed this new era would stop
the great emigration and produce immigration also. At the
Badger dinner Governor Morehead offered the toast:
"The physical and intellectual resources of North Carolina.
Her citizens have long esteemed the one—the Union now
esteems the other." This was typical of the new spirit in
the entire state.

Early in December the Whigs in Orange county started
the ball rolling for the next Presidential and Gubernatorial

elections, by nominating Henry Clay for President, and Governor Morehead to succeed himself, saying: "That we heartily and cordially approve of the Administration of our able and patriotic Governor, John M. Morehead." Early in January, 1842, soon after he had presided at the Bank of North Carolina board meeting, whose condition was excellent, the Democratic Convention met, determined to take advantage of the anomalous Whig situation—having a President who was no President!—, and nominated a Fayetteville man, Louis D. Henry, who might be thought of as so near the eastern and western line as to be of both sections. The contest against Governor Morehead was avowedly because he was a Whig.   Late in the same month news came of the failure of the Girard Bank, Philadelphia, one of the greatest in the Union—and every such event was bound to be disastrous to the party in power.   Governor McNutt of Mississippi was issuing public letters glorying in that state's repudiation of her debts.   The situation was so grave that during the previous summer various Governors were addressed by a W. A. Kentish of London, asking their consideration of a plan to make one head state bank to function like the Bank of England, for each state, and then these to cooperate to secure uniformity.   As a result the Democrats were encouraged and the Whigs had a tremendous fight on their hands.   County Whig conventions were wide awake during the winter and spring endorsing Clay and Morehead, and the Democrats were, if anything, even more active, the Raleigh *Standard* leading the attacks on the Governor, all of them almost as significant as the ice-house episode and all, even though insignificant, proven false.   Candidate Henry began his operations even as early as March, 1842; and in desperation the *Standard* began to speak of "John Moonshine Morehead."

On April 4, 1842, the anniversary of the death of President Harrison, the Whigs held their State Convention in the Hall of the House of Commons, Raleigh; and the *Register,* of that city, said "It was the largest and most imposing political assembly ever convened in North Carolina with the exception of the mass convention of 1840."   It avowed itself for Clay for President and Morehead for Governor, the "whole official conduct" of the latter meeting their "hearty approval" and "his integrity, intelligence, impartiality, dili gence and economy in administering the offices of the State" winning their desires "with one heart and one voice" that he be re-elected. While admitting that a canvass by a Governor for re-election was not ordinarily advisable, they thought the needs of the present in public affairs so important that his opponent ought not to be allowed to preempt the field and thought Governor Morehead ought, in this instance, to make a canvass. Governor Morehead was called from his office on the first floor to the Hall of the Commons on the second.

XI

A

AND

The First Railways

(Continued)

1842

In response to his re-nomination Governor Morehead said: "Mr. President—I should be wanting in candor to myself, were I to say that the Resolution just read is unexpected to me. I could not feel, Sir, that I was an indifferent spectator to the proceedings of my fellow-citizens throughout the State in the numerous primary meetings which have been held for the purpose of appointing Delegates to this Convention. But a few short weeks have passed, since our opponents held a similar meeting in this place, and I was denounced as having done nothing to meet the approbation of the people. And, I did therefore look, Sir, with interest and anxiety, to see what verdict the great body of my fellow citizens would pass upon me. At every meeting, Sir, since held, my conduct as Executive of the State has been cordially approved, and the judgment of these meetings, I am proud to perceive from the Resolution just read, is endorsed by this highly respectable body.

"When, Sir, I entered upon the duties of my Office, as Governor of North Carolina, it was with a determination to *deserve* the confidence of the whole people; and so far, as I had the ability to do so, my conduct has been rigidly shaped to produce that result. From that desk, Sir (pointing to the president's seat), when I took the oath of office, I declared my intention to be the Governor of the *State,* of the *Whole State,* and not of a *Party;* and I have not only endeavored to act up to that declaration, but think I have done so. And, notwithstanding the harshness with which I have been denounced, I am *still* resolved to be the Governor of the State, and not of a Party. It is true, that the position, in which I am now placed, may compel me, of necessity, to mingle in the party politics of the day—I cannot be the candidate of a party, and not show some party feeling—but such feelings shall never enter into the discharge of my *official* duties.

"It would, Mr. President, be extremely gratifying to me, if canvassing the State could be dispensed with, and I am pleased to find that the Convention deprecate in their Resolution, *as a general rule,* the example of an incumbent of the Executive Chair conducting the canvass in person. But, Sir, I am also gratified to perceive, by the terms of the Resolution, that while the example is deprecated, the Whig party have no idea of chaining down their candidate, while hosts of writers, belonging to the opposition, are poisoning the public mind, and even their Candidate is traversing the State, engaged in the same work. The people of Old North Carolina go for fair play, Sir; they will never consent, that in a contest of this kind, one man shall hold my feet, another my hands, and a third stand by *gouging* all the time! No, Sir; but when such foul play is shown, they will come to the rescue.

"Sir, after the manifestations of confidence which I have received at the hands of the Whigs, as well as in primary meetings, as from this Convention, I should not deserve the name of *a true Whig,* if I did not cheerfully accept the nomination. When, in 1840, the banner was committed to my hands, bearing the glorious name of *Harrison,* and those of *Tyler* and *Morehead,* and when, Sir, was run up the last gaff, I took especial care it should never be lowered until victory had crowned our efforts. But, Sir, a shadow has passed over the flag of our prosperity, and the most brilliant name on it has been erased. In its place is left the shadow of Abstraction—I should rather say of *distraction;* but if my own humble name be the only one which shall be emblazoned on its folds hereafter, I will again bear it aloft in triumph from ocean wave to mountain top. No man deserves the name of Whig, who suffers himself to despond. Though death has stricken down our glorious old Chief, and his substitute has deserted our colors, we should never despair. Our Revolutionary fathers waged a seven-years' war to accomplish American Independence, and they would have fought seven times seven years, before they would have given up the Ship. And shall we, their degenerate sons, feel that the measure of our glory is full, because we are called on to labor two short campaigns? If, Sir, there is to be found such a thing as a *wavering* Whig (though I have never seen or heard of one), I would address him in the language of Bruce to his Soldiers—

> "Wha can be a traitor knave?
> Wha can fill a coward's grave?
> Wha so base as be a slave?
> Traitor! Coward! turn and flee.

"Sir, there is no mistake about North Carolina, or her political position. I predicted the success of the Whigs in 1840, and I predict a still more brilliant victory in 1842. I was no false Prophet *then*—I shall not, I am confident, prove one *now*. We have resolved again to deliver our country; but if, by any possibility, we fail, then we shall have only ourselves to blame. We have a decided majority in the State, and our good old mother expects every Whig to do his duty!"[1]

As the Convention closed General Alfred Dockery, the President, said this presidency of a convention that nominated Henry Clay for the national executive and John M. Morehead for that of the state was the greatest legacy he could leave to his children. In the evening the Governor gave a reception to the Convention members and to leading citizens. He at once began to form his itinerary: May 3rd, at Greenville; May 10th, at Snow Hill; 16th, at Waynesboro; 18th, at Halifax; 19th, at Jackson; 24th, at Smith-

---

[1] *Raleigh Register*, 19th April, 1842.

field; 27th, at Hillsboro; and Fayetteville on June 7th. On May 17th *The Register* said in predicting a brilliant victory in August: "All eyes are now turned on North Carolina; and the Whigs throughout the Union regard her as the Gibraltar of sound principles, and as again destined to stop in its mad career the ball of Loco Focoism." This was reinforced by the election of a North Carolinian, Senator Mangum, as President of the National Senate. Governor Morehead's speaking at Hillsboro brought him near the University, where he again performed his duties as President of its governing board.

The most notable debate of the whole gubernatorial campaign of 1842, was when Governor Morehead went directly into the enemies' camp, Fayetteville, the home of his rival, Louis D. Henry. "We have just witnessed the greatest intellectual contest that has ever occurred in North Carolina," says the *Fayetteville Observer*. "The candidates for the office of Governor have been engaged for *ten hours and thirty-five minutes,* without any intermission, in a most animated discussion of all those points of national and state politics which divide the two great parties whose representatives they are. Commencing at eleven o'clock A.M. Mr. Morehead spoke for two hours, when, agreeably to arrangement, he gave way to Mr. Henry, who spoke for three hours and ten minutes (the last hour and ten minutes by the courtesy of Mr. Morehead and his friends, the agreement having been that each should speak but two hours at a time). Mr. Morehead rejoined for two hours and forty minutes, Mr. Henry two hours more, and Governor Morehead forty-five minutes;—closing the debate at 35 minutes past 9 o'clock at night—Mr. Morehead having occupied 5 hours and 25 minutes and Mr. Henry 5 hours and 10 minutes.

"There were hundreds of persons present, many of whom never left the ground to get a mouthful to eat during the whole of the protracted period; many of whom *stood* for hours together in one spot; and many of whom closed their stores and workshops, so that there was a general suspension of business. A number of gentlemen were here from Robeson, Moore, Richmond, Bladen and Sampson counties, whose chief business in town was to witness this first meeting of the rival candidates.

"And what a glorious meeting it has been for the Whigs! Never party had a more honest, a more gallant, a more able, or eloquent leader than John M. Morehead! And never leader had more unequivocal marks of the enthusiasm with which he inspired his auditory. He received the warm congratulations of a large number of his friends, who accompanied him to his lodgings, at the victory, which their joyful faces, not less than the woe-begone countenances of a few of his opponents who were to be seen, so plainly told him that he had gained. It was indeed a victory; a victory not won without a struggle, a powerful struggle, maintained with all the ardor, all the eloquence, all the tact, all the art, for which his adversary has gained no little reputation. The collision was conducted with fairness on both sides, as well by the candidates as by the people; for which all parties deserve great credit.

"It is not possible that we should give our readers any more than the outline of the debate. The Governor commenced by defending himself from the various charges which have been made against him, as well by his opponent as by the press. The charges of his having proscribed public officers for opinion's sake he met fully and satistorily. So far from proscribing any such persons, he had re-appointed Democrats to office whenever he had found them in office. The two Democrats to one Whig, whom he found in the Literary Board, he re-appointed. One of them declined to accept, because of his private business. The other did accept, and held the place till he was about to remove to Baltimore, when he resigned. He filled the vacancies with the most proper persons he could find (ex-Governor Dudley and Mr. Gales)—gentlemen who could advise with him usefully in regard to the duties of the Board. Neither had he proscribed the Democrat who belonged to the Improvement Board—he had re-appointed him also. He had been bitterly assailed by Mr. Henry and his party organs for proscribing for opinion's sake, a

Democrat from the little office of keeper of the public buildings at Raleigh. He showed in reply to this charge, that there was no such officer known to the law till the last act of the Legislature, under which he made the first appointment; consequently, that there could be no proscription from an office which had no existence. That, moreover, the 'proscribed' man who had possession of the Keys, before the office was created, was intemperate; and above all, the Governor was informed that he was a Whig!—and had voted the Whig ticket. So that in no particular was the charge true.

"He stated fully his disposition of the money appropriated by the last Legislature for furniture and repairs of the Governor's house. How he had to expend some of his own money to complete the furnishings of the house; how he had used but $1200 of the $3000 which a committee of the Legislature, with a Democratic member from this county at its head, had reported as necessary to repair the house, fences, etc.; how he had expended the enormous sum of $75 to build an ice-house on the lot! (His own ice-house at home had cost him twice as much.)

"Having disposed of these and other *equally important* charges with which he had been assailed, he passed to an examination of Mr. Henry's letter of Acceptance, and of his political tergiversations, at the close of which he read from the letter a passage declaiming most strenuously on the impropriety of tarnishing the public credit, and the duty of every man to maintain that credit at all hazards. As a fit commentary on these fine sentiments—on paper—the Governor stated that he was informed, and gave Mr. Henry the name of his informant, that at the close of his service in the fat office which Gen. Jackson bestowed on him, he, Mr. Henry, had had the Government draft for his pay protested—the credit of his own friends and favorite administration tarnished—and for what? Why, that he might thus make his draft receivable for public dues at New York, sell the exchange on New York thus created at a premium, and thereby add to his salary of $3500 a year, the additional sum of one or two or 300 dollars! So much for Mr. Hen-

ry's patriotic regard (on paper) for the public credit! Mr.
Henry entered into a long explanation which amounted to
an admission of the fact, justifying it on the ground that
he was entitled to good money (hard money) for his pay,
and as well as we could hear, stating that as far as he could
recollect he had only made about $30 by the operation. Such
is the measure of his patriotism! Weighed against $30,
the public credit, the credit of his own friends, by whom he
had been most liberally rewarded, kicks the beam!

"In his reply, and indeed throughout both his long
speeches, the burden of Mr. Henry's song was, the glory
of Gen. Jackson's services, and a denunciation of Banks of
all sorts, State and National. He lugged in Gen. Jackson
on all occasions. Never did little Van hang on to the General's tail with firmer grasp than Mr. Henry! He had
never differed from Gen. Jackson on but one point, and
that was upon the Deposit Act (an act under which
North Carolina has received upwards of fourteen hundred
thousand dollars). He blamed the General for that act.
But everybody knows that the General made a merit of necessity in that case. He saw that an overwhelming majority of Congress would pass it in spite of his veto.

"But the Banks, Mr. Henry said, were corrupt; they
were 'manufactories of rogues and swindlers;' they were
rotten; political machines; lending their money to effect
political ends; he himself had 'fallen among thieves' in
having anything to do with them. Most effectually did
Governor Morehead turn these charges against their maker.
He said that for his part he didn't know much about Banks;
he had but little to do with them. But *Mr. Henry seemed
to him to be very fond of the company of these 'thieves,
rogues and swindlers,'* for after having been a stock holder
in the old State and Newbern Banks; after having served
as a Director and Attorney in one of these for many years,
he goes right off in 1834, when the new Bank of the State
was chartered, and subscribes for some thirty shares of its
stock, and again consents to become a partner with these
'thieves,' to become Attorney for this 'manufactory of
rogues and swindlers,' and to participate in the profits of its

'roguery.' [This was a deserved rebuke for such vilely false charges against the Banks. We say *vilely false;* for it is an imputation upon those who are directors of the Banks, and, as one, we repel the imputation. Whether true of himself, when he was a director, we know not, nor care not. We have served in that capacity with an honorable man of Mr. Henry's own party, and we are willing that he should say whether he believes or knows that political feeling ever influenced the conduct of himself or his associates.]

"The Governor extorted from Mr. Henry the admission that he was in favor of the U. S. Bank up to the veto Message in July, 1832. He then asked him how he could be favorable to it, if it had done all the mischief that he had attributed to it in 1819–20, 1828–29, etc., and had never regulated the currency nor done any other good thing? Mr. Henry replied that he did not know of these things till after the veto. What! not know of the Bank's evil and corrupt conduct, when one of its branches was located at his own door? No, he knew nothing of them. Well, you surely knew, asked the Governor, that it was breaking down the North Carolina local banks in 1827–28, as you say in your letter? Y-e-s, he did know that. How, then, demanded the Governor, could you favor the re-charter of the Bank which was carrying ruin in its course through the State? This was a poser.

"On the subject of public expenditure, and the relative economy of the late and present administrations, each of the candidates had, of course, a good deal to say. Our readers may judge of the result in this particular, when we inform them, that Mr. Henry actually stated that the present administration had had, in the space of fifteen months, not less than fifty-one millions, on which to administer the government! When Gov. Morehead got him to read his bill of particulars, behold, this enormous 51 millions was composed in part of the loan of $11\frac{1}{2}$ millions, and the sum of five millions, which it is *estimated* Congress will add to the tariff! And these sums, *not one dollar of which has come into the treasury,* are figured by Mr. Henry as composing a part of Whig expenditures for the last fifteen months!! The Governor did not admit that this was a Whig administration, but he showed the humbuggery of this preposterous statement of Mr. Henry's.

"On the subject of Internal Improvements, the Governor arraigned his competitor. The whole tendency of the Letter of Acceptance was to throw odium on Internal Improvements, the 'gambling debts' of the States, created for the prosecution of wild schemes of Improvement, etc. The Governor showed that Mr. Henry had gone as far as the farthest, *not in investing his own money,* but in recommending the investment of the people's money, and the creation of these 'gambling debts.' At one time he was for the State borrowing five millions, and at another three millions, and even from British bankers (of whom he now affects such a horror) ; then he was in favor of the State taking two-fifths of the stock in any works where individuals would take three-fifths, and to crown all, he was of opinion the state ought to undertake certain great works on her own hook, with her funds alone, not asking the people's aid at all. Pressing Mr. Henry to know what he was now in favor of, he procured from him the avowal, that though he had gained wisdom by experience, and was not in favor of the five million loan, yet he was still in favor of, and would stand or fall by the recommendations of the Raleigh Convention of December, 1838. The principal recommendation of that body, which he thus adheres to, was that the State should borrow three millions of dollars to invest in works of Internal Improvement. At a moment of greater leisure, we propose to look into this matter, and let our readers see what a magnificent system of 'gambling debts' Mr. Henry is now in favor of, after all his denunciations of Whig madness on the subject.

"Mr. Henry, in turn, demanded to know of the Governor, whether he was not indebted to the Banks, as had been charged and not denied; arguing that if he was, his judgment in regard to those institutions might be biased by his interest. The Governor's reply carried consternation to his catechist and his party. *He did not owe any Bank one dollar,* so far as he knew. He was not a borrower from them. His only dealings with them were to sell them his bills of exchange when he had such in the course of his business. It was possible that one such draft, accepted by him, had been discounted by some bank, but if it was, it was not done for his accommodation, but for that of the holder of the draft.

"He asked Mr. Henry, since he had answered this question, to inform him how *he* had invested the wealth of which he was the reputed possessor. Mr. H—— replied that he had some real estate, some negroes, some 12 or $15,000 of Ohio State Stocks, some Louisiana Bank Stock, some Raleigh and Gaston Railroad bonds, guaranteed by the State, some Cape Fear and Bank of the State Stocks, but the chief part of his means was loaned out on bonds in the counties of Franklin, Warren, Cumberland, Sampson, etc., etc. The Governor thereupon closed the discussion with a most eloquent description of the effects of breaking down the Banks and resorting to a hard money currency, which seemed to be the result aimed at by Mr. Henry and his party. They had created the Banks, and the people had gone in debt for property purchased at high prices. Strike down the Banks, and the creditors would swallow up all the means of the debtors. A debtor would have to give 100 days' labor to pay for a cow that he could have paid for in ten days when he bought her. 100 bushels of wheat would realize the farmer no more hard money than 10 bushels under the paper money system. It behooved the debtor portion of the community to look well into these matters. They would be at the mercy of the money lenders—such men as Mr. Henry. For his own part, all that he had (and he had made it all by the strong arm, the stout heart, and what little of intellect Providence had blessed him with) was invested in the industrial pursuits within the good old State of North Carolina. He neither sent it out of the State for investment, nor loaned it at interest. He had invested it in manufacturing, mechanical and farming operations, by which he afforded employment to many of his poor neighbors, mechanics, etc.

"This is a hasty, a very imperfect outline, from memory,

of the sayings of this most interesting day.   It is written between midnight and morning, under feelings of the strongest elation, it is true, at the triumph of our cause, and its able advocate; but, as far as it goes, we have endeavored to make it fair.   We only regret that we have not time to make it more full."[1]

In starting his western tour, the Governor spoke at Greensboro, as he had not done in 1840.   Greensboro, as it was in 1842, has been pictured in verse by the Principal of Edgeworth School, Miss M. A. Hoye, just before her death:

> "This thriving village, I am told
> Is but a score and six years old.
> It sprung as if by magic stroke
> Amid the shade of pine and oak:
> For here it may be plainly seen
> By trees of light and darker green
> That there is a dividing line—
> One side is oak, the other pine"———

and boys were boys and girls were girls then as now, for she says:

> "The Edgeworth roof attracts my eye;
> I fain would pass this building by,
> For it may seem against good rule
> To mention first of all my school;
> But what comes first we all agree
> Must first be served. What's this I see?
> The gateway open, I declare,
> And gate unhinged, and gone—gone where?
> Ah, that's the secret—'tis fine fun
> To steal a gate at night and run
> And hide it in some secret place:
> The genus of greatness I can trace
> In minds so eminently wise
> That can such wond'rous schemes devise
> And execute so valiantly!

[1] *Raleigh Register,* 14th June, 1842.   This reference to educational institutions in Greensboro serves to recall the fact that Virginia, North Carolina and South Carolina had, at this time, the fewest persons who could read of all the states of the Union; and that they had the smallest number of newspapers to white population, North Carolina having far the fewest of the three, with only one to 17,500 white people, Virginia coming next with 14,125, and Kentucky and South Carolina following, in that order.   North Carolina had no daily, and but one semi-weekly, althouh it had 26 weeklies, and two periodicals.   In weeklies, only Virginia, Tennessee and Mississippi surpassed her and the last by only one.

> Why they in very troth will soon
>   Equal, if not superior, be
> To cunning fox or sly raccoon
> Which love at midnight hour to stray
> Upon their predatory way!"

And doubtless there is a case of consequences and cause in the juxtaposition of the following:

> "Hark! With the music of my strings
> A distant bell in concert rings.
> It is the Caldwell bell, it calls
> The students to its classic halls:
> It is the hour for evening prayer,
> A hundred noble youths meet there
> With holy shepherds there they meet
> To worship at Jehovah's feet.
> Are they not safer, far, the flock
> Whose guides are faithful, wise and good?"

She also "sings" the two other schools, the factory, and mill, newspaper, the Guards and all the rest that made up "happy Greensboro."[1]

About 1805–7 there was an agitation to remove the court house from "battle-scarred Martinsville" to the "Center" of Guilford county and the two parties took these names. The party of the first part shrewdly secured the decision of the County Court to put up a new building, presumably at their town; but this only put the "Center" people on their mettle and they won. Forty-two acres were secured and the town plan named after the famous Revolutionary hero, General Nathaniel Greene. The deed is dated March 25, 1808. Among forty-six lots all but two were taken and among owners one notes the name of the Rev. Dr. David Caldwell, the famous teacher and divine.[2]

Greensboro met the Governor with a demonstration on Friday, 24th of June, 1842, a mounted company greeted him over a mile out of town, and their spokesman, among other remarks, said: "We welcome you as the champion of Whig principles, who bore the Whig flag triumphantly

---

[1] *The Patriot*, 6th Sept., 1845.
[2] *Ibid.*, 16th May, 1846.

from the ocean wave to mountain tops and crowned it with glorious victory in 1840, and who, we believe, at the sacrifice of your own ease and domestic comfort will bear it again to victory in 1842." The Governor responded with deep emotion and the procession passed on up to the home of Senator James Turner Morehead, his brother, where was held a reception. The Masons were celebrating St. John's day and he became their guest and listened to an address at the Presbyterian Church by Rev. Mr. Kerr. The next day a stage at the side of this church was prepared and at one o'clock Governor Morehead addressed a multitude for about four hours. He recalled how, in 1840, they endorsed him with over 2200 votes, a result that made Guilford looked upon as the Gibraltar of Whig principles in the state. A witness said: "He spoke with all the freedom and fearlessness of one conscious of having done his duty." He attacked Tyler and disclaimed him as a Whig. He said that this period under Tyler were not "Whig times," but "a continuation of Democratic times." He closed with an appeal and a hope that "we should yet see that greatest statesman of the age, Henry Clay, at the helm, when all will be well."[1]

After he left, on his western tour, great news came of his progress. "He does not taunt nor insult his opponents," said one account, "but addresses them as brothers, and in such a persuasive manner, that makes his appeal almost irresistible." At Asheville there was a great barbecue; here he followed Mr. Henry's visit, and held undiminished attention for over three hours. He discussed the banking systems and advocated a National Bank and the "spider web structure" of Mr. Henry had no show before the "heavy battle axe of John M. Morehead"—to quote one enthusiastic Whig. He showed how every President, while President, from Washington down to just before Van Buren had admitted the constitutionality of the National Bank, and "Bank vs. No Bank" was the issue. "The apostle of liberty has visited us," said another paper. "In good faith," said the Greensboro *Patriot,* "we say what we believe, when we

---

[1] *Greensboro Patriot,* 28th June, 1842.

assert that no other county can produce his like." "None
but his powerful frame, animated with a spirit that never
for an instant flags—a soul fired with the most highly honorable personal ambition and the truest love of country,
could endure the fatigue of such a canvass. His country—
his whole country—calls for his powerful efforts; and the
best interests of that country, to all human appearance, at
this moment hangs on his success! . . . Prepare for
another peal of *Guilford Thunder,* that shall fill the ears
of all the people, re-echo from the mountains along her
smiling plains, until its reverberations shall mix with the
murmurs of her seas."[1]

The appointments in July were as follows: 13th, Rutherfordton; 15th, Shelbyville; 16th, Lincolnton; 19th, Morganton; 21st, Statesville; 22nd, Mocksville; 23rd, Salisbury; 25th, Reid's Store; 26th, Charlotte; 27th, Concord;
28th, Stanly; 29th, Lawrenceville; and 30th, Flat Swamp.
By the time the Whig Candidate reached Shelbyville, Mr.
Henry had withdrawn from the canvass, as he said, on account of his health, no doubt having *political* health somewhat in mind. And his instinct was sound, for with the
August election, whose returns were about a month in
arriving at official totals, it was discovered that he was 4592
votes behind the Governor, who received 39,586 votes and,
in so much, preserved the Whig character of North Carolina. In these campaigns he won the sobriquet "Glorious
Old War Horse."

Now attention can be turned to a unique feature of
Governor Morehead's first administration: He was inaugurated on January 1, 1841, just as the Whig Assembly
was closing its session, not to meet again during his term.
So that during his first term he had no Whig legislature;
and at this election of 1842, that body was carried by the
Democrats, so that for his whole two terms, unless the election of 1844 should produce another Assembly of Whigs, he
would not have any law-making body to cooperate in his
plans. What then, up to this time, was the character of his

---

[1] *The Patriot,* 30th July, 1842.

influence as a governor? First, it was the asset of his personal character stimulating every enterprise with which he came in contact. In September he issued the common school fund statement and showed it to be $135,699.05, as indicating development along that line. Secondly, as Whig leader of a naturally Democratic state whose election occurred in August, he became a marked national figure in a Whig administration. Thirdly, his personal example, as he said at Fayetteville, in investing all he had "in the industrial pursuits within the good old state of North Carolina," in "manufacturing, mechanical and farming operations," was a great object lesson in the fact that the way to develop was to develop. Fortunately, his liberal, constitutional views, opposed alike to Abolitionist and great Slave-holders, and his liberal attitude to the colored race, likewise gave him a unique place as a national force, and in that way gave new prestige to North Carolina in national politics. It was in these respects, and not in his great measures carried through a Whig legislature that his two terms as executive were strong. When the Assembly met on November 21st, 1842, however, with a Democratic majority, his message to them showed what would have been done had he had one of his own party in either term, as shall now appear.

The position of North Carolina as a leading Whig state, the position of Governor Morehead as a re-elected Whig executive, and the fact that it was done by the same people who elected a Democratic Legislature, made his first message to that body of more than local significance. It is so perfect an expression of both Governor Morehead and the state, as well as his times, that it is given in full:

"Gentlemen of the Senate and of the House of Commons: The periodical assemblage of a portion of the people, selected for their eminent qualifications, for the important trusts confided to them—to enact laws by which they, as well as their constituents, are to be governed—is an occasion interesting to the philanthropist, cheering to the friends of rational liberty, and an able commentary upon the excellence of our political institutions.

"To that Department of the Government, assigned to

superintend the due execution of the laws, this assemblage
should always be acceptable, as affording an opportunity
to show how the duties of that Department have been discharged—to point out defects of the laws, which experience has proven to exist—and to suggest such amendments
and enactments as the good of the community may require.

"Such is the interesting occasion, fellow citizens, which
brings us together; and, in the name of our common constituents, I cordially greet you, and tender you my hearty
cooperation in the adoption and execution of all measures
that may redound to the welfare of the community.

"Since the last meeting of your Honorable body, although portions of our State have been visited with affliction, and with physical causes destructive to the hopes and
labors of the husbandman[1]—yet the general health of the
land and the bounteous productions of the soil have been
such as to elicit the most profound gratitude towards that
Author, from whom all blessings flow, and to whose superin-
tending Providence we are indebted for all we are, and for
all we hope to be.   And it is our especial duty, as it is that
of every Department of every American Government, earnestly to solicit a continuance of those peculiar favors, which
have rendered the American people the blessed of the earth.

"Within the same period, an event has taken place, in
the death of our lamented Chief Magistrate, which, while
a grateful people has mourned their bereavement, and a
suffering country felt the affliction, yet has it proven the
foresight of our Revolutionary sages, in the adoption of our
Constitution, and has tested its wisdom and stability.   A
similar event, in most other countries, would have been
followed by a resort to force, or, at least to extraordinary
legislation to establish succession.   With us, the successor,
already indicated by the people themselves, glides into the
Chief Magistracy, with an ease and quiet on his part, and
an acquiescence on ours, that proves how fortunate it is
for the human family, when, in the establishment of their
forms of Government, they select Wisdom, instead of Am-

---

[1] Reference is to the cyclonic storm over the lower Roanoke Valley, destroying the crops of that rich section.

bition for their counsellor. And, it is to be fondly hoped, that every future test, like this, will assure the friends of our form of Government, of its strength, and its enemies, how delusive the hope of its destruction.

"The result of the late treaty with Great Britain, gives us pleasing prospects of continued peace; and, however widely some of us may differ from the President, as to the manner in which he has discharged a portion of his duties, yet the meed of praise is due to him, for his earnest and successful efforts, sustained and carried through by the eminent abilities of his distinguished Secretary, to adjust our difficulties with that Power upon principles of Honor and of Justice. Nor is it to be believed, that the good arising from this adjustment, will be confined to the parties immediately concerned.[1] The noble example, set by two of the most powerful, intelligent and honorable nations of the earth, in adjusting their difficulties by a resort to argument, instead of arms, will be worthy the imitation of every member constituting the great family of nations.

"The history of nations ought to have taught, and it is hoped has taught the present generation, that that good which arises from the guidance of reason and the dictates of justice, is more beneficial and permanent, than that which results from the most brilliant triumph of arms, victorious over right and justice.

"In inviting your attention to such matters as ought to engage your deliberations during your present Session, I refer you to the first Article of our Constitution, as amended, whereby it becomes your duty at this Session, to lay off the State into Senatorial Districts, and to apportion the representatives in the House of Commons among the several Counties of the State. The rules, by which you are to be guided in the discharge of your duties, are so explicitly laid down in the Constitution itself, as to preclude all suggestions on the subject.

"At the last Session of Congress an Act was passed to apportion the Representatives among the several States, ac-

---

[1] The Webster-Ashburton Treaty defining the northwestern boundary between Canada and the United States, proclaimed about ten days before.

cording to the Sixth Census. By this Act the number of
Representatives, to which North Carolina is entitled, is reduced from thirteen to nine. It therefore becomes your duty
to lay off the State into nine Congressional and eleven
Electoral districts. In the discharge of this duty justice to
the citizens of every part of the State demands that the districts shall be laid off as nearly equal in Federal Population
as it is practicable to make them, and that they shall assume
such shape as shall be most convenient for the voters and
candidates of every district. Indeed, the principle, that in all
popular elections, every citizen should have the full political
weight to which he is entitled by the Constitutions and Laws
of the country, is so obviously just and undeniable, that it is
deemed scarcely necessary to suggest its adoption for your
guidance in the discharge of your important duties.

"By an Act of Congress, approved the 4th of September,
1841, entitled 'An Act to Appropriate the Proceeds of the
Sales of the Public Lands, and to Grant Pre-emption Rights,'
a payment became due to North Carolina at the public Treasury, on the 1st of July last. On the 24th June preceding,
a communication from the Treasury Department was addressed to this Department, requesting that an Agent should
be designated to receive the payment. I forthwith appointed
Charles L. Hinton, Esq., Public Treasurer, the Agent of this
State, to receive the payment; who proceeded to Washington
for that purpose, but the amount was not then paid, for the
reason, as it was alleged, that the net amount for distribution
had not then been ascertained. On the 4th November, the
Acting Secretary of the United States, informed me that the
accounts had been adjusted, and the sum of $22,917.97 was
found due this State, of which the Treasurer was informed,
and he forthwith requested the Department at Washington
to forward him a draft for the amount. This draft is daily
expected. It becomes your duty to apply this Fund to such
purpose as your wisdom may suggest.

"The Raleigh and Gaston Railroad Company availed
themselves of the Act of the last Session, entitled—'An Act
to secure the State against any and every liability incurred
for the Raleigh and Gaston Railroad Company, and for

the relief of the same,'—by accepting the benefit of the Act, and giving the Executive notice of the acceptance within the time therein prescribed. The Deed of Mortgage, and Deed of Pledge, required by said Act, have been duly executed and registered, and Bonds to the amount of $500,000, conditioned as required, have been executed and delivered to the Treasurer, signed by obligors whom, I believed at the time, to be able to pay and satisfy said Bonds. The Treasurer endorsed $300,000 of the Bonds of said Company, as directed by the said Act to do, and delivered them to the Company; and having therefore, under a former Act, endorsed $500,000, the State stands responsible for the Company, now, to the amount of $800,000. As yet, I am not aware that the Treasurer has been required to pay anything for any responsibility incurred by the State for this corporation.

"At the same Session, an Act somewhat similar, entitled 'An Act for the Relief of the Wilmington and Raleigh Railroad Company,' was passed. That Company availed itself of the benefit of the Act, by fully complying with its requirements, in giving the security, and their Bonds, to the amount of $300,000, have been endorsed by the Treasurer, as by said Act he was directed to do. I am not aware that any demand has been made upon the Treasury, for any liability incurred for this Company; and I am informed that the Company has discharged $50,000 of said Bonds, as required by the Act. Besides the interest, which the State should feel, from pride and utility, in the success of these two noble enterprises, there is an additional interest, which invites your serious attention. For the first of these Roads, we have seen that the State is bound as security for $800,000 —for the latter, she is bound as security now for $250,000, besides being a stock-holder in the same to the amount of $600,000. The first, and most important consideration then, is—How the Roads can be enabled to meet their liabilities, and thereby secure the State. The embarrassment of the country has been, for some time past, and is likely to be for some time to come, so extraordinary, that travel, the most profitable source of revenue to Railroads, has decreased exceedingly, and the productions of industry are so low, and the profits of merchandise so reduced, that the income from heavy transportation has greatly diminished. No doubt is entertained but that both Roads would speedily extricate themselves from debt, and make their stock profitable, could they have full employment. Any Act of legislation that can aid them, in procuring additional employment, without incurring additional responsibility on the part of the State, will certainly be wise and prudent.

"It is more than probable that application will be made to charter a Company to construct a Railroad from some point on the Raleigh and Gaston Railroad, to Weldon, the point where the Portsmouth and Roanoke and Wilmington and Raleigh Railroads meet; thus connecting, by a continuous Railroad, our seat of Government with our own excellent Port of Wilmington, on the one hand, and with one of the best sea-ports in the world on the other. No valid objection to granting this charter is perceived, while there is much to sustain its propriety The distance is short, some fifteen miles, the ground is favorable, and the usual expense of Depots and Cars can be dispensed with, by the use of those belonging to the Roads so greatly interested in this connection. Besides the advantage of transferring heavy articles and such as are inconvenient to handle, directly from the Vessels to the Cars, that will deliver them in Raleigh, and *vice versa,* it will cheapen and quicken transportation, by competition, shorten the route by Railroad to Wilmington, and give us the means of offering our products in the rival markets of Petersburg, Norfolk and Wilmington, within a few hours after leaving the city of Raleigh.

"The next inquiry is, by what means the vast productions of the fertile West can be made to travel Eastward, and reap the advantages of these Railroad facilities. From personal observation, I have found the Roads, leading from Raleigh Westward, for the distance of fifty or sixty miles, and those passing over similar Geological formations, which range from Northeast to Southwest, across the whole State, separating the rich valley of the Yadkin from Fayetteville, decidedly the worst in the State. Thus we find the productions of this range, often seeking a market much more distant than our own, because more easy of access; the towns of Cheraw, Camden, Columbia, and in the far West, Augusta and Charleston are much more familiarly known than even Fayetteville or Raleigh; much less, those Towns farther Eastward; and this grows out of the impracticability, in a great degree, of passing over our Roads with heavy burdens at that season of the year, most convenient to take our products to market. The remedy for these evils is believed to be in good Turnpikes—improvements more within our means and therefore more likely to be made, and answering every desirable purpose. I therefore recommend that a charter be granted, to make a Turnpike Road, from the city of Raleigh to some point Westward, selected with a view to its ultimate continuance to the extreme West, requiring the corporations to commence operations at Raleigh, and to finish specified sections of the Road, within specified periods, and making it forfeit its charter as to all that part of the contemplated Road, which is not finished in the time prescribed, but granting the privilege to charge Tolls on all such parts as are completed, having a due regard to the citizens of the counties through which the Road may pass, so that they shall not be harrassed by unnecessary exactions on those parts of the Road lying in the counties where they reside. Such a charter would hold out inducements to capitalists to embark in the enterprise, as they could abandon it whenever they found it was likely to be injudicious, and yet retain what they had finished. Should this Road be continued to Waynesboro, which might be done at comparatively small expense, the Farmer would have the choice of markets, of Wilmington by the Railroad, or, Newbern by the river Neuse. This Turnpike, it is confidently believed, would aid greatly to sustain the Railroads, and, at the same time to give Industry facilities to which it is now a stranger.[1]

"In connection with these Roads, I will again invite your attention to the facility with which the State can be called

---

[1] Here is evidence of his thought along the line of a Central railroad.

upon for payment. If either of these Companies shall
fail 'to pay the principal and interest as it accrues, the Public
Treasurer is authorized to pay the same, out of any money
in the Treasury at the time,' and for this the faith of the
State is pledged. By reference to the amount of semi-
annual interest, and annual payment of principal, which are
required to be paid, it will be seen, that it is not probable,
nor indeed it is necessary, that there should be in the Treasury at all times, an amount sufficient to meet these contingencies, which, it is to be hoped, will never happen. Yet,
as they may happen, and as the pledge of the State must be
kept, under all circumstances, inviolate, and its faith sustained, I recommend that the Treasurer have authority to
borrow, from our Banks, a sum not exceeding, at any one
time, the amount which the State may be required to pay
between the sessions of the Legislature, and that these loans
be contracted only as the demands are made, and after the
funds belonging to the Treasury are exhausted.

"By a Resolution of the last Legislature, the Treasurer
was directed to borrow, from the Literary and Internal
Improvement Funds, such sums as might be necessary to
defray the expenses of the State, until the 1st Nov., 1842—
'he, at no time, borrowing more than is required for the time
being,' and the officers, having charge of these Funds, were
directed thus to loan them. The inconvenience of this plan,
to supply the wants of the Treasury, is experienced in this:
A large amount of these funds have to lie idle in the Treasury, to be ready when the Treasurer may wish to borrow.
The Boards, having charge of the funds, are thereby restrained from seeking for them permanent investments,
and the profits, which ought to arise from so large an
amount, is greatly diminished, as it is not presumed the
Legislature contemplated paying interest on any more than
was actually used.

"As these liabilities of the Treasury are to continue for
years to come, it is the part of prudence to make provision
to meet them promptly, no matter how sudden and unexpected the call.

"I would respectfully invite your attention to the Public

Highways generally. In the Eastern section of the State, the variety of navigable sounds, rivers and streams, and the excellent adaptation of the face of the country, to good Roads render Legislative negligence on these subjects less oppressive. But from Fayetteville, the highest point of good navigation Westward (and only the navigation in our own State, in that direction, except the slight batteau Navigation of the Dan, as high as the county of Rockingham) to the Buncombe Turnpike, a distance of some two hundred and fifty or three hundred miles, what navigable *Stream, Railroad, Turnpike,* or *McAdamized* highway gives to the laborer facilities of transportation? None—literally, none! This vast extent of territory, reaching from the Blue Ridge in the West to the alluvial region in the East, and extending across the whole State, it is believed, will compare with any spot upon the globe, for the fertility of its soil, the variety of its productions, the salubrity of its climate, the beauty of its landscapes, the richness of its Mines, the facilities for Manufactures, and the intelligence and moral worth of its population. Can another such territory, combining all these advantages, be found upon the face of the whole earth, so wholly destitute of natural or artificial facilities for Transportation?

"I direct your attention to the wants of this portion of the State—it is the business of your wisdom to supply them. Fayetteville seems naturally to invite the commerce of the West. Her river affords as good and durable navigation as most rivers in the South; her exporting port of Wilmington is superior to those of Petersburg, Richmond and many other important towns; and the wisdom of a previous Legislature thought the necessities of this region demanded the advantages which a Railroad could afford. This scheme having failed, it is believed, from the pressure of the times, the next inquiry is—What scheme, that is practicable, will afford the desired facilities?

"Next to Navigation and Railroads, Turnpikes afford the best means of taking produce to market. I therefore recommend that a charter be granted to make a Turnpike from Fayetteville to the Yadkin river, at some point above

the Narrows, or, if deemed most expedient, to some point on
a similar road leading from Raleigh, Westward, thus giving
the West the advantages of both markets; with such favorable conditions in the charter, as heretofore suggested, that
Capitalists will be induced to embark in the enterprise.
And surely this scheme cannot fail for want of means.
Labor will be an excellent substitute for money, and labor
cannot be difficult to obtain, in a region now growing Cotton
at six cents per lb., corn at one dollar per bbl., and wheat so
low that it takes one-half to transport the other half to
market.   Should this Road ever reach the Yadkin, no doubt
is entertained of its continuance across the Catawba, westward—thus giving to this Road the advantages which will
arise from the navigation of these two noble rivers, from
the Falls on the Southern border of the State, now wholly
obstructing their navigation for a greater distance towards
their sources.

"The Western portion of the State, comprising what
may be termed the Mountain Counties, is a vastly interesting
region, and invites your due regard.   To make them more
interesting, we only have to make them more accessible.
The sublimity and beauty of its Mountain Scenery, the
purity of its waters, the buoyancy and salubrity of its atmosphere, the fertility of its valleys, the verdure of its
mountains, and, above all, its energetic, intelligent and hos-
pitable inhabitants, make it an inviting portion of the State.
The face of the country necessarily makes the construction
of Roads very difficult and expensive, and the sparseness of
the population, in many places, forbids the imposition of a
duty so onerous upon them.   These Mountain Roads are
made, at an expense, much less than might be supposed;
and, when well made, are very firm and easily kept in repair.   The rapid descent in the Streams forbids much hope
in Navigation, and, therefore, renders their claim upon the
liberality of the Legislature, to aid them in these Roads
more just and meritorious.   When good Roads shall be established in that region, it is believed the population will increase with rapidity, agriculture improved, grazing will be
extended, and Manufactures and the mechanic Art will

flourish in a location combining so many advantages and inviting their growth. The improved highways will be additional inducement to the citizens of other sections of our State, to abandon their usual Northern Tours or visit to the Virginia Watering places for a Tour much more interesting among our own Mountains, much cheaper and much more beautiful—a Tour in which they will inspire health in every breath, and drink in health in every draught. The large amount of money paid, and to be paid, into the public Treasury, from that quarter, for Vacant and Cherokee Lands, would seem to give stronger claims to aid from the Treasury. It is, therefore, respectfully recommended, that you give to that section of the State, such aid, as in your wisdom its condition may require, and the condition of the public Treasury may justify.

"The Buncombe Turnpike, in which the State is a stock-holder, shows the great advantages arising from such improvements, and its profits, of twelve to fifteen per cent per annum, prove the great use of it.

"There is another inconvenience to which this section of the State labors, and to which I deem it proper to call your attention. This extensive Territory is wholly destitute of Banking facilities, although it is so large that the County, which once embraced nearly the whole of it, was frequently dignified with the appellation of a State. When it is recollected, the large amount that is due to the State, for the sale of Cherokee Lands, it becomes a matter of public interest, that the debtors who reside mostly in that quarter, should have a currency among them in which to make payment.

"Turning our attention to the Eastern part of the State, two improvements, said to be practicable, assume an importance that renders them National in their character. I allude to the opening of Roanoke Inlet, and a connection of Pamlico Sound, by a Ship Channel, with Beaufort Harbor. Frequent surveys of the first of these proposed improvements, made by scientific Engineers, and, more particularly, one latterly made under the authority of this State, by Maj. Walter Gwynn, whose qualifications, endorsed by the General Government, are equalled only by his practical skill, establish the feasibility of this work. The advantages, arising from the improvement to our Commerce, are too obvious to need pointing out. But the view to be taken of its vast importance, is, in the protection it will afford to our shipping, and the lives of our seamen. The difficulty and dangers often encountered at Ocracoke Inlet, render the connection between Pamlico Sound and Beaufort Harbor of vast importance to the convenience and security of our Commerce and Shipping. It will be an extension of that inland navigation so essential to us, in time of war, and give access to one of the safest harbors on our coast, and one from which a Vessel can be quicker at sea than from any other, perhaps, on our Continent. In these improvements the Commerce of the nation[1] is interested; it becomes the duty of the nation to make them, if they be practicable and proper. I therefore recommend, that you bring the attention of Congress to the subject, in the manner most likely to effect the object. The attention of Congress has been repeatedly drawn to the first of these objects, but nothing is yet done. We should assert a continual claim to our right to have this work effected by the General Government. It is beyond the present ability of the State[1] to execute it, and if it were not, it so appropriately belongs to the General Government[1] to execute it, that it might be considered an infringement of its rights for the State[1] to attempt it. You would be saved the trouble of this appeal, if the nation[1] could witness one of those storms so frequent on our coast—could witness the war of elements which rages around Hatteras, and the dangers which dance about Ocracoke—could witness the noble daring of our Pilots, and the ineffectual, but manly struggles, of our seamen—could see our coast fringed with wrecks, and our towns filled with widows and orphans of our gallant tars. Justice and Humanity would extort what we now ask in vain. If

---

[1] These several references to "State," "General Government" and "nation," occurring in this paragraph, especially in the use of capital letters, are unique as an illustration of Governor Morehead's invariable accuracy in the use of capital letters according to the rules of the day, and as illustrating the attitude of mind of the day, also, in his section of the land.

one tithe of the destruction, which happens on our coast, were to happen in Delaware Bay or at the entrance of Boston or New York Harbors, the sensibilities of the whole nation would be aroused, and if its recurrence could be prevented by human means, such appeals would be thundered into the ears of Congress, as would afford the protection desired, regardless of the appropriation. But instead of giving *us* the protection *we* so much need, a beggarly sum is doled out to North Carolina, to repair a dilapidated Fort, or protect an abrading sand-bank.

"On the South side of the Cape Fear, is a considerable extent of Country, watered by the Lumber River and its tributaries, which is heavily timbered, and would become very valuable if accessible to a good market. That river is now used to carry lumber to Georgetown in South Carolina; but the navigation is somewhat obstructed and difficult, and so distant is the market, that the business is not found profitable. It is suggested, by those better acquainted with the geography of that region than myself, that Lumber River can be very easily connected with the Cape Fear by a Canal—that the expense of the Canal, and of opening the river to improve its navigation, will be inconsiderable, compared with the advantages derived from the improvement. I therefore recommend, that a survey be ordered, to ascertain the practicability of uniting these rivers by a good navigable Canal, and that an estimate be made of its probable cost.

"The Judicial Department of our Government has been administered with promptness, fidelity and ability; but I cannot forbear to call your attention to the frequent acts of violence and force committed upon our Jails, whereby prisoners, charged with the highest crimes, are released, rescued, or escape. To such an extent has this been carried, that open force has been used, and that, too, I believe, in the presence of the Jailor to break the Jail, seize the prisoners, and inflict on them summary punishment, for real or supposed offenses. In other instances, the prisoners have been aided in their escape, by external force, clandestinely used. In others, by the use of instruments furnished them in prison. Whether these frequent and repeated offenses against the due administration of Justice, arise from the cowardice, connivance or negligence of Jailors, or from the delinquency of the Magistrates in not building sufficient prisons, are questions submitted for your consideration, with the hope that you will apply the corrective, if the present Laws be insufficient.

"There is another matter connected with the due administration of Criminal Law, that deserves attention. Criminals have been permitted to go at large, and finally to escape, after it has been notoriously known that they have committed offenses. If the present Law on that subject can be improved, I recommend that it be done. Nothing affords such ample protection to the *Innocent,* as the certain punishment of the *Guilty.*

"The President and Directors of the Literary Fund will lay before you, in due time, a detailed Report of their Proceedings, and the state of the Fund, and of the extent of their operations in draining the Swamp Land. It will be your duty, as it is the desire of the Literary Board, to institute the most rigid examination and scrutiny into the manner in which the pecuniary affairs of the Board have been managed. It is due to the People to know how they have been managed; and it is due to the Board, if they have faithfully discharged their duties, that their Fellow Citizens should know that also.

"And, in connection with this examination, I would recommend a scrutiny into the affairs and condition of the University of our State. It is the child of the Constitution, and should be watched over with Parental care by your Body. It is believed that due attention is not paid to that important Institution by the Legislature. Such Reports and examinations are not made as will give the Public full information in relation to its management and utility; and thus Demagogues sometimes make it the hobby, upon which they ride into public favor, by making the grossest misrepresentations.

"The Report of the Board of Internal Improvements will be laid before you during the present Session, which does not promise to be very interesting, as the Board has but little under its charge at this time, besides the small Fund under its control, into which they invite the strictest scrutiny.

"By virtue of the Act authorizing me to appoint an agent in the County of Macon or Cherokee, for the purposes therein specified, I appointed Jacob Siler, Esq., who gave the Bond and Security required, and entered upon the discharge of his duties. His communications to the Treasury Department will give you the information as to his progress. The general pecuniary pressure, the scarcity of circulating medium in the Western part of the State, the want of sufficient Roads to carry Produce to Market, and the outlays necessary to settle a new Country, all combine to make it extremely difficult to pay the debt due the State upon the Cherokee Bonds, and it is believed if payments thereon be rigorously exacted, the result will be, in many instances, ruin to the debtors and loss to the State; but if reasonable indulgence be given, it is probable that most of the debts will be collected. The high price, for which these Lands sold, would seem to justify all reasonable indulgence.

"A Resolution of last Session having authorized me to employ Counsel to defend the Titles of Purchases of Lands in Cherokee County, I engaged the services of Thomas L. Clingman, Esq., who, I presume, will make a Report, during the Session, upon the subject, which will be laid before you.

"The progress of civilization, sustained by the dictates of humanity, would seem to appeal to public liberality, for the establishment of Asylums for the use and benefit of the Deaf, Dumb and Blind, and for the protection of the unfortunate Lunatic. The helpless and suffering condition of many of these afflicted creatures, have long since and often appealed to the public charity of a Christian community. It is referred to you to say how unheeded has been that appeal. It is likewise referred to *you* to say how much longer we shall manifest our gross ingratitude to *Him,* who showers upon us, with the hand of profusion, all the choice blessings of life, while we withhold a beggarly pittance from His afflicted Children.

"The establishment of a Penitentiary, in this State, has

long been a matter of discussion, and it is probable, by this time, that Public opinion has determined upon its expediency. I therefore direct your attention to the subject. Long experience in the practice of the Criminal Courts has satsified me, that offenders are often permitted to escape from a laudable humanity in Jurors, who look upon the severity and ignominy of the punishment that awaits the culprit, upon a verdict of Guilty, until their kindlier feelings conjure up doubts enough to justify a conscientious acquittal. It is believed that a few years apprenticeship in a Penitentiary, substituted for the present mode of punishment, would cause many a verdict to more nearly approximate the truth.

"Whether it be expedient to establish these institutions, and if expedient, whether this is a proper time to do so—whether you will embark the Funds of the State, in any of the schemes of Internal Improvement heretofore suggested—are matters for your consideration.

"To you, the consideration of these matters appropriately belongs—*in* you, the powers of taxation and appropriation are constitutionally vested. You are fresh from your Constituents, and doubtless well advised as to their wishes and wants—to them, you are responsible for the manner in which you shall discharge the high trusts confided to you, and therefore to you are these matters most respectfully referred.

"I would recommend, that whatever schemes of expenditure you may embark in, that you keep within the means at the command of the State; otherwise, the People must be taxed more heavily, or the State must contract a Loan. The pressure of the times, forbids the former—the tarnished honor of some of the States should make us, for the present, decline the latter.

"The mania for State Banking, and the mad career of Internal Improvement, which seized a number of the States, have involved them in an indebtedness, very oppressive, but not hopeless. American credit and character require that the stain of violated faith should be obliterated, by our honest acknowledgment of the debt, and a still more honest

effort to pay it. I therefore recommend the passage of
Resolutions, expressive of the strong interest which the
State feels in the full redemption of every pledge of Public
faith, and of its utter detestation of the abominable doctrine
of REPUDIATION. That State, which honestly owes a debt,
and has, or can command the means of payment and refuses
to pay, because it cannot be compelled to do so, has already
bartered Public Honor, and only awaits an increase of price,
to barter Public Liberty. This recommendation will come
with peculiar force from you. North Carolina has been
jeered at for sluggishness and indolence, because she has
chosen to guard her Treasury and protect her Honor, by
avoiding debt, and promptly meeting her engagements.
She has yielded to others the glory of their magnificent
expenditures, and will yield them all that glory which will
arise from a repudiation of their contracts. In the language
of one of her noblest sons, 'It is better for her to sleep on
in indolence and innocence, than to wake up in infamy and
treason.'

"But when Public Honor is at stake, or Public Liberty
endangered, she will shake the poppy from her brow; and
then, for her high-souled patriotism, for her unwavering
devotion to the love of Liberty, for her loyalty to the Union,
and for her stern integrity, the proudest sister of the Republic may well desire to be her rival.

"The Civil commotion, which has lately disturbed the
patriotic State of Rhode Island, is deeply to be regretted,
and its termination in a conflict might have been attended
with serious consequences to other States.[1] Aside then
from mere sympathy, we cannot be indifferent spectators.
Inequality in the right of suffrage is the ground upon
which resistance to the constituted authorities and overt
acts of rebellion are attempted to be justified. Without
passing upon the merits of the issue between the parties, in
that State, I am constrained to say, that there is a spirit
too often manifested in our country, to enforce our sup-

---

[1] "Dorr's Rebellion" to secure revision of the constitution, which later was
secured in 1842.

posed rights, or to redress our supposed grievances, by appeals to open resistance, rather than to Law, to reason, and to a returning sense of Justice. It is not every grievance, under which a people may labor, that justifies a resort to force for redress; nor is it believed, that in any portion of our enlightened country, in this enlightened age, will a course of policy be persisted in, that is grossly unjust and oppressive. The steady appeal to right and reason, is sure in due time to procure the appropriate remedy. The example of our own State, in her steady efforts to reform her representation, by appeals to the justice of her claims, and the success which eventually crowned those efforts, is proof of the wisdom of that policy. I therefore deem it the duty of all friends of social order, to rebuke, on all occasions, that spirit which is every ready to light the torch of civil discord, and revel in the blood of a brother.

"Our Banks resumed specie payments during the past summer, and it is believed will be able to sustain themselves in future. But, while they afford us a sound Currency, it is to be regretted, that they are not enabled to extend their accommodations, and increase circulation, to that extent the necessities of the community require.

"North Carolina, although an Atlantic State, is to a great extent, in the condition of some of the interior States. She has no large commercial mart, from which is shipped the principal productions of her industry. These are shipped mostly from the Ports of Virginia and South Carolina. The balances against her at the North, contracted for the immense quantity of merchandise purchased there, have to be paid in cash. Our Bank notes have to supply this cost, either by being presented at once for specie, and that taken to the North, and there shaved to the Brokers at a discount (which a prompt redemption in specie cannot prevent), who forthwith present them at Bank for payment in specie, or its equivalent. Thus, the perpetual flow of our Bank notes Northward, to pay balances against us, is met by a counter-current of the same notes Southward—not to pay balances in our favor—not to be thrown again into circulation by the purchase of our produce—but to stop them from circulation, by pushing them into the Banks and drawing out the specie from them. The only means of protection against these continued drains, which our Banks can resort to, is to curtail their circulation—the very thing that operates against the community, but the only thing which can prevent them from being driven again into another suspension. If we had a National Currency at *par* in every part of the Union, by which to pay these balances against us, that Currency would never touch the hands of the Broker. It would be thrown into circulation in every direction, instead of being thrown back upon the Bank that issued it. Our own notes would remain among us—there would be little demand for specie, as but few would return upon the Banks, and they would thus be enabled to throw a much larger amount in circulation, without the risk of their sudden return for specie, and without the risk of being driven again into another suspension. The hopes of having National Currency has been twice thwarted by the President's Vetoes upon Charters for National Banks. Whether he will continue regardless of the will and of the sufferings of the people, time will disclose. Whether the examples of Washington and of Madison are unworthy of his imitation, he must decide. One thing we all know—from the time of the first establishment of the first National Bank, to the present time, whenever we have been without that Institution, our pecuniary affairs have been greatly deranged. In this State, the issue of a National Bank has been fairly submitted to the people by the rival candidates, in the two last gubernatorial elections. The result, each time, proves the majority to be in favor of such an Institution. It is, therefore, respectfully submitted, whether you ought not to aid, by all the means as your command, to carry out this expressed will of your Constituents.

"The disease, under which the National prosperity labors, is the want of facility in Exchanges and a sound uniform National Currency. The remedy, resorted to in some of the States, is the establishment of State Banks, which throw in circulation a supply of notes, which for a moment seems to give relief, but these notes have only to take a turn or two Northward, and back again, to be redeemed with specie, and the vaults are empty—the Bank suspends—the notes become valueless, and the remedy turns out to be a wretched quackery, that aggravates the disease. Banks owned by States, so located as to be subject to these continued drains of their specie, cannot withstand the operation, any more than those owned by individuals.

"The passage of a new Tariff of duties, at the last Session of Congress, it is hoped, will relieve the nation from the temporary shifts of issuing Treasury notes, or of resorting to loans to meet its current expenses, and to pay its debts. Already its effects are visible in the increased activity of American Industry, and in the growling tone of some of the European Journals, and in due time, it is believed, will be visible in the increase of our Revenue. But scarcely has the law gone into operation, before we hear its repeal threatened, because its object is something besides raising Revenue. It is high time, the principles, under which duties may be imposed, should be settled and adhered to. The principle being settled, the extent to which the power may be exercised then becomes a matter of expediency. All agree that duties may be imposed to raise Revenue, but some contend that they can be imposed for no other object. If this latter doctrine be true, then are we shorn of some of the most important prerogatives of a sovereign People—then may we be subjected to the most abject commercial Slavery. If it be admitted that Europe can pour into our Country the excessive productions of her pauper labor, whenever she chooses, and can exclude our productions from her Markets, or tax them so high as to be ruinous to us, and that we have no power to protect ourselves against the influx of the one, or to counteract the oppressive exclusion, or heavy exactions of the other—then, indeed, are we in a helpless condition. The avowal of this doctrine is well calculated to invite Foreign Powers, who are so inclined to forget right, to impose all such tyrannical restrictions upon our commerce, as their cupidity may suggest. Indeed, for some time past, we have been approximating this condition. Europe has been flooding our Country with the products of her labor, at a tax of some 20 per cent, while the productions of American Labor have been either totally excluded from her markets, or taxed from 50 to 2500 per cent. Her writers upon the wealth of Nations descant to us upon the beauties of FREE TRADE. Her political Orators and Journals shout to us, across the Atlantic—'FREE TRADE'—and the glorious privilege of *buying* from whom you please.

"Some of us re-echo *Free Trade,* and the glorious privilege of buying of whom we please. But from none of these do we hear the shout of Free Trade and the glorious privilege of *selling* where we please and to whom we choose. It is as important to us to have the privilege of selling, without exorbitant exactions, as it is to buy without them. If every facility and inducement to purchase the industry of others are opened to us—but every facility and inducement to sell the products of our industry are obstructed or closed, then must we become, most surely, a ruined people. This sentiment was uttered by one of our most distinguished Presidents, in 1824, in relation to a Tariff, and at that time when he was before the people as a candidate for that high office, is fully sustained by eighteen years of subsequent experience. He said—'In short, Sir, we have been too long subject to the *policy of British Merchants.* It is time we should become a little more *Americanized,* and, instead of feeding the *paupers* and *laborers* of Europe, feed our own; or, else, in a short time, by continuing *our present policy,* we shall be rendered *paupers ourselves.*' The policy then recommended by him has not been pursued, and how truly he shadowed forth our present condition. Let us resist the policy of *British Merchants;* let us become a good deal more *Americanized;* let us feed our own paupers and laborers, instead of feeding those of England; let us abandon that policy which leads to Pauperism, and adopt that which will raise paupers and laborers to competency and independence. Let us declare our Commercial Independence and proclaim to the world, we have the power not only to raise Revenue by imposing duties, but that we have the power, by imposing them, to protect American Industry against European Industry, and to counteract by our Legislation any foreign Legislation hostile to our interests. But, at the same time, let us invite all nations to a commercial intercourse with us, upon terms of the most extended liberality, but, they must be terms of equality and reciprocity.

"That the General Government has power to impose duties for the protection of American Industry, against European Industry, and to counteract foreign legislation hostile to our Interests, I think can admit of no doubt. When the States became independent, they had the power unquestionably. All their powers to impose duties, they transferred to the General Government by the adoption of the Constitution. They then ceased to have the power; and, if the General Government has it not, then the power is extinct. Is there an American willing to admit this?

"I do not wish to be understood as advocating a high Tariff. I contend for the power to impose it, if we think our interests require it. I advocate the doctrine of Free Trade, as far as it is practicable; but when it ceases to be practicable, unless at a ruinous sacrifice to us, I abandon it, and say to the world—'We will do unto others as they do unto us.'

"I have thought it proper, on this occasion, to say thus much on this important subject. The American people ought to know the general opinion of the Union upon it; that they may make some calculation what is likely to be the course of policy pursued for the future. Frequent legislation on the subject, from one extreme to another, defeats the best devised plans, baffles the wisest calculations, and often destroys hopes well founded. The suspense in which the people are kept, checks their energy, curbs their enterprise, and kills their prosperity.

"I had long entertained the hope, upon the payment of our National Debt, the proceeds arising from the sales of Public Lands, would be distributed among the States, to which they so justly belong. This Fund would aid the States greatly in the Education of their Youth, and in their schemes of Improvement. But if we wish to expend more than the means now at our command, we shall have to resort to an increase in Taxes upon our citizens. The President has thought proper to interpose himself between us and our just rights and deprive us, for the present, of the Funds arising from that source. He had the power to do so, and we must submit until the time shall arrive, for us to exercise the power vested in us, by removing the obstruction, and taking possession of what is so justly ours.

"The President having called an extra Session of Congress in 1841, prior to the regular Congressional Elections in our State, it became my duty to order an Election for Members of the present Congress, by Proclamation.

"In the death of the Hon. Lewis Williams, the late Representative in the thirteenth Congressional District, the House of Representatives was deprived of its oldest, and one of the most efficient Members, the State one of its ablest and most faithful Representatives, and the community, of one of its best, most honored and most esteemed citizens. A Writ of Election was issued to supply the vacancy, which resulted in the election of the Hon. Anderson Mitchell, of Wilkes.

"By the death of Alexander Troy, Esq., late Solicitor of the fifth Judicial Circuit, the State was deprived of an excellent officer, and of a most estimable citizen. A temporary appointment, by the Presiding Judge, of Hon. Robert Strange, was made to fill the vacancy. It will be your duty to elect his successor. Solicitors for the second and fourth Judicial Circuits are likewise to be elected.

"The Report of the State and progress of Common Schools is necessarily too long for this Communication, and will constitute a part of the Report of the Literary Board.

"Having received the resignations, in file A, of William B. Shepard, Esq., the Senator elect from the first Senatorial District; of Elisha Bostick, a member elect of the House of Commons, from the County of Richmond; and of Robert T. Paine, a member elect of the same House, for the County of Chowan, I issued Writs of Election to supply these vacancies.

"The accompanying File, marked B, contains the resignations of Justices of the Peace, made since the last Session.

"The accompanying File C, contains Resolutions passed by the Legislatures of the following States, viz.: Maine, Massachusetts, Vermont, Connecticut, Rhode Island, New York, New Jersey, Delaware, Pennsylvania, Maryland, Virginia, South Carolina, Georgia, Alabama, Mississippi, Tennessee, Kentucky and Indiana. These Resolutions refer to the following subjects:

"The death of the President and the donation to his Widow;

"The amendment of the Constitution as to the Veto Power, and the Presidential term of service, and the passage of a Law, requiring Electors for President to be elected on the same day throughout the Union;

"The Revenue and Tariff, protective and discriminating;

"The Public Lands, and the distribution of the proceeds of the sales thereof;

"The demand of fugitives from justice, embracing the demand of persons, charged with Negro stealing and the correspondence on the subject;

"The Northeast Boundary;

"The admission of Texas into the Union;

"'The U. S. Bank, or Fiscal Corporation;

"The Bankrupt Law;

"The Sub-Treasury;

"The Repudiation of State debts;

"The surviving Soldiers of the Revolution;

"The Military Academy at West Point;

"The Loan Bill and One Hour rule of the House of Representatives.

"The term of service of Hon. William A. Graham, a Senator of the United States from this State, expires with the present Congress. You will supply the vacancy.

"During the past Spring, I received the Standard Yard Measure and Ounce Weights furnished by the General Government. I advertised for a Contract to make duplicates thereof, to be furnished to the several Counties agreeably to Act of Assembly. Having received no bid, through the agency of a gentleman travelling Northward, I endeavored to get a contract to make them in that direction. A proposition has been received, to execute the work in a style so superior, and at a price so far above anything contemplated by the Legislature, that I did not feel warranted in accepting the proposition. The capacity measures, intended for Standards, were not then ready, and have not been received.

"By a Resolution of the Last Session, I was directed to cause the 1st Volume of the Revised Statutes, to be distributed to such Magistrates as had been appointed since 1836. I have caused all the copies at this place, except such as are required to be retained, to be distributed; and it is believed, a few Magistrates are not yet supplied. There were a few extra copies in some counties, from which I have endeavored to supply those who were not supplied.

"In conclusion, Gentlemen, should the wisdom of your Counsels tend to elevate the moral character of our State, to enlighten its youth, to relieve the helpless, to reform offenders, to protect the innocent, to improve our physical condition, to aid the debtors, to reward industry, and to encourage honesty, integrity and morality, none will be more grateful to you for the essential services, than

"Your Fellow Citizen
"and humble Servant
"J. M. Morehead."[1]

No more statesman-like executive message ever issued from any gubernatorial chair in the United States; and, in its national and international aspect, it is worthy of any occupant of the Presidential chair. It was widely circulated and its principles are still advocated and sometimes has been quoted by his successsors down to the present generation. Here is a conception of transportation that was to become his chief theme for the rest of his life; and his latest successor, as this is written, is still carrying them out to their logical conclusion. The Whigs were of course finding it the produest day of their lives in North Carolina.

Among expressions outside of the State concerning the Whig executive's message was a notable and typical one

[1] *Raleigh Register*, 25th November, 1842; and official reports.

from the *Alabama Times:* "The Message we have read
with great pleasure. It is the Message of a Whig Governor
to a Loco Foco Legislature. It will be remembered that Gov.
Morehead was re-elected in August last, over his Loco Foco
opponent, Louis D. Henry, of Fayetteville, by the same voters
that elected a Loco Foco majority in the two houses of the
Legislature. The language of the Message is marked
throughout with a bold and fearless spirit worthy of the honors the Old North State has bestowed upon its author, and
well worthy of being made an example by older heads than
Gov. Morehead's. Governor Morehead we view as one of
the Old North State's most promising sons. He may be
termed a young man, his age being between 40 and 45. He
is a fine orator, a good scholar, and is justly considered a
man of fine talents. There is something noble in his
ordinary appearance, his private conversation is always remarkably interesting; and when speaking his fine appearance, his manners and gestures are well calculated to make
an impression on all present that he is no ordinary man."[1]

Still further abroad, in the *London Sun,* his vigorous
sentiments on public credit and honor attracted attention.
After expressing itself upon repudiation by certain of the
states, it said: "With this view we republish the following
extract from the Message of the Governor of North Carolina;" and, following the extract, continued: We hope to see
more and more of the same kind of language in the speeches
of American statesmen. The stain produced upon their
character by the repudiating doctrines of the notorious Mc-
Nutt [of Mississippi] sticks so thick over them, that it will
require a great deal of active honesty to wash out the filth.
A few such men as Governor Morehead of North Carolina, might do much to restore the lost credit of the United
States in the European money market."[2]

The *National Intelligencer* of Washington quoted from it
liberally and said it "is very justly commended for its wisdom and its patriotism;" while the *Richmond Whig* in com-
plimenting it, said: "Upon the whole, we must say that the

---

[1] *Raleigh Register*, Jan. 3, 1843.
[2] *Ibid.*, 10th Feb., 1843.

Government of North Carolina is obviously in a most un-
democratic state. It is not in confusion; it is not in debt;
its monied institutions are somewhat more than so-called.
Its public honor seems unshaken, the authority of its laws
gently but firmly maintained over an orderly and moral
people; there is no talk of either Repudiation or Relief;
and such, in a word, is the whole condition of the State,
that the Governor is able, through his Message generally,
rather to propose meliorations and plans of Improvement,
than to offer idle projects for averting the ruin which bad
Legislation and Public Immorality have, in many States,
pulled down, in hideous overthrow, upon the whole community."

What the Democratic Assembly did with his suggestions
is best told in the words of a Raleigh Whig editor: "THE
SESSION HAS BEEN THE LONGEST EVER HELD IN NORTH
CAROLINA! It commenced on Monday, the 21st of November, 1842—and ended on Saturday, the 28th day of
January, 1843—*a period of sixty-nine days!* The people
will scrutinize the captions of the acts passed, which we
publish today, in vain, if they expect to find any equivalent
for the time wasted, or money squandered! They will pore
in vain over this 'beggarly account of empty boxes,' if they
hope to find any realization of the splendid promises made
by the Loco Foco Candidate, whilst canvassing the State.
No provision has been made for the public necessities—*nothing,* ABSOLUTELY NOTHING has been done to promote the
common interest. With a majority of thirty, or thereabouts,
on joint ballot—with the numerical strength to pass *any*
measure—the Loco Foco Legislature adjourned, WITHOUT
HAVING MATURED ONE SINGLE PROPOSITION TO BETTER THE
CONDITION OF THE PEOPLE."[1] One reason for this was the
very radical reapportionment made necessary by the new
census—always a very difficult matter. Three new western
counties were created also; and there were seventy-six private acts. Another feature was the Democratic agitation
against the State banks, but when the State Bank itself

---

[1] *Raleigh Register,* 31st Jan., 1843.

asked to be allowed to close up its affairs, the gage of battle was not accepted; and also much time was spent in trying to instruct Whig national senators by a Democratic Assembly. This is of course the Whig attitude at this time, an attitude which is necessary to the understanding of this narrative. The whole internal improvement plan was turned down on the ground that the railroads, private corporations, had to call for help from the state, in these financially difficult years. Senator William A. Graham, Whig, was replaced in the national Senate by a Democrat, which at once made him a favorite candidate to succeed Governor Morehead, even as early as March, 1843.

This situation made it unnecessary for Governor Morehead to say much at his second inauguration on January 1, 1843, but one may see what he thought of his oath of office, in a letter of December 17th previously to Chief Justice Ruffin concerning the oath of office where he says he expects to qualify on the 31st, and also says: "I look upon the installation of the Executive as anything else than a mere empty pageant or idle show, at least so far as he is concerned. Although the powers of the Executive of our State are very limited, and but little room is left for the discretionary exercise of them—which is the evidence of the excellence of our institutions, which regulates by law everything so far as it is practicable—it becomes the more important to watch over that excellence. The solemnity of the obligations, which the Executive assumes when about to enter upon the discharge of his duties, is well calculated to strengthen that frailty to which poor human nature is too often a victim, and to nerve that firmness necessary to a faithful discharge of those duties. I think there is great propriety in the oaths of office being administered to the Executive by the highest officer of the Judicial Department, in the presence of the Legislature. And it will be additional gratification to me to have these Oaths administered by the high Judicial Officer in the person of yourself."[1]

The amount of detailed purely executive business that

---

[1] *The Ruffin Papers,* Hamilton, Vol. 2, p. 212.

comes before a Governor is startling to one who has occasion to see it for the first time. It was not less so with Governor Morehead. One of the few times in his life, he was ill for several weeks in the summer of 1843, so that on August 24th, he left for a vacation in the old home of his boyhood in Rockingham county where his mother was still living. His health was restored and he was back in Raleigh by the middle of September. The Whigs had become very active again and by October, the *Oxford Mercury* urged that the national ticket be "Clay and Morehead," and recalling how Washington and the world had been impressed by the Whig Secretary of the Navy, Mr. Badger, exclaimed: "Let John M. Morehead be made Vice-President, and the world will find there are more where Mr. Badger came from." The Whig State Convention of 7th December, 1843, which nominated Clay for the Presidency, sent Dudley and Badger to the National Convention and nominated Graham for Governor, also said: "that the Executive Administration by his Excellency, John M. Morehead, has been marked by uniform intelligence and dignity, by unrivalled firmness and perfect integrity: And this Convention, upon a review thereof, cannot forbear to express their high gratification that the Whig party has furnished to North Carolina such a Governor." Upon invitation, the Convention was entertained at "Government House" in the evening by Governor and Mrs. Morehead.

During the spring of 1844 when the Whigs of North Carolina were looking forward to a visit from Henry Clay, still more suggestions of Governor Morehead for Vice-Presidential candidate were made. In the *Register* for February 9th, "A Whig of the West" says he has heard of but one name for that office; "But we have an individual of our own state, who would not only do the citizens of the Old North State great honor, but the American people generally—I allude to His Excellency, John M. Morehead. He is naturally, a great, and, I may say, a good man;" and he shows what need had been shown for a strong man as Vice-President. North Carolina should have the place and "Clay and Morehead" would sweep the land. He urged the delegates to see to it. On the 27th still another, suggested by the former, made a plea: "I have known Gov. Morehead ever since he was a collegian, and as your correspondent justly remarks, he is a great and good man; and I can say with all sincerity, I have never met his superior. Take him altogether, he is one of Nature's noblest sons; no man has a greater reputation among his acquaintances for native intellect." He then compared him to Gen. Harrison.

While these events were in progress a school for the Deaf and Dumb was opened in Raleigh in May, 1845, through the efforts of Governor Morehead, who had said on November 4th, previously: "Impressed with a desire that something should be done for the afflicted children of Providence, I directed the attention of the last Legislature to the subject, but had the mortification to see the recommendation wholly disregarded." This was in a letter in regard to an offer of William D. Cooke of Staunton, Virginia, to undertake a school for Deaf and Dumb if encouraged, since he had observed that the census gave North Carolina as having 82 deaf mutes under 14 years of age, 80 between 14 and 25, and 118 above 25. It finally resulted in the establishment of one in Raleigh. Mr. Cooke's results on a deaf mute of Greensboro, Daniel Albright, had great influence in his success. The school opened in Raleigh the following May. This was due to an appropriation of the late Assembly of $5000 a year from the School Fund for the education of the deaf, dumb and blind, and provision for county tax of $75 a pupil.[1]

The great event of the spring of 1844 was the visit of Henry Clay to North Carolina's capital on his own birthday, April 12th. Ten to fifteen thousand Whigs received him— it even surpassed the Convention scenes of 1840. He was the guest of Governor Morehead at the executive mansion at the foot of Fayetteville street on the night before, and with a great procession headed by an open landau, drawn by four gray horses, in which were the Governor and his

---

[1] In 1843 Governor Morehead had offered Mr. Cooke a large tavern house and out-houses at Leaksville for such a school, offering it free the first year and at a very moderate rental afterwards.

famous guest, he was introduced at the capitol grounds and made a great speech. After he was presented with a silk vest made by a Granville young lady, the barbecue was announced. Speeches fell upon Raleigh's multitude like leaves of Vallombrosa, and cheers were elicited for "Clay, Morehead and Graham," as though that were the next ticket to be voted for. But when the National Whig Convention met in Baltimore on May 1st, it was from Mr. Van Buren's state that a Vice-Presidential candidate was taken, Theodore Frelinghuysen. To face these the Democrats again went to Tennessee and secured James K. Polk, and chose a Pennsylvanian, George M. Dallas, for second place. But the annual elections in the "Old North State" showed that the Whigs had learned a lesson, namely: "Get out and vote!" For, while they gave Graham but 3441 majority— over a 1000 less than they gave Morehead the second time and over 4500 less than the first time, still they not only elected a Whig Executive but a Whig Senate with 2 majority and a 22 majority in a Whig House. Surely North Carolina was the Whig state, *par excellence!*[1] And Governor Morehead was to have a Whig Assembly of his own after all! And the totals were scarcely all in on September 9th, when Death, to show that he was no respecter of parties, claimed the defeated Democratic gubernatorial candidate, Col. Michael Hoke! The prestige of North Carolina rose over the United States even more, if possible, than under the victories of Morehead. Naturally, in November, she went for Clay even more vigorously, but—in vain! Still— the new President, James K. Polk, was a son of North Carolina, not only by birth, but by education, and was not only a fellow-student at the University with Governor Morehead, but while the latter was one of its instructors. North Carolina was mother of at least two Presidents.

---

[1] North Carolina was the only southern state to cast her electoral vote for Henry Clay. The Abolition vote of about 60,000 was taken from the Whigs; and if it had not been, it would make enough to elect Clay, so far as popular vote is concerned. So that the Whigs lost through the Abolitionists, and the Democrats did not really gain. President Polk was a minority executive, owing his election to the Abolitionist defection. There was also a Whig Senate. There were twelve Whig Governors: Georgia, Tennessee, North Carolina, Kentucky, Ohio, Delaware, Maryland, New Jersey, Connecticut, Rhode Island, Massachusetts and Vermont; but there were fourteen Democratic ones.

This event occurred at almost the same time as the meeting of the new Whig Assembly, and as Governor Morehead's previous message, containing his ideas, has been presented in full, the present one need be merely outlined. As to the finances, he objected to the habit of falling back on the common school fund for aid, and measures should be taken to prevent it. In dealing with the railroad debts, he drew attention to the purchase of mortgage on the Portsmouth road, now in the courts with some of its tracks torn up, and noted the possibility of that course with the Raleigh & Gaston road. He felt that what the roads needed was more business, which could be met by a connection of the latter with the Wilmington at Weldon by a road about a dozen miles long, which he had urged before; and the various internal improvements he had urged, especially a system of locks at falls and ship canals at Nag's Head and Beaufort Harbor. He proposed an Agricultural professorship or else a school and model farm; also proposed surveys: geological, mineralogical and agricultural, with a department of statistics. He noted that only Edgecombe and Rowan counties had not adopted the common school system provided, and proposed a state superintendent and better organization. Again he urged asylums or schools for the deaf, dumb, blind and insane or defective; and likewise a penitentiary and revision of the criminal code. Again also he urged more copying of North Carolina material in British archives.[1] He suggested an enclosure for the new capitol grounds; and noting the fact that no swamp lands had been sold, said it was because of the national financial depression, and that they were growing in value. He touched upon free trade as a "humbug" and said a tariff was settled national policy; and again expressed his belief that the national land fund should be distributed. In closing he expressed his only regret, since his term would soon end, namely, that the legislative department "did not assign to me, during my administration, the execution of some work of great and per-

---

[1] On December 21, 1844, he asked that the executive office might take measures to collect and preserve legislative documents of the revolution and it was granted, and his successor at once took it up vigorously.

manent public utility, whereby, in the faithful and zealous performance of the duty, I might manifest to the people of North Carolina, the profound gratitude which I feel to them for the confidence they have reposed in me, and for the kindness with which my official acts have been received by them."

The Whig Assembly only sat 52 days, adjourning on January 6, 1844, just five days after Governor Morehead was succeeded by the new executive. The same editor who almost consigned the former Whig Assembly to perdition, praised this as the most arduous and laborious legislature he had ever known. He considered the most important measures to be: 1. The act to prevent imprisonment of honest debtors; 2. The one in favor of poor debtors; 3. Authorization of foreclosure of the Raleigh & Gaston Railroad for reorganization; 4. Popular vote on building a penitentiary; 5. Surveys for a turnpike west from Raleigh and Fayetteville to the Georgia line;[1] 6. Making Sheriffs and Constables liable for debts uncollected through lack of diligence; 7. Consolidation of Common School code; 8. Appropriation and tax provision for relief and education of Deaf, Dumb and Blind;[2] 9. To prevent fraudulent voting; and 10. For more speedy administration of justice. The amount of humanitarian and educational measures is most striking; while the survey of a western road was a first step in what was to prove probably his greatest life work.

Governor Morehead and his family awakened public pride in and affection for them. Farewells began as early as December 7th, when, in the evening, Stith's Cavalry Corps arrived at the executive mansion at the foot of Fayetteville street for that purpose, whereupon he gave them a military order to dismount and attack his refreshments. The Raleigh Guards came in the afternoon a week later on the same errand and with like results. It was on that evening that Governor Morehead presided at an exhibition of results accomplished in deaf, dumb and blind students which influenced the appropriation that made a school possible. It was

---

[1] He came near getting the turnpike itself.
[2] Guilford, the Governor's county, was the first to vote a tax for it.

on New Year's Eve, however, that a unique farewell dinner
was given him and his family by the members of the Assembly, in which all party differences were forgotten. This
was the eve before their departure and Editor Gales voiced
public sentiment when he said a few days later: "They
came amongst us four years ago, strangers—they depart,
bearing with them the deep regrets and cordial good wishes
of the entire population."[1]

---

[1] A playful pretty incident was part of the welcome of Henry Clay at the
Executive Mansion, mentioned on page 268: When they reached the reception room, Governor Morehead placed his four-year-old, red-headed son, James
Turner Morehead, in his pink silk dress, upon the table, and the child pronounced the welcome to the famous Kentuckian and said he would be the next
President, proving that the bump of prophecy is not fully developed at that
tender age!

XII

A
National Whig Leader
A Presidential Possibility
AND
President of the National Whig Convention
Philadelphia

1845

"The passing from office of such a man as Governor Morehead," said the editor of *The Fayetteville Observer* in a letter of January 1, 1845, "might be deeply regretted, if we did not feel that he is succeeded by one altogether worthy of the high honor, and that he himself cannot be permitted to remain in retirement, so long as eminent talents and unsullied public and private character continue to be appreciated in this good old state. There are few such men in the United States as John M. Morehead, and none better calculated to command respect and to win esteem. I hope to see him adorn a higher station than that from which he now retires with so well deserved a reputation."

The Hillsboro Recorder said: "Governor Morehead retires from his post, having lost nothing of the respect and esteem of those who placed him there. He has served out the time limited by the constitution, with a faithfulness and ability worthy of all commendation; and he will carry with him in his retirement the best wishes of his constituents. May he have a long life of happiness, prosperity and usefulness." This Hillsboro emphasis on his retirement, however, came from Governor Graham's home, and while these two splendid Whigs were so different as hardly to be comparable, they were liable to be so close together in Whig operations as to be objects of a choice between them. Hence the Hillsboro editor's more easy acceptance of the idea of the Ex-Governor's retirement than that of the Fayetteville editor.

After some visiting, Governor Morehead returned to his old home, "Blandwood," in Greensboro, on January 9, 1845, and that was made a gala day. They were met by the Greensboro Guards and officials and proceeded to the east front of the old Court House, where he was officially received. The Governor spoke feelingly of his experiences and at length. "I have returned among you, my fellow-citizens, of Greensboro and Guilford, with a bosom thrilling under emotions of inexpressible pleasure. I am among my early friends and shall in all probability spend here the remainder of my days. I love old Guilford. Why should I not love this beautiful and pleasant spot, consecrated to my heart with the most cherished reminiscences of my life? It is the birthplace of my wife—the birthplace of my children—the scene of my early public efforts—the place where my remains will repose when it shall please the Almighty to call me hence. And what do I owe to you, my neighbors and fellow-citizens—you who have so often endorsed me to the State and to the world with a cordial unanimity almost unexampled in the annals of free elections? The position of Guilford is an enviable one. Let her ever maintain that proud position which she has achieved in the scale of intelligence, and the good influence of her moral and steady habits. Let us still join and continue our efforts to spread intelligence, morality and religion among all people; and never cease while anything good is left for us to perform."[1] And he came home in the spirit of a Cincinnatus, for he who served the commonwealth now served as presiding Judge of Guilford County Court, in which capacity one of the characteristic things he did was to build a humane Poor House, whose humane features secured for it among opponents of it the epithet "Morehead's Folly," just as his Democratic opponents were driven to the desperate expedient of chang-

[1] *Patriot*, Jan. 11, 1845.

ing his name to "John Moonshine Morehead." "Such is the
excellence of our institutions," said Editor Swaim of *The
Patriot* in reference to it, "no matter what honors a man
may have acquired, they are not detracted from, but rather
increased, by being *useful* in any station."

The Whigs of Montgomery county were not inclined to
allow him to retire and nominate him for Congress. "We
have no idea that the Governor will accept," said the
Raleigh Register, "but if he would, what a leader the Whigs
could boast of in the lower House!" Other counties took
it up with such seriousness, that on May 5, 1845, Governor
Morehead felt compelled to address a letter to the Ashe-
borough Convention, in which after he expresses his gratitude for their confidence, he adds: "But after an absence of
so great a length of time from my private and complicated
affairs, devoted wholly to the public service, I find it absolutely necessary to devote a portion of my time and services
to the regulation of my private affairs. And I feel confident
that I have no friend who would not willingly excuse me
from this service, if he were aware of the sacrifice that I
should necessarily suffer, if I were the successful candidate
in the next election."

However, he presided at a meeting on May 19th, called
to condemn the Sub-Treasury bill just passed by the lower
House of Congress and "spoke of the existing war with
Mexico, condemning most unequivocally the President's policy in bringing on the war; but none would be more ready to
sustain the President than himself, in prosecuting this war,
now that we had gotten into it, with vigor and energy, that
it might be brought to a speedy and honorable termination."
He eulogized Webster and condemned Webster's enemies.

Development was contagious wherever Governor More-
head was: In May a new High School was opened in
Greensboro with forty-five to fifty pupils, and the Methodist
Female College buildings were completed. At the Univer-
sity commencement on June 5th, he again presided at the
Alumni Association of which he had been chairman or
President since its formation on May 31, 1843. He was also
chosen to deliver its address in 1846, which was described as

"a fit model for all to come afterward."[1] As a member of
the Trustees he joined in conferring the degree of LL.D.
"upon the just" Whig, late President of the Senate, *pro tem.*,
Mangum, and "the unjust" Democrats, President Polk and
Attorney General Mason, the latter of whom had been his
fellow-students at the University.

The annexation of Texas on July 4, 1845, was looked
upon as almost certain to produce war with Mexico, and the
Whigs expected the Democrats to repeal the Tariff, pass the
Sub-Treasury bill—all of which made financiers and political leaders apprehensive. Governor Morehead came to
Raleigh on January 5, 1846, to attend the stockholders' meeting of the Bank of North Carolina, whose President, Judge
Cameron, was seeking to resign. Governor Morehead took
the lead in expressing warnings as to probable financial conditions of the banks of the land; and now as the Bank of
North Carolina was so ably managed and so prosperous, let
it be kept so by relieving President Cameron of non-essential
duties in order that he might be retained. His ideas were
adopted and Governor Graham, himself and Judge Settle
were made a committee to confer with the President and
convince him—which they did—and the bank continued its
prosperous career.

A few days later, on January 12th, the Whig State Convention at Raleigh re-nominated Governor Graham, and one
of the interesting speeches was by Hon. Edward Stanly:
"In 1840," said he, "they [Democrats] placed in the field a
man of talents—well and favorably known in every portion
of the State—to oppose our own noble-hearted Morehead.
After a thorough canvass, he was found in a minority of
about 8000 votes. In 1842, they selected, to oppose the
incumbent, a gentleman distinguished for his great powers
of *imagination* and for his fluent declamation, and *he* was
informed by some 5000 of these 'Sheep-stealing Whigs' that
he could not be allowed to 'organize and convene' himself
into the gubernatorial chair." He then referred to the campaign of 1844 when their candidate was beaten by over 3000

---

[1] Battle's History of the University gives no further information as to
when he ceased to be President of the Alumni Association.

votes. Governor Morehead's brother, Senator James Turner Morehead, was active in this convention, but he himself was not present.

His proposals for a penitentiary were the chief subject of newspaper epistolary discussion during the winter of 1845–6, nearly all of it favorable. And the results of his Deaf, Dumb and Blind school were heralded and praised in scarcely less degree, Governor Graham being one of those who made an address on the subject. Another feature was the sale and re-organization of the Raleigh & Gaston and Portsmouth railroads and the comparative prosperity of the Wilmington road. There was at this time in the United States 3787 miles of railroad, which cost $113,208,367. The longest was the "Central " [Georgia] with 190 mles ; the next the Baltimore & Ohio with 188 miles ; next the Wilmington & Raleigh [Weldon] with 161 miles ; next the Western of Massachusetts with 156 miles—the shortest being the West Stockbridge [Mass.] with but 3 miles. The most costly one was the Philadelphia & Reading, with but 94 miles, costing $9,457,570. Next to these came the Western and B. & O. roads. Of these roads, the North Carolina railroads totalled 245½ miles at a total cost of $3,160,000—a most reasonable cost compared with any of the rest—not counting the few miles of the Petersburg & Roanoke, Greenville & Roanoke, and the Portsmouth & Roanoke on North Carolina territory to reach the Roanoke river. The campaign divided the interest of the state during the summer of 1846 with the call on North Carolina for a regiment of infantry for the Mexican war, and the news of progress of that conflict.

From public expressions so far away as Raleigh, Edgeworth Seminary was making excellent strides in development. It inspired one of the examining board to write of its excellence, especially in the higher branches of Latin, Algebra, Geometry, Mental Philosophy, Evidences of Christianity and other subjects. At the same time, the first week in June, Governor Morehead was at the University Commencement, as a Trustee and President of the Alumni Association, before whom he gave the annual address, of which one editor said: "We happen to know, that, four days before the delivery of this address, pen had not been put upon paper, in relation to its subject matter. And yet, for useful information, graphic delineation, highly seasoned wit and humor, it has not been our lot to witness a happier effort. The Governor ought to adopt as the motto on his shield: 'Semper Paratus'."

The August elections and the old Whig general, "Rough and Ready" Taylor's victories in Mexico restored Whig prestige with a vengeance! Governor Graham, a Whig Senate and a Whig House by large majorities won in North Carolina, which meant two new Whig national Senators. Thereupon the west began to make a demand for Governor Morehead for the United States Senate, and the eastern Whigs wanted Edward Stanly; others wanted Badger or Osborne. The *Raleigh Register* said Morehead was the North Carolina "Rough and Ready." When November arrived and the Assembly had made Stanly speaker of the lower House and Senator Mangum was willing to accept re-election, Ex-Secretary of the Navy Badger was rewarded for his resignation in protest against President Tyler and sent to the Senate. Later Mr. Stanly was elected Attorney General of the State. The Whig victory did not carry Governor Morehead's penitentiary proposal, however.

This political situation was accompanied by a movement to extend the Raleigh & Gaston line southward through Fayetteville to Camden, South Carolina. The Post Office department had diverted the big mail of the state from the Wilmington route to the Raleigh line and Fayetteville had long been determined on this road. A Railroad Convention was therefore set for November 4, 1846, and wide-spread interest was shown in it even outside the state. This body recommended the building of the road as the metropolitan north and south line; that it is feasible and attractive to capitalists; asked the legislature to charter the North Carolina section of it; appointed a preliminary committee to canvass cost and the like.

On Governor Graham's organization of his second term early in 1847, he did as his predecessor had done before him, placed his own predecessor at the head, next himself, of the Literary Board, as the Common School board was called; Governor Morehead, Charles Manly and Editor Weston R. Gales constituting this body. This was in March, 1847, and at once a sale of Swamp Lands was ordered for May 20th to the amount of 50,000 acres. On April 13th, a meeting was held at the Yarborough Hotel, Raleigh, to arrange to secure an office or "station" there on the new "Magnetic Telegraph" line; and it was at this time that Governor Morehead's board decided to build the Deaf and Dumb School on Moore's Square, Raleigh, while the streets resounded and sparkled with the celebration of Taylor's victories at Vera Cruz and Buena Vista, in which the people called for Taylor as Presidential candidate in 1848. This sentiment was general: Philadelphia Whigs nominated him in town meeting on April 10th. Then, on May 1st [1847], Mr. Webster and his wife, got off the Raleigh & Gaston train, on his Southern tour (but not as Senator Clay had done) and was the guest of the Governor and attended Christ Church on Sunday. Still the journey of such a Whig giant through the South at this time might easily suggest another Presidential candidate besides the hero of Buena Vista. And while Governor Morehead, in May, was at the sale of Swamp Lands, in which they sold enough land to open a road into the vast tract, from Plymouth, President Polk had promoted one Col. Jefferson Davis of Mississippi to be a Brigadier General. But this was hardly over, on the 29th, when President Polk and his suite followed Mr. Webster in a visit to Raleigh, in this case, however, to attend the Commencement of his *alma mater* at Chapel Hill. With him was his Secretary of the Navy, John Y. Mason, whom Governor Morehead, as President of the Alumni Association, introduced as the orator of the day before that body, and who induced that body to erect a monument to the late President Caldwell, the old teacher of both of them. President Polk had appointed four of this Association as ministers to France, Spain, Portugal and Italy. But he was hardly back in Washington before North Carolina was ablaze with Whig Taylor meetings, and the Whig papers were publishing a letter of Gen-

eral Jefferson Davis, in praise of the great hero of the Mexican war, and northern Democrats were intimating that North
Carolina's Whig Governor had not been as cordial to the
Democratic President as he should have been, because he
had Webster at the mansion at the foot of Fayetteville
street and did not have the President as his guest also—
which appeared to be true. Thus does the loom of events
weave so strange a tapestry! North Carolina seemed to
be an unusually beautiful belle to attract such distinguished
political admirers.

And then just as the state election was occuring in August, the first telegraph poles, or "posts," as the press then
called them, had been set up as far as Raleigh and the wires
were rapidly being hung. And the news said that six out of
nine North Carolina Congressmen were Whigs—reversing
the current number there! And this was typical of the
whole lower House of Congress, now returned to the Whigs.
As a consequence the Democrats were at sea, with a half-
dozen candidates to succeed President Polk and the Whigs
were more joyously acclaiming but one, with every new
victory in Mexico, notwithstanding the fact that Henry Clay,
while the returns were coming in, concluded to visit the sea-
shore at Cape May, but stopped long enough in Philadelphia
to receive what amounted to a national demonstration. Then
came James Buchanan's letter saying that the Wilmot Pro-
viso of 1820 saved the country, therefore let its line be
projected from the Missouri boundary to the coast in 1848
and again save the country—and it lifted him out of the
dead level of the half-dozen Democratic candidates.

During this autumn the people of Charlotte were taking
measures to secure a railroad into South Carolina, while
those of Richmond and Danville were seeking to construct
one between those two places. Meanwhile the road from
Raleigh southward was not prospering as it was hoped, but
efforts were making to reorganize the Portsmouth road and
get it in successful operation again. The purchase of a new
locomotive by the Raleigh & Gaston road as well as news
from the Wilmington railway indicated that these roads were
succeeding. The Common Schools fund was growing also,

being $101,775 in 1847, the largest figure yet reached; and at this time there appeared a novel, *Alamance*, from the pen of a talented young man of the state who was soon to fill an office recommended by Ex-Governor Morehead, as head of the Common School system of the State, namely, Calvin H. Wiley, a native of Guilford county and educated there and at the University.

The campaign of 1848 was officially started in Washington, D. C., by Whig members of Congress on the evening of January 27th at a meeting over which Senator Mangum of North Carolina presided, and it was determnied to hold a Whig National Convention. On February 5th, they decided to hold it in Philadelphia at Independence Hall on June 7th. Thereupon the North Carolina counties began to elect delegates to the State Convention to be held in Raleigh on Washington's Birthday; and it was notable that some of them, like Rockingham county, the old home of Governor Morehead, announced themselves for Henry Clay instead of General Taylor, and that some, like Anson county, were silent on the subject, while some others, like McDowell county, were for the hero of Buena Vista. When the State Convention met, however, and had nominated Charles Manly for gubernatorial candidate, they reported resolutions denouncing the President and defending General Taylor from his attacks, but, leaving the ordinary delegates to the National Convention to be chosen by districts, named Ex-Governor Morehead and Hon. John Kerr of Caswell as delegates-at-large for the State, without naming either Clay or Taylor as favorites. The choice of Governor Morehead to lead the delegation, with his well-known admiration for Henry Clay, together with absence of choice of General Taylor was evidence that North Carolina would make a stand for the Kentucky statesman. Governor Morehead was not a member of the Raleigh Convention. Mr. Kerr was a Taylor man.

In March came the close of the war by the ratification of the Treaty, and General Taylor became still more the popular hero; while during the same month, at Harrisburg, the Democratic Convention of Pennsylvania gave their favorite son, James Buchanan, first place for the Presidency.

Early in June, 1848, Governor Morehead began preparations for his trip to Philadelphia. His business affairs had prospered and wonderfully developed in the three years and a half since he left the Executive Mansion in Raleigh. His family also had increased by one more son, Eugene Lindsay Morehead, born on the previous September 16th at "Blandwood," so that he now had four daughters and three sons— and one son-in-law, William R. Walker, a planter on the Yadkin river, to whom his eldest daughter was married on May 31st, just before his departure to take train at Raleigh for Washington and Philadelphia.

Governor Morehead was fifty-two years old and in the maturity of his powers. He found scenes of the greatest enthusiasm in the Quaker City on the days before the convention assembled. The scene on the evening of the 6th of June is thus described in the *Baltimore Patriot:* "The scene yesterday evening in Chestnut Street was animating beyond anything we have ever had here in Philadelphia since the glorious days of 1776, when, from Independence Hall, went forth that great charter of American liberty—the Declaration of Independence. . . . The friends of General Taylor met in Independence Square last night. The large square was crowded to excess—not less than twenty thousand people being present. The enthusiasm exceeded even that shown in 1840."

Instead of meeting in Independence Hall, which was far too small for such a Convention, they gathered in the spacious salon, where had once been exhibited the celebrated Chinese Museum, at Ninth and Sansom streets, northeast corner, which still bore that name. Here the Convention was called to order in the morning of the 7th of June, at eleven o'clock—and a temporary organization formed. The committee on permanent organization was chosen and at the afternoon session, at 4 o'clock, the chairman announced as President of the Convention, Hon. John M. Morehead, of North Carolina, and amid vociferous applause, it was unanimously confirmed. Messrs. King of Georgia and Fuller of New York escorted him to the chair, whereupon Governor Morehead addressed the Convention.

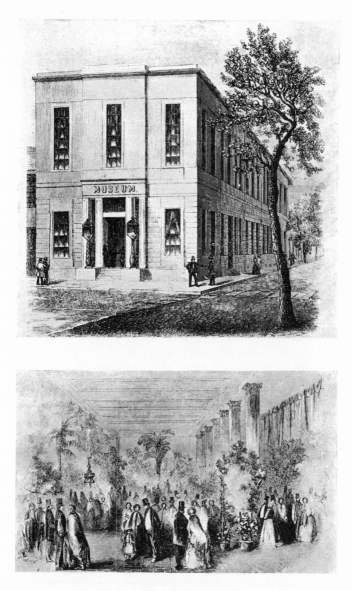

CHINESE MUSEUM
Northeast corner of Ninth and Sansom Sts., Philadelphia, exterior and interior
in which Governor Morehead presided over the Whig Convention
in June, 1848

"The following is the address delivered by Gov. Morehead, on taking the chair as President of the late Whig Convention, at Philadelphia:[1]

"Gentlemen of the Convention:—I do not possess language adequate to express to you my grateful feelings, and to return to you my profound acknowledgments for the distinguished honor conferred upon me by selecting me to preside over the deliberations of this Convention. If, Gentlemen, I possessed qualifications, either by experience or otherwise, for the distinguished position—as I am conscious I do not—the obligations that you have imposed upon me would be far greater than they would deserve, and therefore do I consider my indebtedness to you, at this time, still larger.

"The purpose for which you have assembled here from every part of the land, uniting in common counsel and deliberation, is that of bringing relief to our common country, and devising and executing such schemes as are necessary to her prosperity and happiness. Order, wisdom and decorum should characterize our deliberations, and so sure as they do, success will attend them. [Applause.]

"We should yield, fellow-citizens, on this occasion, all personal preferences. Let us bring forward, for the good of our common country, our united counsels and our united wisdom. Let us rear our standard with the full determination to carry it on to victory. [Applause.] All we have to do is to select a standard bearer who will secure the hearty co-operation of all sections of our country in the common cause of our country's welfare. Let us have inscribed upon our banner 'the prosperity of our country.' [Applause.]

"It has been asserted that 'to the victors belong the spoils.' Let us determine that we will be victors and when victorious, if spoils we must have, let them be the redemption of our country from her present embarrassed condition, and replenishing her exhausted treasury, and restoring her to that flourishing and happy condition from which she had fallen. Let us endeavor to spread over our land industry,

---

[1] *Greensboro Patriot,* 17th June, 1848.

peace and plenty, which shall give to every laborer adequate employment and remunerating wages—which shall cause every sea to be whitened with the sails of our commerce— which shall make the produce of our teeming fields to spread plenty over our own land, enable our people to extend to others that bounty which a Providence has bestowed upon us. [Great applause.]

"Fellow-citizens—If our deliberations are conducted with that order and love of law which characterize the constituents who sent us here, we shall have little cause to fear for our essential triumph. [Applause.] And if our spoils be such as I have described, spoils which will bring prosperity to every door, and cause the land to teem with the blessings of a wise legislation and well-directed industry; if, gentlemen, the results of your deliberations shall be to restore to our country peace, harmony and prosperity: to restore to the constitution its violated rights and powers, and to restore the administration of the laws of our country to its pristine purity, if such should be the effects of your harmonious deliberations, and your patriotic counsels, I shall deem it the proudest legacy that I can bequeath to my posterity, that I had the honor to preside over that council of sages whose deliberations produced these happy results." [Great applause.]

It was the afternoon session of the 8th before they were ready to nominate, and the old Chinese Museum hall resounded to the praises of General Taylor of Louisiana, Henry Clay of Kentucky, John M. Clayton of Delaware, General Winfield Scott, McLean and Webster. The first ballot was significant: Taylor, 111; Clay, 97; Scott, 43; Webster, 22; Clayton, 4; and McLean, 2. On the second ballot, the Clayton and McLean votes and eleven Clay votes increased all the others, Webster's 22 standing solid, so that it stood: Taylor, 118; Clay, 86; Scott, 49; and Webster, 22. With no choice, President Morehead announced the session adjourned until Friday morning. The third ballot showed good work done for the hero of Buena Vista during the night and slight gains for General Scott, but loss to the rest; for General Taylor received 133 and Clay 74—which was the

signal for the Clay forces to scatter to the two military com-
manders, raising General Taylor's vote to 171—thirty more
than was necessary to a choice, whereupon President Morehead announced "in a clear and distinct voice" General
Taylor as the duly elected Whig candidate for President of
the United States. The tremendous applause was taken up
in the streets, and "By means of that astonishing agent—the
Magnetic Telegraph"—said the *Raleigh Register* in its issue
next morning—"we are in possession of the leading acts of
the National Whig Convention . . . giving us information that John M. Morehead—our own Morehead—had been
chosen to preside over the Convention! This is indeed a
compliment DESERVED. . . . North Carolina . . .
has been happily denominated the Thermopylæ of Whig
principles—the most reliable Whig state in the Union; and
it is so. . . . The very moment that our paper was being
put to press on Friday morning, a dispatch was received at
the Telegraph Office, announcing the glorious intelligence
that GEN. ZACHARY TAYLOR! THE HERO OF BUENA VISTA,
*had received the nomination for the presidency on the fourth
balloting."*

After nomination for the Vice-Presidency, President
Morehead directed preparation of ballots, and as Abbot
Lawrence of Massachusetts and Millard Fillmore of New
York were far ahead of the rest on first ballot, a second
one soon selected the New York man by within two of the
same number of votes as that for President, and the objects
of the Convention were achieved.

After the motion was made that the National Whig Convention of 1848 should adjourn, President Morehead said:
"Gentlemen of the Convention—Before severing the tie
which has here united us, permit me to return my profound
thanks for your kindness and forbearance. Your partiality
placed me in this chair, to the duties of which I am unused
and unaccustomed—and that same spirit of kindness has
sustained me in their performance. If I have committed
mistakes or errors, or if in the discharge of my duties here,
I have caused pain to any individual, I have only to say
it was unintentional, and it would cause me serious regret.

Let us, at all events, carry with us no unkind feelings, and I shall feel happy in the impression that no one has any unkind feeling towards me.

"I, too, have been placed here in a peculiar situation; and as various gentlemen, of different delegations, have given expression to their feelings, I trust I may be allowed also to say a few words before we part. I, too, have been defeated in the first wish of my heart; I have not succeeded in the nomination of my favorite candidate—I stand among the vanquished party—but I fall into the hands of my *victor friends,* like a conquered damsel into the hands of her lover, and submit kindly to my defeat.[1] [Loud applause.] I shall enter upon the campaign in the true Whig spirit, determined to succeed, and if, before the election any Whig can be found who will outstrip me in zeal, I hope to take such a Whig by the hand, on the fourth of next March, at the inauguration of Gen. Zachary Taylor.

"It has on a former occasion been my bad fortune not to have my first choice approved. In 1840, the Whigs of North Carolina unfurled the free standard of Henry Clay in that state, and sent his name to the Harrisburg Convention; but the Whigs of that Convention, the representatives of the entire Union, sent back to us that standard inscribed with another name, that of Wm. Henry Harrison—wholly unexpected by us. But I only looked to see if it was still the *True Whig Banner.* I did not ask myself what name was on it. I never thought of inquiring what side of Mason and Dixon's line the nominee was from. It was the Whig Banner, and as such it was placed in my hands. For five months this hand bore that banner through North Carolina, until in the succeeding August, North Carolina, a Slave State, fired the first guns of that volley which shook Democracy from one end of the Nation to the other. Its re-echoes resounded from State to State throughout the entire Union, ' until the great triumph was achieved.

---

[1] Governor Morehead was the only one of the North Carolina delegation who voted for Clay on every ballot. Four others voted for Clay, but one turned to Scott on the third ballot and one to Taylor on the fourth one. Six were for Taylor from the first. The President of the Convention, therefore, did not vote for Taylor, in convention, but accepted him, and worked for him. One of the Taylor men was Calvin H. Wiley. This situation was not calculated to make President Morehead a very probable Cabinet possibility.

"I have mentioned this, gentlemen, for the benefit of Ohio, and I will state one incident from which the Whigs of that State may hope and profit. North Carolina, though she lost the nomination of her first choice, Henry Clay, soon raised on every hill top the banner of Harrison. In one location when a tall pole had been erected with the name of Harrison nailed to the mast, a solitary stranger was seen riding past it; attracted by its inscription he stopped, elevated his eye and seeing the Whig principles inscribed thereon, doffed his beaver and saluted them with three solitary cheers! Nor do I despair before fall that in Ohio will also be seen solitary Whigs cheering the banner of Zachary Taylor.

"I have supported in this body the nomination of Henry Clay—that most illustrious son of our country—his sun is about to set—and I trust his latest hours may be gilded and brightened by our success, which, like the bow of promise, will betoken the spread of peace and prosperity around our land. I have voted for Henry Clay because no man is more largely identified with the glory of our country than he is. No administration could add a particle to his undying fame; no honors could add to his treasure heap! But I yield him to this Convention; yield him cheerfully, and for the future, no man can go more heartily than I will for the Hero of Buena Vista.

"It has been suggested from different States that fears existed of the result of this nomination. We should never fear the consequences when our cause is good. And our cause is not that of Zachary Taylor, but of the Whigs of the Union. Let us when dangers are thickening around us take our cue from his own conduct at Buena Vista, when he said: 'We have got the enemy just where we want him; now is the time to give them a little more grape, Capt. Bragg!' As our leader never surrenders, is there any one of his followers who intends to surrender? [an emphatic response of 'no'] then if we all pull together we cannot be vanquished.

"Before dissolving this body allow me to wish prosperity and happiness to you all, and that you may arrive safely to your homes and friends again. I bid you a long and affectionate farewell, and declare this Convention adjourned *sine die.*"[1]

That night a ratification meeting was held on Independence Square, which was illuminated like day with Drummond lights, transparencies, variegated lamps and the like, while, it is said, 50,000 people seethed and yelled for the Whig candidates. Four platforms, on different sides of the square were required, the main one being next to the Hall. The Whig *Inquirer* editor called the main stand to order at 7 P. M. and, after brief remarks, introduced President John Motley Morehead, whose inspiring account of the nomination was loudly acclaimed, and at mention of the names of Taylor and Fillmore "the shouts which went up were like those which, Byron says, herald in 'a young earthquake's birth' "—to quote from the *Baltimore Patriot*. At the same moment speeches and applause at the other three stands were rivalling those at the main one where they were listening to President Morehead.

Immediately on the next morning President Morehead dispatched to General Taylor at Baton Rouge, Louisiana, the following letter of notification, dated at "Philadelphia, June 10, 1848:"

"Gen. Zachary Taylor:

"Dear Sir: At a Convention of the Whigs of the United States, held in this city on the 7th instant, and continued from day to day until the 9th, you were nominated as a candidate for the Presidency of the United States, at the ensuing Presidential election.

"By a resolution of said Convention, it was made the duty of their President to communicate to you the result of their deliberations, and request your acceptance of the nomination.

"In obedience to said resolve, I, as the organ therein designated, have the honor to make you the foregoing communication and to ask your acceptance of the nomination.

"Permit me, dear Sir, to indulge the hope that he who never shrinks from any responsibility nor fails to discharge

---

[1] *Greensboro Patriot*, 21st June, 1848.

any duty assigned him by his Government, will not now refuse this enthusiastic call of his countrymen.

"I am, dear Sir, with sentiments of very high regard, your most obedient servant,

"J. M. Morehead,
"President of the Whig National Convention."

To Mr. Fillmore, on the same day, he sent the following somewhat similar communication:

"Dear Sir: At a Convention of the Whigs of the United States assembled in this city on the 7th instant, and continued by adjournment until the 9th, Gen. Zachary Taylor of Louisiana, was nominated as a candidate for the Presidency, and you were nominated for the Vice-Presidency of the United States, at the next ensuing Presidential election.

"By a resolution of said Convention it was made my duty to communicate to you the result of their deliberations, and to request your acceptance of the nomination.

"I have the honor to be, dear Sir, your most obedient servant,

"J. M. Morehead,
"President of the Whig National Convention.
"Hon. M. Fillmore."[1]

As Mr. Fillmore was only at the distance of Albany, New York, he soon received his letter, paid its postage as usual, and wrote the following reply, dated seven days later, June 17th:

"Sir: I have the honor to acknowledge the receipt of your letter of the 10th instant, by which I am notified that at the late Whig Convention held at Philadelphia, Gen. Zachary Taylor was nominated for President and myself for Vice-President, and requesting my acceptance of the nomination.

"The honor of being thus presented by the distinguished representatives of the Whig party of the Union for the second office in the gift of the people—an honor as unexpected as it was unsolicited—could not fail to awaken in a

---

[1] *Greensboro Patriot*, 5th Aug., 1848.

grateful heart emotions which, while they cannot be suppressed, find not appropriate language for utterance.

"Fully persuaded that the cause in which we are enlisted is the cause of our country; that our chief object is to secure its peace, preserve its honor, and advance its prosperity; and feeling, moreover, a confident assurance that, in Gen. Taylor (whose name is presented for the first office) I shall always find a firm, consistent Whig, a safe guide, and an honest man, I cannot hesitate to assume any position which my friends may assign me.

"Distrusting, as I well may, my ability to discharge satisfactorily the duties of that high office, but feeling that, in case of my election, I may with safety repose on the friendly aid of my fellow Whigs, and that efforts guided by honest intentions will always be charitably judged, I accept the nomination so generously tendered; and I do this the more cheerfully, as I am willing for such a cause and with such a man, to take my chances of success or defeat as the electors, the final arbitrators of our fate, shall, in their wisdom, judge best for the interests of our common country.

"Please accept the assurances of my high regard and esteem, and permit me to subscribe myself your friend and fellow citizen,

"Millard Fillmore.

"Hon. J. M. Morehead."[1]

The delay in receiving a reply from General Taylor as to his reception of Governor Morehead's notification of his nomination led the latter to publish on July 18, 1848, the following explanation, in the *Greensboro Patriot* [20th July issue]: "Editors of *The Greensboro Patriot*: On the 10th of June, as President of the Whig National Convention, I addressed from Philadelphia to Gen. Zachary Taylor and Hon. Millard Fillmore letters, apprising them of the nominations by that Convention, and requesting their acceptance of the nominations.——Having received no reply from either of the gentlemen, the last of June I addressed them again, and enclosed copies of my letters of 10th June. On the 3rd July I

---

[1] *Greensboro Patriot*, 5th Aug., 1848.

received a communication from Mr. Fillmore, dated at Albany 17th June, which has been forwarded to the *National Intelligencer* for publication.——From General Taylor I have received no communication, and I see by a New Orleans paper that as late as 5th July he had received no communication from me. On yesterday I addressed him again, directly, and also through two friends; so that it is hoped some one of my communications will reach him. His reply shall be published as soon as received.——Yours—— J. M. Morehead."[1]

General Taylor finally received his notification, however, and after over a month, on July 15th [1848] he penned the following reply from his home in Baton Rouge.

"Sir: I have had the honor to receive your communication of June 10th, announcing that the Whig Convention which assembled at Philadelphia on the 7th of that month, and of which you were the presiding officer, have nominated me for the office of President of the United States.

"Looking to the composition of the Convention, and its numerous and patriotic constituency, I feel deeply grateful for the honor it has bestowed upon me, and for the distinguished confidence implied in my nomination by it to the highest office in the gift of the American people.

"I cordially accept that nomination, but with sincere distrust of my fitness to fulfil the duties of an office which demands for its exercise the most exalted ability and patriotism, and which has been rendered illustrious by the greatest names in our history. But should the selection of the Whig Convention be confirmed by the people, I shall endeavor so to discharge the new duties thus devolving upon me as to meet the just expectations of my fellow citizens and preserve undiminished the prosperity and reputation of our common country.

"I have the honor to remain, with the highest respect, your most obedient servant,

"Hon. J. M. Morehead,   "Z. Taylor.
"Greensboro, Guilford Co., N. C."[2]

---

[1] Dashes inserted by the present writer indicate his paragraphing.
[2] *Greensboro Patriot*, 5th Aug., 1848.

This letter reached Governor Morehead in time to appear first in the *Greensboro Patriot* on August 5th and in other papers simultaneously. No explanation accompanied the publication, but it was gradually rumored that the peculiar delay was due to the postal custom of that day, namely, that the person to whom an epistle was of most concern and value should pay the postage, be he sender or receiver; and that these letters were of most concern and value to the candidates, who would naturally expect to pay the postage. Mr. Fillmore did so it seems; but the blunt soldier of the Mexican War, receiving a flood of correspondence which presumed his great interest in his proposed candidacy, before he was nominated, refused to accept the presumption and ordered all un-prepaid mail sent to the Dead Letter Office! Apparently he had not rescinded this order when Governor Morehead's notification of June 10th arrived in Louisiana; and it journeyed on its way to the place where all dead letters go. Whether General Taylor finally came to the conclusion that this letter was of most concern to him and paid the postage, whether some one of the letters reached him without postage, or whether Governor Morehead decided that this notification letter was becoming of more concern to him than to General Taylor, has never yet been discovered, so far as is known.

But whether General Taylor knew it or not, the whole United States knew it as fast as telegraph and courier could scatter it, with the usual enthusiasm for a military hero candidate. President Morehead took boat to Norfolk, arriving on the 13th, and while at the City Hotel, a deputation of citizens waited on him and asked him to address the ratification meeting that evening, which he did amid "thunders of applause," to quote the *Norfolk Herald*. By Tuesday, the 20th of June, President Morehead was in Raleigh, where he addressed the newly organized "Rough and Ready Club" amid the usual enthusiasm. Governor Morehead's slogan: "The Prosperity of Our Country" began to have great vogue, and victory in State and Nation was destined to follow him. The August election for Governor, while successful for the Whig Candidate, Charles Manly, only gave him

874 majority, because the Democratic candidate, David Settle Reid, of Governor Morehead's old home county, Rockingham, advocated a revision of the constitution to remove freehold qualification to vote for State senators. This was naturally attractive to all non-freeholders, and the slogan "equal suffrage" was a most effective one. It is said this slogan was suggested by Stephen A. Douglas, to one of his relatives in that region. When it is observed that this 874 majority for Whig Governor Manly rose to ten times that, of 8581, majority for Taylor over Cass, one can easily see how powerful the "Equal Suffrage" slogan was and also how thoroughly Whig was "The Old North State," the Whig Thermopolae! And also how the President of the Whig National Convention, John Motley Morehead. was the most powerful Whig in North Carolina and one of the most powerful in the United States.

XIII

His Campaign

to

Unite East and West North Carolina

by

Railroad

1849

At the time of the Whig National Convention in June, 1848, the lately increasing interest in the western part of the state, in the approach of railroads from Richmond to Danville on the northern border and a South Carolina line to Charlotte near the southern border, with the magnificent possibility of another cross-state line to connect them, thereby completing a continental line from Maine to Georgia —culminated in a convention at Salisbury in Rowan county, presided over by David F. Caldwell. It was determined, that as soon as the roads reached the two places mentioned, the people should go to the Legislature for a charter. Mr. Caldwell was the leading Guilford representative in the House of Commons.

This movement was of course bound to alarm the east and her two railroads, for they knew the west was determined not to be land-locked much longer. The Raleigh and Gaston road, now the property of the State, it will be recalled, had long been used to base a projected extension southward, through Fayetteville, but in vain. Now, as Governor Graham saw this western movement, headed by Guilford county, and undoubtedly supported by Ex-Governor Morehead, he made the proposition in his message of November 21, 1848, that the best first step in a solution of Raleigh and Gaston troubles as well as general transporta-

tion improvement would be to extend the Raleigh & Gaston
Railroad westward presumably through Hillsboro, Greensboro and Salisbury and thence down southward to Charlotte;
thus he would make the Maine to Georgia line pass from
Richmond through Raleigh and his own home town, instead
of from Richmond to Danville and Greensboro. "Through a
part of North Carolina alone," said he, "a link is wanting, to
complete the grand chain of communication, from one ex-
tremity of our country to the other, and to furnish the whole
nation those facilities of intercourse which the inhabitants
north and south of us enjoy in their several sections." He
argued that branch lines could be built to Fayetteville and
Goldsboro, "and eventually it might realize that scheme of a
central railroad consecrated by the patriotic labors of Caldwell, in an extension from Goldsboro to Beaufort." He
thought it the first improvement which should engage their
energies, and recommended patronage of the state to half or
at least two-fifths. It would be about 160 miles and would
cost about $10,000 a mile. Besides this he recommended the
other projects that Governor Morehead had advocated, and
which were now looked upon as Whig projects. The Assembly, on the 30th, requested him to submit a railroad plan,
which he did on December 4, 1848.

The main feature of his plan was the organization of a
joint stock company—"The North Carolina Railroad Company"—of $2,000,000 capital, half to be taken by the State,
and providing for absorption of Raleigh & Gaston Stockholders. In his later developed plan he seems to have put the
road through the counties south of those of his own and Ex-
Governor Morehead's, but taking in Salisbury—the place
where the June Danville-Charlotte Convention was held, but
he treated it as covering strips both 50 and 100 miles wide.
The west, or that part of it in favor of the Charlotte-Danville link, was by no means convinced of Governor Graham's
presentation, and were still quite determined to have their
link charter. The result was that neither charter was secured, but after Governor Manly's inauguration, and with
his approval, Senator William S. Ashe of New Hanover
[Wilmington] and his friends, among whom was Edward

Stanly of Beaufort county, conceived of the idea of dividing this western plum, instead of giviing it all to the Raleigh
and Gaston, by giving half to the Wilmington & Weldon by
the very simple means of extending it east of Raleigh to the
latter road at Waynesboro [Goldsboro]—a step in the direction of the old Caldwell project to Beaufort harbor, as
Ex-Governor Graham had suggested as a possibility.   A
feature of this plan was that it should be financed, one-third
by the people and two-thirds by the State, up to $3,000,000;
that the Raleigh-Gaston people should put that road in condition to the extent of $500,000, for which the state would
return half their stock and release their bonds; that the
Gaston-Weldon connection of a dozen miles should be built
on a half and half basis; and that the Neuse and Tar rivers
should be improved for the small steamboats recently put
on.   Mr. Stanly led the fight for this in the House and
warned his eastern brethren that if they did not support it,
he would vote for the Danville link.   The result was that
the House passed it on January 19, 1849, with a clear majority of 6 votes, and sent it to the Senate for concurrence.[1]

In this latter body it was destined to have no such clear
sailing.   It came up on the afternoon of January 25, 1849,
for third reading.   Senator Drake called for yeas and nays.
"The moment was one of intense interest," says the *Raleigh
Register,* "The audience generally were ignorant of the views
of the Speaker [Calvin Graves], and when he had announced
that the Yeas were 22, Nays, 22, the stillness was death-
like; until the magical words, 'The Chair decides in the
affirmative,' relieved suspense.   The applause which succeeded was deafening, and it was some minutes before order
could be restored."   The bill became a law on Friday, January
26, 1849.   The men who voted for it besides Speaker Graves,
were Senators Ashe [the author], Bell, Daniel, Davidson,
Gilmer, Hargrove, Hawkins, Joyner, Lane, Lillington, Miller,

---

[1] Hon. D. M. Barringer, in his sketch of state railroads, attributes the success of this vote to another dramatic event of the session attending the passage
of a bill to create an Insane Asylum, which had been so earnestly urged by
both Ex-Governors—Morehead and Graham.   The event was the appearance of
Miss Dorothy Dix before the Assembly and her powerful plea for the insane,
incidentally to which she drew such a picture of the roads of North Carolina
that she broke down the lines of the law-makers in both directions!

Murchison, Patterson, Rowland, Shepard, Smaw, Thomas of
Davidson, Thomas of Haywood, Thompson of Wake, Washington, Woodfin and Worth.   Speaker Graves was Speaker
pro tempore in place of Speaker Andrew Joyner, a Whig,
who had fallen ill; and it had been a great compliment to his
character that, as a conservative Democrat, the Whigs had
elevated him to this position.   Doubtless the leading Whigs
knew his private views on the subject and knew how he
would vote upon this most important of their measures, beside which all others sank into insignificance.   Of course
the author of the bill was a Democrat from the Wilmington
district, and this great measure was secured otherwise by
giving Fayetteville a plank road to it.   Speaker Graves, a
Democrat also, came from a county, Caswell, near the proposed Danville-Charlotte link, which both favored the link
and opposed state aid, and his famous casting vote was
followed by his resignation as Speaker *pro tempore* and re-
instatement of Speaker Joyner, who had recovered; while
the people of Caswell permanently retired him from public
life.   The Whig and progressive elements of the state, however, from that day forward made a hero of him and more
than one project of a statue to him has been proposed.

And still—a North Carolina Central Railroad had been
proposed and even incorporated long before this, and came
to nothing!   It is true Wilmington had never favored it before and it had never secured so good financial conditions;
but it is also true that never before was there so imminent a
threat of a Charlotte-Danville trunk-line link for a trans-
national line that threatened to isolate the east by cutting off
her back-country commerce!   Nature and events were favoring the land-locked west, like the "stars in their courses;"
and let it not be forgotten this project had been a western one
of Caldwell and Morehead, since the "Carleton" papers of
1827; and it was only the grinding of the mills of the gods
that forced the Wilmington representative to finally accept
it as a desperate measure of self-preservation, in an effort to
stay the march of a transnational line down the Piedmont
into Georgia and the southwest.

February was not far advanced when Governor Manly

called his Council to reorganize the Improvement Board;
and the Salisbury Convention, headed by David F. Caldwell
reconvened to help forward the newly proposed North
Carolina Railroad, as though, for the time at least, they had
given up the Danville link, or that part of it not now
covered by the projected road; for, if the new road went to
Greensboro, the link would then be complete except for
crossing two counties—Guilford and Rockingham—a link so
short and so necessary to complete the transnational line,
that, sooner or later, it would be impossible to prevent it.
Following the Salisbury meeting, Guilford county called a
Greensboro meeting for February court; and the Raleigh
Whig editor called for similar meetings in the whole state;
adding that *The Salisbury Watchman* said that they were
trying to form a list of a hundred men to take the whole
stock in Rowan and surrounding counties! The Greensboro
meeting on 20th February provided for ten delegates to another Salisbury convention on June 14th, Senator Gilmer
leading in it. In March, Raleigh had a meeting.

This agitation, it should be noted, and unfavorable comparison with other states in railway matters should be taken
for what it was: Advocacy. For, in 1848, only New York,
Massachusetts, Pennsylvania, Georgia, Virginia, Connecticut, Michigan and New Hampshire had a greater mileage,
and the last three of these but slightly more; so that she was
practically surpassed in her 255 miles of railroad by but five
states in any material degree. It will be observed that
Georgia and Virginia, with 602 and 406 miles respectively,
led the South and ranked next to Pennsylvania, and were on
both sides of North Carolina at Charlotte and Danville offering tremendous railway connection to western North
Carolina; and that the section of the new North Carolina
Railroad between Charlotte and Salisbury or Greensboro
would itself furnish a large section of that longed for link!
Indeed, in the North Carolina Railroad the west was receiving more than three-fifths of the Charlotte-Danville link!
And they could well trust Father Time for the rest! No
wonder they accepted the new project with alacrity. The
remaining 43 miles of air line between Greensboro and Dan-

ville was bound to come later; no one could stop it. Why should they, indeed? Had not Wilmington been trying to do the same thing all along, in the east? Hadn't Raleigh and Fayetteville been trying to do the same thing in the center? Certainly they had; and were even now doing so in connecting Charlotte and Raleigh!

A state convention was agitated during the spring and there seemed to be a new hope in the people. The new incorporating act named fifteen commissioners to put it into effect; and among them was Ex-Governor Morehead, who was also named as the head of the Greensboro sub-committee to open books for stock subscriptions. The act was well drawn and anticipated practically every feature necessary to successful organization. At Hillsboro, Orange county, Ex-Governor Graham led a meeting in urgence of the line's survey through that town and county on March 15th. By April a South Carolinian offered a thousand dollars for the contract of the whole road from Goldsboro to Charlotte. The press began comparing the gains of Boston, which had railroads, with New York, which had none: Boston increased the value of her real estate from $60,000,000 (in round numbers) in 1840 to $97,000,000 in 1847; while, for the same period and estate, New York scarcely increased at all—$187,100,000 to $187,300,000 (in round numbers)! In personal estate, Boston increased from $34,000,000 to over $64,000,000; while New York actually decreased about $8,000,000.

Early in April, the Internal Improvement Board, on which Governor Manly had put Hon. Calvin Graves, met; and also the new Commissioners he appointed to create the new Insane Asylum, of which commission Ex-Governor Morehead was head and Mr. Graves next in order. While they were in Raleigh on the 19th of April a railroad meeting was held and addressed by Governor Morehead and others, and delegates chosen to the Salisbury Convention to be held June 14, 1849. Governor Morehead pointed to Massachusetts, Rhode Island, Georgia and Tennessee as good illustrations of state development. He said at one period when he almost despaired of ever securing such a charter as was now before them, he had favored the Danville-Charlotte link as an outlet for his part of the state; but with the Central Railroad he was heartily satisfied, provided it could be built; that Orange, Guilford, Davidson, Rowan and Randolph would do their full share. Indeed he believed these counties would grade their part of the road, so that the problem was the grading in Wake County and Johnston; "what would Wake and Johnston do? Would they grade their part? If so, he believed the work was assured." It was plain that Governor Morehead had sounded the Keynote of the coming railway campaign in this April address in the Raleigh Court House on the 19th. Before the meeting was over he emphasized the need of the Gaston-Weldon link, chiefly for its access to Norfolk which was at this time seeking annexation to North Carolina, because she was so neglected by Virginia. Indeed, the North Carolina Central Railroad seemed to be as hopeful as the Washington Monument, of which twenty feet was now completed. On May 19th a meeting was held at the tri-county corners below what is now High Point and men pledged themselves to grade from a quarter to a mile of road to the amount of 15 miles. Other meetings were held along the proposed line.

These were busy days for "The Old War Horse:" one day at Edgeworth Seminary, another in a railroad meeting, still another at the University Commencement, where he was both Trustee and President of the Alumni Association, and granting degrees to everybody but himself.[1] Then came the Salisbury Convention, with over 225 delegates from the State and Norfolk and Portsmouth, with twenty odd counties represented. The meeting was held in the Lutheran Church and Governor Morehead was chosen President unanimously and made the keynote address. He was also one of the Committee of 30 to organize the program. Governors Morehead and Graham believed in an appeal to the people, while Governor Swain suggested getting a hundred men to subscribe the million themselves. President Morehead, President Mordecai of the Raleigh & Gaston road and

---

[1] Maria Edgeworth, after whom the seminary was named, died the 21st of May, ten days after the school's commencement. She was 83 years old.

Dr. W. R. Holt were made the Executive Committee to organize subscription. It was plainly evident that the North Carolina Central Railroad was at last to be built! Furthermore President Morehead was authorized to appoint a delegation of three to the Memphis Convention in July to promote a trans-continental railroad.[1] Governor Swain was made chairman of this delegation.

It was interesting to see how men began again to recur to the ideas of Murphy and Caldwell, whose apt pupil was unanimously chosen the head of this Convention and who had personified those broad ideas in his own life ever since the famous Murphy Reports and the "Carlton" letters of President Caldwell! Men began to recur to them in the press as if they had suddenly became current. Murphy and Caldwell were now incarnate in John Motley Morehead. The whole state began to respond to his leadership. The east and the west were about to unite in him—for the first time in reality. It was difficult for the Fourth of July or even politics to get the usual hearing, as the summer of 1849 proceeded. Petersburgh and Norfolk were as much awake to it as North Carolina herself, for they were bound to profit by it. Governor Swain placed himself at the disposal of Governor Morehead and went, at his request, over the Georgia railroads, making a careful study of them and reporting in excellent letters of June 22nd and later.[2] He showed that one road, beginning at a wilderness site in 1837, had made of that wilderness "the flourishing town of Atlanta," and said he, "as the road advanced, the tribe of croakers retired." He thought stockholders of North Carolina roads who had suffered would yet be looked upon as heroic pioneers! Thus the campaign proceeded—even in spite of a cholera epidemic, as well as political campaign; and by August even the Wilmington & Weldon Railroad subscribed $15,000 to the new road. In Davidson county about $30,000 was subscribed and Rowan exceeded that slightly. Raleigh was proposing to take $25,000 as a cor-

---

[1] The Memphis Convention was postponed to October 16th, on account of cholera in July.
[2] *Raleigh Register* of July 25, 1849.

poration. Another Convention, at Greensboro, this time, for
October 18th, was announced, but it was postponed until
November 29th, as Governor Morehead announced on October 5th.[1] This was scarcely issued before Salisbury had a
meeting and agreed to form a company of 20 men to take
$100,000 and asked for the corporation of Salisbury to vote
stock. And yet, in the midst of all this, Governor Morehead
was in New York on the 21st of October, and other places,
inspecting asylums for the insane to guide his board in creating a North Carolina institution. Meanwhile President
Stephen A. Douglas was presiding over the great Trans-
continental Railroad Convention at Memphis on the 15th and
providing a later meeting in Philadelphia.

But Governor Morehead was back in Greensboro early
in November; and at a railroad meeting in their Court House
to increase the $60,000 subscription of Guilford County.
The Swain proposition of a 100 shares was changed to associations taking one of a hundred shares of whatever balance there was. Immediately Associations were formed to
take twelve and a half shares, so that Guilford county was
now responsible for $150,000, not counting late news from
Springfield of some $16,000 subscribed.

This local convention was preparatory to the general
Greensboro Railroad Convention of November 29th.

In November, 1849, about twenty-five counties elected
delegates to this Railroad Convention at Greensboro. They
met in the Presbyterian Church. Governor Morehead
headed the Guilford delegation and, after temporary organization, he rose to nominate a President. He said here was
"the opportunity to elect one that would be an honor to the
state; and proceeded to pass a high eulogium upon Calvin
Graves of Caswell, who had given the casting vote by which
this charter had been passed; and concluded by moving that
he be unanimously appointed President of the North Carolina Railroad Convention." His advice was followed and
President Graves made an address in which he said England

---

[1] A railroad of North Carolina not much mentioned was the Wilmington &
Manchester Railroad from Wilmington into South Carolina, 66 miles in the
state, had 129 miles of the 162 miles road under contract at this time; so that
Wilmington had no objection to "links" for herself.

had expended two hundred million pounds sterling in rail-roads, which often cost over $60,000 a mile merely for right of way; and states of this country were making strides in the same direction. Governor Morehead made a "speech of great power" and moved for a committee on subscription. This was done and he headed it. He was also a Vice-President of the Convention, with five others, among whom was Hon. Richard M. Saunders. The Convention was a vigorous one, and the most forceful figure in it was the Greensboro ex-Governor. Reporting on subscriptions he showed the absolute subscriptions to stock were $190,800; and followed "with a speech full of deep impassioned feeling and great power—listened to with breathless attention and the most intense interest. The gallant and determined spirit of this distinguished gentleman touched every heart in that assembly, and awoke a feeling of enthusiasm and anxiety, deep, startling and fervent as we have ever witnessed."[1] General Saunders, chairman of the Resolution Committee, aided in preserving the program for the whole road or none; and John A. Gilmer of Greensboro presented a form of additional subscriptions to complete the million dollars individual subscription by signers agreeing to take a hundredth part of the unraised balance. Governor Morehead headed a list of fifty-one, and by afternoon $630,000 was regularly subscribed, leaving only $380,000 to be raised. It was then proposed to have conventions in each county through which the road would run, and a committee be appointed to prepare and issue a public address. These latter were Messrs. Saunders, McRae, Griswold, McLeod, Swain, Graham, Trollinger, J. M. Morehead, Thomas, Lord, Fox and Barringer. Governor M—— tried hard to get the convention to double subscriptions and close it up, but did not succeed. The Convention was a great unifying influence, for seldom had men of such opposite views come to act together so fully. The 51 territorially were as follows: Wilmington, 5; Craven, 1; Wayne, 2; Johnston, 1; Raleigh, 6; Franklin, 1; Orange, 4; Alamance, 1; Guilford, 12; Rockingham, 1;

---

[1] Editor *Greensboro Patriot*, 1st Dec., 1849.

Davidson, 4; Rowan, 11; Burke, 1; and Buncombe, 1. Guilford and Rowan leading far ahead of all in unique rivalry. Someone in fun suggested that, when they were at a tie Guilford get ahead and a humorous, witty play was had back and forth until the Quaker firm of Simpson & Gibson put Guilford ahead, and, as they said, in compliment to President Graves. This was the secret of the leadership of Guilford and Rowan.[1]

The Greensboro Convention of November 29, 1849, appointed committees to hold meetings and the chairmen, Graves, John T. Gilmer and Governor Morehead were designated to take the western territory. On January 17, 1850, Governor Morehead wrote a public letter of report to Chairman R. M. Saunders of the Executive Committee of the North Carolina Railroad, in which he said: "We left here on the 3rd inst. and attended meetings at Union Institute in Randolph, Lexington, Salisbury, Concord, Rocky River, Charlotte, Mount Mourne, Statesville, Mocksville, Clemmonsville and Salem—reaching this place [Greensboro], last night. Our efforts were mainly directed to procuring 'the Hundred' individuals or companies who would become responsible for the balance of the stock not covered or taken by independent subscriptions. The number of individuals or companies who added their names to the list has been encouragingly augmented:—Randolph added one; Lexington five; Salisbury four; Concord four; Rocky River two; Charlotte and Mecklenburg nothing; Mount Mourne one; Statesville none, but two or three promised; Mocksville and Davie two; Clemmonsville one; Salem two;—making *twenty-two* added to the fifty-one subscribed at the Convention. I think we may safely calculate on four or five more promised shortly.

"What additions have been made to 'the Hundred' east of this, I am not appraised, save as the four additional names in Raleigh.

"I now feel assured the Railroad will be built, if every good citizen does his duty and proper exertions are made. The best spirit prevailed wherever we went. . . .

---

[1] *Greensboro Patriot*, Dec. 15, 1849, first page, column four.

"This is the great work of the day for North Carolina; and I am pleased to find Whig and Democrat contending side by side which shall do most for its success. . . .

"It is desirable that the Company should be organized at as early a day as possible, that the reconnaissance of the route, preparatory to survey, should be made before the leaves put forth in the spring."[1]

On December 10, 1849, the Committee made its appeal and on the 15th Governor Morehead and Mr. Graves addressed a great meeting at Raleigh, where between $30,000 and $40,000 were added to the Wake county subscriptions. This headed a series of thirteen meetings in various parts of the state to last until January 14, 1850.

To one of these meetings, that at Goldsboro on January 3, 1850, which Governor Morehead was unable to attend, he wrote saying, that "while you are addressing the people of Wayne, let it cheer you to know that I am making the hills of Randolph resound in behalf of the Railroad. It is *the result of the age for North Carolina*. It is truly the great redeeming improvement which is to make us one people— one state—one great community. It is a State improvement —East and West are equally interested in it—and let no croaker against this great State work, ever hereafter talk of patriotism, State pride, etc. How small such opposition will look, when the great valleys of Western North Carolina shall pour along this road its exhaustless productions—and when the Eastern citizen will leave his rich farm in the East in the morning, and take dinner or tea with his wife and children in the West, in their beautiful summer residence, purchased on some mountain side, or in some thriving village, where all the children have the best schools at their command.——This is no fancy picture—it will be realized in less than ten years if this road is built—and no people in the State are more interested than the enterprising and wealthy citizens of Wayne. Let them do but one-half as much as their interest, their patriotism and their State pride, ought to inspire them to do, *and the Road is safe*.——Guilford—poor Guilford has already done more than she is able

---

[1] *Greensboro Patriot*, 10th Jan., 1850.

to do; yet let Wayne and other counties do something worthy of the great cause—worthy of themselves and worthy of the glorious Old North—and Guilford, poor as she is, will still do more—*much more. The Road must be built.* Let that be the watchword of every Wayne man, and the Road is safe. Success, triumphant success, attend your meeting and exertions. Yours in all the bonds that can unite patriots in a glorious State enterprise——J. M. Morehead."[1] In a letter from Mr. Graves at Charlotte he says: "Governor Morehead is making what he calls the second Declaration of Independence with great power."

The rising tide of practical enthusiasm from Goldsboro to Charlotte—the line of the North Carolina Central Road— began to threaten even beyond it to Newbern, where at a meeting on January 23rd, they resolved "that to realize the great enterprise of a Central Railroad binding the commercial ports of the East with the Western farms, once projected by a Stanly, a Gaston and a Caldwell, the North Carolina Railroad should be extended to the town of New Berne;" and, after a speech by Gen. Saunders, they subscribed $70,000 toward the extension eastward to that place.

Thus by February 28, 1850, the railroad Commissioners named in the act, were able to announce that a recent meeting of subscribers held at Hillsboro showed that the required $1,000,000 had been subscribed, but was not all done in a uniform manner prescribed by the act. The Commissioners therefore announced and ordered the opening of books again on March 8th to 23rd, in the indicated places and in Petersburg, Va., at which time $5 per share was to be paid in. They also announced that on March 30, 1850, the Commissioners would meet in Greensboro at which time these moneys were to be deposited, so that a meeting of Stockholders can be called at Salisbury for organization and "commencement of operations on the road." At the Greensboro meeting, however, it was discovered that the Petersburg Railroad charter had a clause that prevented them making their $80,000 subscription good; and that this and

---

[1] *North Carolina Standard*, Jan. 23, 1850.

some unfinished subscriptions in Guilford and Davidson left the fund $60,000 short, although five per cent of the rest was all paid in. By May 1st, however, all but between $12,000 and $20,000 was in sight, according to Governor Morehead's statement to the *Greensboro Patriot* and it was thought the Commissioners could be called by the 16th. Thereupon the *Asheville Messenger* announced that a man in Raleigh had increased his subscription from $2500 to $10,000: "Wonder what 'John' will say now?" It was the 5th of June before the Commissioners met in the Chapel of the University, where Chairman Morehead announced the completion of the $1,000,000 subscription. Thereupon a meeting of the Stockholders was called at Salisbury on July 11, 1850. This University meeting was to allow Governor Morehead and others of the Commissioners to perform their duties as Trustees also.

Two days before the Salisbury meeting another Whig President of the United States died on the night of July 9th. This was such a blow to Governor Morehead as it could be only to a man who had served as President of the convention that nominated him; but the blow fell as he was victorious in the chief part of a great statesmanlike program for North Carolina development for which he had stood for nearly a quarter of a century—since the days of his old University President's "Carlton" papers. So full was he of this great enterprise that he kept it in the public thought abreast, if not ahead of the wide-spread organization of Southern resistance, especially Democratic resistance to Abolition agitations of the north.[1] A large part of the "Carlton" railroad vertebræ of the state, from the mountains to the main, was now to be a reality. The wilderness cries of a Murphy and a Caldwell were at last heard and answered; and the man whom they taught and inspired, John Motley Morehead, was everywhere recognized as their executive and leader of the Old North State's hosts!

---

[1] Governor Morehead was chairman of a Union meeting at Greensboro on October 23, 1850, and among the resolutions was the following: "That we will stand by the Union so long as it is worth preserving, and the Constitution is faithfully administered; and we will maintain, protect and defend the rights guaranteed to us by that Constitution."

XIV

PRESIDENT AND BUILDER

OF

THE NORTH CAROLINA CENTRAL RAILROAD

1850

On July 11, 1850, stockholders and proxies in the North Carolina Central Railroad met at Salisbury and Mr. Duncan Cameron was called to the chair, on motion of General Saunders. Beside the towns of Newbern and Wilmington, there were represented the counties of Wayne, Johnston, Wake, Orange, Alamance, Randolph, Guilford, Rowan, Caswell, Rockingham, Surry, Davidson, Davie, Cabarrus, Mecklenburg, Iredell, Forsyth, Burke and Buncombe. Rowan and Guilford each had two directors and there were eight others, Governor Morehead, Governor Graham and General Saunders being among the number. Governor Morehead was at once elected President of the company, with a salary of $2500—a considerable sum in those days, however insignificant it may appear as the reward of a railway executive now.[1] They then set to work, with Mr. Walter Gwynne as chief engineer. In the summer and fall elections, however, while the Whig leaders were pressing the Central Railway to a conclusion, with the aid of some Democrats like General Saunders, the Democratic leaders, like Editor Holden of the *Raleigh Standard,* were not wildly enthusiastic, to say the least; while David Settle Reid, with the slogan of equal suffrage, overturned the Whig majority and was chosen Governor by about 2700 majority. When the legislature met in November, all of that wrath of the opponents of Calvin Graves and the North Carolina Railroad came to a head on November 26th, when a Wayne county

---

[1] Charles L. Hinton, in a letter of 22nd Aug., 1850, to Governor Graham, says that in the last day or so Governor Morehead had such a fall from his horse that several physicians were called in; but that it proved not to be very serious.

308

representative in the Commons presented a bill to repeal the North Carolina Central Railroad bill! This was to be expected when only twenty-one counties had interest enough to produce stockholders. It is true the bill was against the law of obligation of contracts and so was a species of repudiation, but it did not lack advocates, as likewise the other side did not. It was General Saunders, probably, more than anyone else who headed off his party's efforts to destroy the work of the past years. Secession was advocated with even greater earnestness; and these were going on while the Railroad Directors were in session in Raleigh.

Meanwhile, in the Legislature, Senator Woodfin of Buncombe county, as well as the Newbern and Beaufort people, were taking measures to persuade the State to extend the Central Railroad east and west according to the old Caldwell idea, Senator Woodfin offering a resolution to that effect. But the Directors had scarcely adjourned, when, during December an Industrial Convention was held in the Supreme Court rooms of the capitol, designed to stimulate industries all over the state to get ready to produce traffic on President Morehead's newly organized railroad. On motion of Col. Henry B. Elliott, the Convention unanimously chose Governor Morehead President. It was determined to hold state exhibitions of products in the form of "State Fairs," as was done in other states, under the title "North Carolina Industrial Association." These exhibitions were to be held at Raleigh in October of each year, and were to include agricultural, manufacturing, mining and mechanical products under conditions of generous rivalry. With the permanent organization, Governor Morehead was chosen President of that also, and Governor Swain and others were among the Vice-Presidents. Their first act was to ask the Assembly for geological, mineralogical and agricultural surveys. It is no wonder these gentlemen were indignantly impatient with persistent secession agitation in some quarters of the state and still more outside of it. Indeed they were so busy with this splendid plan of development of the commonwealth that they hardly allowed sufficiently for the disorganizing national influences abroad. So it was a great comfort to them when news came at this time of Georgia's thunderous protest against secession by a vote of 237 to 19! Stephen A. Douglas happened to be visiting in Governor Morehead's old home county at Wentworth on December 27, 1850, at the same time, and his voice was raised for Union against secession in a great Union meeting there. But this was lost sight of in the running fight made in many ways to still defeat the North Carolina Railroad; but the threat of men like Caldwell of Guilford that if the Central charter was touched the Danville-Charlotte link would go on the map instanter softened the ardor of the Anti-Central leaders.

In the midst of all this activity, Governor—or, as it is now proper to call him as head of the Central Railroad— President Morehead was quietly writing announcements of the next session of Edgeworth Seminary on the first Monday in February, 1851, and presenting a list of references from Union Theological Seminary, New York, Rev. Wm. C. Plummer of Baltimore, President Carnahan and Professor Alexander of Princeton and Professor Henry of the Smithsonian Institution, showing that he expected students from all over the Union.

This, however, was by the way. The surveys were being pushed by President Morehead and his engineers; and he saw to it that the great success of Georgia was known to all North Carolina: "It appears," said the *Raleigh Register,* "that before the close of the year 1852, that state will have in operation upwards of *nine hundred miles* of road." Those completed were already paying 8 to 16 per cent on the investment; and after paying $14,000,000 nearly, the state was twice as rich as before. The state in ten years had increased in population fifty per cent, while North Carolina had gained but about twelve per cent! The Georgia Central from Savannah to Macon was the great road.[1]

---

[1] The growth of railroads in Georgia was remarkable: With 40 miles in 1838; 88 miles in 1840; 148 miles in 1844; 213 miles in 1847; the ratio of expenses to receipts decreased from 54 per cent in 1838 to 34 per cent in 1849; and net profits rose from $16,386 in 1838 to $386,232 in 1849; and total receipts rose from $35,753 in 1838 to $582,015 in 1849.—Senator John A. Gilmer of Guilford in a speech in the North Carolina Senate, against the attack on the North Carolina Central Railroad.

Then came the Directors' meeting of May 12, 1851, at Raleigh, that showed the road had been located through Goldsboro, Raleigh, Hillsboro, Graham, Greensboro, Jamestown, Lexington, Salisbury, Concord and Charlotte; and the whole was ordered under contract by July 9th. At this meeting Chief Engineer Gwynne made an elaborate report, describing each of the four divisions: 1. Goldsboro to 6½ miles west of Raleigh; 2. Thence to Guilford county line; 3. Thence to Lexington; and 4. Thence to Charlotte. He wrote with the vision of a statesman as well as engineer, and saw this road's extension over the mountains, for which surveys were already authorized; and to Beaufort, toward which a charter was already granted as far as Newbern. He suggested 10 locomotives, 6 passenger cars, 4 baggage and mail cars, and 80 "burthen cars" as a beginning; and various other features of construction.[1]

While these constructive proceedings were occurring, the State, by early summer, was tense with Union sentiments on the one hand, and, on the other, secession agitation led by a candidate for Congress, Hon. A. W. Venable, and some Abolitionist propaganda in the west, especially in Guilford county, where an Ohio man named McBride was so exciting the people that they formed a Vigilance Committee and persuaded him to seek other territory, where they were not so devoted to the Union and had less detestation of both Disunionist and Abolitionist alike!

On June 25, 1851, while President Morehead was in Raleigh, a meeting of friends of the Central Road was held and resolutions passed suggesting that a ceremony of "breaking ground" be held at Greensboro, on the 11th of July, next day after the Directors' meeting. President Morehead addressed them, telling them that the whole of Wayne county sections, except one and a bridge had been contracted for; indeed that the entire line east of Raleigh was substantially under contract. He believed all would be so before July 11th, and hoped they would all be present at the "breaking

---

[1] President Morehead advertised bids for contracting in May 25, 1851—the work to begin not later than January 1, 1852, and to be completed by January 1, 1854. Payment was to be made, one-half cash and one-half stock in the road. The road was 223 miles long.

ground" ceremonies. Greensboro immediately took it up
with enthusiasm and provided a committee to prepare a great
barbecue and other entertainment to "all friends of North
Carolina!"

The ceremony of "breaking ground" for the North Carolina Central Railroad occurred at Greensboro on Friday,
July 11, 1851, at the time of the meeting of Stock-holders.
"On coming down the street from the place of meeting,"
says the editor of the *Greensboro Patriot*, in the issue of
July 12th, "a crowd of people appeared, ready for the celebration, such as we may safely say was never seen before in
our town, for numbers. It was *one universal jam all out of
doors*. The young gentlemen who acted as marshals had
enough work of it to persuade this vast and unwieldy crowd
into marching shape; but they at length succeeded to a degree
which at first appeared impossible. The procession was
formed on West street—the clergy in front; then the stockholders; then the orders of Odd Fellows and Free Masons,
who turned out in great numbers and in full regalia; closing
with the citizens generally. This immense line moved down
South street to a point on the Railroad survey nearly opposite the Caldwell Institute building, where a space of a
hundred feet each way was enclosed by a line and reserved
for the ceremony of the day. The north side of this space
was occupied by the ladies, whose smiles are always ready
for the encouragement of every good word and work. The
other three sides were soon occupied by the male portion
of the assemblage, from *ten to twenty deep* all around.
. . . Having the misfortune to be among the *outsiders*,
our situation was of course unfavorable for hearing, and
seeing was impossible. But we did hear nearly every word
of Gov. Morehead's clear sonorous voice as he introduced
the Hon. Calvin Graves to the vast assemblage. He did
this in terms eloquent and singularly appropriate to the occasion. After alluding to the necessity so long felt by our
people for an outlet to the commercial world—to the incep-
tion of a great scheme the commencement of which we had
met today to celebrate—to the vicissitudes of the charter before the two houses of the General Assembly, and the fact

that it at last hung upon the decision of the Speaker of the Senate, and that its fate was decided in the affirmative by the unfaltering *'Aye'* of that Speaker—Calvin Graves—he said no other citizen of North Carolina could so appropriately perform the ceremony of removing the first earth in the commencement of this work, on which the hopes of the State so vitally depend, as the man who pronounced that decisive 'Aye.' " Then followed Speaker Graves' address, at the close of which, he dug up a few spadefuls of earth depositing them in a box made for the purpose; upon which Governor Morehead said it was to remain in the box for a hundred years and then opened for their inspection, a pleasantry hugely enjoyed. Over seventy of that hundred years have passed and one wonders where the box is now, as the vast traffic of the Southern Railway noisily rumbles over the spot from which Calvin Graves removed those first spadefuls. The event closed with a barbecue already prepared and the great railway system of North Carolina was started on its course down the decades.

As has been said, President Morehead and the Central Railroad had taken so vital a hold on the people of North Carolina that the call of Ex-Governor Graham to be Secretary of the Navy seemed to cause scarcely a ripple on the surface of public news. But in October, 1851, Guilford county took the lead in nominating for President and Vice-President, both President Fillmore and his Secretary of the Navy, Ex-Governor Graham, to whose wisdom and that of his agent, Commodore Perry, the great modern nation of Japan owes so much. These men stood for the Union, against both Secessionists and Abolitionists equally; while the vocal warfare of the latter two raged as though civil war had already begun in 1851. To these Whigs a destruction of the Union by either seemed impossible. So the great Central Railroad construction proceeded under President Morehead's direction; and the development spirit abroad resulted in the Seaboard and Roanoke line, early in December, again opening up traffic between Weldon and Portsmouth and Norfolk; while news from the Census that North Carolina had 2523 manufacturing establishments aided in intensifying the hopeful outlook. President Morehead's home town was a great source of inspiration at this time in educational lines also, through the work for it by Calvin H. Wiley of that place. By March, 1852, operations were nearly ready to begin on the Gaston-Weldon link between the Raleigh, the Petersburg, the Wilmington and the Norfolk lines. Development was in the atmosphere everywhere in the State, while the building of the Central Railroad proceeded. So it continued, even in June, 1852, when the Whig National Convention put up Scott and Graham as their candidates, and had scarcely done so when the telegraph announced the death of the great Whig leader, Henry Clay, the idol of President Morehead for so many years.

It was time North Carolina was awake on transportation lines. The *American Railway Times* of Boston, during the Winter of 1852–53 made an analysis of contemporary railway conditions, showing that Pennsylvania was then first with 59 roads while North Carolina was almost last with 3; New York was first in number of miles in operation, namely 2129 miles, while North Carolina had but 249; Illinois was first in amount in course of construction, 1698 miles, while North Carolina had but 223; New York was first in cost, $82,000,000, to North Carolina's $4,106,000. The New York Erie railroad was then the longest in the world, 460 miles and with the worst record.

On June 4, 1853, Governor Reid, in accordance with the act of the previous Assembly incorporating both "The Atlantic and North Carolina Railroad Company" and "The North Carolina and Western Railroad Company" requested President Morehead to have surveys made from Goldsboro to Beaufort and from Salisbury to the Tennessee line, and the President at once ordered it. In making a public announcement of it to the press through the *Patriot* of June 18th, he says, among other things: that the commerce of the world was to be had at Beaufort, on the ocean highway within thirty minutes, a great place to coal; that the road would be soon connected with other lines due west to Memphis, and then it was only a question of time until still other lines would go west from there to San Francisco, for the Oriental trade. He said nature had done so much that all that were needed were "MEN, men worthy of the age in which they live." To the press he said: "Onward! and you take the lead."

A few days previously visitors at Beaufort harbor from Newbern told their home papers of development at Sheppard's Point: The *Newbern News* said the new city was to be located there and the three original owners of it decided on the name "Carolina City;" but now there were more in the company, among whom were Governor Morehead, Smith & Colby of New York, Mr. Underwood of Fayetteville and others. They were surveying the plat and had arranged to build a big hotel and several wharves. No building was to be more than one story high and of brick or stone—apparently in view of the possible great storms of this coast. The central street to the main wharf was to be 30 feet wide and have the railroad track in the center. The wharf was ultimately to be built out to White Rock, a formation at which the largest vessels could tie up. The writer had no doubt that it was to become another Charleston, Baltimore or Boston. The proprietors, however, soon changed the name to Morehead City in honor of Governor Morehead who made the achievement possible.[1]

Of Governor Morehead's relation to it, he had the following, in part, to say in a public letter in the *Greensboro Patriot* of August 6, 1853: "For years past, my attention has been directed to the immeasurable value, to North Carolina, of the great Harbor of Beaufort; and my surprise was, that so little regard was paid to its importance by those who knew it better than I did, and resided in its immediate vicinity.——Some eighteen months since [about February 1, 1852] I sent a friend to examine the Harbor, who commenced negotiations for an interest in the lands at Sheppard's Point, which eventuated in a purchase by me of an interest, in October last—long before the Railroad Bill was introduced into the Legislature, under which the survey is about to be made, and when no one knew that such a survey would be ordered

---

[1] *Greensboro Patriot*, June 18, 1853.

—and, if ordered, that I would be connected therewith. I suppose no one . . . would expect me to abandon that interest, because I may be placed in a delicate position relative thereto, by the subsequent action of the Legislature."[1] In addition to this, he took occasion to publish his reply to a fellow owner at Sheppard's Point, who just a month before, assumed they would act on personal advantage in the matter: "The first matter to be looked to," Governor Morehead wrote in part, "is, *not our mutual advantage, but the great interest of the State;* and if any point in that Harbor shall prove upon examination, to have better water and be more accessible than Sheppard's Point, in which I have some interest, I shall disregard Sheppard's Point, and go for the other."[1]

On July 14, 1853, the regular meeting of stockholders of the North Carolina Railroad Company occurred at Salisbury, with Gov. Wm. A. Graham as chairman.[2] President Morehead's report showed that contractors were obligated to finish by January 1, 1854, but that unavoidable delays of one company caused him to extend its time to April. There were present, either by proxy or in person, 564 stockholders representing 8148 shares. To one familiar with political history and conditions of North Carolina, it is not difficult to see how easily political interests crept into these meetings. Governor Morehead and his old time rival, Judge R. M. Saunders, were the favorites of the two elements, and their relative standing in this meeting was represented by the vote for them for a vacant directorship: Morehead, 3958, and Saunders, 3812, with 62 scattering, resulting in reelection of Morehead, both as director, and almost unanimously as President, an office for which he received the munificent sum of $2500. The four divisions of the line, on July 1, 1853, had a force of 1158 men, 358 boys, 511 cars, 732 horses and mules, 29 oxen, 16 track-layers, besides wagons and wheelbarrows. This was the first meeting at which the eight new directors representing the State's shareholding were present, with the four chosen by the private stockholders. The eight were appointed by Governor Reid, Governor Morehead being

---

[1] *Greensboro Patriot*, Aug. 6, 1853.
[2] Track-laying began on this road at Goldsboro on June 23, 1853.

one of the stockholders' four, voting 80 shares, probably
his own. They provided for immediate survey of the eastern
and western extensions. *The Carolina Watchman,* of July
21st, expressed the "gratification felt by a large portion of
the stockholders" at the reelection of President Morehead.
"He has filled the office from the time of its creation, and
has been over the operations on the road from the beginning." "The place which Governor Morehead has occupied,
and continues to fill, is a difficult one; and we presume there
is no one in the State who could hold the balances on such an
even poise, as to give entire satisfaction to every man concerned." The editor thought the source of difficulty was
some stock-holders becoming contractors and not making
enough money out of it. Its political character was illustrated in September when the *Democratic* organ, the
Standard, of Raleigh, intimated Governor M—— was too
anxious to have the railway shops at Greensboro, and twitted
him on a desire to have a Danville, Virginia, connection—
not wanting the west to have even one to Raleigh and Wilmington's two! The *Patriot,* like other Whig papers, of
course defended him: "Where is the man in the state of
North Carolina who could have done so much to set on foot
and carry forward this gigantic enterprise as Gov. Morehead
has done? He is being tried in a field where some of the
stoutest men in the Union have been broken down. He
stands just at that point of internal improvement history in
North Carolina, where other men in other states have stood,
who did the drudgery and endured the odium, while their
successors reaped the glory of success." *The Patriot* added:
"We have heard Gov. M——, some time since, casually express the opinion that such connection would be advantage-
ous to the Central Road by bringing on to it more trade
than it would carry off from it." But there was understood among all that there had been a tacit agreement with
the east not to do it; but the editor warned the east that suggestions of hypocrisy might defeat their own aims. The
project referred to was an extension north from Greensboro
to the Richmond and Danville Railroad which was being
completed towards Danville at this time, but with a slowness

that led the Danville editors to recommend to that road the Morehead system of letting contracts only for comparatively short distances and to a larger number of contractors. The *Patriot* editor endorses this attitude and adds: "there has been more hard work done, in a shorter time, and with less money, on the North Carolina Central Road than on any other road ever built."[1]

Asheville asked Governor Morehead to attend her railroad convention on August 25th, and his reply on the 15th was typical of his spirit and method at this period: "I am into the cause," he wrote, "soul and body, and if the state be true to herself, old as I am, I yet hope to live to see her, by her improvements, among the first states of this glorious Union." "The time for growling legislation is past—the spirit of the age is onward! onward!!" He pointed the way from Beaufort to San Francisco and the trade of China and South America. The survey was then complete to a dozen miles west of Morganton. An engineer at Asheville said there were five great roads over the mountains in the eastern part of the United States now in operation. He said the Raleigh and Gaston was extended to Weldon and both this road and the Wilmington-Weldon road were earning 7% on their investment, clear profit. The former nearly had a branch complete from Ridgway to Clarksville on the Roanoke; and a road from Fayetteville to the coal mine is begun. The North Carolina Railroad, begun January 1, 1852, "is now more than two-thirds graded," and they were laying track between Goldsboro and Raleigh, and preparing to lay track between Charlotte and Salisbury. The forces would meet near Greensboro in the autumn of 1855, "thus presenting the only case in the United States in which the contractors (and *native* contractors and *native* laborers) have executed $600,000 worth of work before they asked for or received one dollar; and the only case in which a railroad 223 miles long has been put into full and successful operation, in four and one-half years from the time when

---

[1] *The Greensboro Patriot*, 1st Oct., 1853. The best single brief account of the North Carolina Railroad is Chief Engineer Gwynne's last report in the *Raleigh Register* of March 12, 1856.

the first shovelful of earth was removed by the hand of man from its native resting place. North Carolinians may justly pride themselves in this achievement. The contractors will, in the fall of 1855, present you, not a flag of triumph, but a noble monument to their own energy and skill—a well constructed railroad complete in all its parts and adapted to the growing demands of an enterprising public."[1]

During the winter of 1852-3, it became evident that the success of the North Carolina Railroad and its President and the consequent prestige of both, should not accrue to the Whigs, who had failed in both the state and national campaigns. Besides President Morehead had made a few speeches for Scott and Graham—in vain, to be sure; but it was held against him, even though Director Saunders had made Democratic speeches. They therefore began to consider means of displacing all Whig directors, and within a year and a half, or by June, 1854, the last two Whigs on the state's part of the directory, were replaced by Democrats.[2] They pointed, however, to the fact that the stockholders elected all Whigs on their part—which could not be denied. The State had eight and the stockholders four; but even so, at the Salisbury meeting in July, 1853, President Morehead was re-elected almost unanimously. Chief Engineer Gwynne's salary was increased from $3000 to $5000 and he was given the surveys of the eastern and western ex-

---

[1] *The Greensboro Patriot,* Oct. 15, 1853. Civil Engineer Theodore S. Garnett at the Asheville convention. It is well to note that Virginia had over a thousand miles of railroad in use at this time in seventeen railroads, from one 4 miles long to the Baltimore and Ohio with 242. Its longer roads were, besides the B. & O., the Virginia Central with 106 miles, the Richmond and Danville with 90 miles, the Seaboard and Roanoke with 80 miles, the Richmond, Fredericksburg & Potomac with 76 miles, the Orange & Alexandria with 75, the Virginia & Tennessee with 73, the Southside with 63, the Petersburg with 59, etc.— *Alexandria Gazette.*

The Gaston-Weldon line was completed in April, 1853.

[2] It is amusing to see the Democratic leader, Editor Holden of the *Raleigh Standard,* in May and June, industrially praising Calvin Graves' "commanding fame" for his vote that secured the North Carolina charter—the man whose name even to this day, is mentioned as "never getting a public office again" for it! Editor Holden, also, on May 27, 1854, gravely gave a list of six Democrats who "made the railroad:" Graves, Ashe, Dobbins, Gen. Saunders, and Governors Reid and Bragg. To such extremities do political advantage lure political leaders! What these particular men did, under the circumstances of the moment, no one can nor should desire to deny; but the Democrats were afraid of the Whig leader and set out to destroy his prestige, as a party maneuver. Editor Holden did not recall to his readers that in 1848 43 Whigs and 17 Democrats favored it, while 14 Whigs and 38 Democrats were against it in the House, and in the Senate 17 Whigs and 6 Democrats were for the bill and 5 Whigs and 17 Democrats against it; 60 Whigs and 23 Democrats for, and 19 Whigs and 55 Democrats against!

tensions. The rumblings of opposition were much like those connected with the famous ice-house of 1842; and about as baseless. They thought he would want the railway shops at Greensboro—certainly about as near central to the line as could be, if it were true; and they thought he still wanted the Danville link, and the editor of the *Patriot* (Greensboro) plainly asserted that President Morehead had said not long since that it would be a good thing and bring more trade than it would take away.

The year 1854 saw the completion of the Wilmington & Manchester Railroad and the Western Railroad from Fayetteville contracted for; and as many in the North Carolina counties below Danville had stock in the Richmond & Danville road, they were again agitating for the Danville link, which was perfectly natural, in view of the fact that the North Carolina Central Railroad was finished from Charlotte to Concord by September of that year, the first passenger car passing over it on September 6th. It was at the Directors' meeting on the 30th of that month, at Greensboro, that it was decided to use the English term "station" instead of the French one "depot," which was commonly used in some states.

Meanwhile the Atlantic road from Goldsboro to Beaufort Harbor had obtained all subscriptions necessary by its meeting at Newbern on June 21st, and secured its charter; and by December 16, 1854, Chief Engineer Gwynne reported the route from Goldsboro to Sheppard's Point, Morehead City, as 95.84 miles, which was by nearly four miles the shortest route.[1] On January 1, 1855, President Morehead announced the "Central" as open for business from Goldsboro to "Durham's" [Durham]; and by the 20th, the Assembly had provided for charters the state's part in both the eastern and western extensions. The first freight tariff had been published in October. On February 24, 1855, President Morehead announced that $1,000,000 more stock authorized by the Assembly would be raised; and by April 1st, trains would be running as far as Hillsboro. As a fact,

---

[1] Craven County, of which Newbern is the county seat, took the $150,000 necessary to get the charter.

MRS. JOHN MOTLEY MOREHEAD
From a portrait by William Garl Broune, 1855

the trains were running to Mebane by June 30th, about 32 miles east of Greensboro, while they had reached Lexington at the same time about 35 miles west of Greensboro, showing that the line would undoubtedly meet near the latter place soon.

With the completion of the North Carolina Central Railroad practically a fact, and because of Governor Morehead's interest in the eastern extension, as well as because of the opposition politically, he resigned on July 12th, both as a director and as President, and his old time leader of the '20s, Charles F. Fisher of Salisbury, was chosen his successor. This was followed on August 16, 1855, by the stockholders of the Atlantic road deciding on Sheppard's Point as the ocean terminal, that is, Morehead City, and contracts for building the road were assigned, 26 miles to Governor Morehead and 16 miles to a Mr. Wood.

It was on the following December 14, 1855, that the "Pello," the first railway engine, entered Greensboro, and the 16th of that month set for a Jubilee and celebration of the event, with Governor Morehead as the chief speaker. By this time the meaning of this great work, with actual construction begun, both of an ocean port and railway from the sea to Tennessee, was beginning to illumine the minds of everybody. A line of fine steamers was put on Pamlico Sound from Beaufort and Morehead City to Washington on the Neuse river, one boat named the *"Astoria"* and the other the *"Governor Morehead,"* and were in operation in August, 1855, when Morehead City was decided upon as the ocean terminal of the Atlantic road.

The approach of the meeting of the two ends of the Central road near Greensboro caused a western correspondent of the *Patriot* to voice a general feeling among Whigs, that if the Whig ticket next time, were "Fillmore and Morehead," instead of "Scott and Graham," it might not fail. "Individually," he wrote, in the *Greensboro Patriot* of December 21, 1855, "I would rather hail John Morehead as President of the Senate than anyone now on the face of the globe." The editor seconds the nomination with: "There is no purer politician in the Union, and, none, we venture to

say, who would more thoroughly command the respect of
the people North and South and whose *influence* would be
felt so sensibly for good."

The enthusiasm was at its highest on the 29th of the next
month, January, 1856: "On Thursday last," said the *Patriot*
of February 1st, "about 3 o'clock P. M. the last bar of iron
was laid on the North Carolina Railroad. The meeting of
the two ends took place some 4½ miles west of this place.
After their work was completed, the hands of the two companies got into the cars and rode down to Greensboro, amid
the happy greetings and rejoicings of our citizens. And
after a half hour of hilarity they returned to Jamestown to
enjoy some of the inner man comforts." The next day mail
and passenger trains made their first trip and the following
schedule was announced: "On and after Thursday, the 31st
day of January, 1856," etc., to the effect that trains, mail
and passenger, would leave Goldsboro at 2.10 A. M. and arrive at Charlotte at 6.04 P. M.; and leave Charlotte at 5
P. M., reaching Goldsboro at 8.48 A. M., the absence of any
reference to sleeping accommodations being a part of the
conceptions of the period.

By the following May [1856] news of the progress of the
Atlantic road began to appear. The *Newbern News* of May
2nd, said that a force of 600 men and 130 horses were at
work on Governor Morehead's section of the Atlantic road,
which was in immediate charge of Mr. G. P. Evans, and that
track-laying would begin at the "Point" in Morehead City
in a month or so. It also said that Edward Stanly and Mr.
C. B. Wood were likewise contractors. Seven days later
it was announced in the *Patriot* that the Richmond & Danville road's completion to Danville was to be celebrated with
a barbecue on June 19th next. The July meeting of the
North Carolina Central stockholders, on motion of Ex-Governor Swain, disapproved of the running of Sunday trains
on their line—and presumably the smoke of "Pello" and its
fellow engines, did not thereafter contaminate the Sabbath
atmosphere of North Carolina. The atmosphere of the
Piedmont and mountains was stimulating the survey of the
Western North Carolina Railroad, as the western extension

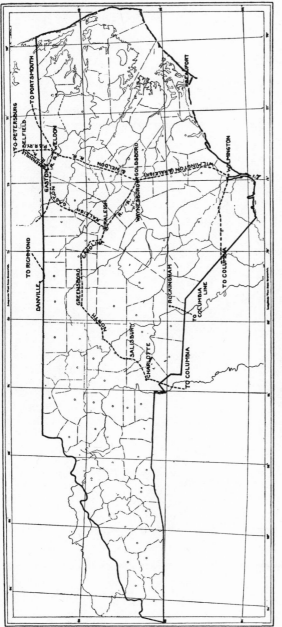

RAILROAD MAP OF NORTH CAROLINA IN 1856
Prepared by the author
(After Bartholomew, Edin.)

from Salisbury was called, and over 77 miles through Morganton was completed by the autumn of that year, when the "Land of the Sky," which it was to make accessible, was in its glory.

The dreams of Archibald DeBow Murphy and President Joseph Caldwell were in process of realization. Rails were slowly creeping from Cape Lookout's harbor to the passes of the Great Smoky Mountains on the Tennessee line. Not horses, as the "Carlton" papers proposed, but steam locomotive engines were already flying with passengers, mail and freight over a considerable portion of the line; while the foundations of a great ocean port were being laid in Beaufort Harbor. Not only so but these nearly realized dreams —realized by their old pupil and executive—were being extended by John Motley Morehead to include a transcontinental line to Memphis or the Ohio and the Pacific coast, with connection with the Oriental nations at the one end of the line, and steamship lines at the other to connect with New York, the West Indies and South American ports and those of Europe at Liverpool. Such were the vision and first steps of achievement of John Motley Morehead in the autumn of 1856.

XV

Building

The Eastern Extension and an Ocean Port
Morehead City
and
Whig Leadership Again

1856

In the early '50s, the Democrats had been calling themselves the Democratic Republicans or Republican Democrats,
thus showing a desire to capture the name "Republican" and
all that it then signified. With it they won not only the State
ticket, but pushed out the Whig National candidates, Scott
and Graham, by the narrow margin of 603 votes in North
Carolina. Neither Scott nor Graham had the power to hold
the "Old North State" in the Whig column, while, in many
northern states, the Abolitionist vote was also cutting down
the Whig majorities. In the mid-winter of 1853–4, the
Guilford county Whigs, in the presence of this sad experience with the Orange county leader, determined to put the
political harness back on "The Old Whig War Horse,"
President Morehead of the North Carolina Railroad, who
was accustomed to victory in all he undertook and especially
Whig victories. On January 2, 1854, at their Whig meeting
in Greensboro they both passed broad Whig resolutions,
among them being one for a Bank of the United States, and
selected President Morehead to head their delegation to the
State Convention and assumed the name "Republican
Whigs." The Whig State Convention that followed on
February 21st, nominated General Alfred Dockery of Richmond county, as candidate for Governor on a "Republican
Whig" ticket. General Dockery failed at the August elections by 2095, however; and, as if this were not bad enough,

President Morehead's railroad had its first collision on the following October 17th, about ten miles east of Raleigh, due to a negro flag-man sleeping at his post.

The years 1855–6 saw a breaking up of the old parties. For some four years, in certain parts of the United States, where foreign, and especially Roman Catholic immigration, was so great, a secret political society, whose members met inquiry by saying: "I know Nothing," grew under various names until in 1855 it carried four New England States, New York, Kentucky and California. This drew from the Whig party quite largely, under the name "American Party." The Abolitionists also drew largely from the Whigs and at Philadelphia, in 1856, nominated John C. Fremont. The Whigs of North Carolina turned to the "American Party" and had their State Convention on October 19, 1855, at Raleigh, at which they emphasized the Constitution and Union, and provided for a general gubernatorial nomination Convention on April 10th at Greensboro. To this move-met Governor Morehead gave his hearty allegiance and at the April meeting at Guilford Battle-Ground, he presided. For Governor there was nominated John A. Gilmer of Greensboro; and they nailed to the mast-head the names of "Fillmore and Donelson," the "American" party national candidates. In this atmosphere those who adhered to the old party called themselves, proudly, "Old Line Whigs," and there was a considerable sentiment, in North Carolina, to hold their old organization together, and Governor More-head, at least, and his followers were inclined to persuade them to support their own old President, Millard Fillmore, whose able contrast to their apostate Whig President, Tyler, awakened in them a great affection.

On September 19, 1856, the Whigs of Guilford County met at Greensboro, with Governor Morehead as Chair-man, and as he was already a State delegate-at-large to the Whig National Convention at Baltimore, he was authorized to appoint ten delegates to that meeting, which was set for September 17th. This "Old Line Whig Convention" met in the hall of the Maryland Institute on that day, and twenty-two states were represented: 1. Of the distinctive northern states were Illinois, Indiana, Ohio, Pennsylvania, New York, Connecticut, Massachusetts, New Jersey, Delaware and Minnesota; the border states were Maryland, Kentucky and Missouri; while the Southern states were Virginia (including what is now West Virginia), North Carolina, Tennessee, Georgia, Alabama, Florida, Mississippi, Arkansas, and Louisiana, with District of Columbia. The enthusiasm was very great, and the Virginia and North Carolina delegates found it necessary to call for more room. David Paul Brown, the brilliant lawyer from Philadelphia, was chairman of the organizing committee and they made Hon. Edward J. Bates of Missouri President of the Convention, and Governor Morehead, Governor Graham and others were on the platform with him. There were many speeches and the resolutions, among other things, stood for the Constitution and Union and deprecated the two main parties, one of which avowedly represented only sixteen northern States and the others the South chiefly. They approved the candidates, Fillmore and Donelson, but ignored the doctrines of the "American" party. In one of the speeches, namely, that by Mr. Banks of North Carolina, the speaker said: "I have consulted my political father, him for whom I cast my first vote in 1840—Governor Morehead." [Applause.] Among calls for various speakers were repeated demands for Governor Morehead, and probably his most notable speech in his whole life was this at the "Old Line Whig" Convention at Baltimore, in the Hall of Maryland Institute on the evening of Wednesday, September 17, 1856. It made his name ring throughout the land, for it was prophetic of the greatest tragedy in the life of himself and his country.

"Mr. President," said he, as he rose to respond to repeated calls, "I cannot but respond to the call which has been made upon me on this occasion. It would be strange if I did not feel any interest in the meeting of the Whig party here. The very stars may fly from their orbits, meteors may fly through space and fade away to mere nothingness, but so long as I live I will be found revolving around the great center of Whig principles. Eight years ago, Mr. President, I had the honor to fill the seat you now occupy."

"The President: Did you use this gavel?

"Mr. Morehead: I do not know as it was that very one. But the one I did use brought Millard Fillmore into the Presidency once, and I challenge you to do the same thing again. [Laughter and applause.] The great Whig Captain, Henry Clay, was then up before us for the Presidency. My State was unanimous for him; we held out so long as there was any hope, until State after State gave way and still the Chairman of her delegation voted 'Clay' to the last. [Applause.] It was the last time we could hope to bring our gallant chieftain forward, the last opportunity of showing that republics are not ungrateful; and I never gave him up until absolute necessity compelled me to do it. But that meeting gave us another Whig chieftain, under whose banner the Whigs fought as did our soldiers at Buena Vista.

"In that Convention I looked to Massachusetts to stand by North Carolina, as we stood by her in 1776. One month after British soldiers shed American blood upon American soil on the 19th of April, 1775, the people of the Old North State proclaimed to the world that they were a free and independent people and would no longer submit to British domination, and pledged our lives, our fortunes, and our sacred honors to protect the liberties we claimed as our right. I looked to Massachusetts to stand by us for the second in command, a distinguished son of hers now no more. But the choice of that convention was against me, and they selected that man whose name is now proposed to us. I had seen him but once before that time, and but once or twice since, and then but for a few minutes. When we went into that campaign, the spirits of our friends were very much subdued, when we found that our glorious old captain had been set aside, and it took us some time to gather up our soldiers. But, in a few weeks, we went into the campaign and no Whigs fought more gallantly under the banner of Taylor and Fillmore than the soldiers of North Carolina, and we triumphed in the Old North State.

"But Providence in its dispensation soon removed our head from us, and Millard Fillmore occupied his place. Every eye was upon him, and when I witnessed the position he assumed then, saw him take the stand of an American statesman entertaining broad views of government, working for the whole Union, setting aside his old cherished early prejudices, and take the Constitution for his guide and sole support, in defiance of the prejudices of either section, I saw in him the right man to rule over this great and glorious people. I no longer hesitated in believing that Millard Fillmore was the man the Whigs of the United States should support. He gave us one of the most glorious administrations this government has ever been blessed with. He retired from the Presidential chair with the plaudits of all good men who were honest in the expression of their convictions. And how did he leave our once distracted country? In peace, in prosperity and happiness, tending in every respect toward that great destiny, which, I hope, we will yet reach. He left this country to visit foreign climes, and what do we see? In the space of four short years, a country once abounding in everything pleasant, happy and peaceful, with prospects brilliant as the rising sun, has, under Democratic rule, become involved in discord, brother's hands dipped in brother's blood, women and children fleeing from the ruins of their once happy homes, in one section of the country, rebellion stalking abroad at noon-day, and the great government of the United States unable to quell an insignificant insurrection or to give protection to the humblest portion of the nation. Civil discord and dismay are spreading over the whole country. Patriots, true patriots, are looking around them to find where they shall flee for protection.

"To whom can they look but to him who, in 1850, Clay and Webster, and all good and true men, rallied around. In vain they look for Clay and Webster; they are gone to 'that bourne from which no traveller returns.' But there is Millard Fillmore! [Cheers.] This distracted country casts her eyes across the waters and invites him once more to return to her shores, and with outstretched arms she welcomes him back. And where is the man who has more moral courage to march up to the discharge of his duty than has Millard Fillmore? I will stand up in his support,

and if I must fall, I will fall with my winding sheet the
glorious constellation of 31 States."

"Mr. President, you will pardon me for saying, that I
regretted to hear from your lips of wisdom on yesterday a
reference to the fragments of the Whig party. The Whig
party in fragments! The Whig party is dead!

"The President: No longer so. [Applause.]

"Mr. Morehead: No, sir; no longer is the Whig party
dead. Here are around me evidences that the Whigs are
alive, and so long as the goddess of liberty has residence
upon this terraqueous globe, Whigs will live. They lived before the revolution; they brought us to be the great people
we now are. The glorious Whig portrait of George Washington, whose genius presides on all occasions where Whigs
meet together in behalf of their glorious country, who led
the glorious stars and stripes in victory through many a
bloody field of battle—that glorious old Whig and his principles can never die. It is true the Whig party were defeated
four years ago; and it was a melancholy defeat for the country; she has regretted it ever since in sackcloth and ashes!
Our people were deluded, and we stood aside and gave them
an opportunity for a sober second thought, and they have
had a dozen sober second thoughts since. They have begun to repent of their evil delusion, and will it their interest
and duty to fall into our ranks and aid us in restoring this
country to its former condition of peace and prosperity.

"What is the present condition of the country, and what
has been its condition whenever the Democrats have been in
power? Spoils, spoils have been their cry. If they would
be content with the spoils, we would let them have the spoils,
though the overflowing treasury of the last four years has
been enough to corrupt any people but Americans, and it
has corrupted a portion of them. But down South they are
proclaiming, as they proclaim everywhere else, that there is
no hope for the country but in Democracy; that Fillmore
has no strength; that none but the Democrats can save the
South from the Black Republicans of the North. They have
lashed the political ocean into a tempest and have madly
leaped into it; and now they come to us and cry, 'help me

Cassius, or I sink. [Cheers.] Let the ambitious Cæsar go down; it were better that he should be lost and Rome be saved, than that Rome should sink and the tyrant live.

"I have been amused at the course the Democracy have been pursuing. I remember that in 1840, it was said that our gallant old chieftain from Ohio had been placed in the hands of a committee and permitted to say nothing but what had first passed through their lips. I should like to know who is the spokesman of the candidate of the Democratic party now? What has become of Jimmy Buchanan? The last account I had of him, he had gone into the Cincinnati platform [laughter] and bid good-bye to the friends of James Buchanan. It will be with him as with their last President, who was so green as to suppose that the Democratic party meant what they said by their platform. When they began to tear up the planks, he nailed them down again with his veto nails, but they tore them up again and scattered them to the winds. And so it will be with James Buchanan. If he can stick to the platform, it will be only on some lonely plank, like the people of Lost Island in the Gulf of Mexico— on the plank of the Ostend manifesto, going down the Gulf to see how Cuba is. [Laughter and applause.] Who is his spokesman now? How shall we address a question to him? Where is he? Who is he? What is he? So far as he is concerned, he is out of the question.

"There is another candidate in the field, Mr. Freemont. Who entitles him to the confidence of the people of this great nation? But the Democrats are the last men who should find fault with him; their course has brought him into the field. They set the eminent example in 1852 and he is now following in their footsteps. They then brought forth a candidate preeminently distinguished for his equestrian performances in Mexico, and the Black Republicans have brought forth a man perhaps a little more distinguished in the same way. He is a fast man, can, perhaps, ride farther than any other man in a day, but if placed at the helm of government would drive it to destruction at a gallop. Now, I am not willing to entrust him with that command. Give me our old helmsman; a man who took command of the ship of State once before when she was tossed to and fro, and brought her safely into port, with the aid of such men as Webster and Clay and others. He is the man for me; to him I would trust our ship of state.

"What shall we do when we leave this Assembly? Heretofore we have had a sad lot of our own; but now we have not. Heretofore the Democrats have said we were for the spoils, when they were after the same thing themselves. But now we are not for office, we have strictly no Whig candidate in the field, we form an outside body, we have determined to support a tried man, whom we believe will give more peace and prosperity to this country than any other man. We have re-elected him because we believe he is entitled to our confidence. Why should we not take him up? Because, it is said, he is the candidate of another party! Why, sir, if the Democratic party had nominated such a man as George Washington, would you not support him? Had they taken up Millard Fillmore, should you not then support him? And if the American party will stand by us, we will elect Millard Fillmore. [Cheers.] And if they will not, I give them notice now that we Whigs intend to elect him anyhow. [Cheers.] If they do not like our man, let them get a better one if they can. [Laughter.] We want a Whig President, and we will have a Whig President. One thing is certain, if he be President at all, he will be an American President, and that is what we want.

"Now about geographical discrimination. I want but one geographical limit—let us be bounded by the Lakes on the North, the Gulf of Mexico and the Rio Grande at the South, the Atlantic on the East and the Pacific on the West, and within that let us all be a glorious brotherhood of Americans. [Cheers.] Talk about the North and the South! Where is the North? Is there any North in this glorious republic? Which is the Northern part of your Constitution and which the Southern? What part in this great republic was the land of Washington, Adams, Franklin and *id omne genus?* Shall I not bequeath to my children, as my father bequeathed to me, that land cemented by the blood of Warren? Shall I not look upon the battle fields of

Lexington, Bunker Hill and Boston as my country? I tell
you I will, or die in the attempt to look upon them a such.
[Cheers.] Shall not the land of Sumner and Marion be my
land? Aye, sir, as long as time shall last it shall be so.
If Wilson and Sumner do not like me to have a foothold in
a State with them, then let them leave the sacred land of
Massachusetts, for I will not give it up. If Greeley and
Beecher seek to elbow me from the State of New York, they
will find hard elbowing, and they will have to go out themselves. I never will consent that one foot of the soil of this
glorious Union shall ever be considered anything else but
'My own, my native land!' [Applause.] He who expects
me to fight for the North against the South, or for the East
against the West, will find it with me as they will find it
with our glorious leader; they will be mistaken in their man;
I am for the whole country. Go to Maine, and where is
Massachusetts? At the South. Go to Massachusetts and
where is the gallant state of Maryland? At the South. Go
to Maryland, and where is North Carolina? Aye, *North!*—
thank God, *North* Carolina! [Applause.] We have a
North under the blazing sun of the South: and yet they say
they will have this North.

"Dissolve this Union! Let the fiery hotspurs of the
South design it when they may; let the plotting traitors of
the North design it when they will; let the pulpits of the living God send forth their Sharpe's rifles, and their powder
and bullets; but the people of the Union will not let them
disturb it. [Applause.] With your Constitution in one
hand and your Bible in the other, and with patriotism in
your hearts, you will prove victorious against all the traitors
that ever trod the earth. [Cheers and applause.]

"Dissolve this Union! Sir, it never can be dissolved
until the blood of the heroes of '76 has been so polluted and
diluted that the last drop of it has left us. While there is
a spark of the blood of '76 in American veins, so long will
this Union stand! [Applause.] Dissolve this Union!
Never, never, never! Why, sir, you may invite all the foreign foes into our land; you may robe our cities in flames;
make our homes smoking ruins, and send our wives and

children screaming through the streets, but when our country appears as if in the last gasp of expiring agony, a mighty voice like the sound of a trumpet will speak forth, proclaiming liberty and union as the watch-word, and that will save the Union! [Applause.]

"Mr. President, I was gratified to hear you say yesterday that you came a thousand miles and would have come three thousand, if necessary, to meet your brethren and friends in this convention. I was delighted, too, yesterday, to hear the eloquent voice of my friend from Massachusetts, who eight years ago stood side by side with me; it showed me that the North is not so far from some of us as some people imagine, but that there is a bond of brotherhood which connects this Union together and will never permit it to be rent asunder. And permit me here, Mr. President, to advert also to a remark made by yourself last night in private conversation, when you said that this country was knit and rivetted together by the great Mississippi, binding degree of latitude with degree of latitude, that will never allow this great Union to be severed. [Applause.]

"And let me say to the Whigs assembled here, let us go home and tell our friends, that we have stood by and seen the tricks and fanaticism of those who have brought this crisis upon the country, and we have said not a word, but given them full swing in their mad course, letting them cut their own throats as much as they pleased. [Laughter and applause.] Perhaps it may purify the country to let them go on in such a career of madness and folly. The towering form of Gen. Scott sent into Kansas would have quieted that distracted people and secured peace. [Applause.] But, sir, no political capital would have been made out of it. And another thing: Who is the prime minister of this administration?

"The man who, perhaps more than any other, has attempted to worry that great chieftain. He was Secretary of War when Gen. Scott was sent to Mexico without orders necessary to fulfill his mission, which occasioned the saying about the hasty plate of soup. New York has some bad men mixed up with her good men, like other States.

[Laughter.]   Gen. Scott waited month after month, impatient to take Vera Cruz, and at length he had to strip the ships of their guns, and in spite of the administration worrying at his heels, he went and took the city by storm—he took it, to use his own emphatic language, with a fire in front and in the rear. [Laughter and applause.] The conquest he achieved in Mexico was one that was never excelled in the records of this country's warfare.

"And then what was his reward at the hands of the administration? He was put on trial before Buchanan and Marcy and sent to a court martial. If ever my blood boiled, it was eight years ago, when I met the old chieftain at Washington on his way to that court martial. I asked him where he was going. He said: 'To the town of Fredericksburg, Md.' 'For what?' I asked. 'To attend a court martial,' said he. 'What is the charge against you?' I inquired. 'God only knows—you must ask the administration, not me. I never have been disgraced in the field, but their design is to disgrace me before the country.' Fellow citizens, can any of you tell what Gen. Scott was arraigned for? I think not.

"But to return to North Carolina. I shall return home, and if I can only hear the assurance that the glorious State of New York will do its duty, I am sure I have only to tell my fellow citizens in North Carolina so, and victory will perch on our banner, and unless you are very speedy of foot and strong of arm, we will outstrip you. [Applause.]

"I heard a remark, while on my way here, from a Democrat, that the Whig party was only as a brake upon the great Democratic train that was sweeping over the land. That was intended as a cut, but it was like an unfaithful blunderbuss—it hit the man behind harder than the object in front. [Laughter.] The Democratic train is rushing on to destruction with an open draw-bridge ahead, and, with inevitable ruin in prospect, is shouting out to the Whigs, 'Break up, or we are gone.' [Laughter.] Sir, thank God, we *are* on board, and we will let them go on and plunge heels over head into the abyss. [Applause.] Certain it is, that either

they or the country have got to be destroyed, and we are
for saving the latter.   [Applause.]"[1]

Here was the same old ring of *The Laird of Muirhead*

> "Afore the King in order stude
> The stout laird of Muirhead,
> Wi that same twa-hand muckle sword
> That Bartram fell'd stark dead.

> "He sware he wadna lose his right
> To fight in ilka field;
> Nor budge him from hs liege's sight,
> Till his last gasp should yield."[2]

This speech was read all over the United States and
touched the hearts of every lover of the Constitution and
the Union.   It made such an impression that one boy at
least, in a northern home, heard its author discussed over a
dozen years afterwards, when "the train had rushed on to
destruction into the open draw-bridge ahead;" and "a
mighty voice" did, "like the sound of a trumpet" "speak
forth, proclaiming liberty and union as the watch-word,"
and did "save the Union!"

One other address must be noticed, namely, one he delivered about a month later, October 24th, in his native
county, Pittsylvania, Virginia, just across from Rockingham
county, North Carolina, the home of his childhood and
youth.   This address was on the occasion of a visit to a
mass-meeting at the court house:

"Governor Morehead, of North Carolina, having been
introduced by the President, arose and said (after loud and
long continued applause with which he was welcomed
had subsided) that the times, being sadly out of joint, he
came over to the Old Dominion, to find out, if he could,
the causes which had brought the country to its present
deplorable condition, which he portrayed in a masterly manner.   He then reviewed, briefly but graphically, the whole
field of politics, from 1824 to the present time [October,
1856]—said he was one of the few, if not the only man, who

---

[1] *The Weekly Raleigh Register*, 1st Oct., 1856.
[2] See Scott's ballad, *ante*.

had voted three times as an elector for Gen. Jackson—
showed the inconsistency of those Jackson men who now
cooperate with the Democracy—how Virginia had, on
former occasions, disappointed the country by repudiating
her own worthiest sons, when put in nomination for the
Presidency, and by voting for northern men with southern
principles, who had betrayed the best interests of the nation
—said a northern man, not with Southern but with national principles, was now a candidate for her support, and
it remained to be seen whether the old Mother of States
would be again overreached and deceived by the wily arts
of Democracy.   He animadverted with much severity on
Polk's Administration, alluding to the treatment which those
great chieftains, Taylor and Scott, received at his hands.
He had recently learned, he said, for the first time, during
a tour through some of the northern states, the name of
the present Chief Magistrate, who is known at the South as
The Fainting Gen. Pierce! His name is pronounced *Purse,*
by his northern friends and neighbors, and a most appropriate name it is for the head of such an administration.   Perhaps some *General Purse,* if not one at the head of the government, could give an account of the thirty millions of dollars which have so mysteriously disappeared from the vaults
of the Treasury.

"He said the Whigs had remained passive for several
years—had nothing to do with the elevation of the powers
that be.   If they were dead, as had been stated, their ghosts
would frighten every Democrat in the country; before the
Ides of November Whigs would be glad of the aid of the
American Party; but having nominated Mr. Fillmore, they
intend to elect him, with or without its assistance.

"The Ex-Governor painted a truthful but glowing picture of disunion, a contingency flippantly spoken of by
demagogues—a consummation to which he would never
submit; would never consent to a state of things which
would render it necessary for him to get a passport to cross
the line that separates the Old North State from the Old
Dominion; to go to a foreign land when he wishes to worship
at the shrine of the Father of his Country; but that when-

ever his inclination prompted, he would make his home on the banks of the Hudson or amid magnolia groves of the far South; it was all his country; his father had fought for it; he would never give it up. The Democracy, after getting the country into its present disturbed and unhappy condition, prescribe the same remedy that a farmer would for a horse with a broken leg, namely, to *Knock it in the head.* If the Union were dissolved, it would not be into two confederacies, but into thirty-one states. The same causes which make nation quarrel with nation, section with section, man with man, men with their wives, would operate to keep the whole country in continual war: there would be no place where peace and contentment could be found. To remove from one state to another would be to jump out of the frying pan into the fire.

"Comparing the three parties of the country to three ships, he brought up, first, the old hulk of Democracy, loaded down to the water's edge with public plunder, buccaneers over-burdened with spoils, her prow set for Cuba, with colors flying, inscribed on one side—'Buchanan! Democracy! Cuba! No Improvement by the General Government.' On the other—'Might makes Right! Pacific Railroad!' The old rickety craft gives a lurch in the first gale and goes down with a bubble to be heard of no more. Then comes the piratical Black Republicans, with their black flag and motley crew. Next comes the old Ship of State, with Fillmore for her commander, with the stars and stripes fluttering to the breeze; 'The Union! The Constitution!' glittering in letters of gold on her trembling pennant, the eagle perched upon the top of the main-mast, overlooking the gallant crew—storms might comes from the North, from the South, waves might roll and breakers roar,

> "The strained mast might quiver as a reed
> The rent canvas, fluttering, strew the gale,
> But still would she on!"[1]

Nevertheless the effect of the new Republican-Abolitionist party in 1856 was to draw heavily from the Democratic

---

[1] *Greensboro Patriot,* Oct. 24, 1856.

ranks in the North—one northern boy's two grandfathers and father changed from Democrats to Republicans that year—and this so consolidated the South that, in North Carolina alone, the pendulum in the gubernatorial election swung to the unprecedented Democratic majority of over 12,000; while in the national election Buchanan was victorious, and the Whigs were dead.

Meanwhile, by 1857, North Carolina was taking on a new prosperity under the stimulus of her new railroad. National Treasury statistics showed her, with a population of 921,852, having a property valuation of $239,603,372. This gave her greater wealth than California, Connecticut, Iowa, Maine, Michigan, Missouri, New Hampshire, New Jersey and some few others. And not the least of these sources of stimulation were the prospects of a new great port terminal of the trans-state lines, as illustrated in the following letter:

Governor Morehead's enthusiastic development of his plans for Morehead City is well illustrated in a letter of his of February 9, 1857, from "New-Berne," as his letter spells it: It is written to the editors of *The Patriot and Flag,* and says:

"On Monday last the barque *Damon,* Captain Bartlett, of Bangor, Maine, entered the port of Beaufort with a cargo of rails for the Atlantic Railroad of 476 tons. She passed the bar and entered the port at dead low water.

"On Friday, the 'T & J' barque, Captain J. D. Coffin, of Halifax, Nova Scotia, entered the same port in low tide with 580 tons rails and drawing over 15 feet of water. They are lying in New Port Channel, near each other, in front of the terminus of the railroad where the Wharf is to be built, and about 3000 feet from the shore, and in water some 20 or 30 feet deep. They might have brought in much larger cargoes if the vessels had been larger.

"I wish all North Carolina could have seen both these magnificent barques entering the port under a cloud of canvass, all sails set (as I saw the T & J) and see them round to and cast anchor within a few feet of the shore, where they now ride so quietly on the bosom of this safe land-locked harbor, that every outline is mirrored from its placid surface.

"These are splendid ships, well arranged and well commanded by their quiet and gentlemanly Captains, whose bearing would grace the drawing-room, and is the reverse of that rough address and exterior which is so often attached to an *Old Salt.*

"The cabins are handsomely fitted up, and Mrs. Bartlett and an interesting daughter grace Captain Bartlett's, and have partaken with him in the rough weather which both experienced on their voyage from New Port, Wales, from which place they sailed about the 15th of December last.

"Twelve months more will show the wisdom of driving the Atlantic Road forward to completion, and the world will find out that North Carolina has one of the best and safest ports on the Atlantic Coast.

"Yours respectfully

"J. M. Morehead."[1]

By August 21, 1857, Governor Morehead, as President of The Sheppard's Point Land Company, was able to announce that on November 11th, following, the first lots in the new city would be sold at public auction, and the Atlantic and North Carolina Railroad would be ready for business on New Year's Day following. Here is the vision President Morehead had of this new city's future place in the world: "The interior communications by water and land must make this a great commercial city. The vast productions of the fertile valleys of the Roanoke, Tar and Neuse Rivers and the commerce of those great inland seas—the Albemarle, Carrituck, Croatan and Pamlico Sounds on the north, whilst Bogue Sound will bear on its bosom, the agricultural products, lumber, naval stores and fine ship timber of the regions lying South. The North Carolina Railroad, among the best in the Union, 223 miles long, is completed to Charlotte, where it connects through the South Carolina and Georgia Railroads with Atlanta and the southwest; and by its western extension, now in rapid progress, it is contem-

---

[1] *The Weekly Raleigh Register,* 18th Feb., 1857.

plated to reach the trade of Memphis and the Mississippi Valley by the net-work of all the railways that connect at Atlanta, Chattanooga, or with the Eastern Tennessee Railroad. The ports of Beaufort, Chattanooga, Memphis and San Diego in the Pacific are about the same parallel of latitude; and if that parallel be extended across the Pacific, it will reach Shanghai, the nearest great port on the Eastern continent; therefore, if the Pacific Railroad be constructed (and that should be done forthwith), why may not this new city become the Atlantic mart for the commerce of the East Indies? Two short railroads will connect the two great coal fields of the state, lying on the south of the North Carolina Railroad, with that road; and it is confidently expected that a vast coal trade will be carried on through the new city; if so, may not Beaufort become a great coaling port, not only for purposes of commerce, but to furnish the supplies to steamers passing so near the entrance going north and south; and may not the new city become the 'entre depot' between the North and the South, to which our able and distinguished countryman, Lieut. Maury, refers in his unrivalled statesmanlike paper on the commerce of the Amazon, South America, and the Gulf of Mexico? The City of Morehead is situated on a beautiful neck of land or dry plain, almost entirely surrounded with salt water; its climate salubrious; its sea breezes and sea bathing delightful; its drinking water good; and its fine chalybeate spring, strongly impregnated with sulphur, will make it a pleasant watering place. . . . It will be the first instance of an entire new city on the Atlantic Coast being brought into market at once; and capitalists may never have again such an opportunity for good investments, for a great city must and will be built at this place.——J. M. Morehead, President of Sheppard's Point Land Company."[1]

The November sales were successful, in that over 60 lots were sold in Morehead City for some $13,000, while at the plat called "Carolina City" lots were sold for a total of $17,000. A regular boat was running between Morehead

---

[1] *Greensboro Patriot*, 6th Nov., 1857.

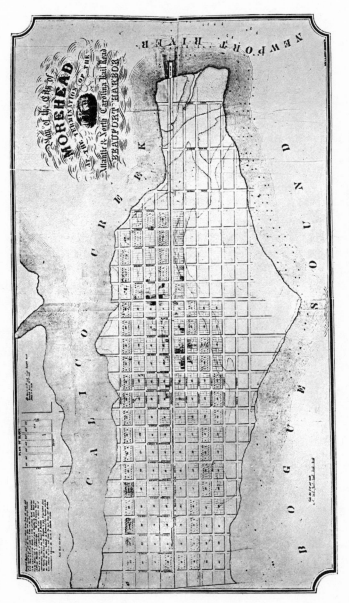

THE ORIGINAL MAP, SHOWING FIRST LOTS PURCHASED, NOVEMBER 11, 1857
In possession of Lindsay Patterson, Winston-Salem, N. C.

City and Beaufort on an hour schedule. An editorial letter
to the *Greensboro Patriot* of 17th September, 1858, says:
"Ever since our school-boy days we had heard of Beaufort
harbor, having learned from our geography that there was
such a place away down on the sea-coast, many hundred
miles distant, where the people lived on fish, and used
oyster-shells as cups, with which to drink water out of old
pine stumps; but we had never had an opportunity to visit
that section of the country, and see for ourselves, whether
or not the men of that region—as had been reported and
believed in the interior by many—were scaly, had broad
tails and thorny fins growing from their backs, the result of
living on fish and diving after crabs. Well, we went, we
saw, and we have returned. We saw not only the mighty
ocean, the deepest inlet and finest harbor on the Atlantic
coast, south of Norfolk; but we found the waters covered
over with vessels of various sizes and descriptions, freighted
with produce of every section of the state, transporting it
from our shores to distant parts of the world, and bringing
in return whatever was most pleasant and desirable. We
found there, also, an active, good looking, thriving and intelligent population, men of character and stability, who
were putting forth all their energies to avail themselves of
the many advantages and the great market facilities with
which nature has so bountifully blessed them. Beaufort is
situated immediately on the Sound, right opposite the inlet,
and has a population of some twelve or fifteen hundred,
contains three very neat churches, three hotels, all said to
be good houses. . . ."

He then describes the inlet approach: "The inlet at
Beaufort Harbor is, we understand, about three-quarters
of a mile wide, extending from the Point on the Shackelford banks on the east to the point at Fort Macon on the
West. Ships drawing from eighteen to twenty feet can
cross the bar with safety. Ships crossing the bar, enter the
harbor near the Shackelford banks, then bear up in a
westwardly direction toward Fort Macon. From the bar
at the inlet, across the Sound to Beaufort, is about three
miles, this being about the widest part of the harbor. The

channel is in the form of a half-moon, one horn running
eastwardly along the Shackelford banks, called Core Sound,
and the other westwardly by Morehead and Carolina cities,
which are situated on Bogue Sound. The deepest water
is along Newport river, which runs in nearly a north
direction, between Morehead City and Beaufort, touching
the railroad wharf in the former place. The main channel
is about one mile wide, so that the inside of the channel
would be some two miles from Beaufort, though vessels
drawing from nine to ten feet water can approach the Beaufort wharves at full tide. Running up the channel about
three miles from the bar, we come to the railroad wharf at
Morehead City, where vessels drawing eighteen feet can approach with ease, and unload and take in lading with the
greatest safety."

He then shows that one turns from the channel to the
left into Bogue Sound, three miles farther, to Carolina
City, where vessels drawing only twelve feet could land;
but this narrative is concerned only with his description of
Morehead City, the real port. "Sheppard's Point, or Morehead City, is situated very much like the City of New York.
On the south is Bogue Sound, on the east right at the point
is Newport River, through which runs the main channel,
and out to which the railroad wharf extends. On the north
is Calico Creek, extending westwardly . . . nearly
three miles, and running almost parallel with Bogue Sound.
This channel, from the railroad wharf for nearly a mile
along the Point, is now, at full tide, from six to nine feet
deep, and if properly dredged, could, for that distance up,
admit vessels drawing from ten to twelve feet of water,
while the dirt taken from the channel would be amply
sufficient to raise the ground between the channel and the
mainland, above high tide, affording a long extent of
wharves. The railroad wharf, taken in connection with the
warehouse at Morehead City, when completed, will be a
magnificent affair. The wharf having to extend for a considerable distance from the Point to reach the channel, it
was for a long time predicted that it would be impossible
for one to be constructed sufficiently firm and durable to

resist the action of the tides and the violence of storms. All doubt on this score, however, has been removed, and it is universally conceded that the work not only can, but that in a few months it will be completed."

He tells how the Chief Engineer and Governor Morehead explained everything to him and how they proposed having wharves on both sides of the peninsula—Sheppard's Point. "Let only one-third the amount be expended at Morehead City as has been on the bay at Baltimore, and every obstruction will be removed and vessels of the largest size can load and unload at the wharves with the greatest ease, while they are most securely protected from storms. The railroad warehouse, when completed, will be a magnificent work. It stands just at the end of the wharf, surrounded by water twenty feet deep, supported by ninety-three large iron piles which have been driven into the ground by an immense force. . . . The extent of the warehouse is 165 by 90 feet, with the railroad track passing through its entire length on both sides—the track branching on the wharf—so that freight can be taken immediately from the cars and placed aboard the vessels."

Then a pleasing incident occurred: Governor Morehead had told him all of the tropical nature of this coast so near the Gulf Stream, and spoke of fig trees large as apple trees, and proposed they sail up Calico Creek [naturally] to a Mrs. Piggott's and enjoy some figs and melons. The editor and the Chief Engineer were disinclined, until Governor Morehead added that she had some pretty daughters, whereupon they accepted with alacrity—although the editor lays all blame on the engineer. They feasted on three varieties of figs, the White, the Red and the Blue Fig, mentioning them in this order, as though conscious of their patriotic colors, and avowing the Blue to be the "best flavored." Five or six bushels to a tree was a not unusual crop. Then came the two daughters—"Hebes," the editor calls them, while the engineer and he both seem to have forgotten both figs and melons in their presence, and Governor Morehead again illustrated his power as a diplomat. The staid editor advises Guilford young men, that if they want to help found a great port they would find no such difficulty as Romulus did—"a scarcity of ladies," for—

"I've been to the West, I've been to the East,
And I've been to North Carolino;
But the prettiest girl I ever saw
Was tripping along through the Pino."[1]

And yet this was a year of one of the greatest panics and failures in national history. Fifteen great railways of the land with a total of over $180,000,000 liabilities failed to meet their debts; but those of North Carolina, under the inspiration and wisdom of Governor Morehead's years of leadership, were not among them; although stock was depreciated and President Fisher was charged with incompetency. Newbern celebrated the opening of the Atlantic road on April 29th, with free excursion trains from all over the state bringing over 10,000 people, and with ceremonies lasting three days. Thus, by May, 1858, Governor Morehead's new road was in operation and all the lots sold in Morehead City.

---

[1] Chorus of an old ballad.

XVI

He Enters The Assembly

TO

Defend and Extend the Railway

West and North

A Great Vision of Transportation

1858

With the Morehead City and railroad projects accomplished facts in the spring of 1858, there was a demand that Governor Morehead enter the Assembly to defend and extend railroad development.[1] He had spent a good deal of time in Greensboro, and in September previously he had organized the Greene Monument Association proposing that either the national or state governments, if the former would not, erect a monument to General Greene at Guilford Battle-Ground, and he was made President of this body.

A pretty picture of him at "Blandwood," that adjoined Edgeworth Seminary, which he was enlarging at this time, is given by an old pupil—a picture of Governor Morehead accidentally meeting two young pupils of this girls' seminary, who had wandered into the unusually beautiful grounds of "Blandwood," in *Reminiscences of School Life,* by An Edgeworth Pupil: "At first a little startled at the sight of two crouching children, Governor Morehead halted, but something in our wistful eyes and home-hungry faces told the tale. Extending both hands he drew us to him; kindly he patted our heads, then sitting down with us, he talked pleasantly to us of our homes, and cheerfully gave

---

[1] At a meeting of stock-holders of the Atlantic and North Carolina Railroad at Newbern on the 24th of June, 1858, Governor Morehead was present and plainly indicated that the road's capital stock must be increased from $1,600,000 to the necessary amount, while Governor Bragg asserted that the road's management was sound and the construction properly done.

us free access not only to these intermediate grounds, which for the first time we had on that occasion dared enjoy, but he also invited us to 'Blandwood,' his own beautiful home. He then passed on, and we returned to the Seminary a happy couple. . . . His name on history's page has its reward; over these Southern lands 'tis a household word. And remembering his wisdom and justice in our country's weal, what fitter talisman need we ask. But his private life, who shall tell us of that? Who? Let the countless throngs so often gathered at Blandwood's pleasant halls tell us. Let the gay and fashionable pleasure seeker tell us. Let noble lords and handsome ladies tell us. And the statesman, let him speak of his compeer, this scion of the 'Old Dominion' gentility. But are these all? No, no. Let the prattling child, the weary invalid, the aged matron, the gray-haired sire, the orphan and widow, the poor and homeless. Yea, these and hundreds of school girls, all may tell us of *one* whose sympathies and charities flowed in every channel of want."[1]

As antiphonal to this, from the eastern end of the state is another reminiscence, this time from a boy instead of a girl!

Governor Morehead was once visiting the father of a seventeen-year-old boy, in 1858, near La Grange, N. C., and considerably over a half century later that boy wrote his impressions. "I heard him [Gov. M——] say, as they were sipping their toddies in the parlor, that a man ought to be a half-hour taking a drink. He said to take it all at one swallow was too great a shock to the system; but sipped slowly, it diffused itself in the system gradually and was more beneficial. I adopted his plan and followed it all through my life. If Morehead had put on clerical robes, no Pope or priest ever had a more benevolent face or a more magnetic presence."[2] This father was a director of the Atlantic and North Carolina Railroad.

As has been said, his Guilford county friends and others

---

[1] Clippings in possession of Mrs. W. R. Walker, Spray, N. C.
[2] C. S. Wooten, Mt. Olive, N. C., in a letter to Judge W. P. Bynum, 2nd Sept., 1921, in response to an invitation to attend the presentation of a portrait of Governor Morehead to the Court at Greensboro, N. C.

interested in further railroad development persuaded him
that it was his duty to take up the cause in the House of
Commons. The specific aims will appear as the campaign
and sessions proceed; for he was successful at the August
election, receiving 1581 votes, the highest of any except
for McRae for Governor and Gorrell for the Senate. Then
it began to appear what was the real discontent of the people,
even while, in September, the Western North Carolina Railroad was completed as far as Statesville. This note was
sounded in the *Greensboro Patriot* about the time for the
meeting of the Assembly: it was charged that the Democrats
put in controlling Directors from the Wilmington and Weldon Railroad, and subordinated the North Carolina Railroad
to the Wilmington interests—and that was what was the
matter of it! So it was the same old fight of east and
west; and the west again brought out their old club to battle
with, namely, the Danville link! And Governor Morehead
was chosen to again weild this Excalibur! This promised a
tense condition in the legislative halls at Raleigh and was
bound to make such a battle as those halls had not seen since
Calvin Graves voted "Aye" and created the Central railroad!
All the more was it a gigantic battle because the odds were
so great: the House had a Democratic majority of thirty-
eight and the Senate a majority of twelve! And the Guilford David was a Whig against this Democratic Goliath!
And Governor Ellis' majority was 16,247.

And still there was a reason for this Democratic land-
slide, locally, for the state was becoming alarmed at a bonded
indebtedness of $6,879,505, of which was $533,500 balance
on the Atlantic and North Carolina Railroad, a $400,000
loan to that line, and a loan of like amount to the Western
North Carolina Railroad—or a total of $1,333,500 for rail-
road extensions east and west, alone. In addition to this
a total of 640,000 in bonds must soon be issued to the
Western—or last mentioned road—to increase it to
$1,973,500, or nearly one-third of the entire state debt.
The state's stock was of course a sinking fund in all this,
but the people were concerned about it.

The program of the Guilford leaders was, first, to reorgan-

ize the North Carolina Railroad Directory plans so as to give
the stock-holders control, which meant, practically, western
control; and, secondly, if this failed, to get a charter for the
Danville link. They held that the mismanagement of the
Central road was not so much due to President Fisher as the
Democratic eastern directory's policy of subordinating the
road to Wilmington interests. This of course also meant
that it was against Morehead City and Beaufort interests,
as well as the Atlantic railroad! As a part of the battle it
was proposed to have stock-holders of both the Atlantic
road and the Western road have a majority on the North
Carolina Central directory instead of the Wilmington road!
To prepare the way for these, the Danville connection club
was put upon the table at an early date.

The Assembly gathered at Raleigh capitol on November
15, 1858, and the Ex-Governor from Greensboro took his
seat as a representative in the Commons. He was at once
put on the Internal Improvement Committee and on the
Joint Standing Committee on Finance. The press of the
east began to teem with arguments against the "link," or
"Danville Connection," as it was more commonly called.
They said that even when the Richmond and Danville
Railroad was first proposed, it was, like the Petersburg and
Norfolk roads, designed to tap the Roanoke valley and western North Carolina which was growing so rapidly. That
Richmond, as the largest tobacco market in the Union—with
possession of the regular order of the French government, and with the largest flouring mills in the world commanding the South American market, would make competition from any port in North Carolina of no avail: all
western commerce of the state would become a Richmond
tributary; and it would debilitate every railroad in the state.
They showed the well-grounded great fear of an oncoming Piedmont trans-national line from Maine to New
Orleans; and looked upon the advocates of the Greensboro
and Danville Railroad as the greatest menace the state had
had in modern times! They were looked upon as wreckers
by the eastern press; even the Whig leader, *The Raleigh
Register,* joined the cry. They recalled to Governor More-

head his speech at Petersburg, Virginia, on Nov. 8, 1849, when they claimed he said that, if the Central road was built, with a re-constructed Raleigh & Gaston road, neither he nor his people would ever ask for a Danville road; and charged him, as Virginia born, with being ready to sacrifice his adopted state, and break up her whole system of improvements. This was the kind of press attacks upon him by mid-December, 1858, and upon his following in Person, Rockingham, Caswell and Guilford counties, among whom were Democrats like Speaker Settle, his old Latin teacher, who was considered another Calvin Graves! Evidently the move to put eastern and western extension Directors, instead of Wilmington ones, on the Central Railroad board, with its accompanying club, the Danville link, was breaking up political families. Certainly it was striking terror into the eastern political leaders, like a life and death struggle.

The Morehead minority report of 1858 shows that even without the Danville connection that trade is coming from Virginia, not to it; and even with the Danville connection produce would change cars twice to reach Richmond, 192 miles, while it can reach Newbern port, 187 miles, Morehead City, 222 miles, or Wilmington, 211 miles, with no change—reaching the Atlantic in far less time than to reach Richmond, which is an interior port 160 to 170 miles from the Atlantic, but slightly superior as a port to Newbern, not equal to Wilmington, and greatly inferior to Morehead City. This report shows that the Greensboro-Danville road makes the transnational line 96 miles shorter than the Knoxville or Wilmington routes.[1]

The Danville connection bill was set for Tuesday, the 28th of December, mid-holiday season. The attack was centered upon the leader, Governor Morehead, whose speech was long continued. It came up again for second reading on January 10, 1859, and indeed it seemed to be before the House in some form much of the time. The bill was known as "House Bill, 92, to charter the Greensboro and Danville Railroad Company:" and it was in committee of the whole

---

[1] *Greensboro Patriot* of Dec. 24, 1858.

almost every day.   On Wednesday, January 12, 1859, it was
again continued, Speaker Settle's remarks for it being followed by Mr. Green of Franklin county in reply; "after
which," says the *Raleigh Register* editor, who was, in this
matter at least, inimical to the "link," "Mr. Dortch took the
floor and gave Governor Morehead a complete dressing."
Mr. Norwood took the floor on Thursday and was followed
by Mr. Bridgers.   These attacks were continued on Friday
and on Saturday, whereupon Governor Morehead rose,
and even the editor who thought the "Old War Horse"
had received "a complete dressing" was compelled to say,
in his report of it, that "it was an admirable one of its kind!"

Some interesting inside history of the appearance of a
Rockingham Coal Fields railroad bill, after the Greensboro
and Danville bill was rejected is given by the *Fayetteville
Observer*.   It seems that Rockingham county, Governor
Morehead's old home and seat of his great Leaksville plant,
wanted the link as much as he did; but, as it was safely
Democratic, the eastern leaders thought they could hold it,
until they saw how much in earnest that county really was.
To save the county to Governor Ellis, the Wilmington member of the House introduced this bill and got it passed;
whereupon the Wilmington Senator so amended it that he
thought Governor Morehead and his friends would reject it
—which they did not choose to do!   For an act passed two
years before, to charter a road from High Point, *via* Salem
and Germanton to Virginia would enable a Danville connection to be made, and what was more the Salem road went
directly by Governor Morehead's steam mills there, and both
roads helped his lands and plants at Leaksville and his great
possessions at Holtsburg on the Yadkin River!   The
Observer charged Wilmington with mistakes all the way
along: the Weldon road which takes 8000 bales of cotton
out of Edgecombe alone to a Virginia port; the Manchester
road which carries produce off to Charleston; and finally
the Charlotte & Rutherford would be a South Carolina
feeder still more—two roads for Virginia and two for
South Carolina![1]

---

[1] *Greensboro Patriot,* 14th Oct., 1859.

Several reports of the great debate on the "Danville Connection," as it was called, in January, 1859, exist, but this from the *Fayetteville Observer,* is brief, friendly and picturesque: "He [Governor Morehead] had been assailed by Bridgers of Edgecombe, Dortch of Wayne, and other leading Democrats, opponents of the Danville Connection. Mr. Bridgers had imputed an 'avaricious spirit' to the Governor. In reply he said that he had invested *eighty-seven thousand dollars* in railroads for the improvement of North Carolina. He desired to know how much the gentleman from Edgecombe had thus invested? 'Do you desire an answer now?' said Mr. Bridgers. "Certainly!' And Mr. Bridgers replied that he owned *one share* (nominal value, $100) in the Wilmington and Weldon road (which runs through his own county). Would that we had more 'avaricious' spirits as Governor Morehead, and fewer such patriots as Mr. Bridgers. If we only had Governor Morehead in this town, we could guarantee the speedy completion of the Coalfields Railroad, with or without State aid. . . . Having thus effectually disposed of Mr. Bridgers, it was Mr. Dortch's turn next. This gentleman had delivered himself of some 'startling developments' in regard to extravagance on the North Carolina Railroad whilst under the Presidency of Governor Morehead. This of course derived great weight from the fact Mr. Dortch had long been one of the State's Directors in the road, and was therefore presumed to have availed himself of his opportunities to secure full and reliable information on all the financial operations of the Governor. He was one of those sentinels placed by Democratic Governors to see that the state had justice done to her. He arraigned Governor Morehead before the House as guilty of extravagant expenditures of the State's money. And what reply could the culprit make to a charge from such a high and well informed authority? He [Gov. M——] quietly produced a Report from an Examining Committee, certifying that the North Carolina Railroad was the cheapest built railroad in the country. And to this Report was signed the name of this same Mr. Dortch! And so on through the catalogue of Gov. Morehead's accusers. He brushed them off like mosquitoes—those lean fellows who keep up a prodigious buzzing without having the power to sting! . . . Long live the old patriot and statesman, to labor for his State and to confound his enemies, whether political or personal!"

Another report says of it: "The debate of which I have spoken might be said to have been closed by a three hour speech from Governor Morehead, though Mr. Norwood followed him for about an hour. Morehead occupied part of two days in its delivery. His personal character had been assailed, the spirit of his youth was roused, and never before, nor will there again this season, be heard in this capitol such a speech. It towered far above anything we have ever heard there. Always impressive and speaking with ability, his full powers were then brought out. We have never heard such withering sarcasm, more forcible arguments, or more finished and entrancing eloquence. A member opposed to him in politics, and on this question, remarked to us that, he always thought Mr. Morehead was the first man in North Carolina, and now he knew it! . . . All have heard Gov. Morehead, in one or another of the many great efforts of his life, but this was the crown upon all.'"[1]

To this account, let the memories of a young man of that time be added: "I knew Governor Morehead," wrote J. S. T. Baird of Asheville, on April 29, 1912, "and had the honor to serve with him in the House of Commons (as we then called it) at the session of 1858–9. I was then quite a young man, and for courtesies and kindnesses shown me by him during the session, I learned to hold him in very high esteem. Though differing in our political views, he was nevertheless kind to give me much valuable advice and assistance in my legislative duties. While there were quite a number of able men of the Whig party in the House at that session, such as W. N. H. Smith, David Outlaw, John Kerr, Atlas J. Dargan, O. H. Dockery, Tod R. Caldwell, and others, Governor Morehead stood preeminent above

---

[1] Clipping in possesson of Mrs. W. R. Walker, Spray, N. C.

them all and was their recognized leader. Col. Bridgers was among the ablest of the Democratic members and shared the leadership with such men as Ransom, Dortch, Flemming and others. There was much attempted railroad legislation at that session. Governor Morehead, who, during his administration as Governor many years before had shown himself a staunch friend and promoter of railroad building in the state, was friendly to about all schemes that were presented at that session, while Colonel Bridgers was not so much so. The people of this section [western] of the state were deeply concerned and were making strenuous efforts for the extension of railroads through our mountain country, but there was much opposition by members from the east and other sections of the state. I am not positive, but my recollection is that it was while the extension of the Western North Carolina Railroad was under discussion that Colonel Bridgers made his attack on the railroad record of Governor Morehead.[1] After the lapse of fifty-four years, it is impossible for me to recall many of the incidents of the debate, but this much I do remember: that Colonel Bridgers' attack on Governor Morehead was futile and did the Governor no harm, for he vindicated himself in the most thorough manner. . . . I cannot close this without again expressing the many pleasing recollections that I have of Governor Morehead, as well as the great admiration I had for him. Truly he was a great and good man, and his venerable form and benign features are ever before my mental vision, while the memory of his many kind and courteous acts is forever enshrined within my heart. He deserves to stand high on the roll of those whose names and whose character have shed lustre upon the pages of North Carolina's history."[2]

His great speech in this most notable debate, however, was unable to overcome the eastern vote, and the second reading, on Saturday, January 15, 1859, was lost by a vote of 65 nays and 37 yeas, but one of which yeas was east of

---

[1] As has been seen it was the Greensboro & Danville line, or "connection" with the latter place, instead.
[2] Letter to R. D. W. Connor. N. C. Historical Commission, Misc. Papers, Ser. 1, Vol. IV, p. 108.

Raleigh, namely of Beaufort county. Guilford's three votes were the highest from any one county, Davidson, Wilkes and Mecklenburg following with two, while Rowan, Cumberland, Harnett, Caswell, Rutherford, Robeson and Beaufort were divided.

This was not the end of the battle, however, for three days later, on January 18, 1859, the Internal Improvement Committee, of which Governor Morehead was a member, reported out a substitute for the Greensboro and Danville bill, recommending its passage. On consideration of the Chatham Railroad bill on January 21st, Mr. Caldwell of Guilford county offered an amendment giving the road power to build also between Greensboro and Danville, which was promptly defeated by 74 to 25, but the bill was passed. Instantly Mr. Simpson's substitute bill, No. 92, was called up for third reading, but the "link" people didn't want it *then,* and got an adjournment. It was called up again next day, whereupon the enemies of it began to offer amendments designed to kill it: connection with any Virginia road to work forfeiture, even if by stage or other means; it should not carry passengers, except free negroes entering the State (!); and freight or passengers could not be carried from the Central road to the Virginia road. It was then passed third reading and the name changed to the "Rockingham Coal Fields Company." This passed second reading in the Senate on February 14, 1859, where one Senator saw in it a purpose to get a railroad from Greensboro to Danville without connections at Danville, in expectation of applying to a future legislature for the right to connect, and sought an amendment making such application work forfeiture of charter, but this was rejected. Senator Ashe secured an amendment keeping the new line twenty miles from the Central road, and it passed second reading and also third reading 23 to 17. Then its title was changed to the "Dan River Railroad Company" and the House was asked to concur, which it promptly did. It opened the Dan River coal fields to the Danville and Richmond road.

Governor Morehead did other useful things in the session of 1858–9 as a member of the Commons, but this battle so overshadowed all others that they were eclipsed in public attention. This coal-fields road was in no sense a "link" although it went down to the region of Governor Morehead's properties at Leaksville, and really gave him an outlet for his Rockingham county plants. The echoes of this battle continued for months afterwards, because it was of great concern to the whole Atlantic seaboard states as the completion of a trans-national line from Maine to New Orleans. It will be well to note one or two most interesting comments, choosing one from Richmond and one from Fayetteville: In June, 1859, "A Virginian" wrote to the *Richmond Whig* the following letter on Governor Morehead and enclosed one from the *Fayetteville Observer* on the same subject, requesting its publication, and which follows his own: He says the latter letter is about Governor Morehead "who has done more to develop the resources of his native [?] Commonwealth, and to aid the deserving poor people around him, than has been effected by all the other public men of North Carolina together.

"Gifted by nature with wonderful mental and physical powers, and with unsurpassed industry, enterprise and public spirit, he has, through a long life, devoted all his energies to the improvement of the various interests of his state. Nor has he been wanting in efforts to unite Virginia and North Carolina by the strong ties of reciprocal interest and mutual benefit.

"His liberal subscription to the Richmond and Danville Railroad and his Herculean efforts in the Legislature of his State to procure a charter for a connecting link between that improvement and the North Carolina Central road, whilst they subjected him to the grossest injustice and to the most malignant opposition, on the part of those who are opposed to the connection, have won for him a name and fame which his opponents may envy, but to which they can never attain. . . . he stands before his admiring countrymen as a patriot of enlarged views, whose comprehensive grasp takes in, not only all of his beloved Commonwealth, but looks also to the good of his sister States. As the great advocate and patron of internal improvements, he may be justly

regarded as *the De Witt Clinton of the South*. It may truly
be said, that such a man as John M. Morehead is not only
an ornament to his State, but a benefactor to his species.

"But to the extract referred to:"

The Fayetteville writer tells of a visit to Leaksville
and Governor Morehead's plant there: "Being attracted
by the magnitude and number of buildings, I stopped a few
hours to look around. Here was a large stone building, the
cotton factory, constructed in the most substantial manner,
and of the most durable materials. It is situated at the
mouth of a magnificent canal, leading from Smith's river,
and operated by the largest and finest metal wheel that I
have ever seen. Near by are the oil mills, flour mills, and
saw mill—all operated by the water of the same canal,
which appears to have a fall of at least 25 feet, and at a
slight expense could be made to propel millions of dollars
worth of machinery.[1]

"After surveying this immense water power and canal,
capable of being made to control the entire current of
Smith's river, I looked upon the hills that jut in towards
the manufacturing establishments, to see the neat and substantial dwellings—some brick and others frame—where the
hundreds of laborers and their families live, who earn honest and respectable support from the capital here invested.
The store-house and factory appear to have been built some
years, and all the establishments and plans show that intelligent enterprise and capital have accomplished much
here for the benefit of the country, when such improvements
were in their infancy in North Carolina. Seeing such results from the sagacity and enterprise of an individual when
there was no prospect of railroads in that portion of North
Carolina, I was naturally led to reflect, what this portion of
the State might become, with its rich lands, abounding in
iron and coal, and its immense water power, with the advantages of a railroad? But this would not suit your Wilmington neighbors; and hence the people of that portion of

[1] Governor Morehead, at this time, had steam mills at Salem (now Winston-
Salem), thousands of acres in Rockingham with this great plant at Leaksville,
and considerable possessions at Holtsburg on the Yadkin river.—*Greensboro
Patriot* of 14th Oct., 1859.

North Carolina must be denied the benefits and blessings resulting from such improvement. In reflecting upon what I have witnessed and learned, I am satisfied that no man in the State of North Carolina has been more identified with her material interests than J. M. Morehead. He has been, and probably is now, identified with the farming, manufacturing, mechanical, mercantile and educational pursuits of the people of the state. He knows their wants and interests, perhaps, better than any other man. He has done more to give impulse and success to the internal improvement system than any man in the State. The North Carolina Railroad would never have been constructed had he not taken hold of it and brought his potent influence to raise the means and put the work forward almost to completion. Within six months or less he would have had the road completed. But here low party malignity had to do its dirty work. It forced him to resign that position which he had filled with such signal ability, that it might reap the rewards due to another. It was an act of black ingratitude, and some of its perpetrators are now reaping its bitter fruits.

"He did more to build the Atlantic and North Carolina Railroad than any man in the State. Altho' he was not the President, he subscribed the money and did the work, and today, I am told, owns more stock in the road than all other stockholders collectively. Yet he has never even been tendered a Director's place in the company. This is base ingratitude and places the company in no enviable light, altho' I do not suppose that Governor Morehead wants any position on the road.

"During the sitting of the last Legislature, there was developed a bitter partizan spirit against him. He had mind and capacity enough in his objects of legislation to comprehend the whole state of North Carolina. He was for giving the additional aid necessary to complete the Albemarle and Chesapeake Canal; he was for going forward with the Western Extension [of the N. C. R. R.]; he advocated the Danville connection; and he was for the Fayetteville Coal Fields Road as well as other useful improvements to the State. His more comprehensive and statesman-like policy did not suit all the local and petty interests represented in the Legislature, and an attempt was made to hunt him down by those pigmy politicians and factionists.

"Men who would not dare to meet him in discussion in the legislative halls or elsewhere by misrepresentation and slander, by whiskey and ground-peas in the lobbies, hotels and groceries, endeavored to do their dirty work of robbing an honest man of his good name and just fame. The decree had gone forth that Morehead *delendus est.*

"His public and private life were ransacked to find some fault or blemish with which to damn him. Truly *'montes parturiunt et ridiculus mus nascitur.'* The result is too well known. How like chaff before the wind he scattered the imputations of his adversaries, and how triumphantly he vindicated himself, and put to the blush every accuser, is too familiar to your readers.

"His speech, both in eloquence and its vindication of truths would have immortalized almost any statesman; but to J. M. Morehead, who had proved the victor in an hundred hard-fought battles, it was only one among the many triumphs of his life, when his opponents dared to meet him face to face. . . .

"North Carolina has but few such men as J. M. Morehead. A statesman of manly bearing and frank views on all questions—tried in the severe ordeals of public and private life, he is known to possess the integrity of a Cato; a man of brains and of great practical intellect, identified with almost every honorable and liberal pursuit in the country, and having devoted the best of his life and services to the improvement, both public and private, of the State. These are qualities which justly endear him to his fellowmen, and well may they be proud of him.

"It was these high attributes of character, illustrated through his whole life that caused the people to elect him twice triumphantly to the Gubernatorial chair by such majorities as no other man has ever received, with parties so equally divided and the strongest opposition that could be arrayed against him. He has never asked the people for office, which they did not confer; indeed, he never sought

office, but has often served in public positions at the sacrifice
of his individual interests.   And when partizan feeling shall
have subsided and the revilers and private traducers of his
just fame and great name shall have moulded into dust,
and been forgotten, posterity will cherish the name and
memory of J. M. Morehead, and rank him with North Carolina's most gifted statesmen and greatest benefactors."[1]

Such was the result of the great fight for the last link in
a trans-national Piedmont railway.   And what was it?
The result was that, if the Richmond and Danville road extended its line to the Dan River Railroad whose terminus
would be at Leaksville, then the "link" still necessary to the
trans-national line would be reduced to but twenty-eight
miles—the distance between Leaksville and Greensboro!
So great a part of the "link" had Governor Morehead secured in the past ten years!   And then he went back to
Morehead City to continue his efforts to build up a great
port terminal of the North Carolina Railroad "system" as
it would now be called.   For was not the Raleigh & Gaston
road now a part of the "system?"   And was not Wilmington
and the Roanoke valley trying to make the Wilmington
& Weldon a part of it likewise?   Now, his activities at
Morehead City were like a great symbolical picture, showing
a giant building a mighty port terminal metropolis of the
commonwealth, with Wilmington, a rival, beholding it and
observing, near at the giant's hand, a bludgeon marked
"Twenty-eight miles of trans-national link, Greensboro to
Leaksville.   For the Dog-In-The-Manger, who can neither
eat hay, nor allow those to eat it who can!"   For such Wilmington was considered by all who had favored the sea-to-
Tennessee vertebral railroad, from President Caldwell to
Governor Morehead.   Would Wilmington and the Roanoke
heed the warning?   Could the Cape Fear metropolis surrender her primacy to a program avowedly designed to displace her—even though it was also designed to be a veritable
unification of the commonwealth—its greatest need since the
Piedmont became populous?   It was not in human, nor

---

[1] From a clipping from the *Richmond Whig* in possession of Mrs. W. R.
Walker, Spray, N. C.

metropolitan nature, to do it; and so the picture of the giant creating a new port terminal and metropolis, while his Greensboro-Leaksville bludgeon lay close at hand as a warning to Wilmington, still stands, late in 1859; while a storm is brewing beside which, a hurricane off Hatteras would be a mere zephyr, and which would bring disaster to both!

And yet as soon as that Assembly of 1858–9 adjourned in February, Governor Morehead boarded the train eastward for Morehead City to continue building a great unifying port for the state.

A letter from Morehead City, dated March 10, 1859, and signed "Beaufort," gives a vivid picture of progress there: "The wharf, as you know, is built upon iron screw-piles—a novelty in this country as well as Europe, and is just finished. And the warehouse built thereon, and the whole structure for enclosing the wharf are raised and will be under cover by the last of next week. The arrangements here for loading and unloading vessels and cars are superior to anything I have ever witnessed, either North or South. The warehouses, being some fifty-five feet narrower than the wharf, and placed nearer one side of the same, the railroad track forks before reaching the warehouse, and a track runs on each side of the same and between it and the vessels lying at the side of the wharf; so that if the cars are ready, the goods are taken directly from the vessel, and put directly on board the cars without any delay or cost. If cars are not ready, the goods which are valuable and need locking up, are carried across the tracks, and put in the warehouse until the cars arrive. Those more bulky are left outside the tracks on the wharf, though not exposed to the weather, as the whole is under cover, and enclosed by large sliding doors remaining entirely around the wharf.

"Here the steamer drawing twenty feet of water, and the locomotive weighing twenty or thirty tons, with its whole train, may be along side each other; and this, too, on each side of the wharf at the same time, while in front other vessels may be loading or discharging cargoes.

"For admirable arrangement, I have never seen anything to compare to it. And it reflects great credit on the engineers, who planned it and superintended its construction; on the railroad authorities whose wisdom and liberality have done so much to facilitate commerce, and to the contractors for the admirable execution of the work.

"Three vessels are lying at the wharf, loading and discharging cargoes, to wit:

"Schr. John Clark, Capt Sull, from New York, with merchandise. Cargo discharged and loading with Naval Stores and wheat for New York.

"Schr. E. J. Tabbot, Capt. Pegram, from Boston, loaded with lime; return cargo Naval Stores.

"Schr. George D., Capt. Dill, from Charleston, loaded with salt, and to load with Naval Stores for Baltimore. This vessel ran, as I am informed, from Charleston to Morehead City in about 30 hours.

"The above vessels are lying at the wharf loading and discharging cargoes.

"A barque of some eight hundred tons is expected here tomorrow from Baltimore, chartered to take five thousand barrels rosin direct to Liverpool, a porton of the cargo being now on the wharf.

"Schr. Oliver H. Lea is expected here in a day or two, with merchandise from New York for western merchants.

"A freight train arrived this evening with fourteen loaded cars, and to load back with merchandise, salt and lime. Salt at 90 cents per sack and lime at 85 cents per barrel, from vessels.

"I see a number of good houses going up and the population rapidly increasing; indeed there are few places more changed than this since I saw it some twelve months ago.

"I found your townsman, Gov. Morehead, here, the founder of this city, the builder of the wharf and warehouse at the eastern end of the railroad. He was giving directions and instructions to his workmen, some thirty in number, in his usual quiet way. He is evidently gratified with this consummation of his wishes—the connection of the mountains and the ocean railway.

"I shall be deceived if a brilliant future does not await this place.

"I saw other vessels lying in the harbor at a distance; but learned no particulars as to them. If I remain here a few days I may write you again."[1]

Here was a man of vision—a man who had some time before said to a well-known opponent: "You are a younger man than I am, and have not yet learned that in politics, as in everything else, it is best always to keep cool and take things easy."[2]

---

[1] *Greensboro Patriot,* March 25, 1859.
[2] *Social Reminiscences of John M. Morehead* by Mrs. Mary Bayard Clarke. It was about this time that Governor Morehead had his portrait painted in 1859 by William Garl Broune. Several copies were made by the artist for various children and the Governor's Mansion at Raleigh. The one here used as frontispiece is in possession of Major John Motley Morehead III, at his home, "Blandwood," in Rye, N. Y. It represents the Governor with the charter of the North Carolina Central Railroad in his right hand.

A note at this point may conveniently draw attention to the fact that the pseudonym "Carlton" has been discovered in several places, too late for correction, as "Carleton."

XVII

DEFENDER OF THE UNION
IN
THE STATE SENATE
AND
WHIG NATIONAL CONVENTION
1859

In the middle of October, 1859, like a thunder-bolt out of a clear sky, came news of an uprising at Harpers Ferry, at the junction of the Shenandoah and Potomac rivers, on the Baltimore and Ohio Railroad, led by one John Brown, a Kansas fanatic, maddened by the long bloody struggle in that state between abolition and slave factions, who sought to start a violent revolution to free the southern slaves. The old Whig and "American" or "Opposition" element in North Carolina had become bitter against both "Black Republicans" and Democrats alike; while the Democrats were enraged that this "Opposition" was unable to see that there was now no longer any middle ground between "Black Republicans" and the Democrats, for any opposition to stand on. The "Opposition," as they began to call themselves, as opposed to both "Black Republicans" and Democrats had a strong voice in Senator John A. Gilmer of Guilford county, at Washington, and the more bitter the acts of the "Black Republicans" and Democrats became, the more incensed the Whig "Opposition" became against both! This October revolutionary episode kindled the flame still higher. Even the *Raleigh Register,* probably leading journal of the "Opposition" element, had an editorial on November 30, 1859, that was very significant, remarking that there was not a powder-mill south of Delaware; not a factory for arms or foundry for cannon south of this same Harpers Ferry, and yet Virginia and Kentucky had saltpetre mines. With this were warnings to have volunteers in each county and at least three arsenals should be established; and that a Northerner on a Southern street should be an object of suspicion. Commercial independence from the north was advocated early in December. The execution of John Brown was followed by renewed hatred of such books as that by Hinton Helper; and news began to arrive of Union meetings in various northern centers. Brown, however, had broken as many ties of union between north and south in a day nearly as had grown by slow accretions since 1776. Like a flame in a wheat field, the commercial boycott of the north spread over the south. The secession of southern medical students in the great medical schools of Philadelphia nearly disrupted those bodies in December. Senator Gilmer and others, at Washington, were trying to head off the mad frenzy, by a Union party, as the new year 1860 arrived.

While these events were proceeding there was an arrest in Greensboro of Rev. Daniel Worth, a Wesleyan Methodist, and Democratic Abolitionist, who was charged with spreading Helper's *Impending Crisis* and inciting to insurrection, and the trial was with difficulty kept from becoming a mob.

Late in January, 1860, came the news that after thirty-nine ballots in the national House of Representatives, a "Black Republican" had been chosen speaker, against Representative Smith of North Carolina, "in one of the fiercest struggles ever witnessed on the floor of" that body. The animus of the fight arose from bitterness of opposition to John Sherman of Ohio, who had spoken favorably of Helper's *Impending Crisis*. North Carolina was especially bitter against this book in the slave-holding parts of the commonwealth, because it was a North Carolina product. Hinton Rowan Helper was a native of Mocksville, in what is now Davie, but was then Rowan county, in 1829, so that he was a young man of but twenty-six years when it was issued in 1857. The Republican party used it as a campaign document and during the first four years nearly 150,000 were in circulation. It was dedicated to the non-slaveholding citizens of the South, of whom there were a great many in this general region, beside the Quakers, who of course did not have them.[1] The Moreheads did have them, however; yet they were among that large number in the South who would have been glad if it could be re moved without revolution and danger of uprisings of an ignorant uncontrolled race.

On January 24, 1860, a Whig Opposition meeting was held in Greensboro, at which Governor Morehead was present; and resolutions were passed condemning the "rule or ruin" Democrats, who could have organized the lower House at Washington, with a conservative Southern Whig, who loved the Union, but preferred to see a "Black Republican" to such a man! They applauded Senator John A. Gilmer, who joined with such men as Crittenden, Harris, Conrad, Clemmens of Tennessee, Etheridge and similar patriotic Union leaders, in connection with a late Philadelphia meeting of the Executive Committee. They also favored the Opposition Convention at Raleigh for Washington's Birthday, next. At this latter gathering, Governor Morehead was not present, but this body selected the defeated Vice-President William A. Graham, as their first choice for the Whig Presidential nomination and praised their Congressmen Smith, Gilmer, Vance and Leach for their conservative course in the late struggles at Washington.

---

[1] Helper's book, when republished, had added to it—what was not in the original edition—a "Compend" of recommendations: (Just who was responsible for them is not known.)

"1st. Thorough organization and independent political action on the part of non-slaveholding whites of the South.

"2nd. Ineligibility of slaveholders—never another vote to the trafficker in human flesh.

"3rd. No co-operation with slaveholders in politics—no fellowship with them in religion—no affiliation with them in society.

"4th. No patronage to slaveholding merchants—no guestship in slave-waiting hotels—no fees to slaveholding lawyers—no employment of slaveholding physicians—no audience to slaveholding parsons.

"5th. No recognition of pro-slavery men except as ruffians, outlaws and criminals."

It was this addition to the reprint, unknown to many supporters of the book, which, in itself, contained no such sentiments, that added fuel to the flame created by the John Brown fire-brand. Mrs. Stowe's book—*Uncle Tom's Cabin*—which had been circulating since 1852—had no such influence upon the South, of course, as this book by a North Carolinian, especially after the "Compend" appeared in it.

A considerable source of irritation, especially in North Carolina, was added to this in May, 1860, by a disagreement between the railroads of that state and the Postmaster General on rates for mail carrying, in which all the roads refused to carry the mail, except the Wilmington & Weldon, the Atlantic and the Western. Thereupon the Post Office Department banned those parts of the state, refusing to forward their mail. Wagon mail carrying had to be resorted to from the nearest roads that did carry.

During this month, on May 16, 1860, the "Opposition" held its national meeting at Baltimore, as the "National Constitutional Union Convention," in the old church building at the corner of Fayette and North Streets. It was called to order by Hon. John J. Crittenden of Kentucky, as chairman of the Executive Committee. Ex-Governor Hunt of New York was made President of the Convention; and the delegation from North Carolina was headed by Governor John Motley Morehead as delegate-at-large. General Coombs of Kentucky, in an amusing skit, expressed the attitude of the Convention by offering platforms for Republicans, Democrats and this "Opposition" to them both: "First, then," said he, "for the *harmonious* Democracy, I propose the Virginia and Kentucky resolutions of 1798–99 —one in favor of excluding slavery from the territories, and the other in favor of forcng it into them—[laughter] to be adopted unanimously without debate, under the previous question, and no questions asked afterwards. [Laughter.] For the 'irrepressible conflictionist,' about to assemble at Chicago, I suggest the 'Blue Laws' of Connecticut; first in reference to the right of a man to kiss his wife on Sunday—[laughter] and second, in reference to the burning of witches; provided that wives shall have the privilege to be kissed, and witches to be burned. [Laughter.] The third is the Constitution as it is, and the Union under it, now and forever. [Immense applause.]" Governor Morehead's first activity in the Convention was to oppose the unit rule and to insist on free discussion. There were ten candidates in the field on the first ballot, in which, under Governor Morehead's leadership, North Carolina cast her full 10 votes for Graham; but as John Bell of Tennessee had far the most votes of any of the ten candidates, and Graham was fourth in number [Bell, Houston of Texas, Everett and Graham], while on the second ballott Bell absorbed many of the other votes, only Houston and Graham showing any increase at all, Arkansas led in transferring her vote to Bell, and was followed by Mississippi, Massachusetts, North Carolina, Virginia and the rest to make it unanimous. In the presentation of Vice-Presidential candidates Governor Morehead, following Missouri, Tennessee and New York, announced North Carolina as for Edward Everett. The Bell and Everett ticket was the choice of the Convention and they were announced as "The only National Candidates for President and Vice-President in the United States."

With the echoes of the Baltimore Convention scarcely silent, the contrasting scenes of a May Day celebration on May 5, 1860, were being enacted in Greensboro by the students of Edgeworth Seminary. Miss Mary Corinna Morehead, the Governor's daughter, was to be crowned Queen at the throne erected in the grove of the school grounds. It was at 5.30 P. M., escorted by fourteen Maids of Honor, ten Floras, with flowers to scatter in her path, a Scepter and Crown Bearer, the Queen, with Lady Hope and the Archbishop on either side, approached with her two First Maids of Honor, ten Pages and the Guilford Grays. The beautiful ceremony of coronation was followed by the poetical speech of the Queen and her presentation of a flag to the Guilford Grays:

"In the name of my subjects, the fair donors of Edgeworth, I present this banner to the Guilford Grays. Fain would we have it a banner of peace, and have inscribed upon its graceful folds 'Peace on earth and good will to men;' for our womanly nature shrinks from the horrors of war and bloodshed. But we have placed upon it 'the oak'—fit emblem of the firm, heroic spirits over which it is to float. Strength, energy and decision mark the character of the sons of Guilford, whose noble sires have taught their sons to know *but one fear*—the fear of doing wrong.

"Proudly in days past have the banners of our country

waved over yon Battle-field, where our fathers fought for freedom from a tyrant's power. Their motto, 'Union is strength,' and we their daughters would have this our banner unfurled only in the same noble cause, and quivering through our soft Southern breezes, echo the same glorious theme, Union! Union!!''

These Grays were organized but a few months before when Southern and Northern fanatics were threatening the Union. Ensign Gorrell in his speech recalled the Brown raid and retaliatory acts of the South that called them into being and the present hope that it had all subsided.[1]

The growing crisis in both State and national affairs made the districts and counties pick out their strong men for the next Assembly. In the 36th Senatorial district of North Carolina—that of Governor Morehead, he himself, was put up for the State Senate and in August elected easily as a "Unionist." Again, however, the Democrats had a majority of 12 in the Senate and 10 in the House, the "Unionists" numbering 19 in the former and 55 in the latter. Governor Morehead, as a Unionist, like the rest of his party, saw no reason why any man, with the requisite number of votes, should not be inaugurated President, without any danger to any institution protected by the Constitution, be he even the "Black Republican" candidate, Abraham Lincoln. They had no fears for the Constitution even under him; so that they held that the *onus* would rest on whomsoever first took steps of revolution or secession, as Democrats were so commonly threatening, in case the "Black Republican" candidate should be elected. This was the national meaning of Governor Morehead's election to the State Senate; but, there was also a state meaning to it; for he and his followers, who had secured all but twenty-eight miles of the trans-national Piedmont line—the Greensboro-Leaksville link, had no notion of considering the outcome of the railway battles of the last Assembly as final.

The breaking up of political families now extended to the Democracy as well as the Whigs. The autumn visit of

---

[1] *Greensboro Patriot*, May 18, 1860.

Stephen A. Douglas to Raleigh brought it out in North Carolina vividly. The *Raleigh Standard,* Senator Clingman and Governor Ellis espoused the cause of the "Little Giant," while Weldon N. Edwards, "the political executor of Nathaniel Macon" was so against Douglas that he said he would prefer the election of Lincoln! Then there was the Breckenridge elector of the Raleigh district, Mr. Venable, who joined his own wing of the party in declaring for a dissolution of the Union, if the "Black Republican" from Illinois were elected. The news of this brought a significant comment from the Bell and Everett leading North Carolina organ, the *Raleigh Register,* when it said that if a choice between the two, Douglas and Lincoln, were compulsory, it would unhesitatingly be for "The Little Giant."

The "Opposition" or "Unionist" candidate for Governor reduced his opponent's majority to about half of that of Governor Bragg; which shows the Unionist strength in North Carolina at this critical period; for a gubernatorial majority of but 6093 in a vote of 112,702 for the whole state —59,396 Democrat and 53,303 Unionist—is a remarkable Unionist showing. And Guilford county led all the rest in a majority of 2137 to 457, among others with largest majorities being Iredell, Wilkes, Stanly, Randolph and Beaufort counties. By the accompanying map it will be seen that, in a general way, the Unionist counties were a great block central and westward from and including Raleigh, with another block generally from Newbern northeastwardly. Many counties on both sides, however, were close. In a general way, also, the Democrats had the great eastern central block on both sides of the Wilmington & Weldon Railroad and the Roanoke valley—the regions of great plantations and large slave-holdings.

Between this date and the November national election, the fear of the "Black Republican" success increased, and a consequent increase of disunion expression and actual preparation by the organization of "Minute Men." "Already the effects of disunion threats are manifesting themselves," says the *Raleigh Register* of November 14, 1860. "Negroes have gone down 30 per cent, and soon other prop-

erty will begin to depreciate. And for what?—a miserable
abstraction. Should an attempt be made to execute these
threats, men now wealthy will be reduced to poverty."
The national election confirmed their worst fears, although
the Raleigh *Standard,* the Breckenridge leader in a Breckenridge State, was for accepting the result lawfully. The
Douglas ticket had but little support in North Carolina and
there was but little change in totals from those of the
August gubernatorial vote; a few counties changed, by slight
vote, to Bell, but Raleigh's county changed to Breckenridge,
while the counties, in many cases were so close, that the
totals for the state were not greatly different from the
August gubernatorial results. Therefore, although North
Carolina went for Breckenridge and Lane, her leading
Democratic editor being for lawful acceptance of the result,
it can readily be seen that this was a Unionist state—at this
moment. The *Raleigh Register* charged South Carolina
with a purpose to secede in order that, Georgia following,
the reduced Southern representation in Congress would
leave the "Black Republicans" in control and forced to do
something that would drive the rest of the South along with
those two States! For the whole North above New Jersey,
Maryland, Kentucky and Missouri went overwhelmingly
for Lincoln, carrying the country almost two to one.

This was the situation on November 19, 1860, when the
Assembly met in the capitol at Raleigh and Ex-Governor,
now Senator Morehead, took his seat in the north Senate
Chamber. The whole South was in a state of convulsion,
financially, politically, industrially, educationally—a crisis
even before secession was actually begun. Senator John
Motley Morehead was trying to keep his head and thereby
aid the state in doing the same thing. He presented two
bills in an ordinary way as though nothing had happened.
He was put on the Committees on Internal Improvement,
Education, and Privileges and Elections; and yet Governor
Ellis' message was essentially a secessionist one, and the
Clerk of the House of Commons had even modified the oath
of office of members in that direction. Governor Ellis
recommended both a State Convention and a Southern Con-

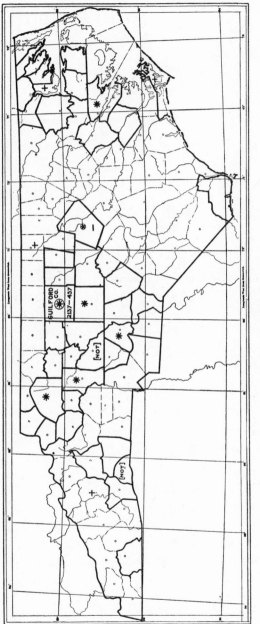

MAP OF NORTH CAROLINA, 1860
Prepared by the author

Showing Unionist vote for Governor: 1. Counties with greatest Union majority, marked * (Highest ⊛);
2. Union, returns not complete, marked +; 3. Turned to Breckenridge in November, marked —

ference—on the basis of "in the Union if possible, out of it if necessary." Union meetings were held in various parts of the State, but it was December 7th, before a noticeable ebullition occurred in the Senate, when Senator Turner of Orange, made a striking speech in which he said: "The people of North Carolina are not ready for disunion; nor are they ready to be chained to the car of South Carolina and be dragged out of the Union into discord and civil war. Senators will find that the Union men of North Carolina will take a firm, fixed, immovable stand for the Union of the States, and the Constitutional rights of each of the States, and no power can drive them from it, short of the bayonet and sword."

It was on Thursday, December 13, 1860, that Governor Morehead first made himself felt in a speech on Senator Turner's amendment to a resolution regarding a conference with South Carolina. "Mr. Morehead addressed the Senate at some length in an able and eloquent manner," says the *Register* reporter. "He said that he opposed this conference with South Carolina, because she did not want to confer with any State; that if she wishes to go out of the Union, let her go; but when she wishes a conference with us, and she respectfully asks a conference, then we will confer with her. He thought that North Carolina's being so alarmed about a dissolution of the Union would destroy all the moral effect of the secession of the State of South Carolina. He took a strong ground against the right of a state to secede from the Union, though he acknowledged an inherent right of revolution in all men and all governments; but if a state did secede, there was no provision in the Constitution for forcing her into the Union, because such an event was not contemplated by the framers of that instrument. He thought the Union could yet be saved. There was already a returning sense of justice in the Northern States." This address was answered by Senator Brown, who, in return, was replied to by the Guilford county Senator. The resolutions were abandoned the next day.

Events came swift and fast as the new year, 1861, opened. The United States ports at Charleston and even below Wilmington were among the first objects of attack. By January 14, 1861, the Senate passed resolutions asking the President to withdraw troops from South Atlantic states before a collision, in order that efforts might be made to restore peace by conference; and these were about to appoint commissioners to go to the President, when adjournment occurred. In the midst of such a situation the City of Morehead incorporation bill was passed by the Senate; and on the 15th, as a member of the Committee on Federal Affairs, Senator Morehead recommended amendment to the national constitution on fugitive slaves; and on the 17th he made an extended eloquent appeal for the Union, in connection with discussion of a call for a State Convention; and the bill passed both houses that day.

On January 24th, submissions from Virginia and Alabama having been referred to the Committee on Federal Relations, that body recommended appoinment of Commissioners to meet similar ones from other states at Washington on February 4, 1861, and also similar ones to a like Southern meeting at Montgomery, Alabama, on the same date. Senator Morehead was one of only nine who voted against it. While they were discussing it, the House resolutions on the same line, but more complete, were received and discussed. In these resolutions, Commissioners were named, those to Washington being Hons. John M. Morehead, Daniel M. Barringer, Chief Justice Thomas Ruffin, Ex-Governor David S. Reid and George Davis, Esq. Those to Alabama were Ex-Governor Swain, M. W. Ransom and J. L. Bridgers. These resolutions were concurred in, the meeting being set for February 4, 1861, at Washington, with Senator Morehead as Chairman of the Washington Commissioners.

And then, on January 31, 1861, came the ghost of the Greensboro and Danville road asking to be brought to life! Senator Barringer moved it as a substitute for another bill, while Senator Bledsoe tried to make it—no doubt in a humorous sense—from "The Shops [at Greensboro] to Leaksville." Senator Thomas, once opposed, now favored the Danville link. Senator Dobson favored it because it asked no money from the State. Then Senator Bledsoe said

Senator Morehead had himself abandoned it, and referred to the matter of 1849; whereupon Governor Morehead said he had never deserted the Danville connection. He then paid his respects to Senator Bledsoe and the county of Wake, whom the Senator said was opposed to it. "Take out of the county of Wake the money which the State of North Carolina had thrown into it, and it would soon be the most magnificently insolvent county to be found anywhere, either in or out of the State." Whereupon he advocated the Danville connection with great ability, and the bill passed second reading 23 to 17. On Friday, February 1, 1861, Senator Barringer from committee introduced a bill for a Greensboro and Dan River Railroad, and it passed first reading. This was the last day Senator Morehead was present, as the Assembly had given him the Peace mission to the national capital.

While he was gone, however, a more or less continuous fight was on, by means of the Milton & Yancyville Junction Railroad bill, to get and defeat a Danville connection, on the principle that it would be as "sweet" by any "name." On February 15, 1861, however, the Senate received from the House a bill to incorporate The Greensboro and Leaksville Railroad; and it passed third reading on the 16th, and granted a charter.

Also while he was away the Governor Swain commission to the Alabama Convention at Montgomery, Alabama, returned and reported on February 11, 1861, that on their arrival the Convention had adjourned, so they communicated with the Southern Congress and found that a decided minority only were in favor of reconstruction; that a "Provisional Government of the Confederate States of America" was adopted on the 8th and that General Jefferson Davis of Mississippi was elected President on the 9th, and that North Carolina was invited to join them. The Assembly adjourned on the 25th of February, 1861, awaiting a report from Senator Morehead and his fellow Peace Commissioners from the national capital, who were having no such brief session as those to Alabama.

XVIII

The Peace Conference
Governor Morehead's Last Efforts
to
Preserve the Union

4th February, 1861

Just why was North Carolina attempting to make peace by sending Commissioners both to Washington and Montgomery, and why was Governor Morehead at the head of the one and Governor Swain of the other? Both were western men and both strong Union men and not excelled in influence by any other men in the state. They best represented the commonwealth. The census of 1860 shows how that commonwealth was composed. Guilford county, Governor Morehead's home, next to the county containing Raleigh, had the greatest white population in the state, 15,738, the county below her coming next with 14,968 and the next nearest being in the 13,000s in that part of the state. She had about one-fifth that number of slaves, namely, 3625, and but 693 free negroes. In total population—both white and negro, 20,056—Raleigh's county again stood first, while Granville county, next north, in the Roanoke valley, with over one-half colored, came second—23,396, making Guilford third in total population. Halifax county, also on the Roanoke, with over two-thirds colored and far the greatest number of free negroes—2450—in all counties of the state, was fourth in total population. Granville, with 11,085 slaves, was the greatest slave county in North Carolina, although those other lower Roanoke counties, Edgecombe, Halifax, Warren and Raleigh's and Wilmington counties came next in the 10,000s. No county in the state but had slaves, Watauga having the fewest, 104. The total was

331,081 slaves, while the total free negroes was so great as
30,097. This latter added to the 631,489 white population
made the free population 661,586—almost exactly twice the
slave population. On the other hand, the negro population
—both slave and free—were over half of the white or about
one-third the total population. Seven counties had above
1000 free colored people: about half of the Pasquotank
county negroes were free, the greatest proportion where
there was a large colored population. Watauga had 82 free
out of her 104 negroes; and but one county, Haywood, had
no free negroes, and but one other with so small a number
as 2—Madison county—all mountain counties. As Wake,
the capital's county, was generally looked upon as somewhat neutral, an almost North Carolina District-of-Colum-
bia, in a sense, Governor Morehead, from the largest white
inhabited county in the state and from the dominant white
district of the commonwealth very properly headed the
Peace Commission designed to conciliate the north; while
Governor Swain, also of the west, but of most excellent
diplomatic qualities and consequently highly regarded by
the east, was sent on the even more hopeless mission to
Montgomery.

This latter was in response to the Alabama Convention's
invitation to all states below Mason-Dixon line to confer
on best measures on February 4, 1861. They were neither
delegates to the Confederate Provisional Congress nor to the
Alabama Legislature. The Convention had adjourned *sine
die,* and no other delegates seemed to have thought it necessary to come; so on the third day, they concluded to submit
the North Carolina sentiments to the Congress, which thereupon invited them to do so, but also invited North Carolina
to join the new Confederate government, giving them a copy
of the Constitution when it was adopted on the 8th instant.
They remained until after President Davis was chosen
on the 9th and made their report on the 11th—a mission
all in vain.

Meanwhile, likewise, on Monday, February 4, 1861, at
Virginia's invitation, delegates from eleven states—five
south of the Mason-Dixon line (Delaware, Maryland, Vir-

ginia, Kentucky and North Carolina) and six north of that line (New Hampshire, Rhode Island, New Jersey, Pennsylvania, Ohio and Indiana) met at Willard's Hall in Washington. Virginia's aims were based upon an adjustment, along the lines of the Crittenden Resolution, by amendment to the national constitution, limiting slave territory, but protecting slave property in transit. To such Whigs as Governor Morehead it boded no good that Ex-President Tyler headed the Virginia delegation. Curiously enough there were two Ex-Governors Morehead in the Conference, cousins, too, one from Kentucky, Charles S., and the other from North Carolina; and the former called the conference to order. On the second day Governor J. M. Morehead was put on the Credentials Committee, and witnessed the man he had many times called a Whig traitor, elevated to the presiding officer's chair, Ex-President John Tyler. By this time Vermont, Connecticut and New York were present and Massachusetts announced as on the way, as was Tennessee. Iowa also joined, and New York had one delegate with more on the way, and Illinois was coming. On the 7th the Conference called on President Buchanan and also appointed a committee to formulate measures.

Among the delegates were such men as Salmon P. Chase, George S. Boutwell, Thomas Ewing, David Dudley Field, Reverdy Johnson, Wm. M. Meredith, Thomas Ruffin, David Wilmot, and others. Death marred the first days in the passing of temporary Chairman Wright of Ohio. Other delegates were equally well-known to their generation, but, in some cases, not so well to succeeding ones. Delegates had varied powers—some were bound by Legislatures, some merely executive appointees. The Virginia invitations had the nature of an ultimatum to the free states and the majority report tended to even anticipate it; but the minority report favored the Crittenden Kentucky plan of a Constitutional Convention for amendment on these questions—let the Convention settle it. This was proposed in the face of the fact that seven states had seceded and organized a new government. On Monday, the 18th of February, 1861, the beginning of the third week, Mr. Boutwell of Massachusetts,

while holding the general position that Governor Morehead
of North Carolina held as to constitution and union, plainly
announced the northern doctrine that, if a state attempted to
secede, the whole force of the United States would be
used to prevent it, and "we shall march our armies to the
Gulf of Mexico, or you will march yours to the Great Lakes.
There can be no peaceful separation." This was the turning point in the Conference and it was in this connection
on the following day that Governor Morehead of North
Carolina first spoke and as a peace-maker between those
who did and those who did not want debate limited.

"I regret extremely," said Governor Morehead (N. C.),
"to hear talk of *sides* in this Conference. I came here to act
for the Union—the whole Union. I recognize no *sides*—
no party. If any come here for a different purpose I do not
wish to act with them; they are wrong. I hope from my
heart that we can all yet live together in peace; but if we are
to do so we must act, and act speedily."[1] Chief Justice
Ruffin expressed similar sentiments with great feeling:
"I was born before the present Constitution was adopted.
May God grant that I do not outlive it. I cannot address
you on this subject without manifesting a feeling which fills
my heart." He wanted the popular voice at once, for
unless it helped North Carolina she would "be drawn into
that mad career of open defiance, which is now opening so
widely against the government."

While a detailed account of this most interesting Conference is not possible here, some illustrative expressions
will show its unique place in the events of Governor Morehead's life. "I regard the present course of New England
as very unfair," said Mr. Rives of Virginia. "She is herself responsible for the existence of slavery—she is our
fiercest opponent; and yet New Jersey and Pennsylvania,
who have not this responsibility, have always stood by the
South, and I believe they always will." "The gentleman
from Massachusetts may congratulate himself that there
are no negroes [slaves] in that commonwealth." "Say,

[1] *Proceedings*, p. 113.

and let it be said in the Constitution, that you will not interfere with slavery in the District, or in the States, or in
the Territories. Permit the free transit of our slaves from
one State to another, and in the language of the patriarch,
'let there be peace between you and me'."

The effort of Governor Wickliffe of Kentucky to withdraw the resolution which precipitated this storm, was prevented by Governor Morehead (N. C.) and made regular
order for the next day. Then David Dudley Field addressed
them, holding that the Fathers would not put slavery guar-
antees more definitely into the Constitution than they now
were, nor would he. "Not to save the Union?" asked Governor Morehead (N. C.). "No, Sir! No!" was the reply.
"Then you will let the Union slide?" again interjected the
North Carolina leader. "No, never!" said the New York
jurist. "I would let slavery slide and save the Union.
Greater things than this have been done. This year has
seen slavery abolished in all the Russias." He then stated
the position of such Southern States as were not yet out of
the Union: "If you will support our amendments, we will
try to induce the seceded States to return to the Union.
We rather think we can induce them to return; but if we
cannot, then we will go with them." He closed eloquently
with Longfellow's "O Ship of State!"

On the 23rd, after Mr. Logan of Illinois had said, in
discussion of an Iowa proposal, "We should act as if the
fate of a great nation depended on our action," Governor
Morehead (N. C.) thought it time for him to speak: "I thank
God I hear a voice such as I have just heard from *that* section of the country! I have been a member of a recent
Legislature of North Carolina, in which there was a majority
of secessionists. I have been jeered at in that body for the
opinions I have expressed, for I told those gentlemen repeatedly that if we could once get the ear of the North, the
North would do us justice. They pointed me to the raid of
John Brown—to the meeting in Boston, where the gallows
of John Brown was carried with solemn ceremonies into
the Cradle of Liberty. They pointed me to the man who
presided over that meeting, since elevated to the high and

honorable position of Governor of Massachusetts. Notwithstanding all this, I have replied that the masses of the northern people would deal fairly by us. I have told these secessionists to their teeth that Lincoln was properly elected under the Constitution, and he ought to be inaugurated. Their reply was 'Kansas, and the John Brown raid!'

"Now, I ask this Conference to look for one moment at the effect of the amendment which is proposed. It withdraws all constitutional protection from us north of 36° 30'. Adopt it, and what has Massachusetts to do but to import her foreigners into the country south, and take possession of it. New York will back her, and we shall be swept from the face of the earth.

"If the gentleman from New York means to say that the nation can put its foot on the neck of the States and crush them into submission, let him go into Virginia and join another John Brown raid. Virginia will treat him as she did John Brown. No! the gentleman has not studied the motto of the Union. There is the *E pluribus* as well as the *unum*. If the new President proposes to come down to the South and conquer us, he will find that the whole temple shall fall. We can be crushed, perhaps, but conquered, *never!*"

Eight states were out of the Union by this time. President Tyler was hopeful of bringing them back. Governor Morehead again spoke on the beginning of the fourth week, the 25th, on the property status of slaves internationally. Indeed he spoke briefly several times in moulding the proposed constitutional amendment, as he also did on the 26th. On the latter day, he spoke on a proposed mode of freeing fugitive slaves: "We know," said he, "from past experience what the abolitionists of the free states would do under such a provision as this in the Constitution. [He was qualifying it by keeping the freed negroes in the state where owned.] There will be an underground railroad line along every principal route of travel. There will be depots all along these lines. Canoes will be furnished to ferry negroes over the Potomac and Ohio. John Brown & Co. will stand ready to kill the master the very moment he crosses the line in pursuit of his slave. What officer at the North will dare to arrest the slave when John Brown pikes are stacked up in every little village? If arrested, there will be organizations formed to rescue him, and you may as well let the 'nigger' go free at once. You are opening up the greatest scheme of emancipation ever devised." His amendment was agreed to, 17 to 3. On the same day he opposed an amendment of Mr. Fields which practically acknowledged a right of secession under certain conditions, even though Mr. Field no doubt considered them impossible conditions. "I should regret extremely," said Governor Morehead, "to have this amendment adopted, and to have the Constitution made practically to assert a right of secession. I have denied that right always in my State, in public and in private. I am aware that on this point I differ from the general sentiment of the South, and I hold there is no right of secession, and on the part of the General Government no right of coercion. I claim that a State has no right to secede, because that right is not found in the Constitution, and the theory of the Constitution is against it." The amendment was rejected 11 to 10. With the majority report so nearly finished, Ex-Governor Reid of North Carolina expressed his purpose not to agree to them, whereupon Chief Justice Ruffin and Governor Morehead (N. C.) disagreed with him: "I came here," said the latter, "to try to save the Union. I have labored hard to that end. I hope and believe the report of the majority, if adopted, will save the Union. I wish to carry these propositions before the people. I believe that the people of North Carolina and of the Union will adopt them. Give us an opportunity to appeal to the generosity of the people of the whole Union. Certainly no Southern man can object to submitting these propositions to the popular vote."

When the vote on sections was taken, *seriatim,* Chief Justice Ruffin and Governor Morehead dissented from their State's vote against Section 1. The vote stood 11 States against 8 for, with Indiana declining to vote at all—and nearly every State having one or more dissenters. The vote was accompanied by considerable excitement, because it looked as if the whole program was to fall; but a motion to reconsider was secured; and on the 27th it was passed by 9 to 8, with North Carolina among the latter, and New York divided because of the absence of Mr. Field. Thereupon the whole seven sections were successively adopted with even better majorities. In two other cases Chief Justice Ruffin and Governor Morehead (N. C.) dissented from their State's vote; and on but sections 3 and 4 did North Carolina's vote go to the affirmative. Twenty-one States were present at this last voting—all states north of and including North Carolina, Tennessee and Missouri, including Kansas and Iowa, and up to Michigan and Wisconsin. Against Chief Justice Ruffin of Graham and Governor Morehead of Greensboro in North Carolina's delegation were George Davis of Wilmington, Governor Reid of Rockingham county, and D. M. Barringer of Raleigh.

On the same day, President Tyler presented the proposed amendment as "Article XIII" to Congress, and the Senate rejected it promptly by a vote of 28 to 7. It was too late. The oath of office of President Lincoln gave him no alternative but to preserve the Constitution of the United States at all costs, and the action of South Carolina and similar States left but one course to pursue. Political power, by the election, had passed from the South to the North for the first time, practically. A large element—a growing element in the North had been and still were ignoring the Constitution and its recognition of slave property; and the extreme part of that element was even saying that that instrument was "a covenant with hell." These elements elected President Lincoln, who was bound by oath to preserve that Constitution. Great elements of the South stood where Lincoln stood, but the extreme element saw him representing the extreme element in the North and also ignored the Constitution. Every move that had touched slave property was a violation of the Constitution as much as secession was—a point that is liable to be overlooked. Before an avowed, wide-spread purpose in the North to break slavery, and with no care to do it by constitutional methods, it was natural that an equally extreme purpose should arise and spread widely in the South to ignore the Constitution also. With two great elements, North and South, fanatical in their purpose to overturn the Constitution, it could not but result in civil war to preserve that Constitution, by those who would follow President Lincoln. By the grim humor of events, the Abolitionist element, who declared the Constitution "a covenant with hell" and sought to break it, now were following President Lincoln in preserving that "covenant with hell!" No wonder the Secessionists could not do otherwise than identify the President with them and act accordingly. It is true that when the Abolitionists found just what Mr. Lincoln's purpose was, namely, to preserve the Constitution, without regard to slavery, and did so for nearly three bloody years, they were inflamed against him for it, but followed him because he was marching against slave-holders. Had the slave-holders obeyed the Constitution he would have found his greatest protection in that same "Black Republican" President, but because he sought to break it by secession, he forced the President to be his enemy, so long as the Constitution was threatened. It will be seen, therefore, that Governor Morehead even yet had the same attitude, as Mr. Lincoln, except that, Lincoln, like Washington and Jackson believed that the Constitution, like any government that is a real one, had the power of self-preservation and coercion.

This, however, leaves untouched the question of the conflict of moral and political movements, and the power of new wine to break old bottles. This was a realm into which Governor Morehead did not enter apparently. His was the realm of practical statesmanship; not that of the political or moral philosopher. He was a man of great vision, but it was not in this field—so there is no occasion for this narrative to enter it.

The great Whig leader arrived home at Greensboro on March 2nd, just two days before President Lincoln's inauguration.

"The Peace Congress having finished their labors," said the *Greensboro Patriot* of Thursday, March 7, 1861, "and having adjourned, Governor Morehead reached home by the

Express train on last Saturday evening. He found waiting at the Station an anxious crowd, desiring to know what had been done, and what was the prospect for peace. In order to impart this information in the most satisfactory manner to all, Gov. Morehead repaired at once to the Court House, which was in a short time nearly filled. Having been travelling all day, the Governor declined making a speech, but taking a seat on the bench where all could see and hear, he proceeded in a conversational way to detail briefly what had taken place in the Peace Conference. It was composed, he said, of some of the most distingushed men of the nation. Many of them quite old and feeble; and who had retired from public life. A committee of one from each state was appointed at the beginning of their session to prepare business. Hon. Thomas Ruffin was on this committee from North Carolina. In this committee, the Governor said, there was much able debating. The Governor spoke in the highest terms of Mr. Ruffin [Chief Justice]; that he exerted a great, if not a greater influence than any other member of the Conference; that he did not see how they could have got along without Judge Ruffin. That the Conference was composed of a great many distinguished lawyers, to all of whom Mr. Ruffin was known by reputation, having served so long as Chief Justice of our Supreme Court. The Governor said, that when they first met, New York nor Massachusetts were represented, and that everything went on quite harmoniously until the delegates from those States took their seats; that as soon as the members from New York and Massachusetts came, they commenced throwing fire-brands among them. New York had nine delegates, five of whom seemed determined to oppose all compromise, but that the other four were disposed to bring about an adjustment. That the four Union delegates dared the other five to submit the matter to the people of New York, and they would be voted down by 100,000 majority. When the final voting came on, the vote of New York was not cast either way, as one of the no-compromise delegates, for some cause or other, was not present, which made a tie, and so the vote of the State was not cast.

"Rhode Island, said the Governor, stood by the South from the beginning. So did New Jersey. The delegates from Ohio, headed by Thomas Ewing, were very conservative and did all they could to bring about an adjustment. That the vote of North Carolina was cast against the propositions as passed, but that Mr. Ruffin and himself voted for them. The Governor thinks that the South should be satisfied with the plan as adopted, and that it is everything we had any reason to hope for. He did not think that the present Congress, as the time was so short, and as so much bad feeling had been gotten up, would be able to carry the plan through. The Governor seemed quite sanguine that time would bring all things right, but that if nothing could be done, that the border states, together with the border free states, would form a new Constitution for themselves, and take possession of the United States. That they would never go out of the Union, but would stay in the Union, hold to the capitol and Mount Vernon, and let the New England states slough off. He said a great deal more, but . . . we will add no more."

The Commissioners made their report and were discharged. On March 5, 1861, the next day after President Lincoln's inauguration, Governor Morehead wrote Chief Justice Ruffin as follows: "I was at Raleigh yesterday and found our friends Badger and Moore [B. F.], Ryan and others well pleased with our resolutions. They said the secessionists were trying to make dissatisfaction with the 1st Section—professing not to be able to understand it— and particularly they seemed not to understand—according to the course of the common law.'——They all put the proper construction on it—but to put that quibble to rest——we came to the conclusion that it would be as well for someone to write you a letter on the subject, and get your reply and publish it.——I drop you this line, that you may have the subject under consideration, and the reply ready and if no application is made for an explanation I would respectfully suggest that you prepare such an article for publication with or without your name as you prefer. Our resolutions give general satisfaction, but I understand our colleagues repre-

sent them as a rickety affair, and Brother Davis, I am informed, made a strong speech against them at Wilmington
which was rapturously received by not unwilling ears.——I
am exceedingly anxious to see the inaugural. I fear its
effect very much. Chase is in the Cabinet, it is said, if so
there is danger. Nothing certain in Raleigh when I left
last evening, but it was said that Seward, Bates, Blair,
Wells, Chase, Cameron and Montgomery [Blair] are the
Cabinet. If so, the South refused seats in it I expect;
and it was said the inaugural would demand the return
of all property seized, the collection of duties, etc., etc.
If so, I fear all hope is gone——but let us keep cool and
all may come right yet. P. S.—I go to Charlotte
by the 2 o'clock train today, where I may get mobbed,
but I shall risk it; and if I am, you must come up
and share the Honors with me. Charlotte is a young
Charleston."[1]

---

[1] *The Papers of Thomas Ruffin,* Vol. 3, p. 137. Long dashes indicate
paragraphs.

XIX

In
The Confederate Provisional Congress
Richmond

July, 1861—February, 1862

While Governor Morehead was still in Washington on the last day of February, 1861, North Carolina voted on whether to call a Convention. His own county, Guilford, had gone 2771 to 113 against it; and the three delegates elected were all Union men, one being the Governor's brother. No other county approached it except Randolph, the next south of it, with 2466 to 45. Not counting Davie, the returns of which were not in, thirty-five counties were against a Convention and forty-eight for it, with a somewhat similar territory to that of the recent election, but with some changes. The matter was not settled by counties, however, but by votes, and while 48 counties voted 46,409 *for* a Convention, 35 counties were able to get what they wanted, namely, no convention by 46,603 votes, some of which were from all counties. The smallest number of votes *against,* in any one county, was 17 in Edgecombe; while the smallest *for* it, in any one county, was 34 in Yadkin. This meant that, by the small margin of but 194, with Davie not counted, the State of North Carolina saw no cause to consider a danger to the Union—at that time, February 28, 1861. Those counties, however, that were overwhelmingly for action were Buncombe, Cleveland, Duplin, Edgecombe, Franklin, Gaston, Halifax, Mecklenburg, Nash, New Hanover, Wayne, Warren, Rutherford, Person, Onslow, Lincoln, Jones, Jackson, Hyde, Granville, and a few others —chiefly the Charlotte region intimately associated with South Carolina, as also the Wilmington region, with some of the Roanoke valley.

During this month of March, 1861, the Guilford Grays

celebrated their first anniversary and that of the eighty-fifth
of the Battle of Guilford Court House, and they were joined
by the Orange Guards, the Danville Grays, and the Rowan
Rifle Guards, which was a notable affair and a significant
one, for these were from "No Convention" counties.   Still
no one knew what a day would bring forth, and the secessionist elements were even then having a convention at
Goldsboro, while in almost every county either Unionists
or Disunionists were holding meetings.   The Union delegates elected, in case a convention was called, were so much
in the majority, that the *Warrenton News* thought that, if
the vote had been plainly on "Secession" or "No Secession,"
it would have been still more overwhelmingly for the latter.
And while the Confederation was grownig, a songster in the
Fayetteville Observer was carrolling "Dixie" with—

> "I'm glad I'm not in de land ob cotton;
> Old times dar, am all forgotten;
>   Let us stay! Let us stay in North Caroline;
> In Carolina I was born,
> The land of Backer, Pine and Corn;
>   Let us stay! Let us stay in North Caroline—
> We'll cling to North Callina—Hooray! Hooray!
>   Old Rip's the land on which we'll stand,
>   To live and die like freemen:
>   Away! Away! we'll live and die like freemen,
>   Away! Away! we'll live and die like freemen.

> "That glorious spunk is still alive,
> That bore us out in seventy-five;
>   Let us stay! Let us stay in North Caroline;
> The Cotton boasters still may shout,
> Their mammy's do not know they are out.
>   Let us stay! Let us stay in North Caroline—
> We'll cling to North Callina—Hooray! Hooray!
>   Old Rip's the land, &c.

> "Our gallant sons will fight and bleed,
> We'll beard 'Old Abe,' we won't secede;
>   Let us stay! Let us stay in North Caroline.
> The coward flies when danger's near,
> But call the roll you'll find us 'here.'
>   Let us stay! Let us stay in North Caroline—
> We'll cling to North Callina—Hooray! Hooray!
>   Old Rip's the land, &c.

"We'll force Old Abram to do right,
By standing firm, but not by flight,
  Let us stay! Let us stay in North Caroline.
But when the die is cast—our fate,
Our destiny is with our State.
  We will stay! We will stay in North Caroline—
  We'll cling to North Callina—Hooray! Hooray!
    Old Rip's the land on which we'll stand,
    To live and die like freemen!
    Hooray! Hooray! Hooray for Rip Van Winkle!
    Hooray! Hooray! Hooray for Rip Van Winkle!"

But the Goldsboro Convention meant business and began to organize a "Southern Rights Party" with a view to another vote on a Convention. This was met by efforts to organize a "Union Party," starting in Raleigh under the chairmanship of B. F. Moore, Esq. A South Carolina paper said at this time: "Terrapin like, Virginia, Kentucky and Missouri are beginning to *poke* out their heads and legs preparatory to *crawling,* under the fire laid upon their backs by the Lincoln Administration. But North Carolina and Tennessee, under a stream of molten lava pouring upon them, would not even *shake* their *tails.*" It thought they would better remain a barrier between North and South, whereupon the *Patriot* editor reminded them that their great boasting was due to the fact that the states that wouldn't "shake their tails" were protecting them! On April 18, 1861, however, the *Greensboro Patriot* said: "It is with deep regret and most painful anticipation of the future, that we announce to our readers that the war has commenced; that the first gun has been fired and that Fort Sumter, instead of being evacuated, as should have been done, has been violently seized upon, and that the flag of the Confederate States, now floats above its walls. . . . Events of the most startling character, so crowd upon each other, that the mind becomes bewildered and confused, no time being afforded for reflection. But yesterday, all was quiet, peace and happiness; today, terror, excitement and confusion rules the hour. The Stars and Stripes, the Flag which we have been taught to reverence, and which we all so much love, which has commanded the respect of the civilized world, and beneath whose ample folds, we have, for three-quarters of a century, found safety and protection, has been dishonored, and that, too, by the hands of those, who of all others, should have been the first to defend it." He then shows that the fact that seven states had seceded, and even formed a government, without molestation of the United States had led them to believe that Uncle Sam would let his erring Cotton States children go, and the Southern boundary of the nation would be the south lines of North Carolina and Tennessee. He plainly expressed the doctrines of James Madison that, while not allowing the right of secession, except as revolution, that the constitution gave no power of coercion. In the same issue, however, he prints President Lincoln's call for 75,000 men "to suppress said combinations, and cause the laws to be duly executed," which, as it is observed, said nothing about secession, but only enforcement of laws. The *Patriot,* however, seems unable to conceive of either side actually invading the other, as he had been unable to conceive of the fall of Sumter; and he announced his determination to at once begin issuing a campaign paper to be called *"The Stars and Stripes!"* As this paper was looked upon as one of the first two or three leading Unionist papers of the State and as generally expressing the views of Governor Morehead, though not his organ, it may be viewed as the expression of himself and his constituency. In the same issue also he printed Secretary of War Cameron's telegraphic call upon Governor Ellis at Raleigh for two regiments, and the latter's very natural reply that he regarded "the levy of troops made by the Administration, for the purpose of subjugating the States of the South, as in violation of the Constitution, and as a gross usurpation of power." *"You can get no troops from North Carolina,"* he underscored, as James Madison had given him interpretation to do. Even then the Editor of *The Patriot* called upon the people to be calm, for "like the mistletoe on the oak," "in a short time the mistletoe will be blown away," but "a million and a half of strong Union men" "in the north, who love the Union," "will do us justice." "Wait." Like Madison, too, he said: "Woe to

the ambition that would meditate the destruction of either"
[Constitution or Union]. On April 25th, however, he was
ready to say: "We would merely suggest the idea, that
instead of calling a Convention would it not be as well, for
the Legislature, just simply to declare the State of North
Carolina in a state of revolution; and then provide all the
necessary measures for carrying on the war, vigorously co-
operating with our Southern brethren in resisting every attempt of the tyrant Lincoln to subdue the South." He went
still further, and outlined reconstruction after victory,
namely, that one condition of the treaty should be that
"North Carolina is a free and independent sovereign State"
and then determine whether she wishes to reconstruct the
Union or join the Confederacy.

On April 17th Virginia, in secret action, seceded, and
on the same day, Governor Ellis of North Carolina, drew
his call for a special meeting of the Assembly for May 1,
1861; but Virginia did not announce her action until April
24th and Ellis' proclamation was published in the *Patriot*
of April 25th. He also called upon the militia and among
those that responded were the Guilford Grays and Minute
Men under Captain W. S. Hill. The arsenal at Fayetteville was captured by a thousand volunteers. "On Tuesday"
[23d April] said the *Patriot,* "our streets were filled with
an excited crowd. They were addressed by Mr. J. W.
Thomas of Davidson, Governor Morehead, Hon. R. C. Pur-
year, Hon. J. A. Gilmer, Ralph Gorrell, Esq., Samuel P.
Hill, J. R. McLean, R. P. Dick, Thomas Settle and perhaps
others. The speeches of these gentlemen all breathed the
true spirit of resistance to tyrants, and that the time had
come for North Carolina to make common cause with her
brethren of the South in driving back the Abolition horde.
North Carolina may rest assured that the people of Guilford
are all right." The Guilford Grays, under Capt. John Sloan,
were at Fort Macon on duty. Two other companies were
organizing; and the *Patriot* announced its abandonment
of its campaign paper—*The Stars and Stripes.* A company
of Home Guards, also, under Capt. Jos. A. Houston, was
organized and the ladies were forming organizations to pro-

vide supplies and hospital appurtenances. And while such preparations were making, Edgeworth Seminary announcements were appearing as usual, telling of twenty years of successful work and a growth to a faculty of seven gentlemen and four ladies. It is a curious fact that when the Guilford Grays started for Goldsboro on the first call, both Senator Gilmer and Judge Dick—Whig and Democrat—and Richard Sterling, as well, said to them substantially: "Go! Defend your State! Carry with you the Stars and Stripes, and fight under that banner! Repel any armed force that puts foot on North Carolina soil—whether it come from South Carolina, Virginia or Yankeedom!" And they went with three days' rations, expecting soon to return.[1]

The special session of the Assembly gathered at Raleigh on May 1, 1861, as called, and at once ordered another vote on Convention for May 17th, and as there was no doubt as to need for it, it was to meet on the 20th. The Governor was directed to immediately prepare 20,000 volunteers for a year, and 10,000 State troops for the war, with a $5,000,000 defense fund. In all this Ex-Governor Morehead was as active a leader on committees, military and others, as he had been on internal improvement, railways, education or anything else. The Assembly was completely unified for defense and, as the choice of fighting Abolitionists or Slaveholders, one or the other, was forced upon them they were already a unit as to which must be done. On the 8th, Governor Morehead secured passage of a bill for creation of a Military Board of three to advise with the Executive. Great dispatch was the order of the day and the session adjourned on May 13, 1861, to June 25th.

The Convention met at Raleigh on the 20th of May and on the 21st the members signed the Ordinance of Secession and two days later ratified the "Constitution of the Confederate States of America." Governor Morehead being a member of the State Senate was not a member of the Convention. On the 27th of May, 1861, President Davis Proclaimed North Carolina a part of the Confederacy. Chief

---

[1] A. M. Scales in *Greensboro Daily News*, 20th Sept., 1908.

Justice Ruffin was probably the ablest leader of this Convention and before it adjourned on the 28th he aided in electing among the eight district delegates to the Confederate Congress, his companion in Peace Conference activities at Washington, State Senator John Motley Morehead, who at once resigned his state post, and prepared to go to the Confederate capital.

The "Provisional Congress of The Confederate States of America," as it was called technically, held its first session at its temporary capital, Montgomery, Alabama, from February 4 to March 16, 1861. The second session, due to the Fort Sumter developments, was called to meet there also on April 29th and did not adjourn until May 21, 1861; so that it was in recess, on the 27th, that President Davis proclaimed North Carolina's entry into the Confederacy, and Governor Morehead was elected to this body. Meanwhile, during June, the preparations for a clash of arms about the national capital, led to the third session of the Confederate Congress being called to meet at Richmond on July 20, 1861, and the Virginia capital becoming the Confederate capital.

Therefore, when, on July 20th, the delegates assembled in the state capital, just the day before the battle of Bull Run, the first business was the presentation of the Virginia and North Carolina delegates, the latter of whom were announced by Mr. Toombs of Georgia and among them being Governor John Motley Morehead of Greensboro. The message of President Davis, to which Congressman Morehead listened, drew emphatic attention to President Lincoln's position that the states had no other power "than that reserved to them in the Union by the Constitution, *no one of them having ever been a State outside of the Union.*"[1] This was on Saturday. The following day President Davis witnessed the defeat of the national forces at Bull Run and announced the results to the Congress at Richmond. Chief Justice Ruffin did not arrive until the 25th and it was the 26th before any record of Governor Morehead is had,

---

[1] This of course excepted Texas, which was a "State," or, more properly, a "nation" wholly independent of all other bodies.

CONFEDERATE CAPITOL, RICHMOND
From a five-dollar bill of 1864

namely, a nay vote in opposition to secret sessions, in which the majority of his delegates joined him, but without success. On August 2nd a similar phenomena occurred in connection with features of a general embargo act, but with success attending his nay. Likewise on August 7th, on a vote to adjourn on the 19th to meet in November, he voted nay, in a minority of his own state, but in vain; but on another vote on adjournment on August 8th, he and Mr. Ruffin voted nay, in minority of their own state, but were successful in preventing adjournment.[1]

The Congress had been organized by the aggressive leaders of the secession before the Virginia and North Carolina members had appeared, so that up to this date there is no evidence of their membership of committees. On this very day, August 8, 1861, Governor Morehead wrote Chief Justice Ruffin from Richmond: "I have had two short conversations with the President on the subject of seeing our troops (for it seems difficult to get a good sitting with the President so as to have a *consultation* with him). If I understood him correctly, he is now willing to receive volunteers for any period of time, provided we will arm and equip them—as he says they find great difficulty to do it as fast as they tender their services. . . .

"Since the great fight and victory at Manassas I think the Government has come to the conclusion, that it is not indispensable to victory, that the troops should be regulars—on the contrary it may sometimes turn out that it is better they are not and this perhaps happened at Manassas. For the opinion prevails with many, and even the enemy seemed so to have concluded from the dispatches in the earlier part of the day, that we, once or twice, had fairly lost the battle, according to the usual rules of *regular* fighting—but our *green volunteer troops* were not up to their regular rules and when regulars might have concluded that they were fairly whipped and therefore ought to yield the day—the volunteers knew nothing about it—and only concluded when hard pressed and driven back that it was only marching and

---

[1] Thomas Ruffin of Goldsboro is here referred to, a distant relation of the Chief Justice it is said.

counter marching—and constituted nothing more than the regular emergencies of a battle field, and as they had gone in for whipping the enemy—*it had to be done*. And it was gloriously done, by every man making himself a hero and fighting with a *valor* never surpassed anywhere. Every hero fought as if the Salvation of the Republic depended upon the vigor of his own right arm, and he determined to know nothing but *victory or death.*" After describing the confusion on the battlefield, "without waiting to charge or fire by platoons, companies or regiments," "*each one pitched into his man hand to hand*" and the enemy concluded they were fighting "Devils not men" hence the "unprecedented panic." "Regulars could do no more." "The war spirit possesses the whole land, and Congress [Confederate, of course], in secret session all the time it transacts business, will respond to the public sentiment—this is perhaps as much as I ought to say *at this time.*" He says regiments are flocking in the direction of Alexandria and Arlington, intimating an attack on Washington with artillery that will "satisfy all Black Republicans that they have no business south of Mason and Dixon's line, in other words—Yankeeism will not flourish in the land of 'Dixie'." "I regret exceedingly you are not with us in this Congress."

Much time during August was given to financial questions and on August 10th, Governor Morehead was made the North Carolina representative on the Committee "To Secure The Financial And Commercial Independence of The Confederate States." On the surface of affairs he apparently took but little initiative either in preparing bills or in any recorded discussons, although he supported President Davis in his railroad proposition to which attention may presently be turned. He was absent during the last days of the session, which closed on August 31st.

President Davis recalled them on September 3rd, however, because of an oversight by which an appointment bill had not reached him for signature. There were few in attendance and they did what was necessary and adjourned the same day. Governor Morehead was not present. They adjourned to November 18, 1861.

The November session brought a recommendation from President Davis of personal interest to Governor Morehead, although he was not there on the 19th to hear it—did not arrive, indeed, until the 20th, so far as the record indicates. This was President Davis' calling attention to the fact that the Confederacy had but two through transportation lines north and south, one along the seaboard and one in western Virginia to New Orleans; but that a third was needed and "might be secured by completing a link of about forty miles between Danville, in Virginia, and Greensborough in North Carolina. The construction of this comparatively short line would give us a through route from north to south in the interior of the Confederate States, and give us access to a population and to military resources from which we are now in great measure debarred. We should increase greatly the safety and capacity of our means for transporting men and military supplies. If the construction of this road should, in the judgment of Congress, as it is in mine, be indispensable for the most successful prosecution of the war, the action of the government will not be restrained by the constitutional objection which would attach to a work for commercial purposes, and attention is invited to the practicability of securing its early completion by giving the needful aid to the company organized for its construction."

This message was read on Tuesday, and on the following Saturday, the 23rd, Governor Morehead, who was still in Greensboro, and was to leave for Richmond the next day, wrote Judge Ruffin that he had received an offer from a well-known South Carolina legislator that if he or any other reliable man would take hold of the Danville link that the Sea Island planters would furnish the slaves to do the grading in quick time and glad to do it because of the safety of the slaves and would make a very low figure. The Governor writes, however, of these facts, namely: *Three Charters* cover the Danville project—the Coal Fields line from the Virginia line to some six or eight miles below Leaksville, the Brodnax charter from Leaksville to Germanton, and the Greensboro-Leaksville charter. "This is not right," says Governor Morehead's letter. "It should be

one corporation throughout or at least there should be but
one change and that should be at Danville or Leaksville—
it will be the same if the Danville road is extended to Leaksville (ignoring the intermediate charter) or the Greensboro
and Leaksville road is extended to Danville. Now had we
not better have our charter so modified as to effect this
object. The Convention of both States are in session and
can give the necessary charter."

He then argues the question of route. Referring to the
large stream of travel between north and south, he thought
"that day is gone—I confidently believe *never to return.*"
So he now considers it solely from a military view, suggesting the Leaksvilile route because of the coal and iron on Deep
and Dan rivers. He confidently assumes the permanence
of "Our Southern Republic." He also considers that a
road from Leaksville and Greensboro to Lynchburg, Va., is
a military necessity. Judge Ruffin replies with suggestions, which he takes up in a letter of December 4, 1861,
from Richmond.[1] President Lincoln's suggestion of a military railroad through Cumberland Gap he thinks has western
North Carolina in view. Again he suggests a line through
Leaksville, but thinks it ought to run as direct from Greensboro to Danville as military necessity will allow. An arm
may go to the coal and iron fields, which might be a part
of the Virginia-Tennessee line. Judge Ruffin made an effort, but it was finally put up to the Confederate Congress
which passed it on February 8, 1862, leaving it optional
with the President whether to connect with the North Carolina Central or not. It was now desired that the North
Carolina Convention pass a bill, which it did do by the
10th. The optional feature is the only outward evidence
of the old "connection" fight which was carried up by both
sides to the Confederate Congress, but, as the result indi-

---

[1] In this letter he answers Judge Ruffin's desire that he come on to Raleigh
and aid by saying: "I should be willing to lend my aid to make the connection
between the N. C. and Danville roads, but I do not think my presence in
Raleigh would lend any aid to effect the object. My efforts to effect that object
have been so often thwarted by the Eastern Roads and the N. C. Road itself,
that my presence would arouse the old hostility notwithstanding the pressing
urgency of the measure; which I think is greatly increased by reading the
message of Lincoln—recommending a Military Road for Kentucky through
Cumberland Gap. He evidently has his eye on Western N. C."—*Ruffin Papers,*
Hamilton, Vol. III, p. 200.

cates, the "link" was bound to come and did come thus as a military measure. President Davis had again urged it on December 17th, and a considerable fight had been made over it on January 30, 1862, and was continued again on February 6th, and on the 7th was passed 9 to 3 (states), only Alabama, Florida and Georgia voting against it, and North Carolina being divided. It therefore took the vote of the Southern Confederacy to decide Governor Morehead's great question of the Greensboro-Danville link, on which North Carolina was so bitterly divided, and President Davis was authorized to build it as a military measure. It was not done, however, without a systematic protest, headed by Mr. Toombs of Georgia, on Constitutional grounds; but on February 10, 1862, President Davis announced that he had signed the bill and that closed the matter so far as the Confederate Congress was concerned. So was it to be as far as North Carolina was concerned, for she passed a like bill on the same day!

Governor Morehead wrote, on the day President Davis signed the bill to Judge Ruffin whose letter he had just received containing "the joyous intelligence of the passage of the Railroad Charter." "On the same day," writes the Governor in reply, "we passed the bill for the same purpose appropriating $1,000,000 to be expended in such a way as the President may direct, which is now a law, so the Greensboro and Danville connection is now a fixed fact and I congratulate you on it; for when finished it will take you across to go to Dan and see how the crop is growing, and if needs be—go home the same way. Don't you think I may congratulate myself, too?

"Motion to re-consider was disposed of today, and the law was approved by the President, and the thing is safe. I will see the President in a day or two and get his views as to the manner in which the Confederate State may be connected with the enterprise.

.   .   .   .

"Our city is in gloom—the defeat at Roanoke Island is a calamity; the Albemarle and Roanoke are exposed, and I should not be surprised any day to hear the enemy have Weldon.

"They have the Tennessee River open to Florence [Muscle Shoals]—can take possession of the Railroads leading to Memphis, and can pour by steamers any amount of men into Florence, nearly the heart of Alabama, take possession of all roads to Mobile and New Orleans, and cut off Memphis; reach the Mississippi below there and go toward New Orleans, leaving the defenses above at Columbus, etc., useless. I do not like the indications—and our nation was as one—and, too, the field—we are in danger. Stirring times may be expected before the Inauguration."

A week later the Provisional Confederate Congress ceased to exist, on the 17th, when it adjourned; and on the 18th the new regular government with Senate and House was inaugurated at Richmond—and Governor Morehead was in neither body. His influence had secured the Confederacy the third and best trunk line, the last link in what would have been a great Piedmont line from Maine to the mouth of the Mississippi; and it was to prove the last piece of railroad to aid President Davis and the Confederate executive in escaping from the fall of Richmond.

XX

The Closing Years

OF

"The Father of Modern North Carolina"

1862–1866

When Governor, or Congressman, Morehead reached Greensboro from Richmond late in February, 1862, he had finished his public career, although he was no doubt not yet aware of it, and was in his sixty-sixth year. His eldest daughter, as has been noted, was married; his second daughter was the wife of Waightstill W. Avery; his third was Mrs. Col. Peter G. Evans of the 63rd North Carolina, whose husband's death was to occur within almost a year; his first son, Col. John Lindsay Morehead was on the staff of the War-Governor Vance; his fourth daughter, since 1858, had been Mrs. Julius A. Gray, whose husband was a Greensboro banker, later to be a railroad president like his father-in-law; Governor Morehead's second son, Col. James Turner Morehead was Adjutant with Col. Evans' 63rd Cavalry, destined to be desperately wounded at the same time his brother-in-law, head of his regiment, was killed; while the Governor's youngest son and child, Eugene Lindsay Morehead, was then nearly ready to enter the University— destined to serve as a Lieutenant, later in the war, in defending the ocean front of the state at Wilmington and Fort Fisher.[1]

---

[1] It should be noted that most of Governor Morehead's sons and also sons-in-law devoted themselves to development of the lines in which he had been interested. For example (not to mention more, and referring the reader to *The Morehead Family of North Carolina and Virginia* by Major John Motley Morehead of New York), his son, Major James Turner Morehead, was a leader in the political reconstruction of the state in the early '70s; developed manufacturing so much at Spray, as to raise it from a 300 village to above 6000; was the first non-professional leader in geological survey of the

399

The Governor's great project, Morehead City, and his railroad up to Newbern, were in the hands of the enemy, who, in the west, were carrying out the program he predicted. By April, 1862, the Confederate Congress were restive at the probable loss of western Virginia-Tennessee rail outlet to the South and the threatening moves against the coast line, and asked President Davis what was the status of the Danville "link," or, as it was now called, the Piedmont Railroad, the title given it in its North Carolina Convention charter. They became still more anxious in September, when the great McClellan failure in Virginia began to encourage plans to invade Pennsylvania and her coal and iron fields. By November 10, 1862, the Secretary of War was able to announce to the Governor of North Carolina that the Greensboro-Danville link was in progress with 800 hands, and the suggested impressment measures of both whites and negroes and mules and wagons in both states. Labor and iron rails were the great difficulty, but Governor Vance impressed the former and as Charlotte had two railroads that had not yet reached their terminii, the one to Statesville was stripped of its rails so that it was not completed until May, 1864.[1] This work was urged on by the Federal raids from Newbern on the Wilmington & Weldon line on 16th December, 1862, and in July, 1863; although the road was re-secured and repaired. It was all the more needed in the first half of 1863 in the supplies for the great campaign into Pennsylvania that was broken at Gettysburg; and was still more needed in the gradual retreat to and beyond Richmond that was to close the conflict.

It was about five days after the defeat at Gettysburg and the fall of Vicksburg, both on July 4, 1863, that Gover-

---

state, especially in mineralogy; was a leader in creating the Midland Railroad, purchasing the old Western and attempting the Cape Fear and Yadkin Valley Railroad, suffering with others the losses caused by the panic; won world-wide recognition as a practical scientist by his laboratory discovering commercial carbide and showing the power of the electric arc in smelting refractory ores. At his plant acetylene gas was discovered by his son; and it produced most of the chromium of the world, with the result that New York became his headquarters for the rest of his life. Hickory timber was marketed through his spoke and handle factory, and he had a boat line from Madison and Leaksville to Danville to handle his products.

[1] The July 7, 1864, report of the Raleigh & Gaston Railroad says that it had lost half its ordinary receipts since the Danville link was completed.

nor Morehead, sixty-seven years old on that same day, wrote his friend Judge Ruffin: "I have just returned from the discharge of a melancholy but pious duty, the depositing of the body of my venerable, beloved mother beside the body of my honored father in the spot selected thirty-one years ago by herself as her final resting place. When last I saw her some two weeks since, at Major Hobson's in Davie [county] she charged me to see that she was buried by father's side. She expired on Monday morning as calmly as an infant sleeps, in her 92nd year. The lamp of life became extinguished for the want of material to support it."

Just what had happened in eastern North Carolina by this time? In the summer of August, 1861, General Butler's naval forces took the forts at Hatteras Inlet; and early in 1862 General Burnside's naval force, with his aid, captured Roanoke Island. This opened up the way to attack Newbern, then the second largest town in the state, and it fell on March 14, 1862; while they occupied Morehead City, Beaufort, Carolina and Newport, using Newbern as a base. On April 25th, the Federal gun-boats shelled Fort Macon, guarding the Morehead City inlet, into surrender. By this time North Carolina had put about 41,000 equipped men into the Confederate army, and on a new call, twenty-eight more regiments were formed. Then came the head-ship of General Lee and his driving back of McClellan's armies, and the state gave 15,000 more men. This was late in June, 1862. In those awful battles, as Dr. D. H. Hill says: "every fifth Confederate flag floated over North Carolina bayonets; and every fifth man who dropped a gun in death was grieved for in a North Carolina home. Nearly every fourth wounded man who was borne off in a litter or who limped to the wretched hospitals in the rear wore a North Carolina uniform." Fort Fisher, below Wilmington, at this time, was aiding the very successful blockade running at this port. Meanwhile General Lee had sent forces to threaten Washington again to counteract attacks on Richmond, and late in August, 1862, the second battle of Manassas let Lee's forces into Maryland, and the great aggressive campaign into Pennsylvania was begun that, as has been said, ended on July 4, 1863.[1] The Federals and Confederates in eastern North Carolina during this time had contested for the line of the Wilmington & Weldon road, without much change.   But early in 1864 fierce fighting was renewed under new leaders, especially about Plymouth near the mouth of the Roanoke to get control of the Roanoke river, on which was being built an iron-clad, the *Albemarle*, and Plymouth was captured, the Federals giving up Washington, at the head of Pamlico.   General Grant's new leadership in Virginia, however, called off the Confederate forces in east North Carolina to "bottle up Butler" between the James and Appomattox.   In Grant's great concentration upon Richmond and the campaign of Sherman to the sea, General Butler was to prepare the way in December, 1864, by reducing Fort Fisher, as it was proposed to bring Sherman up from the South through eastern North Carolina in the rear of Lee.

Just before this demonstration, the following illuminating picture of the sorrows of war was written to the Confederate commander in eastern North Carolina:

"As I am not posted about the state of affairs about Wilmington," writes Governor Morehead to General Bragg on November 22, 1864, from Greensboro, "I hope I may be excused, if this letter shall be deemed inopportune upon its arrival.

"My wounded son, Turner, the Provost Marshal of this place, is to be married on 6th December.   He is only a few years older than my youngest child, Eugene L. Morehead, now a private in Capt. Barron's [?] Heavy Artillery on Bald Head Island.

"He has been absent since March.   His mother is very feeble, but insists she must see him—and will go to Wil-

---

[1] During the latter part of 1863 the Confederate currency question was the most discussed subject in the Southern press. Governor Morehead took part in it advocating the sharp restriction of the amount in circulation. Some editors ridiculed it, whereupon the Greensboro *Patriot* attacked that editor saying: "Governor Morehead, as an able and far-seeing statesman, is too well known by the people to require any words from us."   It is known that there were people who wanted him to dispose of his Confederate bonds while it was possible to realize on them but he refused, saying it would at once affect the credit of the bonds; and he never did. He took his medicine with the rest in manly fashion.

mington for that purpose if it becomes necesssary. The loss
of two sons-in-law in this war, one son shot through the
head and an invalid for life, three nephews at home on
crutches, besides some half-dozen, who have fallen in the
service, are stubborn facts well calculated to impress her
mind with the fear, that she may never see her youngest
again.

"She requests me to say, that if you think there is any
probability of an attack, shortly, she does not wish her son
to be absent from his post; but if such an attack is not
apprehended, we shall be greatly obliged, that a furlough
be granted to him to attend the marriage, if it be for only a
few days—postponing a more extended furlough to a more
convenient season.

"Should you grant him this favor, we shall be much
obliged, if you will give the proper order that he may arrive
by 3rd Dec. at least, as the wedding is some fifty miles
distant. I make no other application except this, to any
one.

"I would respectfully suggest that confusion is becoming
worse confounded, by the unfortunate mode of doing business, between the railroad lines, by three trans-shipments.
I do not know that I can impress it on your mind more
forcibly than by statement of facts, which I witnessed on
last Sunday morning on my arrival from Goldsboro—
through a night of heavy rains.

"Above, below and around the depot there were hundreds,
if not thousands of sacks of salt, lying on the ground, some
piled up—others lying promiscuously around as they were
tumbled out of the cars—the ditches filled with them, and
the rain-water poured up against these piles of salt. There
were various instances of this and all without any cover.
Other property was equally exposed.

"Through freight to and from Danville will be worth
millions to the company.

"With high regard
"Yr. obt. Svt.
"J. M. Morehead.

"P. S.

"Your letter was duly rec'd and Mrs. M. requests me to thank you sincerely for your kind invitation to her to visit Wilmington, but her health forbids the risk of the journey, which she hopes sometime to make.

"Lest it might be infer'd that Government agents were negligent, it is proper to say the salt and other property referred to above did not belong to the Conf'dt. Govt.

"J. M. M."[1]

Whether his request was granted is not known, but on January 12th, next, 1865, Commodore Porter reduced Fort Fisher. Thereupon, in March, the Johnston forces, falling back before Sherman's army coming up from the South, had a battle at Southwest Creek. Then they fell back to Bentonville, Johnston county, between Goldsboro and Raleigh, and on the 19th had a battle, after which Johnston retired towards Raleigh on the 21st. Meanwhile the great closing battles about Richmond were being fought and on April 10, 1865, General Johnston heard of Lee's surrender and on the 26th, at the house of a Mr. Bennett, near Durham, Generals Sherman and Johnston agreed on terms of surrender.

Meanwhile the Richmond and Danville road was the means of escape by the Confederate Government. Greensboro in 1865 is pictured rather happily—or unhappily, if the conditions are what one has in mind rather than the quality of the pictures, one of which is by Mrs. (Letitia H.) William R. Walker, daughter of Governor Morehead: "General Beauregard and staff came to Greensboro in March, spending several days at Blandwood, Governor Morehead's mansion, speeding on the last of our Confederate troops to join Lee. Suspense was ended on April 9, 1865, when Lee surrendered to Grant at Appomattox. Before leaving Richmond, the officials had the wounded and sick sent on to Greensboro, where every available room was filled, and had been full all winter with the sick and dying. The women, to their honor, be it said, ministered to them daily

---

[1] Braxton Bragg Papers. N. C. Hist. Comm.

with loving care and sympathy.   The Confederate Navy and
the army stores at Richmond were also sent, by the
Manassas Gap Railroad, to Greensboro, under the care of
Commander Lee, a brother of General Lee.   These stores
he kindly distributed to the sick and returning soldiers until
the surrender of Johnston, when he turned over the lot
to the soldiers and citizens to prevent their capture
by the federal troops.

"Commander Lee was a charming genial old man,
whose patient endurance of army rations enlisted the
sympathy of my mother, who begged his company every
day, for dinner, while he was in the city 'to enjoy lettuce
and onions.'   The earth seemed to yield her grateful increase
of turnip greens, lettuce and onions.   These, with hot
cornbread, seemed to be all the starving and uncomplaining
soldiers wanted.

"President and Mrs. Davis remained over one night in
Greensboro in their car, declining the invitation from my
father, 'lest the Federal troops should burn the house that
sheltered him for one night.'[1]   Memminger and his wife
remained over several days with us for a rest, bringing
with them Alexander Stephens of Georgia, so pale and
care-worn, but the price was on his head, and we tearfully
bade him God-speed.   Never can I forget the farewell scene
when the brave and grand Joseph E. Johnston called to say
farewell, with the tears running down his brave cheeks.
Not a word was spoken, but silent prayers went up for his
preservation.   The Salisbury road was filled with the
retreating troops—wretched, half-clad, starving and very
many shoeless.   Eyes wept until the fountain of tears was
exhausted.

"But one fine morning, amid the sounding of bugles and
trumpets and bands of music, the Federals entered Greensboro fully thirty thousand strong, to occcupy the town for
some weeks.   Gen. Cox was in command.   He, Burnside,
Schofield and Kilpatrick, with their staffs, sent word to the

---

[1] This sufficiently answers Secretary of the Confederate Treasury Stephen
B. Mallory, who intimates otherwise in his article in *McClure's Magazine*, Vol.
XVI, p. 107.

Mayor that they would occupy the largest house in town that night, and until their quarters were established. In charge of Major Howlett, they came to Blandwood, which already sheltered three families and several sick soldiers. My father met them courteously and received them as guests, a fact which General Cox appreciated, and after placing his tent in the rear of Judge Dick's house, he rode up every afternoon to consult with Hon. J. A. Gilmer and my father on the conditions of the country. He was a most courteous and elegant man, and, in delicate ways, displayed his sympathy with us; no triumph of the conqueror in tone of voice and manner; spoke tenderly of the misfortunes of war, and in spite of ourselves, won our heart's confidence.

"Very soon a note was received from the General announcing the arrival of Mrs. Cox and the hope was expressed that 'Mrs. Gilmer and Mrs. Walker would do him the honor to call upon his wife.' Our superior officers ordered a compliance with his wishes, but what to wear was the perplexing question. An old silk, dating back five years in style, came from the recesses of my trunk, the 'skyscraper' was the head gear, shoes and gloves that had run the blockade and been purchased at enormous figures. Thus equipped we called upon the lady from Cincinnati! She received us in Mrs. Dick's parlor, in a yellow morning wrapper, was simple in manner, dignified, bordering on stiffness, in contrast with the genial manners of her husband. As you may imagine, the discourse was on very general topics—the skies, the climate, etc., of North Carolina—never an allusion to the events of the last four years!

"A grand review of all the troops was to be held on the next Saturday, and a pavilion was built in the center of the town—the upper story to be occupied by the Federal ladies. By 9 o'clock a four-horse ambulance with out-riders was sent with a note from General Cox again 'begging the honor of Mrs. Gilmer's and Mrs. Walker's company with Mrs. Cox to witness the review.'

"Mrs. Gilmer flatly told her husband that she refused to add one more spectator to the pageant, for it was an enemy's bullet, which had maimed her only son for life. Vio-

lent, decisive words and very ugly ones, too, were spoken
by the other lady, but a peremptory order was given and
with bitter tears, accompanied by one of our soldiers, she
went to the pavilion, to be received so graciously by Mrs.
Cox. Sullen, speechless and vindictive, no eulogy was paid
the magnificent pageant, the gorgeous display of thousands
of new uniforms, glittering sabers and bayonets, and all
flushed with victory and marching to the music of splendid
bands.

"These troops remained several weeks encamped on the
hills around the town, and at sunset each evening, the prac-
ticing of the various bands of music would again open the
floodgates of tears. But, with the morning sun, the avaricious desire for their 'greenbacks' seized the ladies of the
town; pies, chicken and fruit, beaten biscuit, ice-cream
and cake poured into the camps. One company sent me a
message that 'the ice-cream was not rich enough—needed
more eggs.' A few drops of tumeric (often used for yellow
pickle) covered the difficulty and gave satisfaction.

"The reorganization of our domestic life in homes and
farms came up for consideration. Wages were paid to
negroes before the troops left the town, and their behavior
was respectful and creditable. The philanthropic North
sent out agents to purchase lands for homes, churches and
school-houses; thus Warnerville sprang into existence.
White women came as teachers, and a lonely life they led
with their only friends. As the farms were well advanced
with the growing crops the negroes remained and received
wages and gave no trouble. Sorgum was introduced during
the war, while coffee, so-called, of parched rye and sweet
potatoes, refreshed the inner man.

"It was a sweet and heroic service during the war to
wear home-spun cloth, leather shoes and home-knit stock-
ings, but when all was over and patriotism no longer demanded this sacrifice of self and comfort, behold we had no
money with which the ward-robe was to be replenished, no
laws to protect person or property. Egyptian darkness
covered the land for months until the manhood of the South

asserted itself and adjusted the disjointed condition of affairs. . . ."

"This account of the feelings and actions of the people of Greensboro and the troubles they went through shows that it is no wonder they shrink from the unexpected, limelight flash of publicity turned upon them by these innocent Cupids, which, singularly enough, were drawn by Kenyon Cox, a son of General Cox, who occupied Greensboro with Federal troops."[1]

"But it was on March 19, 1865," wrote Mrs. (Rev.) J. Henry Smith of Greensboro, some years ago, "the date of the battle of Bentonville, N. C., that the war in its stern and startling reality came to our very doors. It was one of the fiercest of the war and the last great battle of the Confederacy, in which Johnston defeated Sherman's forces and sent them retreating through the streets of Goldsboro, while he attempted to join Lee in Virginia.

"On that memorable night, without warning or preparation, the wounded were brought to Greensboro in such numbers as to fill the churches, court house and every available space in the town." Then she describes the women's work with the sick and dying and how, like a thunder-bolt out of a clear sky, came the news of Lee's surrender. "The Confederate soldiers," said she, "were all transferred to Edgeworth Seminary, and our occupation was gone," although they were allowed to visit them. She also pays tribute to General Cox, "a Christian gentleman and Presbyterian elder."

Still another picturesque account appeared in the *Greensboro Patriot* of March 23, 1866: "During these eventful years, Greensboro was a central railroad thoroughfare of great importance to the Confederacy. Huge trains of cars swept through almost hourly, bearing their great loads from the Southern States and mountain regions to the great consumer and fighter—the Army of Northern Vir-

---

[1] The magazine and article referred to was *McClure's*, in which Ex-Secretary of the Confederate Navy, Stephen B. Mallory, had an artcle on "Last Days of the Confederate Government." The last paragraph, above, is from an article in the *New York Tribune*, by Carrie Elizabeth Herrell, of High Point, N. C., defending Greensboro and giving Mrs. Walker's article in proof.

ginia." Then he describes the great final military movement. "Our gallant young Governor [Vance] remained at
the capital until Sherman's advance was entering the limits
of the city, when, mounting his horse, he slowly rode westward, and, arriving at Greensboro, made it the temporary
capital of the State." Beauregard came up to meet the
forces of Stoneman. "As April, 1865, dawned upon the
world, Greensboro was no longer the beautiful, quiet, delightful place of yore." He then describes the confusion
and how Stoneman was diverted from Greensboro by a
telegraph operator's fictitious answer to his inquiries by telegraph; but how soldier mobs, in the disorganization, fought
over the supplies, and a mob of old women from the surrounding country tried it, but in vain. Then he tells how
Lee's soldiers began to drift in and how finally "The Confederate Government" arrived in "a leaky old car" that stood on
the switch, and how President Davis declined several invitations to make his home in some residence; how there was to
be seen on the streets "D. H. Hill, the veteran general, with
his strange face—and Stuart and S. D. Lee and Cheatham
and Walthall, and Stephenson and Loring and Butler of the
Cavalry, and Iverson, who captured Stoneman in Georgia,
and Lomax of the Virginia Cavalry, and Beauregard looking like a fox and the old 'Doctor of Strategy' Joe Johnston
and Admiral Semmes. A host of heroes!" He then describes meeting Secretary of War John C. Breckenridge,
whom he thought, as a specimen of manhood, "had not his
superior living." He tells of the money train and how it became stolen but partly recovered and used to buy forage for
Johnston's men. How President Davis and General Breckenridge on horseback and the rest in ambulances left toward
Salisbury, as the railroad had been torn up by Stoneman.[1]
Gen. Johnston signed the articles of surrender to Sherman in
Mr. Ralph Gorrell's yard in Greensboro under the ancient
oaks. The Federal commander, General Hartsuff and his

---

[1] In Correspondence of Jonathan Worth, Vol. I, p. 381, it says Govs.
Graham and Swain, as Commissioners of Gov. Vance, went to meet Sherman
before Raleigh was reached in order to get good treatment for the capital; but
that President Davis, then at Greensboro, ordered their arrest, but they were
prisoners within the enemy lines before Davis' order reached Hampton. They
got back, and Johnston evaded arresting them, and Davis left for the west.

staff, were the first to enter Greensboro to parole the Confederates. This interesting sketch, in closing, says: "We fought a brave fight—we were conquered—we submit."[1]

By December, 1865, the people had elected Jonathan Worth of Guilford county Governor against Editor W. W. Holden of the Raleigh *Standard,* who had been provisional governor. In his efforts at reorganization in the spring following, he writes Governor Morehead a confidential letter on April 25, 1866: "The appointment of Directors on our [Rail] Roads is my most important duty and is most embarrassing to me because of want of information. . . . I am sure there were some very good Old Union Democrats and Whigs who did not vote for me. I think it would be wrong and impolitic to seem to proscribe them. The ultra war men, in view of their own and the State's interests, had better remain in the background for the present. I may be justified in appointing a very few of them, in such counties as Warren and Franklin."

He mentions four men for two roads and adds: "What say you to these?" But for the Atlantic & North Carolina from Morehead City he says: "You ought to be one. Would you prefer the appointment from the state or the stockholders? I would like to have a full conference with you. I shall take no action until June." On May 2nd, he writes another correspondent regarding this line's presidency and shows that the office hangs between Newbern and Morehead City interests——. "Morehead City and Governor Morehead will insist that we will sacrifice the interests of the State to party and Newbern, if we reappoint ——." For Governor Morehead and the other friends of this road were at this time urging consolidation of it with the North Carolina Central Railroad. This latter railroad, at this time, about June 1st, had built in its own shops at Greensboro a handsome engine and named it "The Governor Morehead" —"as handsome as any we ever saw," said the editor of *The*

---

[1] "During the war I was with Sherman," said a man named James Burson, in an interview in a Texas paper some years since, "and I was a guard in front of Governor Morehead's house—yes, sir, and I walked up and down in front of that house for three weeks guarding and protecting them."—From a clipping in possession of Mrs. W. K. Walker of Spray, N. C.

Patriot. A letter from Josiah Turner, Jr., to Governor Worth on June 20, 1866, said Governor Morehead would certainly be a stock-holder director. On June 19th, Governor Worth says Governor Morehead and party, on a special train, will examine the North Carolina Central to Goldsboro on the 26th, and go to Newbern and Beaufort on the 27th, to be at the annual meeting of the Atlantic road at the latter place on the 28th.

And now comes, about two weeks after this Beaufort meeting, what is probably John Motley Morehead's last public effort. A bill had been introduced in the Senate of North Carolina to consolidate the Atlantic, the Central and the Western railroads, which were essentially one, as it was. On July 17, 1866, Governor Morehead wrote an appeal to the stockholders of the "Central" to support this movement: Among other things, he said: "Here let us pause and take a survey of what has been done in *seven* years toward this great work. From Beaufort harbor to Goldsboro the Atlantic and North Carolina Railroad Company have built ninety-six miles. From Goldsboro to Charlotte you (the North Carolina Railroad) have built two hundred and twenty-three miles. From Salisbury to within four miles of Morganton the Western North Carolina Railroad has built seventy-six miles . . . making in all three hundred and ninety-five miles, from which deduct forty-three miles from Salisbury to Charlotte, and we have actually built this great line three hundred and fifty-two miles in one continuous line. Think of it! Seven years! In the lifetime of a State or nation seven years is but as a moment in its existence. In the great day of a nation's improvements seven years would not be the sun-rise of that day. We have done this great work in the twilight of our great day of internal improvement—a day which dawned so beautifully upon us, but which became enveloped in that gloom which shrouds the nation in mourning. But let us not despair. *The day which dawned so beautifully upon us will yet reach its meridian splendor.* Then let us be up and doing . . . and then the hopes, the dreams of the great and good Caldwell and Gaston will be realized

. . . You have the honor of being the pioneers in this great work executed in sections. Do yourselves now the honor to consolidate the whole and complete the original design. You, the most powerful and most independent of the three corporations, can, with much grace, propose to your sister corporations consolidations upon terms of justice and equity manifesting selfishness in naught but your name. Yield not that. The new consolidated corporation should be still 'The North Carolina Railroad Company.' This will be a corporation worthy of you, of your State, and of the great destinies that await it." "What this destiny was," writes R. D. W. Connor in 1912, "no man had foreseen so clearly as he. The traveller of 1912 along the line of the North Carolina Railroad sees the fulfillment of Morehead's dreams of 1850." Then, the same writer describes the wealth of development of modern North Carolina and adds: "The foundation on which all this prosperity and progress rests is the work done by John M. Morehead or inspired by him." [1]

Within but little over a month from the day Governor Morehead penned that letter on consolidation of the east and west rail lines, namely, on August 27, 1866, this great-hearted constructor of a commonwealth was dead—but, as has been seen, dead only in body. Taken with liver trouble, in which that organ rapidly ceased to function, he was removed to Rockbridge Alum Springs, Virginia, in the mountains northwest of Lexington. [2] Here distinguished men visited him, amongst them Mr. William Southerlin of Danville; and they found his mind clear and vigorously occupied with his great plans to such a degree that they were astonished. "My God," said Mr. Southerlin, "is it pos-

---

[1] Address on presentation of a bust of Governor Morehead—one of four in as many niches in the rotunda of the capitol at Raleigh, on December 4, 1912. The bust was presented by two grandsons of the Governor, John Motley Morehead and J. Lindsay Patterson.

[2] In a letter to Chief Justice Thomas Ruffin on Aug. 16, 1866, he says: "I am alive and that is all—as yellow as a pumpkin—jaundiced from top to toe, and feel as if I cared for nothing on earth." He was concerned about the arbitration of his claims to the Atlantic line, which Mr. Gray, in a letter of October 27, 1867, says the Governor said was about $80,000, a large portion of his estate. By August 22, 1866, his last thoughts were for his wife and news of this arbitration in Chief Justice Ruffin's and Governor Graham's hands, which was finally settled favorably to Governor Morehead's estate.—Letters in the *Ruffin Papers*, Vol. IV.

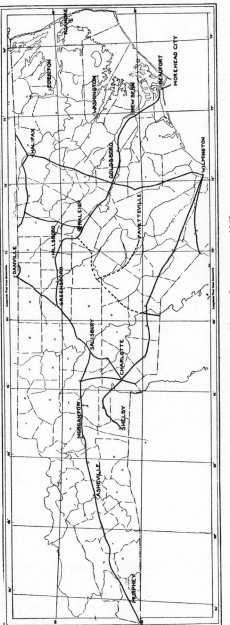

RAILROAD MAP OF NORTH CAROLINA IN 1865
Prepared by the author
(After Hamilton, 1914)

sible he can be in a dying condition! He has laid out fifty
years work for us in this conversation alone."[1]   And this
was in the midst of that awful wreck of the whole South
by civil war, which was yet to be even more awful in that
dark reconstruction period that reminds one, who knows,
of some of the present day horrors of parts of Europe;
but this great spirit's vision saw through that, and far beyond, this great modern state of North Carolina, refusing
to have his soul's eye blinded by the wreckage about him.
He was like those valiant Chicagoans, who began clearing
foundations still burning; and letting their contracts, by
which, like a Phœnix from the flames, rose the great modern
city whose motto is: "I Will."   In this sense, he was, as a
distinguished North Carolina statesman recently said to the
writer, "The Father of Modern North Carolina;" for, after
the period passed, which may well be called the "dark ages"
of the state, the commonwealth picked up the lines where
Governor Morehead has dropped them in 1861, and has
ever since been working at their development, the vast
road development of the present Governor Morrison being
but one part of it.

But in those closing days at Alum Springs, he discussed
religion with his minister friends, and wrote his wife the
comforting message that "*he* trusted in the Saviour, in whom
she trusted."   Then came a day when he was removed from
the room that had a view of the mountains: "Ah, Doctor,"
said he, "I have looked for the last time on that beautiful
mountain."   The end came on August 27, 1866, and people
recalled his farewell address to the North Carolina Railroad
stockholders in Greensboro, at the close of his Presidency
on July 12, 1855: "Living, I have spent five years of the
best portion of my life in the service of the North Carolina
Railroad—dying, my sincerest prayers will be offered up
for its prosperity and its success—dead, I wish to be buried
along side of it in the bosom of my own beloved Carolina!"
His body was laid to rest in the church yard of the First
Presbyterian Church, within sound of the rumblings of the

---

[1] Mrs. Mary Bayard Clarke's *Social Reminiscences* in *In Memoriam,* a
booklet on Governor Morehead.

great traffic of the vast railway systems of today.[1] A monument stands over his grave; and it has been proposed that
at this great junction of modern systems of transportation,
when the original North Carolina Railroad was completed
and the last spike driven, that a beautiful new columned
Union Station shall arise dominated at its front by a dis-
tinguishing statue of President John Motley Morehead, the
whole to be a permanent celebration of his great work. And
yet a greater monument already exists in the development of
modern North Carolina itself, to the inquirer concerning
which one may say, with another: *"Circumspice!"*

A town-meeting, on the 29th and 30th, mourned their
greatest citizen. The Guilford Bar Association said great
and tender things about him, and listened to Thomas Settle,
Jr., recall the chief features of his career and how he had
so often heard it said that "John M. Morehead was the greatest man the State of North Carolina had ever produced."
He also recalled how, in the presence of current disaster
of civil war, Governor Morehead had said to him: "I was
always a great Providence man; I leave all these things to
Providence, well assured that He will bring good out of it
yet"—in which respect he voiced perfectly the sentiments of
his father before him. And the home county of his youth,
Rockingham, on October 30th, at Wentworth, and its Bar
Association on February 26, 1867, listened to a great
address by Hon. John Kerr, who recalled how young Morehead's industry in Dr. Caldwell's school was so great it
impaired in his health at times and caused his father to keep
him at home; and traced his career with great ability.
Referring to the great conflict in the Senate in 1858–9, Mr.
Kerr said: "Just before he rose to answer his assailants,
seeing that he was deeply excited, I stepped across the
aisle and whispered thus in his ear, 'Governor, do your *best*.
You are the most abused man in North Carolina.' With an
eye flashing light through water at me, he promptly re-

---

[1] The funeral took place at his residence, "Blandwood," on August 31, 1866,
at ten o'clock. On November 23, 1866, his sons, John L. Morehead and J.
Turner Morehead and his son-in-law, Julius A. Gray, advertised Edgeworth
Seminary for rent; and it is interesting to note that on December 24, 1868,
John Motley Morehead Caldwell, as principal, announced the re-opening of the
seminary.

sponded, 'How shall I deal with them, my friend—shall I treat them *gently*, or shall I make myself the Wellington of the occasion, and *vanquish* them completely?' *'Play Wellington,'* said I. 'I will,' he replied, with energetic action. . . . *And he did play Wellington, if ever man did,* on battle field or in parliament. Never was there a more brilliant victory won, than he achieved that day." Mr. Kerr told of how he worked hard to aid in feeding and clothing the soldiers and how he remembered aged fathers and mothers left behind, and wives and ltitle ones; how his steward at Leaksville was directed to take care of large numbers. His kindliness to his slaves was such that some of them said, after he died, that, could he have lived, they would prefer being his slaves to being free, took the name Morehead and they and their children have been proud of it to this day. His losses were great, because he took Confederate money and bonds, staking, as he said, all he had on the cause. He was, said Mr. Kerr, a great son, brother, husband and father. A sister said she had never seen him give way to his temper; and his love for his brother Abraham, the poet, was like that of Jonathan for David. As a lawyer Mr. Kerr said he was entitled to be ranked as "great;" he had genius and talent both in high degree, but it was as an advocate that he shone with particular splendor. "His presence was imposing—his voice was exceedingly pleasant in its tones—his argumentation was logical—his wit sparkling—his illustrations striking—and his flow of soul under the excitement of his causes, captivating to all hearts. He assailed with great force his adversaries' positions—and defended his own with consummate skill. He was always self-possessed—always courteous. He had the best control of his temper of any man I ever knew. It was in vain to attempt to get the advantage of him by exciting his anger." He was scholarly in his knowledge from practical surveying to metaphysics and theories of Hooker, Reid and Dugald Stewart, and *belles-lettres* were no less at his command.

An exquisite "Tribute" to him appeared in the *Greensboro Patriot* of February 15, 1867, from the pen of Lawyer

William Lafayette Scott, to whom Governor Morehead had been a hero since childhood, when his favorite pet was named "Morehead." His boyish picture of his hero is given: "He was about two-score-and-two years old; the weight of years had not stooped his shoulders; his hair was only slightly 'besprent with rays and gleams of silver light,' his face was smooth shaven; a mild luster usually lit his blue eyes, but in moments of animation, they sparkled like the brightest stars; his forehead was not high, but massive; his nose slightly Roman; his chin prominent; his lips compressed; not infrequently, when in deep thought, he indulged in a whispering whistle; and his dress was elegant, but never ostentatious. Such was he as I first saw him, nor can that image ever pass from my memory. . . . Never have I seen, in the walks of life, nor has my imagination conceived, a man so all-gifted as he was." He tells of "halcyonian evenings" in the latter half of 1865 and the early half of '66 when Governor Morehead would come down town and sit with neighbors and friends in reminiscence or discussion, narrative, history—"a living book," the joy of young and old.

His old University Dialectic Society paid its tender tribute on September 21, 1866; and the stockholders of the North Carolina Railroad, on July 12, 1867, registered their testimony as to his "deliverance of the state from commercial and agricultural bondage" through their "great central trunk railway." The Piedmont Railroad, the present link between Greensboro and Danville, and the heart of the great Southern Railway System, expressed their gratitude to him on September 13, 1866, and gave to the station nearest Greensboro the name of "Morehead." Even his ancient enemy, the *Raleigh Standard*, sounded his praises in generous accents.

Then the dark ages of reconstruction, which, his eyes were fortunately prevented from seeing by his passing at the "three-score-and-ten" mile post, gradually faded and a new generation, his own sons and nephews among them, picked up the lines as they fell from his hands in 1861; and began to again develop that program "of fifty years," at which Maj. Southerlin, a Danville connection director, had exclaimed. It is now half a dozen years more than that half century, since he died; and "modern North Carolina" is the only term that adequately distinguishes the "Tar-Heel" state of the last quarter of a century from all periods preceding. "The traveller along the line of the North Carolina Railroad" [now the Southern Railway]" writes Mr. R. D. W. Connor in 1912, "sees the fulfillment of Morehead's dreams of 1850. He finds himself in one of the most productive regions of the new world. He traverses it from one end to the other at a speed of forty miles an hour, surrounded by every comfort and convenience of modern travel. He passes through a region bound together by a thousand miles of steel rails, by telegraph and telephone lines, and by nearly two thousand miles of improved country roads. He finds a population engaged not only in agriculture, but in manufacturing, in commerce, in transportation, and in a hundred other enterprises. Instead of a few old-fashioned hand-looms turning out annually less than $400,000 worth of 'homemade' articles, he hears the hum of three hundred and sixty modern factories, operating two millions of spindles and looms by steam, water, electricity, employing more than fifty millions of capital, and sending their products to the uttermost ends of the earth. His train passes through farm lands that, since Morehead began his work, have increased six times in value, that produce annually ten times as much cotton and seventy-five times as much tobacco. From his car window instead of the four hundred and sixty-six log huts that passed for school-houses in 1850, with their handful of pupils, he beholds a thousand modern school-houses, alive with the energy and activity of one hundred thousand school children. His train carries him from Goldsboro, through Raleigh, Durham, Burlington, Greensboro, High Point, Lexington, Salisbury, Concord, Charlotte—villages that have grown into cities, old fields and cross-roads have become thriving centers of industry and culture. Better than all else, he finds himself among a people, no longer characterized by their lethargy, isolation and ignorance, but bristling with energy, alert to every opportunity, fired with the spirit of the modern world, and with their faces steadfastly set toward the future."

"The foundation on which all this prosperity and progress rests,"—Mr. Connor continues, "is the work done by John M. Morehead or inspired by him. No well-informed man can be found today in North Carolina who will dispute his primacy among the railroad builders of the State. The North Carolina Railroad, the Atlantic and North Carolina Railroad, the Western North Carolina Railroad, the connecting link between the North Carolina and the Richmond and Danville railroads from Greensboro to Danville, all bear witness of his supremacy in this field. In one of the finest passages of his message to the General Assembly in 1842 he urged the building of good couty roads; today [1912] there are five thousand miles of improved rural highways in North Carolina. He recommended the building of a Central Highway from Morehead City through Raleigh to the Tennessee line; today we have just witnessed the completion of a great State Highway piercing the very heart of the State almost along the very route he suggested seventy years ago. He suggested plans for extensive improvements of our rivers and harbors; today a 'thirty-foot channel to the sea' has become the slogan of our chief ports and the National Government is spending annually hundreds of thousands of dollars in the improvement of the Cape Fear, the Neuse, the Pamlico and other rivers of eastern North Carolina. He urged the construction by the National Government of an inland waterway for our coastwise vessels through Pamlico Sound to Beaufort harbor; seventy years have passed since then; this enterprise has become national in its scope, the Federal Government has assumed charge of it, and the whole nation is anticipating the completion in the near future of an inland waterway from Maine through Pamlico Sound and Beaufort harbor to Florida. First of all our statesmen Morehead realized the possibility of establishing at Beaufort [Morehead City] a great world port; and although this dream has not been realized, there is not lacking today men noted throughout the business world for their practical wisdom, inspired by no

JOHN MOTLEY MOREHEAD
A Bust by Ruckstuhl in 1912, in one of four niches in the
Capitol Rotunda, Raleigh

other purpose than commercial success, who have not hesitated to stake large fortunes on the ultimate realization of this dream also. A twentieth century statesman sent before his time into the world of the nineteenth century, as a distinguished scholar has declared, 'would have been more at home in North Carolina today than would any other of our ante-bellum governors. He has been dead forty years [at the time this was written], and they have been years of constant changing and unceasing development. But so wide were his sympathies, so vital were his aims, so far-sighted were his public policies, and so clearly did he foresee the larger North Carolina of schools, railroads and cotton mills, that he would be as truly a contemporary in the twentieth century as he was a leader in the nineteenth'."[1]

But this was a decade ago, when those railroads in which the state stock was valued at $7,000,000; today it is valued above $15,000,000; while the whole mileage of the commonwealth is nearly 5000 miles. They have built up her greatest cities in the Piedmont section, instead of any great ocean port, and these treat New York as their port. "Western North Carolina," said Mr. B. Frank Mebane, the great manufacturer at Spray and Leaksville, "is a suburb of New York, which is little more than a night's ride and we all have offices there." Winston-Salem, the largest city of the State, over 48,000, a great tobacco center; Charlotte, until 1920 the largest city, with above 46,000, a manufacturing center, are both Piedmont cities, after which follows Wilmington, now third (once first), with over 33,000, still the port of North Carolina. Asheville, with over 28,000, the metropolis of the "Land of the Sky," identified with Piedmont life, comes fourth. Raleigh, with over 24,000, because

---

[1] The extract is from a sketch by Dr. C. Alphonso Smith in Ashe's *Biographical History of North Carolina*, Vol. 2, and quoted by Professor R. D. W. Connor in his address at the unveiling of the bust of Governor Morehead in the capitol rotunda at Raleigh in 1912. As interesting added testimony, in 1921, Col. G. S. Bradshaw of Greensboro, in his address of presentation of a portrait of Governor Morehead to the Court House there, said: "Not a great lawyer as Ruffin or Pearson—not as versatile and accomplished as Murphey, not as learned as Gaston, not as brilliant as Badger, not as profound as Moore, not as eloquent, perhaps, as Stanly or Miller—not as polished as Graham, yet judged by the fruits of his life and the far-reaching influence of his achievements he was greater than any one of them and accomplished more than all of them. No name is more securely and permanently enshrined in the heart of North Carolina than that of Governor Morehead."

the capital, while no city is large enough to be *the* metropolis, takes on many of the features of the leading city, and it essentially belongs to the Piedmont. Durham, west of Raleigh, with nearly 22,000 is the great American Tobacco Company center, in the same region; while Greensboro, the "Gate City," with nearly 20,000 within her borders and surrounded by factory towns galore, typical of Governor Morehead's theories, is in the very heart of the Piedmont; and High Point, the great furniture center, with over 14,000, is in the same county, and comes next. Other cities above 10,000 are Salisbury, Gastonia, also in the Piedmont; and Newbern, Rocky Mount and Wilson in the east. Many of these and others, however, are not representative of actual population that includes country factory towns identified with them, which is a striking feature of the state and ever increasing.

This remarkable factory development is due largely to the great growth of hydro-electric power by two North Carolina corporations, the Southern and the Carolina, the former radiating from the Catawba falls and the latter in the east. She stands fifth in amount of electrical energy developed east of the Mississippi.[1] And this power is in a state, which, in a decade, "has climbed," as the late Governor Bickett said before the North Carolina Society of Philadelphia, in 1920, "from the twenty-second to the fourth state in value of agricultural products." Only Texas, Iowa and Illinois surpass her. She is first in amount of cotton to the acre and value of tobacco crop. She is second only to Massachusetts in cotton manufacture and second only to Michigan in furniture factories. She is sixth in amount paid into the national treasury, and the richest, per capita, of any state from the Potomac to the Rio Grande. More automobiles are owned in North Carolina than any Southern state except Texas—illustrations that serve to indicate what this "modern" state is, and what a distinguished North Carolina statesman of today meant when he said that "Governor Morehead may be called The Father of Modern North

---

[1] Charlotte is the largest distributing center of hydro-electric power in the world.

Carolina;" while another, Ex-Secretary of the Navy Daniels, has predicted that a great port, the dream of Governor Morehead, will yet be realized in the region of Cape Lookout, the entrance to Beaufort harbor and Morehead City. And even so it will take generations to realize all the dreams of Governor John Motley Morehead for the development of North Carolina.

INDEX

Index